# The Rhythm and Reason of Reality

*Prose and Poetry in*
*A Course In Miracles*

Compiled by
Steve "Michael" Russell
with a
Preface by Ray Comeau, Ph.D

ENDEAVOR ACADEMY
*Certum Est Quia Impossibile Est*

The Rhythm and Reason of Reality:
*Prose and Poetry in A Course In Miracles*
Compiled by Steve Russell

International Standard Book Number (ISBN-10): 1-890648-91-4
(ISBN-13): 978-1-890648-91-6

Library of Congress Control Number: 2011940661

Published By:
Endeavor Academy
501 East Adams Street, Wisconsin Dells, WI 53965, USA
Phone: +1 608-253-1447
www.themasterteacher.tv
www.endeavoracademy.com
Email: publishing@endeavoracademy.com

# CONTENTS

Acknowledgements ..................................................... 9
The Rhythm and Reason of Reality ........................ 11
Facing Your Dilemma ............................................. 11
PREFACE ................................................................ 13
Introduction ............................................................. 17
Portals to Rhythmic Reality .................................... 21
Iambic pentameter lead sentences from Chapters 13 thru 24 ......................................................................... 21

Chapter 25
THE JUSTICE OF GOD ......................................... 25
Introduction ............................................................. 25
The Link to Truth .................................................... 25
The Savior from the Dark ....................................... 26
Perception and Choice ............................................ 28
The Light You Bring ............................................... 29
The State of Sinlessness ......................................... 30
The Special Function .............................................. 31
The Rock of Salvation ............................................ 33
Justice Returned to Love ........................................ 35
The Justice of Heaven ............................................ 38

Chapter 26
THE TRANSITION ................................................. 40
The "Sacrifice" of Oneness ..................................... 40
Many Forms; One Correction ................................. 41
The Borderland ....................................................... 42
Where Sin Has Left ................................................ 43
The Little Hindrance ............................................... 44
The Appointed Friend ............................................. 47
The Laws of Healing .............................................. 47
The Immediacy of Salvation .................................. 50
For They Have Come ............................................. 52
The End of Injustice ............................................... 53

Chapter 27
THE HEALING OF THE DREAM ......................... 55
The Picture of Crucifixion ..................................... 55
The Fear of Healing ............................................... 57
Beyond All Symbols .............................................. 60
The Quiet Answer ................................................... 61
The Healing Example ............................................. 62
The Witnesses to Sin .............................................. 64
The Dreamer of the Dream .................................... 65

Chapter 28
THE UNDOING OF FEAR ..................................... 71
The Present Memory .............................................. 71

Reversing Effect and Cause .................................... 73
The Agreement to Join ............................................ 75
The Greater Joining ................................................ 77
The Alternate to Dreams of Fear ............................ 78
The Secret Vows ..................................................... 79
The Ark of Safety ................................................... 80

Chapter 29
THE AWAKENING ................................................ 83
The Closing of the Gap .......................................... 83
God's Witnesses ..................................................... 86
Dream Roles ........................................................... 87
The Changeless Dwelling Place ............................. 88
Forgiveness and the End of Time ........................... 89
Seek Not Outside Yourself ..................................... 90
The Anti-Christ ....................................................... 91
The Forgiving Dream ............................................. 93

Chapter 30
THE NEW BEGINNING ........................................ 95
Introduction ............................................................ 95
Rules for Decision .................................................. 95
Freedom of Will ..................................................... 97
Beyond All Idols .................................................... 98
The Truth behind Illusions ................................... 100
The Only Purpose ................................................ 101
The Justification for Forgiveness ......................... 103
The New Interpretation ........................................ 104
Changeless Reality ............................................... 106

Chapter 31
THE FINAL VISION ............................................ 108
The Simplicity of Salvation ................................. 108
Walking with Christ ............................................. 110
The Self-Accused ................................................. 112
The Real Alternative ............................................ 113
Self-Concept versus Self ...................................... 114
Recognizing the Spirit .......................................... 117
The Savior's Vision .............................................. 118
Choose Once Again ............................................. 121

LESSON 78 ........................................................... 124
Let miracles replace all grievances. ..................... 124
LESSON 91 ........................................................... 126
Miracles are seen in light. .................................... 126
LESSON 92 ........................................................... 128
Miracles are seen in light, and light and strength are one. ......................................................................... 128

| | |
|---|---|
| LESSON 93 .................................................... 1 3 0 | LESSON 121 .................................................. 1 6 7 |
| Light and joy and peace abide in me. ..... 1 3 0 | Forgiveness is the key to happiness. ...... 1 6 7 |
| LESSON 94 .................................................... 1 3 2 | LESSON 122 .................................................. 1 6 9 |
| I am as God created me. ............................. 1 3 2 | Forgiveness offers everything I want. ..... 1 6 9 |
| LESSON 95 .................................................... 1 3 3 | LESSON 123 .................................................. 1 7 1 |
| I am one Self, united with my Creator. .... 1 3 3 | I thank my Father for His gifts to me. ..... 1 7 1 |
| LESSON 96 .................................................... 1 3 5 | LESSON 124 .................................................. 1 7 2 |
| Salvation comes from my one Self. .......... 1 3 5 | Let me remember I am one with God. ...... 1 7 2 |
| LESSON 97 .................................................... 1 3 7 | LESSON 125 .................................................. 1 7 4 |
| I am spirit. ..................................................... 1 3 7 | In quiet I receive God's Word today. ....... 1 7 4 |
| LESSON 98 .................................................... 1 3 8 | LESSON 126 .................................................. 1 7 5 |
| I will accept my part in God's plan for salvation. . 1 3 8 | All that I give is given to myself. ............... 1 7 5 |
| LESSON 99 .................................................... 1 4 0 | LESSON 127 .................................................. 1 7 7 |
| Salvation is my only function here. .......... 1 4 0 | There is no love but God's. ........................ 1 7 7 |
| LESSON 100 .................................................. 1 4 2 | LESSON 128 .................................................. 1 7 9 |
| My part is essential to God's plan for salvation. .... 1 4 2 | The world I see holds nothing that I want. ............ 1 7 9 |
| LESSON 101 .................................................. 1 4 4 | LESSON 129 .................................................. 1 8 0 |
| God's Will for me is perfect happiness. ... 1 4 4 | Beyond this world there is a world I want. ........... 1 8 0 |
| LESSON 102 .................................................. 1 4 5 | LESSON 130 .................................................. 1 8 1 |
| I share God's Will for happiness for me. ............. 1 4 5 | It is impossible to see two worlds. .......... 1 8 1 |
| LESSON 103 .................................................. 1 4 6 | LESSON 131 .................................................. 1 8 3 |
| God, being Love, is also happiness. ........ 1 4 6 | No one can fail who seeks to reach the truth. ...... 1 8 3 |
| LESSON 104 .................................................. 1 4 7 | LESSON 132 .................................................. 1 8 5 |
| I seek but what belongs to me in truth. .. 1 4 7 | I loose the world from all I thought it was. ........... 1 8 5 |
| LESSON 105 .................................................. 1 4 8 | LESSON 133 .................................................. 1 8 7 |
| God's peace and joy are mine. .................. 1 4 8 | I will not value what is valueless. ............. 1 8 7 |
| LESSON 106 .................................................. 1 5 0 | LESSON 134 .................................................. 1 8 9 |
| Let me be still and listen to the truth. ..... 1 5 0 | Let me perceive forgiveness as it is. ....... 1 8 9 |
| LESSON 107 .................................................. 1 5 2 | LESSON 135 .................................................. 1 9 1 |
| Truth will correct all errors in my mind. .. 1 5 2 | If I defend myself I am attacked. ............. 1 9 1 |
| LESSON 108 .................................................. 1 5 4 | LESSON 136 .................................................. 1 9 4 |
| To give and to receive are one in truth. .. 1 5 4 | Sickness is a defense against the truth. ............... 1 9 4 |
| LESSON 109 .................................................. 1 5 6 | LESSON 137 .................................................. 1 9 7 |
| I rest in God. ................................................. 1 5 6 | When I am healed I am not healed alone. ............. 1 9 7 |
| LESSON 110 .................................................. 1 5 8 | LESSON 138 .................................................. 1 9 9 |
| I am as God created me. ............................. 1 5 8 | Heaven is the decision I must make. ...... 1 9 9 |
| | LESSON 139 .................................................. 2 0 1 |
| REVIEW III .................................................... 1 6 0 | I will accept Atonement for myself. ......... 2 0 1 |
| Introduction .................................................. 1 6 0 | LESSON 140 .................................................. 2 0 3 |
| LESSON 111 .................................................. 1 6 2 | Only salvation can be said to cure. ......... 2 0 3 |
| LESSON 112 .................................................. 1 6 2 | |
| LESSON 113 .................................................. 1 6 3 | REVIEW IV .................................................... 2 0 5 |
| LESSON 114 .................................................. 1 6 3 | Introduction .................................................. 2 0 5 |
| LESSON 115 .................................................. 1 6 4 | LESSON 141 .................................................. 2 0 7 |
| LESSON 116 .................................................. 1 6 4 | LESSON 142 .................................................. 2 0 7 |
| LESSON 117 .................................................. 1 6 5 | LESSON 143 .................................................. 2 0 7 |
| LESSON 118 .................................................. 1 6 5 | LESSON 144 .................................................. 2 0 7 |
| LESSON 119 .................................................. 1 6 6 | LESSON 145 .................................................. 2 0 7 |
| LESSON 120 .................................................. 1 6 6 | LESSON 146 .................................................. 2 0 7 |

| | |
|---|---|
| LESSON 147 | 207 |
| LESSON 148 | 207 |
| LESSON 149 | 207 |
| LESSON 150 | 207 |
| | |
| LESSON 151 | 208 |
| All things are echoes of the Voice for God. | 208 |
| LESSON 152 | 210 |
| The power of decision is my own. | 210 |
| LESSON 153 | 212 |
| In my defenselessness my safety lies. | 212 |
| LESSON 154 | 215 |
| I am among the ministers of God. | 215 |
| LESSON 155 | 217 |
| I will step back and let Him lead the way. | 217 |
| LESSON 156 | 219 |
| I walk with God in perfect holiness | 219 |
| LESSON 157 | 220 |
| Into His Presence would I enter now. | 220 |
| LESSON 158 | 221 |
| Today I learn to give as I receive. | 221 |
| LESSON 159 | 223 |
| I give the miracles I have received. | 223 |
| LESSON 160 | 225 |
| I am at home. Fear is the stranger here | 225 |
| LESSON 161 | 227 |
| Give me your blessing, holy Son of God. | 227 |
| LESSON 162 | 229 |
| I am as God created me. | 229 |
| LESSON 163 | 230 |
| There is no death. The Son of God is free | 230 |
| LESSON 164 | 232 |
| Now are we one with Him Who is our Source | 232 |
| LESSON 165 | 234 |
| Let not my mind deny the Thought of God | 234 |
| LESSON 166 | 235 |
| I am entrusted with the gifts of God. | 235 |
| LESSON 167 | 237 |
| There is one life, and that I share with God | 237 |
| LESSON 168 | 239 |
| Your grace is given me. I claim it now. | 239 |
| LESSON 169 | 240 |
| By grace I live. By grace I am released. | 240 |
| LESSON 170 | 242 |
| There is no cruelty in God and none in me. | 242 |
| | |
| REVIEW V | 244 |
| Introduction | 244 |
| LESSON 171 | 246 |
| LESSON 172 | 246 |
| LESSON 173 | 246 |
| LESSON 174 | 246 |
| LESSON 175 | 246 |
| LESSON 176 | 246 |
| LESSON 177 | 246 |
| LESSON 178 | 246 |
| LESSON 179 | 246 |
| LESSON 180 | 246 |
| | |
| Introduction to Lessons 181 to 220 | 247 |
| LESSON 181 | 248 |
| I trust my brothers, who are one with me. | 248 |
| LESSON 182 | 250 |
| I will be still an instant and go home | 250 |
| LESSON 183 | 252 |
| I call upon God's Name and on my own. | 252 |
| LESSON 184 | 254 |
| The Name of God is my inheritance. | 254 |
| LESSON 185 | 256 |
| I want the peace of God. | 256 |
| LESSON 186 | 258 |
| Salvation of the world depends on me. | 258 |
| LESSON 187 | 260 |
| I bless the world because I bless myself. | 260 |
| LESSON 188 | 262 |
| The peace of God is shining in me now | 262 |
| LESSON 189 | 264 |
| I feel the Love of God within me now. | 264 |
| LESSON 190 | 266 |
| I choose the joy of God instead of pain. | 266 |
| LESSON 191 | 268 |
| I am the holy Son of God Himself. | 268 |
| LESSON 192 | 270 |
| I have a function God would have me fill | 270 |
| LESSON 193 | 272 |
| All things are lessons God would have me learn. | 272 |
| LESSON 194 | 274 |
| I place the future in the Hands of God. | 274 |
| LESSON 195 | 276 |
| Love is the way I walk in gratitude | 276 |
| LESSON 196 | 278 |
| It can be but myself I crucify. | 278 |
| LESSON 197 | 280 |
| It can be but my gratitude I earn. | 280 |
| LESSON 198 | 281 |
| Only my condemnation injures me. | 281 |
| LESSON 199 | 283 |
| I am not a body. I am free. | 283 |
| LESSON 200 | 284 |
| There is no peace except the peace of God | 284 |

| | |
|---|---|
| REVIEW VI | 286 |
| Introduction | 286 |
| LESSON 201 | 287 |
| LESSON 202 | 287 |
| LESSON 203 | 287 |
| LESSON 204 | 287 |
| LESSON 205 | 287 |
| LESSON 206 | 287 |
| LESSON 207 | 288 |
| LESSON 208 | 288 |
| LESSON 209 | 288 |
| LESSON 210 | 288 |
| LESSON 211 | 288 |
| LESSON 212 | 288 |
| LESSON 213 | 289 |
| LESSON 214 | 289 |
| LESSON 215 | 289 |
| LESSON 216 | 289 |
| LESSON 217 | 289 |
| LESSON 218 | 289 |
| LESSON 219 | 290 |
| LESSON 220 | 290 |
| | |
| PART II | 291 |
| Introduction | 291 |
| | |
| What is Forgiveness? | 293 |
| LESSON 221 | 294 |
| Peace to my mind. Let all my thoughts be still. | 294 |
| LESSON 222 | 294 |
| God is with me. I live and move in Him. | 294 |
| LESSON 223 | 294 |
| God is my life. I have no life but His. | 294 |
| LESSON 224 | 294 |
| God is my Father, and He loves His Son. | 294 |
| LESSON 225 | 295 |
| God is my Father, and His Son loves Him. | 295 |
| LESSON 226 | 295 |
| My home awaits me. I will hasten there. | 295 |
| LESSON 227 | 295 |
| This is my holy instant of release. | 295 |
| LESSON 228 | 295 |
| God has condemned me not. No more do I. | 295 |
| LESSON 229 | 296 |
| Love, Which created me, is what I am. | 296 |
| LESSON 230 | 296 |
| Now will I seek and find the peace of God. | 296 |
| | |
| What is Salvation? | 297 |
| LESSON 231 | 298 |
| Father, I will but to remember You. | 298 |
| LESSON 232 | 298 |
| Be in my mind, my Father, through the day. | 298 |
| LESSON 233 | 298 |
| I give my life to God to guide today. | 298 |
| LESSON 234 | 298 |
| Father, today I am Your Son again. | 298 |
| LESSON 235 | 299 |
| God in His mercy wills that I be saved. | 299 |
| LESSON 236 | 299 |
| I rule my mind, which I alone must rule. | 299 |
| LESSON 237 | 299 |
| Now would I be as God created me. | 299 |
| LESSON 238 | 299 |
| On my decision all salvation rests. | 299 |
| LESSON 239 | 300 |
| The glory of my Father is my own. | 300 |
| LESSON 240 | 300 |
| Fear is not justified in any form. | 300 |
| | |
| What is the World? | 301 |
| LESSON 241 | 302 |
| This holy instant is salvation come. | 302 |
| LESSON 242 | 302 |
| This day is God's. It is my gift to Him. | 302 |
| LESSON 243 | 302 |
| Today I will judge nothing that occurs. | 302 |
| LESSON 244 | 302 |
| I am in danger nowhere in the world. | 302 |
| LESSON 245 | 303 |
| Your peace is with me, Father. I am safe. | 303 |
| LESSON 246 | 303 |
| To love my Father is to love His Son. | 303 |
| LESSON 247 | 303 |
| Without forgiveness I will still be blind. | 303 |
| LESSON 248 | 303 |
| Whatever suffers is not part of me. | 303 |
| LESSON 249 | 304 |
| Forgiveness ends all suffering and loss. | 304 |
| LESSON 250 | 304 |
| Let me not see myself as limited. | 304 |
| | |
| What is Sin? | 305 |
| LESSON 251 | 306 |
| I am in need of nothing but the truth. | 306 |
| LESSON 252 | 306 |
| The Son of God is my Identity. | 306 |
| LESSON 253 | 306 |
| My Self is ruler of the universe. | 306 |
| LESSON 254 | 306 |
| Let every voice but God's be still in me. | 306 |

| | |
|---|---|
| LESSON 255 | 307 |
| This day I choose to spend in perfect peace. | 307 |
| LESSON 256 | 307 |
| God is the only goal I have today. | 307 |
| LESSON 257 | 307 |
| Let me remember what my purpose is. | 307 |
| LESSON 258 | 307 |
| Let me remember that my goal is God. | 307 |
| LESSON 259 | 308 |
| Let me remember that there is no sin. | 308 |
| LESSON 260 | 308 |
| Let me remember God created me. | 308 |
| | |
| What is the Body? | 309 |
| LESSON 261 | 310 |
| God is my refuge and security. | 310 |
| LESSON 262 | 310 |
| Let me perceive no differences today. | 310 |
| LESSON 263 | 310 |
| My holy vision sees all things as pure. | 310 |
| LESSON 264 | 310 |
| I am surrounded by the Love of God. | 310 |
| LESSON 265 | 311 |
| Creation's gentleness is all I see. | 311 |
| LESSON 266 | 311 |
| My holy Self abides in you, God's Son. | 311 |
| LESSON 267 | 311 |
| My heart is beating in the peace of God. | 311 |
| LESSON 268 | 311 |
| Let all things be exactly as they are. | 311 |
| LESSON 269 | 312 |
| My sight goes forth to look upon Christ's face. | 312 |
| LESSON 270 | 312 |
| I will not use the body's eyes today. | 312 |
| | |
| What is the Christ? | 313 |
| LESSON 271 | 314 |
| Christ's is the vision I will use today. | 314 |
| LESSON 272 | 314 |
| How can illusions satisfy God's Son? | 314 |
| LESSON 273 | 314 |
| The stillness of the peace of God is mine. | 314 |
| LESSON 274 | 314 |
| Today belongs to Love. Let me not fear. | 314 |
| LESSON 275 | 315 |
| God's healing Voice protects all things today. | 315 |
| LESSON 276 | 315 |
| The Word of God is given me to speak. | 315 |
| LESSON 277 | 315 |
| Let me not bind Your Son with laws I made. | 315 |
| LESSON 278 | 315 |
| If I am bound, my Father is not free. | 315 |
| LESSON 279 | 316 |
| Creation's freedom promises my own. | 316 |
| LESSON 280 | 316 |
| What limits can I lay upon God's Son? | 316 |
| | |
| What is the Holy Spirit? | 317 |
| LESSON 281 | 318 |
| I can be hurt by nothing but my thoughts. | 318 |
| LESSON 282 | 318 |
| I will not be afraid of love today. | 318 |
| LESSON 283 | 318 |
| My true Identity abides in You. | 318 |
| LESSON 284 | 318 |
| I can elect to change all thoughts that hurt. | 318 |
| LESSON 285 | 319 |
| My holiness shines bright and clear today. | 319 |
| LESSON 286 | 319 |
| The hush of Heaven holds my heart today. | 319 |
| LESSON 287 | 319 |
| You are my goal, my Father. Only You. | 319 |
| LESSON 288 | 319 |
| Let me forget my brother's past today. | 319 |
| LESSON 289 | 320 |
| The past is over. It can touch me not. | 320 |
| LESSON 290 | 320 |
| My present happiness is all I see. | 320 |
| | |
| What is the Real World? | 321 |
| LESSON 291 | 322 |
| This is a day of stillness and of peace. | 322 |
| LESSON 292 | 322 |
| A happy outcome to all things is sure. | 322 |
| LESSON 293 | 322 |
| All fear is past and only love is here. | 322 |
| LESSON 294 | 322 |
| My body is a wholly neutral thing. | 322 |
| LESSON 295 | 323 |
| The Holy Spirit looks through me today. | 323 |
| LESSON 296 | 323 |
| The Holy Spirit speaks through me today. | 323 |
| LESSON 297 | 323 |
| Forgiveness is the only gift I give. | 323 |
| LESSON 298 | 323 |
| I love You, Father, and I love Your Son. | 323 |
| LESSON 299 | 324 |
| Eternal holiness abides in me | 324 |
| LESSON 300 | 324 |
| Only an instant does this world endure. | 324 |

| | |
|---|---|
| What is the Second Coming? | 325 |
| LESSON 301 | 326 |
| And God Himself shall wipe away all tears | 326 |
| LESSON 302 | 326 |
| Where darkness was I look upon the light | 326 |
| LESSON 303 | 326 |
| The holy Christ is born in me today. | 326 |
| LESSON 304 | 326 |
| Let not my world obscure the sight of Christ | 326 |
| LESSON 305 | 327 |
| There is a peace that Christ bestows on us | 327 |
| LESSON 306 | 327 |
| The gift of Christ is all I seek today. | 327 |
| LESSON 307 | 327 |
| Conflicting wishes cannot be my will. | 327 |
| LESSON 308 | 327 |
| This instant is the only time there is. | 327 |
| LESSON 309 | 328 |
| I will not fear to look within today. | 328 |
| LESSON 310 | 328 |
| In fearlessness and love I spend today. | 328 |
| | |
| What is the Last Judgment? | 329 |
| LESSON 311 | 330 |
| I judge all things as I would have them be. | 330 |
| LESSON 312 | 330 |
| I see all things as I would have them be. | 330 |
| LESSON 313 | 330 |
| Now let a new perception come to me. | 330 |
| LESSON 314 | 330 |
| I seek a future different from the past | 330 |
| LESSON 315 | 331 |
| All gifts my brothers give belong to me. | 331 |
| LESSON 316 | 331 |
| All gifts I give my brothers are my own. | 331 |
| LESSON 317 | 331 |
| I follow in the way appointed me. | 331 |
| LESSON 318 | 331 |
| In me salvation's means and end are one. | 331 |
| LESSON 319 | 332 |
| I came for the salvation of the world. | 332 |
| LESSON 320 | 332 |
| My Father gives all power unto me. | 332 |
| | |
| What is Creation? | 333 |
| LESSON 321 | 334 |
| Father, my freedom is in You alone. | 334 |
| LESSON 322 | 334 |
| I can give up but what was never real. | 334 |
| LESSON 323 | 334 |
| I gladly make the "sacrifice" of fear. | 334 |
| LESSON 324 | 334 |
| I merely follow, for I would not lead. | 334 |
| LESSON 325 | 335 |
| All things I think I see reflect ideas. | 335 |
| LESSON 326 | 335 |
| I am forever an Effect of God. | 335 |
| LESSON 327 | 335 |
| I need but call and You will answer me. | 335 |
| LESSON 328 | 335 |
| I choose the second place to gain the first. | 335 |
| LESSON 329 | 336 |
| I have already chosen what You will. | 336 |
| LESSON 330 | 336 |
| I will not hurt myself again today. | 336 |
| | |
| What is the Ego? | 337 |
| LESSON 331 | 338 |
| There is no conflict, for my will is Yours. | 338 |
| LESSON 332 | 338 |
| Fear binds the world. Forgiveness sets it free. | 338 |
| LESSON 333 | 338 |
| Forgiveness ends the dream of conflict here. | 338 |
| LESSON 334 | 338 |
| Today I claim the gifts forgiveness gives. | 338 |
| LESSON 335 | 339 |
| I choose to see my brother's sinlessness. | 339 |
| LESSON 336 | 339 |
| Forgiveness lets me know that minds are joined. | 339 |
| LESSON 337 | 339 |
| My sinlessness protects me from all harm. | 339 |
| LESSON 338 | 339 |
| I am affected only by my thoughts. | 339 |
| LESSON 339 | 340 |
| I will receive whatever I request. | 340 |
| LESSON 340 | 340 |
| I can be free of suffering today. | 340 |
| | |
| What is a Miracle? | 341 |
| LESSON 341 | 342 |
| I can attack but my own sinlessness, And it is only that which keeps me safe. | 342 |
| LESSON 342 | 342 |
| I let forgiveness rest upon all things, For thus forgiveness will be given me. | 342 |
| LESSON 343 | 342 |
| I am not asked to make a sacrifice To find the mercy and the peace of God. | 342 |
| LESSON 344 | 342 |
| Today I learn the law of love; that what I give my brother is my gift to me. | 342 |

LESSON 345...................................................343
I offer only miracles today, For I would have them be returned to me. ...................................................343
LESSON 346...................................................343
Today the Peace of God envelops me, And I forget all things except His Love. ...................................343
LESSON 347...................................................343
Anger must come from judgment. Judgment is The weapon I would use against myself, To keep the miracle away from me. ...................................343
LESSON 348...................................................343
I have no cause for anger or for fear, For You surround me. And in every need That I perceive, Your grace suffices me. ...................................................343
LESSON 349...................................................344
Today I let Christ's vision look upon All things for me and judge them not, but give Each one a miracle of love instead. ...................................................344
LESSON 350...................................................344
Miracles mirror God's eternal Love. To offer them is to remember Him, And through His memory to save the world. ...................................................344

What am I? ....................................................345
LESSON 351...................................................346
My sinless brother is my guide to peace. My sinful brother is my guide to pain. And which I choose to see I will behold. ...................................................346
LESSON 352...................................................346
Judgment and love are opposites. From one Come all the sorrows of the world. But from The other comes the peace of God Himself. ...................346
LESSON 353...................................................346
My eyes, my tongue, my hands, my feet today Have but one purpose; to be given Christ To use to bless the world with miracles. ...................................................346
LESSON 354...................................................346
We stand together, Christ and I, in peace And certainty of purpose. And in Him Is His Creator, as He is in me. ...................................................346
LESSON 355...................................................347
There is no end to all the peace and joy, And all the miracles that I will give, When I accept God's Word. Why not today? ...................................................347
LESSON 356...................................................347
Sickness is but another name for sin. Healing is but another name for God. The miracle is thus a call to Him. ...................................................347

LESSON 357...................................................347
Truth answers every call we make to God, Responding first with miracles, and then Returning unto us to be itself. ...................................................347
LESSON 358...................................................347
No call to God can be unheard nor left Unanswered. And of this I can be sure; His answer is the one I really want. ...................................................347
LESSON 359...................................................348
God's answer is some form of peace. All pain Is healed; all misery replaced with joy. All prison doors are opened. And all sin Is understood as merely a mistake. ......348
LESSON 360...................................................348
Peace be to me, the holy Son of God. Peace to my brother, who is one with me. Let all the world be blessed with peace through us. .......................................348

FINAL LESSONS ...........................................349
Introduction .................................................349
LESSONS 361 to 365....................................350
EPILOGUE ....................................................351

MANUAL FOR TEACHERS .........................352
HOW IS CORRECTION MADE? ..................352
AS FOR THE REST........................................353

CLARIFICATION OF TERMS ........................354
THE EGO – THE MIRACLE ..........................354
FORGIVENESS – THE FACE OF CHRIST .........355
TRUE PERCEPTION – KNOWLEDGE...............355
JESUS – CHRIST ............................................356
EPILOGUE ....................................................358

## ACKNOWLEDGEMENTS

Thanks to Marty Preston and Judy Blue Eyes for encouraging me in this project, and to all who sat with me in the library while I pondered metric irregularities and replaced spaces with carriage returns

# THE RHYTHM AND REASON OF REALITY

*A Course In Miracles* is a direct communication from God through Jesus Christ indicating the apparent conditional situation between God and man, which is one of false separation, and the manner in which that apparent schism is and was repaired. Its sole purpose is to bring enlightenment through the transformation of your mind.

### Facing Your Dilemma

Let's look at *A Course In Miracles* as an effect of supra-consciousness; that is, with Jesus Christ as its true Causation. The acceptance or admission that *A Course In Miracles* originated from an absolutely unearthly Source, while it appears simple, is the single most difficult barrier to enlightenment that the immature consciousness faces. No matter how overwhelmingly predominant the evidence, both in method of origination and in content, that this is indeed so, the assertion is finally, inevitably, an act of faith. You must remember that human conceptual consciousness is explicitly formulated in a self-perpetuating structure of thought that denies singularity. Nothing could be more devastating to the dualistic mind construct, that is, limited perceptual reality, than the realization that *A Course In Miracles* is indeed not of this world, but actually Truth speaking to falsity. In other words, God-man speaking to man!

> *"This course has come from him because his words*
> *have reached you in a language you can love*
> *and understand."* (Manual For Teachers)

# PREFACE

I have so much gratitude for Steve "Michael" Russell. With his musician's ear, he heard the underlying rhythm running through the prose paragraphs of Jesus' unworldly masterpiece, A Course in Miracles, and with his poetic sensibilities he saw the blank verse emerging from the prose of the Course.

As you can see in his Introduction, he saw the blank verse emerge from the prose, sporadically along the way in the early chapters of the Text, and in Chapters 26-31, the prose paragraphs morph entirely into poetic stanzas, and the same morphing occurs in the Workbook, Lessons 98-365.

While sitting at his computer in the early 90's, reading the Course on his computer screen, he heard the rhythm in the lines, recognized the iambic pattern in the syllables of slack STRESS, slack STRESS, and realized the pattern of five sets of iambs per line. This is iambic pentameter, a poetic convention that appeared in the time of Shakespeare. To illustrate, I selected the first paragraph of Lesson 132, I loose the world from all I thought it was.

What KEEPS the WORLD in CHAINS but YOUR be LIEFS? And WHAT can SAVE the WORLD ex CEPT your SELF? be LIEF is POW er FUL in DEED. The THOUGHTS

And Russell counted, or more accurately, felt the rhythm, and after five sets of iambs, he hit the Enter Key, and the rest of the prose paragraph fell away.

What KEEPS the WORLD in CHAINS but YOUR be LIEFS?

And then again:

And WHAT can SAVE the WORLD ex CEPT your SELF?

And:

be LIEF is POW er FUL in DEED. The THOUGHTS

you HOLD are MIGHT y, AND il LU sions ARE

as STRONG in THEIR ef FECTS as IS the TRUTH.

a MAD man THINKS the WORLD he SEES is REAL,

and DOES not DOUBT it. NOR can HE be SWAYED

by QUES tion ING his THOUGHTS' ef FECTS.

it IS but WHEN their SOURCE is RAISED to QUES tion THAT

the HOPES of FREE dom COMES to HIM at LAST.

And now a poetic stanza emerges from the prose paragraph, marching stately across the page.

To shift the metaphor from hearing to seeing, what he saw emerging from the prose paragraphs is like sitting in a movie theatre, watching the action on the screen, and then putting on your 3D glasses, and suddenly, you are viewing a panorama that was there all the time, only you could not perceive it without your glasses.

The only reason I am writing this Preface is to take it one step further by demonstrating exactly how Jesus postures our voice by using a variety of poetic rhythms and techniques. Within the context of the basic iambic cadence, Jesus varies His rhythm to posture our voices to say the words exactly as He intended, while reading His words, either silently, or aloud. One way He realizes His intention is to employ the rhythmic metrics that have been used in English poetry for over four centuries.

You are already familiar with the iamb, slack STRESS: chris TINE

Here are four others:

1. Trochee, STRESS slack: RAY mond

2. Spondee, STRESS STRESS: CHRIS TINE (spoken by an irate mother)

3. Dactyl, STRESS slack slack: JON a than

4. Anapest, slack slack STRESS: ger trude STEIN

Here are illustrations of each, Lesson 340, I can be free of suffering today.

FA ther, I thank You for today, and for 1

the freedom I am certain it will bring.

THIS DAY is holy, for today YOUR SON 3

will be redeemed. His suffering is done.

For he will hear Your Voice directing him 5

to find CHRIST'S VIS ion through forgiveness, and

be free forever from all suffering.

THANKS for to/ DAY, my/ FA ther/ i was BORN

into this world but to achieve this day,

and what it holds in joy and freedom for 10

Your holy Son and for the world he made,

which is released along with him today.

Be glad today! Be glad! There is no room

for anything but joy and thanks today.

our FA/ ther HAS/ redeemed His Son this day.

Not one of us but will be saved today.

Not one who will remain in fear, and none

the father will not gather to Himself,

awake in Heaven in the Heart of Love.

Please notice that in your reading of this Lesson, your voice maintained a primarily iambic rhythm, only the underlined syllables indicate where your voice varied from the basic cadence, and in each variation, Jesus is posturing your voice to read those words with particular emphasis.

In line 1, Jesus use the trochee, FA ther, emphasizing that God, the Father, is standing out from the other four sets of iambs.

In line 3, two spondees are used to emphasize THIS DAY and YOUR SON.

In line 6, the spondee /CHRIST VIS/ is used, making clear the result of forgiving the sights seen through the body's eyes that cause all our suffering.

In line 8, Jesus breaks away completely from the iambic pattern, using a dactyl, THANKS for to, and an anapest, i was BORN, framing two trochees, DAY my, and FA ther, indicating our gratitude for being born as His Son.

"OK. Enough of that," you may be saying to yourself.

"You just used three sets of iambs," I say.

"STOP IT!"

"Now, that's a. . .OK, I'll stop."

Here is one more thing, very briefly. Jesus also utilizes the basic poetic techniques of sound to posture our voices, demonstrating how the sounds resonate in our ears, blending sound and sense. There are primarily three techniques:

1. Alliteration: the repetition of initial sounds.

The hush of heaven holds my heart today. (Lesson title, 286)

2. Consonance: the repetition of consonant sounds.

Here are the last two sentences of the same Lesson:

Today we will not doubt the end which God

Himself has promised us. We trust in Him,

and in ourself, who still is one with Him.

3. Assonance: the repetition of vowel sounds.

My heart is beating in the peace of God. (Lesson title, 267)

Here are the last two sentences of the same Lesson:

Father, my heart is beating in the peace

the Heart of Love created. It is there

and onlY there that I can be at home.

Finally, in His unworldly masterpiece Jesus is always posturing our voice by a perfect blend of sound and sense, rhythm and reason, whether we are reading His prose paragraphs, or His poetic stanzas. His singular intent is to lull us into a state of mind profoundly receptive to the Word of God.

Ray Comeau, Ph.D.
Endeavor Academy
Wisconsin Dells, WI

# INTRODUCTION

Those of you who have discovered the unearthly masterpiece, *A Course In Miracles*, will no doubt be aware of, and grateful for, its divine message of the remembrance of God and reality through love and forgiveness, that are only made possible in the realization that this world is a dream of your own making. You may remember reading, amongst the literature concerning the scribing of the *Course,* references to the use of the poetic form called *iambic pentameter*. Most of you won't know exactly what this means, some notwithstanding your own claims to the contrary. Of those who do know what the term means, most will not be able to easily discern the poetic form within the prosaic layout of the *Course*.

The purpose of this volume is to present the poetry of the *Course* in a totally accessible manner. You need know nothing about poetic forms and meters to begin enjoying it immediately. You may, however, wish to read this introduction, since the search to ascertain the extent of the poetic form within the Course has revealed another astounding dimension in its structural integrity.

Iambic pentameter is usually described as "lines consisting of five *iambs*", which in turn are described as "metric feet of two syllables each, the second syllable being the stronger". Such a description is useful to few. Put simply, a line of iambic pentameter sounds like this:

*Da-**dum** da-**dum** da-**dum** da-**dum** da-**dum**.*

This form is also called "blank verse", a more general term denoting even rhythm without rhyming. Because the *Course* is presented entirely as prose, the extent to which this form is used is a surprising and exciting discovery.

The Text of *A Course In Miracles* can be seen as three distinct parts, two of twelve chapters each, and the last of seven chapters, each differentiated from the other by the use of meter. Within this structure, a gradual transition is made from prose to blank verse. Normal spoken English and prose is arhythmic, having sometimes one, sometimes two syllables between accents. The first twelve chapters of the *Course* are written in such prose, and the portrait of the human condition given is prosaic indeed. The very last sentence of Chapter 12 is the first glimpse of what, metrically speaking, is to come: "Your *Father could* not *cease* to *love* His *Son*."

The second part begins with the first seven sections of Chapter 13 becoming increasingly iambic ~ one syllable between accents ~ until in section seven, "The Attainment of the Real World," each paragraph contains on average only three or four irregularities. This is the metric characteristic of the second twelve chapters. Frequently, paragraphs begin with emphatic statements of light reality, given in iambic pentameter. "There is a light that this world cannot give;" is the first such occurrence. "You do not really want the world you see;" "We cannot sing redemption's hymn alone;" "Your faith in nothing is deceiving you." These glorious statements are each elucidated conceptually in the paragraphs that follow from them, but each also offers an opportunity to enter into real communication. For instance, you could read *"You do not really want the world you see,"* and then read on to see what this means, or you could simply say: "Oh wow! That's actually true!" and spring immediately into Heaven. You are being prepared for a new mode of data transmission.

Deeper into the second part, increasingly strong "insertions" of iambic pentameter occur; longer passages that persist further into the paragraphs. For instance, in Chapter 21:

*Thus they define their life and where they live,*
*adjusting to it as they think they must,*
*afraid to lose the little that they have.*
*And so it is with all who see the body*
*as all they have and all their brothers have.*
*They try to reach each other, and they fail,*
*and fail again.*

Coincident with the approach of total iambic pentameter, Jesus makes this statement (in Chapter 22): "*This is a crucial period in this course,* for here the separation of you and the ego must be made complete." And this:

*This course will be believed entirely*
*or not at all.*
*For it is wholly true or wholly false,*
*and cannot be but partially believed.*

Chapter 25 is the beginning of the final part. In Chapters 25 and 26 the final transition is made into perfect iambic pentameter, making feasible the presentation as poetry in the same manner as the works of Shakespeare are presented, with two columns of the short blank verse lines to a page. Encoded into the ongoing presentation of conceptual ideas is the true communication the *Course* aims to teach. Each line is a perfectly whole package of information. It is at this last part that this volume takes up the Text.

Some parts of these two chapters are still not regular enough to allow breakdown into lines, and so are presented as prose. Also, the regular iambic pentameter in these two chapters, and early in Chapter 27, often contains lines that have one extra syllable, or short lines of only four or six syllables. These discrepancies are used to emphasize ideas in the same manner that the single lines of iambic pentameter were used in the second part, only rather than lifting you into communication, they drop you out momentarily, the aim being to teach you to recognize the difference.

In the remaining chapters of the Text, the iambic pentameter is perfect. Jesus never abbreviates words to achieve this, but does make use of words with an adaptable syllable count: *Heaven* as one or two syllables, *idea* as two or three. Maintenance of the meter accounts for what frequently seemed to be unusual syntax - but which now makes perfect sense, read as poetry.

A transition from prose to poetry also occurs in the Workbook, but it is much simpler, and quicker. The first ninety lessons are plain prose, with the exception of Lesson 78, which is totally poetic. The transition occurs entirely within seven lessons. Lesson 91 is prose. The following lessons have increasing percentages of verse, but the distinction is kept very clear. Any paragraph will either be entirely prose, or entirely poetry, and within the poetry there are very few uneven or short lines. Lesson 98 is pure poetry, and it is astonishing to discover that *everything* in the *Workbook* from Lesson 98 on is in iambic pentameter ~ the introductions to Reviews, the "instructions on themes of special relevance," such as *What is Forgiveness?*, the prayers and the Epilogue.

The Manual for Teachers and Clarification of Terms are post-production add-ons to *A Course In Miracles,* and refer to Jesus in the third person, indicating different authorship, actually a collaboration. They contain very few but very beautiful poetic passages, and these are also included here, as is a collection of iambic pentameter "zingers" from within the second part of the text.

Attempts to read the poetic form directly from the original prose layout often result in diminished comprehension. Conversely, the presentation as blank verse guarantees placing correct emphasis for understanding (though not understanding itself), and the elegance and eloquence of Jesus' poetry, and the regular rhythmic lope, offer an expanded experience of the *Course* to the musical mind. The final and most exciting discovery of all is that whole communication occurs without the need to understand concepts at all.

The magnitude and beauty of the *Course*, simply as a work of literature and without regard to its miraculous content, adequately belie any notion of its human authorship. The divinity of the ideas expressed is beyond question. Certainly the poetic and prosaic forms contained in *A Course In Miracles* are there because that was necessary for the healing of God's Son, since this is the Holy Spirit's only purpose.

~ Michael Russell

# PORTALS TO RHYTHMIC REALITY

## Iambic pentameter lead sentences from Chapters 13 thru 24

Your Father could not cease to love His Son.
(Ch12.VIII)

There is a light that this world cannot give.
(Ch13.VI)

Awaking unto Christ is following
the laws of love of your free will, and out
of quiet recognition of the truth
in them.
(Ch13.VI)

You do not really want the world you see…
(Ch13.VII)

Christ is still there, although you know Him not.
(Ch13.VII)

We cannot sing redemption's hymn alone.
(Ch13.VII)

Determine, then, to be not as you were.
(Ch13.X)

*Now* it is given you to heal and teach…
(Ch13.X)

Release from guilt as you would be released.
(Ch13.X)

Your faith in nothing is deceiving you.
(Ch14.II)

The Holy Spirit asks of you but this…
(Ch14.VII)

There is no substitute for truth. And truth
will make this plain to you as you are brought
into the place where you must meet with truth.
(Ch14.VIII)

You have one test, as sure as God, by which
to recognize if what you learned is true.
(Ch14.XI)

You cannot be your guide to miracles,
for it is you who made them necessary.
(Ch14.XI)

Can you imagine what it means to have
no cares, no worries, no anxieties,
but merely to be perfectly calm
and quiet all the time?
(Ch15.I)

Think you that you can judge the Self of God?
(Ch15.V)

The Holy Spirit cannot teach through fear.
And how can He communicate with you,
while you believe that to communicate
is to make yourself alone?
(Ch15.VII)

We who are one cannot give separately.
(Ch15.X)

Fear not to recognize the whole idea
of sacrifice as solely of your making.
(Ch15.XI)

This is a course in how to know yourself.
(Ch16.III)

Your bridge is builded stronger than you think…
(Ch16.III)

Across the bridge it is so different(Ch16.VI)
As God ascends into His rightful place
and you to yours, you will experience
again the meaning of relationship
and know it to be true. Let us ascend
in peace together to the Father,
by giving Him ascendance in our minds.
(Ch17.IV)

To substitute is to accept instead.
(Ch18.I)

Let not the dream take hold to close your eyes.
(Ch18.II)

What could God give but knowledge of Himself?
(Ch18.VI)

What would you see without the fear of death?
(Ch19.IV)

The holy do not interfere with truth.
(Ch20.III)

The blind become accustomed to their world
by their adjustments to it.
They think they know their way about in it.
(Ch21.I)

Thus they define their life and where they live,
adjusting to it as they think they must,
afraid to lose the little that they have.
And so it is with all who see the body
as all they have and all their brothers have.
They try to reach each other, and they fail,
and fail again.
(Ch21.I)

I am responsible for what I see.
I choose the feelings I experience,
and I decide upon the goal I would achieve.
And everything that seems to happen to me
I ask for , and receive as I have asked.
(Ch21.II)

Begrudge not then this little offering.
(Ch21.II)

Faith and belief and vision are the means
by which the goal of holiness is reached.
(Ch21.III)

Where would the answer be but in the Source?
(Ch21.V)

You *are* your brother's savior. He is yours.
Reason speaks happily indeed of this.
This gracious plan was given love by Love.
And what Love plans is like Itself in this:
Being united, It would have you learn
what you must be. And being one with It,
 it must be given you
to give what It has given, and gives still.
Spend but an instant in the glad acceptance
of what is given you to give your brother,
and learn with him
what has been given both of you.
To give is no more blessed than to receive.
But neither is it less.
(Ch21.VI)

The Son of God is always blessed as one.
(Ch21.VI)

Take pity on yourself, so long enslaved.
(Ch22.IN)

This is a crucial period in this course,
for here the separation of you and the ego must
be made complete.
(Ch22.II)

This course will be believed entirely
or not at all. For it is wholly true
or wholly false,
and cannot be but partially believed.
(Ch22.II)

The ego's whole continuance depends
on its belief you cannot learn this course.
(Ch22.III)

These eyes, made not to see, will never see.
(Ch22.III)

If you were one with God and recognized
this oneness, you would know His power is yours.
But you will not remember this while you
believe attack of any kind means anything.
(Ch22.VI)

Nothing around you but is part of you.
(Ch23.IN)

Be certain that it is impossible
God and the ego, or yourself and it,
will ever meet.
You seem to meet,
and make your strange alliances on grounds
that have no meaning.
For your beliefs converge upon the body,
the ego's chosen home, which you believe
is yours.
(Ch23.I)

What *you* remember *is* a part of you.
For you must be as God created you.
Truth does not fight against illusions,
nor do illusions fight against the truth.
Illusions battle only with themselves.
Being fragmented, they fragment. But truth

is indivisible, and far beyond
their little reach. You will remember what
you know when you have learned you cannot be
in conflict. One illusion about yourself
can battle with another, yet the war
of two illusions is a state
where nothing happens. There is
no victor and there is no victory.
And truth stands radiant, apart from conflict,
untouched and quiet in the peace of God.
(Ch23.I)


The "laws" of chaos can be brought to light,
though never understood. Chaotic laws
are hardly meaningful, and therefore out
of reason's sphere. Yet they appear to be
an obstacle to reason and to truth.
(Ch23.II)

How can some forms of murder not mean death?
Can an attack in any form be love?
What form of condemnation is a blessing?
Who makes his savior powerless
and finds salvation?
(Ch23.II)

Where God created life, there life must be.
(Ch23.II)

To learn this course requires willingness
to question every value that you hold.
Not one can be kept hidden and obscure
but it will jeopardize your learning.
No belief is neutral.
(Ch24.IN)

You have come far along the way of truth;
too far to falter now. Just one step more,
and every vestige of the fear of God
will melt away in love.
(Ch24.II)

Here is your savior *from* your specialness.
He is in need of your acceptance of
himself as part of you, as you for his.
(Ch24.II)

Forgiveness is the end of specialness.
(Ch24.III)

Without foundation nothing is secure.
(Ch24.III)

Forgive the great Creator of the universe,
the Source of life, of love and holiness,
the perfect Father of a perfect Son,
for your illusions of your specialness.
(Ch24.III)

The slaves of specialness will yet be free.
Such is the Will of God and of His Son.
(Ch24.III)

Rejoice you have no eyes with which to see;
no ears to listen, and no hands to hold
nor feet to guide. Be glad that only Christ
can lend you His, while you have need of them.
(Ch24.V)

The Father keeps what He created safe.
(Ch24.VII)

# Chapter 25
# THE JUSTICE OF GOD

## Introduction

The Christ in you inhabits not a body. Yet He is in you. And thus it must be that you are not within a body. What is within you cannot be outside. And it is certain that you cannot be apart from what is at the very center of your life. What gives you life cannot be housed in death. No more can you. Christ is within a frame of holiness whose only purpose is that He may be made manifest to those who know Him not, that He may call to them to come to Him and see Him where they thought their bodies were. Then will their bodies melt away, that they may frame His holiness in them.

No one who carries Christ in him can fail to recognize Him everywhere. *Except* in bodies. And as long as he believes he is in a body, where he thinks he is He cannot be. And so he carries Him unknowingly, and does not make Him manifest. And thus he does not recognize Him where He is. The son of man is not the risen Christ. Yet does the Son of God abide exactly where he is, and walks with him within his holiness, as plain to see as is his specialness set forth within his body.

The body needs no healing. But the mind that thinks it is a body is sick indeed! And it is here that Christ sets forth the remedy. His purpose folds the body in His light, and fills it with the holiness that shines from Him. And nothing that the body says or does but makes Him manifest. To those who know Him not it carries Him in gentleness and love, to heal their minds. Such is the mission that your brother has for you. And such it must be that your mission is for him.

## The Link to Truth

It cannot be that it is hard to do the task that Christ appointed you to do, since it is He Who does it. And in the doing of it will you learn the body merely seems to be the means to do it. For the Mind is His. And so it must be yours. His holiness directs the body through the mind at one with Him. And you are manifest unto your holy brother, as he to you. Here is the meeting of the holy Christ unto Himself; nor any differences perceived to stand between the aspects of His holiness, which meet and join and raise Him to His Father, whole and pure and worthy of His everlasting Love.

How can you manifest the Christ in you except to look on holiness and see Him there? Perception tells you *you* are manifest in what you see. Behold the body, and you will believe that you are there. And every body that you look upon reminds you of yourself; your sinfulness, your evil and, above all, your death. And would you not despise the one who tells you this, and seek his death instead? The message and the messenger are one. And you must see your brother as yourself. Framed in his body you will see your sinfulness, wherein you stand condemned. Set in his holiness, the Christ in him proclaims Himself as you.

Perception is a choice of what you want yourself to be; the world you want to live in, and the state in which you think your mind will be content and satisfied. It chooses where you think your safety lies, at your decision. It reveals yourself to you as you would have you be. And always is it faithful to your purpose, from which it never separates, nor gives the slightest witness unto anything the purpose in your mind upholdeth not. Perception is a part of what it is your purpose to behold, for means and end are never separate. And thus you learn what seems to have a life apart has none.

*You* are the means for God; not separate, nor with a life apart from His. His Life is manifest in you who are His Son. Each aspect of Himself is framed in holiness and perfect purity, in love celestial and so complete it wishes only that it may release all that it looks upon unto itself. Its radiance shines through each body that it looks upon, and brushes all its darkness into light merely by looking past it *to* the light.

The veil is lifted through its gentleness, and nothing hides the face of Christ from its beholders. You and your brother stand before Him now, to let Him draw aside the veil that seems to keep you separate and apart.

Since you believe that you are separate, Heaven presents itself to you as separate, too. Not that it is in truth, but that the link that has been given you to join the truth may reach to you through what you understand. Father and Son and Holy Spirit are as One, as all your brothers join as one in truth. Christ and His Father never have been separate, and Christ abides within your understanding, in the part of you that shares His Father's Will. The Holy Spirit links the other part - the tiny, mad desire to be separate, different and special - to the Christ, to make the oneness clear to what is really one. In this world this is not understood, but can be taught.

The Holy Spirit serves Christ's purpose in your mind, so that the aim of specialness can be corrected where the error lies. Because His purpose still is one with both the Father and the Son, He knows the Will of God and what you really will. But this is understood by mind perceived as one, aware that it is one, and so experienced. It is the Holy Spirit's function to teach you how this oneness is experienced, what you must do that it can be experienced, and where you should go to do it.

All this takes note of time and place as if they were discrete, for while you think that part of you is separate, the concept of a oneness joined as one is meaningless. It is apparent that a mind so split could never be the teacher of a Oneness Which unites all things within Itself. And so What is within this mind, and does unite all things together, must be its Teacher. Yet must It use the language that this mind can understand, in the condition in which it thinks it is. And It must use all learning to transfer illusions to the truth, taking all false ideas of what you are, and leading you beyond them to the truth that *is* beyond them. All this can very simply be reduced to this:

*What is the same can not be different,*
*and what is one can not have separate parts.*

## The Savior from the Dark

Is it not evident that what the body's eyes perceive fills you with fear? Perhaps you think you find a hope of satisfaction there. Perhaps you fancy to attain some peace and satisfaction in the world as you perceive it. Yet it must be evident the outcome does not change. Despite your hopes and fancies, always does despair result. And there is no exception, nor will there ever be. The only value that the past can hold is that you learn it gave you no rewards which you would want to keep. For only thus will you be willing to relinquish it, and have it gone forever.

Is it not strange that you should cherish still some hope of satisfaction from the world you see? In no respect, at any time or place, has anything but fear and guilt been your reward. How long is needed for you to realize the chance of change in this respect is hardly worth delaying change that might result in better outcome? For one thing is sure; the way you see, and long have seen, gives no support to base your future hopes, and no suggestions of success at all. To place your hopes where no hope lies must make you hopeless. Yet is this hopelessness your choice, while you would seek for hope where none is ever found.

Is it not also true that you have found some hope apart from this; some glimmering, - inconstant, wavering, yet dimly seen, - that hopefulness is warranted on grounds that are not in this world? And yet your hope that they may still be here prevents you still from giving up the hopeless and unrewarding task you set yourself. Can it make sense to hold the fixed belief that there is reason to uphold pursuit of what has always failed, on grounds that it will suddenly succeed and bring what it has never brought before?

Its past *has* failed. Be glad that it is gone within your mind, to darken what is there. Take not the form for content, for the form is but a means for content. And the frame is but a means to hold the picture up, so that it can be seen. A frame that hides the picture has no purpose. It cannot be a frame if it is what you see. Without the picture is the frame without its meaning. Its purpose is to set the picture off, and not itself.

Who hangs an empty frame upon a wall and stands before it, deep in reverence, as if a masterpiece were there to see? Yet if you see your brother as a body, it is but this you do. The masterpiece that God has set within this frame is all there is to see. The body holds it for a while, without obscuring it in any way. Yet what God has created needs no frame, for what He has created He supports and frames within Himself. His masterpiece He offers you to see. And would you rather see the frame instead of this? And see the picture not at all?

The Holy Spirit is the frame God set around the part of Him that you would see as separate. Yet its frame is joined to its Creator, one with Him and with His masterpiece. This is its purpose, and you do not make the frame into the picture when you choose to see it in its place. The frame that God has given it but serves His purpose, not yours apart from His. It is your separate purpose that obscures the picture, and cherishes the frame instead of it. Yet God has set His masterpiece within a frame that will endure forever, when yours has crumbled into dust. But think you not the picture is destroyed in any way. What God creates is safe from all corruption, unchanged and perfect in eternity.

Accept God's frame instead of yours, and you will see the masterpiece. Look at its loveliness, and understand the Mind that thought it, not in flesh and bones, but in a frame as lovely as Itself. Its holiness lights up the sinlessness the frame of darkness hides, and casts a veil of light across the picture's face which but reflects the light that shines from it to its Creator. Think not this face was ever darkened because you saw it in a frame of death. God kept it safe that you might look on it, and see the holiness that He has given it.

Within the darkness see the savior *from* the dark, and understand your brother as his Father's Mind shows him to you. He will step forth from darkness as you look on him, and you will see the dark no more. The darkness touched him not, nor you who brought him forth for you to look upon. His sinlessness but pictures yours. His gentleness becomes your strength, and both will gladly look within, and see the holiness that must be there because of what you looked upon in him. He is the frame in which your holiness is set, and what God gave him must be given you. However much he overlooks the masterpiece in him and sees only a frame of darkness, it is still your only function to behold in him what he sees not. And in this seeing is the vision shared that looks on Christ instead of seeing death.

How could the Lord of Heaven not be glad if you appreciate His masterpiece? What could He do but offer thanks to you who love His Son as He does? Would He not make known to you His Love, if you but share His praise of what He loves? God cherishes creation as the perfect Father that He is. And so His joy is made complete when any part of Him joins in His praise, to share His joy. This brother is His perfect gift to you. And He is glad and thankful when you thank His perfect Son for being what he is. And all His thanks and gladness shine on you who would complete His joy, along with Him. And thus is yours completed. Not one ray of darkness can be seen by those who will to make their Father's happiness complete, and theirs along with His. The gratitude of God Himself is freely offered to everyone who shares His purpose. It is not His Will to be alone. And neither is it yours.

Forgive your brother, and you cannot separate yourself from him nor from his Father. You need no forgiveness, for the wholly pure have never sinned. Give, then, what He has given you, that you may see His Son as one, and thank his Father as He thanks you. Nor believe that all His praise is given not to you. For what you give is His, and giving it, you learn to understand His gift to you. And give the Holy Spirit what He offers unto the Father and the Son alike. Nothing has power over you except His Will and yours, which but extends His Will. It was for this you were created, and your brother with you and at one with you.

You and your brother are the same as God Himself is One, and not divided in His Will. And you must have one purpose, since He gave the same to both of you. His Will is brought together as you join in will, that you be made complete by offering completion to your brother. See not in him the sinfulness he sees, but give him honor that you may esteem yourself and him. To you and your brother is given the power of salvation, that escape from darkness into light be yours to share; that you may see as one what never has been separate, nor apart from all God's Love as given equally.

**Perception and Choice**

To the extent to which you value guilt, to that extent will you perceive a world in which attack is justified. To the extent to which you recognize that guilt is meaningless, to that extent you will perceive attack cannot *be* justified. This is in accord with perception's fundamental law: You see what you believe is there, and you believe it there because you want it there. Perception has no other law than this. The rest but stems from this, to hold it up and offer it support. This is perception's form, adapted to this world, of God's more basic law; that love creates itself, and nothing but itself.

God's laws do not obtain directly to a world perception rules, for such a world could not have been created by the Mind to which perception has no meaning. Yet are His laws reflected everywhere. Not that the world where this reflection is, is real at all. Only because His Son believes it is, and from His Son's belief He could not let Himself be separate entirely. He could not enter His Son's insanity with him, but He could be sure His sanity went there with him, so he could not be lost forever in the madness of his wish.

Perception rests on choosing; knowledge does not. Knowledge has but one law because it has but one Creator. But this world has two who made it, and they do not see it as the same. To each it has a different purpose, and to each it is a perfect means to serve the goal for which it is perceived. For specialness, it is the perfect frame to set it off; the perfect battleground to wage its wars, the perfect shelter for illusions which it would make real. Not one but it upholds in its perception; not one but can be fully justified.

There is another Maker of the world, the simultaneous Corrector of the mad belief that anything could be established and maintained without some link that kept it still within the laws of God; not as the law itself upholds the universe as God created it, but in some form adapted to the need the Son of God believes he has. Corrected error is the error's end. And thus has God protected still His Son, even in error.

There is another purpose in the world that error made, because it has another Maker Who can reconcile its goal with His Creator's purpose. In His perception of the world, nothing is seen but justifies forgiveness and the sight of perfect sinlessness. Nothing arises but is met with instant and complete forgiveness. Nothing remains an instant, to obscure the sinlessness that shines unchanged, beyond the pitiful attempts of specialness to put it out of mind, where it must be, and light the body up instead of it. The lamps of Heaven are not for mind to choose to see them where it will. If it elects to see them elsewhere from their home, as if they lit a place where they could never be, then must the Maker of the world correct your error, lest you remain in darkness where the lamps are not.

Everyone here has entered darkness, yet no one has entered it alone. Nor need he stay more than an instant. For he has come with Heaven's Help within him, ready to lead him out of darkness into light at any time. The time he chooses can be any time, for help is there, awaiting but his choice. And when he chooses to avail himself of what is given him, then will he see each situation that he thought before was means to justify his anger turned to an event which justifies his love. He will hear plainly that the calls to war he heard before are really calls to peace. He will perceive that where he gave attack is but another altar where he can, with equal ease and far more happiness, bestow forgiveness. And he will reinterpret all temptation as just another chance to bring him joy.

How can a misperception be a sin? Let all your brother's errors be to you nothing except a chance for you to see the workings of the Helper given you to see the world He made instead of yours. What, then, *is* justified? What do you want? For these two questions are the same. And when you see them as the same, your choice is made. For it is seeing them as one that brings release from the belief there are two ways to see. This world has much to offer to your peace, and many chances to extend your own forgiveness. Such its purpose is, to those who want to see peace and forgiveness descend on them, and offer them the light.

The Maker of the world of gentleness has perfect power to offset the world of violence and hate that seems to stand between you and His gentleness. It is not there in His forgiving eyes. And therefore it need not be there in yours. Sin is the fixed belief perception cannot change. What has been damned is damned and damned forever, being forever unforgivable. If, then, it is forgiven, sin's perception must have been wrong. And thus is change made possible. The Holy Spirit, too, sees what He sees as far beyond the chance of change. But on His vision sin cannot encroach, for sin has been corrected by His sight. And thus it must have been an error, not a sin. For what it claimed could never be, has been. Sin is attacked by punishment, and so preserved. But to forgive it is to change its state from error into truth.

The Son of God could never sin, but he can wish for what would hurt him. And he has the power to think he can be hurt. What could this be except a misperception of himself? Is this a sin or a mistake, forgivable or not? Does he need help or condemnation? Is it your purpose that he be saved or damned? Forgetting not that what he is to you will make this choice your future? For you make it *now*, the instant when all time becomes a means to reach a goal. Make, then, your choice. But recognize that in this choice the purpose of the world you see is chosen, and will be justified.

### The Light You Bring

Minds that are joined and recognize they are,
can feel no guilt. For they cannot attack,
and they rejoice that this is so,
seeing their safety in this happy fact.
Their joy is in the innocence they see.
And thus they seek for it, because it is
their purpose to behold it and rejoice.
Everyone seeks for what will bring him joy
as he defines it. It is not the aim,
as such, that varies. Yet it is the way
in which the aim is seen that makes the choice
of means inevitable, and beyond
the hope of change unless the aim is changed.
And then the means are chosen once again,
as what will bring rejoicing is defined
another way and sought for differently.

Perception's basic law could thus be said,
"You will rejoice at what you see because
you see it to rejoice." And while you think
that suffering and sin will bring you joy,
so long will they be there for you to see.
Nothing is harmful or beneficent
apart from what you wish.
It is your wish that makes it what it is
in its effects on you.
Because you chose it as a means to gain
these same effects, believing them to be
the bringers of rejoicing and of joy.
Even in Heaven does this law obtain.
The Son of God creates to bring him joy,
sharing his Father's purpose in
his own creation, that his joy
might be increased, and God's along with his.

You maker of a world that is not so,
take rest and comfort in another world
where peace abides. This world you bring with you
to all the weary eyes and tired hearts
that look on sin and beat its sad refrain.
From you can come their rest. From you can rise
a world they will rejoice to look upon,
and where their hearts are glad. In you there is
a vision that extends to all of them,
and covers them in gentleness and light.
And in this widening world of light
the darkness that they thought was there
is pushed away, until it is
but distant shadows, far away,

not long to be remembered as
the sun shines them to nothingness.
And all their "evil" thoughts and "sinful" hopes,
their dreams of guilt and merciless revenge,
and every wish to hurt and kill and die,
will disappear before the sun you bring.

Would you not do this for the Love of God? And for *yourself*? For think what it would do for you. Your "evil" thoughts that haunt you now will seem increasingly remote and far away from you. And they go farther and farther off, because the sun in you has risen that they may be pushed away before the light. They linger for a while, a little while, in twisted forms too far away for recognition, and are gone forever. And in the sunlight you will stand in quiet, in innocence and wholly unafraid. And from you will the rest you found extend, so that your peace can never fall away and leave you homeless. Those who offer peace to everyone have found a home in Heaven the world cannot destroy. For it is large enough to hold the world within its peace.

In you is all of Heaven. Every leaf
that falls is given life in you. Each bird
that ever sang will sing again in you.
And every flower that ever bloomed has saved
its perfume and its loveliness for you.
What aim can supersede the Will of God
and of His Son,
that Heaven be restored to him for whom
it was created as his only home?
Nothing before and nothing after it.
No other place; no other state nor time.
Nothing beyond nor nearer. Nothing else.
In any form. This can you bring to all
the world, and all the thoughts that entered it
and were mistaken for a little while.
How better could your own mistakes be brought
to truth than by your willingness to bring
the light of Heaven with you, as you walk
beyond the world of darkness into light?

### The State of Sinlessness

The state of sinlessness is merely this:
The whole desire to attack is gone,
and so there is no reason to perceive
the Son of God as other than he is.
The need for guilt is gone because it has
no purpose, and is meaningless without
the goal of sin. Attack and sin are bound
as one illusion, each the cause and aim
and justifier of the other. Each
is meaningless alone, but seems to draw
a meaning from the other. Each depends
upon the other for whatever sense
it seems to have. And no one could believe
in one unless the other were the truth,
for each attests the other must be true.

Attack makes Christ your enemy, and God
along with Him. Must you not be afraid
with "enemies" like these? And must you not
be fearful of yourself? For you have hurt
yourself, and made your Self your "enemy."
And now you must believe you are not you,
but somethingalien to yourself
and "something else,"
a "something" to be feared instead of loved.
Who would attack whatever he perceives
as wholly innocent? And who, *because*
he wishes to attack, can fail to think
he must be guilty to maintain the wish,
while wanting innocence?
For who could see the Son of God
as innocentand wish him dead?
Christ stands before you,
each time you look upon your brother.
He has not gone because your eyes are closed.
But what is there to see by searching for
your Savior, seeing Him through sightless eyes?

It is not Christ you see by looking thus.
It is the "enemy," confused with Christ,
you look upon. And hate because
there is no sin in him for you to see.
Nor do you hear his plaintive call,
unchanged in content in whatever form
the call is made, that you unite with him,
and join with him in innocence and peace.
And yet, beneath the ego's senseless shrieks,

such is the call that God has given him,
that you might hear in him His Call to you,
and answer by returning unto God
what is His Own.

The Son of God asks only this of you;
that you return to him what is his due,
that you may share in it with him. Alone
does neither have it. So must it remain
useless to both. Together, it will give
to each an equal strength to save the other,
and save himself along with him. Forgiven
by you, your savior offers you salvation.
Condemned by you, he offers death to you.
In everyone you see but the reflection
of what you choose to have him be to you.
If you decide against his proper function,
the only one he has in truth,
you are depriving him of all the joy
he would have found if he fulfilled the role
God gave to him. But think not Heaven is lost
to him alone. Nor can it be regained
unless the way is shown to him through you,
that you may find it, walking by his side.

It is no sacrifice that he be saved,
for by his freedom will you gain your own.
To let his function be fulfilled is but
the means to let yours be. And so you walk
toward Heaven or toward hell, but not alone.
How beautiful his sinlessness will be
when you perceive it! And how great will be
your joy, when he is free to offer you
the gift of sight God gave to him for you!
He has no need but this; that you
allow him freedom to complete the task
God gave to him. Remembering but this;
that what he does you do, along with him.
And as you see him, so do you define
the function he will have for you, until
you see him differently and let him be
what God appointed that he be to you.

Against the hatred that the Son of God
may cherish toward himself, is God believed
to be without the power to save what He
created from the pain of hell. But in
the love he shows himself is God made free
to let His Will be done. In your brother
you see the picture of your own belief
in what the Will of God must be for you.
In your forgiveness will you understand
His Love for you; through your attack believe
He hates you, thinking Heaven must be hell.
Look once again upon your brother, not
without the understanding that he is
the way to Heaven or to hell, as you
perceive him. But forget not this; the role
you give to him is given you, and you
will walk the way you pointed out to him
because it is your judgment on yourself.

### The Special Function

The grace of God rests gently on forgiving eyes,
and everything they look on speaks
of Him to the beholder. He can see
no evil; nothing in the world to fear,
and no one who is different from himself.
And as he loves them, so he looks upon
himself with love and gentleness. He would
no more condemn himself for his mistakes
than damn another. He is not an arbiter
of vengeance, nor a punisher of sin.
The kindness of his sight rests on himself
with all the tenderness it offers others.
For he would only heal and only bless.
And being in accord with what God wills,
he has the power to heal and bless all those
he looks on with the grace of God upon his sight.

Eyes become used to darkness, and the light
of brilliant day seems painful to the eyes
grown long accustomed to the dim effects
perceived at twilight. And they turn away
from sunlight and the clarity it brings
to what they look upon. Dimness seems better;
easier to see, and better recognized.
Somehow the vague and more obscure
seems easier to look upon;
less painful to the eyes than what
is wholly clear and unambiguous.
Yet this is not what eyes are for,
and who can say that he prefers
the darkness and maintain he wants to see?

The wish to see calls down the grace of God
upon your eyes, and brings the gift of light

that makes sight possible.
Would you behold your brother? God is glad
to have you look on him. He does not will
your savior be unrecognized by you.
Nor does He will that he remain without
the function that He gave to him. Let him no more
be lonely, for the lonely ones
are those who see no function in the world
for them to fill;
no place where they are needed, and no aim
which only they can perfectly fulfill.

Such is the Holy Spirit's kind perception
of specialness; His use of what you made,
to heal instead of harm. To each He gives
a special function in salvation he
alone can fill; a part for only him.
Nor is the plan complete until he finds
his special function, and fulfills the part
assigned to him, to make himself complete
within a world where incompletion rules.

Here, where the laws of God do not prevail
in perfect form, can he yet do
one perfect thing and make one perfect choice.
And by this act of special faithfulness
to one perceived as other than himself,
he learns the gift was given to himself,
and so they must be one. Forgiveness is
the only function meaningful in time.
It is the means the Holy Spirit uses
to translate specialness from sin
into salvation. Forgiveness is
for all. But when it rests on all it is
complete, and every function of this world
completed with it. Then is time no more.
Yet while in time, there is still much to do.
And each must do what is allotted him,
for on his part does all the plan depend.
He *has* a special part in time
for so he chose,
and choosing it, he made it for himself.
His wish was not denied but changed in form,
to let it serve his brother and himself,
and thus become a means to save
instead of lose.

Salvation is no more than a reminder this world is not your home. Its laws are not imposed on you, its values are not yours. And nothing that you think you see in it is really there at all. This is seen and understood as each one takes his part in its undoing, as he did in making it. He has the means for either, as he always did. The specialness he chose to hurt himself did God appoint to be the means for his salvation, from the very instant that the choice was made. His special sin was made his special grace. His special hate became his special love.

The Holy Spirit needs your special function, that His may be fulfilled. Think not you lack a special value here. You wanted it, and it is given you. All that you made can serve salvation easily and well. The Son of God can make no choice the Holy Spirit cannot employ on his behalf, and not against himself. Only in darkness does your specialness appear to be attack. In light, you see it as your special function in the plan to save the Son of God from all attack, and let him understand that he is safe, as he has always been, and will remain in time and in eternity alike. This is the function given you for your brother. Take it gently, then, from your brother's hand, and let salvation be perfectly fulfilled in you. Do this *one* thing, that everything be given you.

## The Rock of Salvation

Yet if the Holy Spirit can commute
each sentence that you laid upon yourself
into a blessing, then it cannot be a sin.
Sin is the only thing in all the world
that cannot change. It is immutable.
And on its changelessness the world depends.
The magic of the world can seem to hide
the pain of sin from sinners, and deceive
with glitter and with guile. Yet each one knows
the cost of sin is death. And so it is.
For sin is a request for death, a wish
to make this world's foundation sure as love,
dependable as Heaven, and as strong
as God Himself. The world is safe from love
to everyone who thinks sin possible.
Nor will it change. Yet is it possible
what God created not
should share the attributes of His creation,
when it opposes it in every way?

It cannot be the "sinner's" wish for death
is just as strong as is God's Will for life.
Nor can the basis of a world
He did not make be firm and sure as Heaven.
How could it be that hell and Heaven are
the same? And is it possible that what
He did not will cannot be changed? What is
immutable besides His Will? And what
can share its attributes except itself?
What wish can rise against His Will, and be
immutable? If you could realize
nothing is changeless but the Will of God,
this course would not be difficult for you.
For it is this that you do not believe.
Yet there is nothing else you could believe,
if you but looked at what it really is.

Let us go back to what we said before,
and think of it more carefully.
It must be so
that either God is mad, or is this world
a place of madness. Not one Thought of His
makes any sense at all within this world.
And nothing that the world believes as true
has any meaning in His Mind at all.
What makes no sense and has no meaning is
insanity.
And what is madness cannot be the truth.
If one belief so deeply valued here
were true, then every Thought God ever had
is an illusion. And if but one Thought
of His is true, then all beliefs the world
gives any meaning to are false, and make
no sense at all. This is the choice you make.
Do not attempt to see it differently,
nor twist it into something it is not.
For only this decision can you make.
The rest is up to God, and not to you.

To justify one value that the world upholds
is to deny your Father's sanity
and yours. For God and His beloved Son
do not think differently. And it is the
agreement of their thought that makes the Son
a co-creator with the Mind Whose Thought
created him. So if he chooses to
believe one thought opposed to truth, he has
decided he is not his Father's Son
because the Son is mad, and sanity
must lie apart from both the Father and
the Son. This you believe. Think not that this
belief depends upon the form it takes.
Who thinks the world is sane in any way,
is justified in anything it thinks,
or is maintained by any form of reason,
believes this to be true. Sin is not real
*because* the Father and the Son
are not insane. This world is meaningless
*because* it rests on sin. Who could create
the changeless if it does not rest on truth?

The Holy Spirit has the power to change
the whole foundation of the world you see
to something else; a basis not insane,
on which a sane perception can be based,
another world perceived. And one in which
nothing is contradicted that would lead
the Son of God to sanity and joy.
Nothing attests to death and cruelty;
to separation and to differences.
For here is everything perceived as one,
and no one loses that each one may gain.

Test everything that you believe against
this one requirement, and understand
that everything that meets this one demand

is worthy of your faith. But nothing else.
What is not love is sin, and either one
perceives the other as insane and meaningless.
Love is the basis for a world perceived
as wholly mad to sinners, who believe
theirs is the way to sanity. But sin
is equally insane within the sight
of love, whose gentle eyes would look beyond
the madness and rest peacefully on truth.
Each sees a world immutable, as each
defines the changeless and eternal truth
of what you are. And each reflects a view
of what the Father and the Son must be,
to make that viewpoint meaningful and sane.

Your special function is the special form
in which the fact that God is not insane
appears most sensible and meaningful
to you. The content is the same. The form
is suited to your special needs, and to
the special time and place in which you think
you find yourself, and where you can be free
of place and time, and all that you believe
must limit you. The Son of God cannot
be bound by time nor place nor anything
God did not will. Yet if His Will is seen
as madness, then the form of sanity
which makes it most acceptable to those
who are insane requires special choice.
Nor can this choice be made by the insane,
whose problem is their choices are not free,
and made with reason in the light of sense.

It *would* be madness to entrust salvation
to the insane. Because He is not mad
has God appointed One as sane as He
to raise a saner world to meet the sight
of everyone who chose insanity
as his salvation. To this One is given
the choice of form most suitable to him;
one which will not attack the world he sees,
but enter into it in quietness
and show him he is mad. This One but points
to an alternative, another way
of looking at what he has seen before,
and recognizes as the world in which
he lives, and thought he understood before.

Now must he question this, because the form
of the alternative is one which he
cannot deny, nor overlook, nor fail
completely to perceive at all. To each
his special function is designed to be
perceived as possible, and more and more
desired, as it proves to him that it
is an alternative he really wants.
From this position does his sinfulness,
and all the sin he sees within the world,
offer him less and less. Until he comes
to understand it cost him his sanity,
and stands between him and whatever hope
he has of being sane. Nor is he left
without escape from madness, for he has
a special part in everyone's escape.
He can no more be left outside, without
a special function in the hope of peace,
than could the Father overlook His Son,
and pass him by in careless thoughtlessness.

What is dependable except God's Love?
And where does sanity abide except
in Him? The One Who speaks for Him can show
you this, in the alternative He chose
especially for you. It is God's Will
that you remember this, and so emerge
from deepest mourning into perfect joy.
Accept the function that has been assigned
to you in God's Own plan to show His Son
that hell and Heaven are different, not the same.
And that in Heaven *They* are all the same,
without the differences which would have made
a hell of Heaven and a heaven of hell,
had such insanity been possible.

The whole belief that someone loses but
reflects the underlying tenet God
must be insane. For in this world it seems
that one must gain *because* another lost.
If this were true, then God is mad indeed!
But what is this belief except a form
of the more basic tenet, "Sin is real,
and rules the world?" For every little gain
must someone lose, and pay exact amount
in blood and suffering. For otherwise
would evil triumph, and destruction be
the total cost of any gain at all.
You who believe that God is mad,

look carefully at this, and understand
that it must be [that] either God or this
must be insane, but hardly both.

Salvation is rebirth of the idea
no one can lose for anyone to gain.
And everyone *must* gain, if anyone
would be a gainer. Here is sanity
restored. And on this single rock of truth
can faith in God's eternal saneness rest
in perfect confidence and perfect peace.
Reason is satisfied, for all insane
beliefs can be corrected here. And sin
must be impossible, if this is true.
This is the rock on which salvation rests,
the vantage point from which the Holy Spirit
gives meaning and direction to the plan
in which your special function has a part.

For here your special function is made whole,
because it shares the function of the whole.

Remember all temptation is but this;
a mad belief that God's insanity
would make you sane and give you what you want;
that either God or you must lose to madness
because your aims can not be reconciled.
Death demands life,
but life is not maintained at any cost.
No one can suffer for the Will of God
to be fulfilled. Salvation is His Will
*because* you share it. Not for you alone,
but for the Self That is the Son of God.
He cannot lose, for if he could
the loss would be his Father's,
and in Him no loss is possible.
And this is sane because it is the truth.

### Justice Returned to Love

The Holy Spirit can use all that you give to Him for your salvation. But He cannot use what you withhold, for He cannot take it from you without your willingness. For if He did, you would believe He wrested it from you against your will. And so you would not learn it *is* your will to be without it. You need not give it to Him wholly willingly, for if you could you had no need of Him. But this He needs; that you prefer He take it than that you keep it for yourself alone, and recognize that what brings loss to no one you would not know. This much is necessary to add to the idea no one can lose for you to gain. And nothing more.

Here is the only principle salvation needs. Nor is it necessary that your faith in it be strong, unswerving, and without attack from all beliefs opposed to it. You have no fixed allegiance. But remember salvation is not needed by the saved. You are not called upon to do what one divided still against himself would find impossible. Have little faith that wisdom could be found in such a state of mind. But be you thankful that only little faith is asked of you. What but a little faith remains to those who still believe in sin? What could they know of Heaven and the justice of the saved?

There is a kind of justice in salvation of which the world knows nothing. To the world, justice and vengeance are the same, for sinners see justice only as their punishment, perhaps sustained by someone else, but not escaped. The laws of sin demand a victim. Who it may be makes little difference. But death must be the cost and must be paid. This is not justice, but insanity. Yet how could justice be defined without insanity where love means hate, and death is seen as victory and triumph over eternity and timelessness and life?

You who know not of justice still can ask, and learn the answer. Justice looks on all in the same way. It is not just that one should lack for what another has. For that is vengeance in whatever form it takes. Justice demands no sacrifice, for any sacrifice is made that sin may be preserved and kept. It is a payment offered for the cost of sin, but not the total cost. The rest is taken from another, to be laid beside your little payment, to "atone" for all that you would keep, and not give up. So is the victim seen as partly you, with someone else by far the greater part. And in the total cost, the greater his the less is yours. And justice, being blind, is satisfied by being paid, it matters not by whom.

Can this be justice? God knows not of this. But justice does He know, and knows it well. For He is wholly fair to everyone. Vengeance is alien to God's Mind *because* He knows of justice. To be just is to be fair, and not be vengeful. Fairness and vengeance are impossible, for each one contradicts the other and denies that it is real. It is impossible for you to share the Holy Spirit's justice with a mind that can conceive of specialness at all. Yet how could He be just if He condemns a sinner for the crimes he did not do, but thinks he did? And where would justice be if He demanded of the ones obsessed with the idea of punishment that they lay it aside, unaided, and perceive it is not true?

It is extremely hard for those who still believe sin meaningful to understand the Holy Spirit's justice. They must believe He shares their own confusion, and cannot avoid the vengeance that their own belief in justice must entail. And so they fear the Holy Spirit, and perceive the "wrath" of God in Him. Nor can they trust Him not to strike them dead with lightning bolts torn from the "fires" of Heaven by God's Own angry Hand. They *do* believe that Heaven is hell, and *are* afraid of love. And deep suspicion and the chill of fear comes over them when they are told that they have never sinned. Their world depends on sin's stability. And they perceive the "threat" of what God knows as justice to be more destructive to themselves and to their world than vengeance, which they understand and love.

So do they think the loss of sin a curse. And flee the Holy Spirit as if He were a messenger from hell, sent from above, in treachery and guile, to work God's vengeance on them in the guise of a deliverer and friend. What could He be to them except a devil, dressed to deceive within an angel's cloak. And what escape has He for them except a door to hell that seems to look like Heaven's gate?

Yet justice cannot punish those who ask
for punishment, but have a Judge Who knows
that they are wholly innocent in truth.
In justice He is bound to set them free,
and give them all the honor they deserve
and have denied themselves
because they are not fair,
and cannot understand
that they are innocent.
Love is not understandable to sinners
because they think that justice is split off
from love, and stands for something else. And thus
is love perceived as weak, and vengeance strong.
For love has lost when judgment left its side,
and is too weak to save from punishment.
But vengeance without love has gained in strength
by being separate and apart from love.
And what but vengeance now can help and save,
while love stands feebly by with helpless hands,
bereft of justice and vitality,
and powerless to save?

What can Love ask
of you who think that all of this is true?
Could He, in justice and in love, believe
in your confusion you have much to give?

You are not asked to trust Him far. No more
than what you see He offers you, and what
you recognize you could not give yourself.
In God's Own justice does He recognize
all you deserve, but understands as well
that you cannot accept it for yourself.
It is His special function to hold out
to you the gifts the innocent deserve.
And every one that you accept brings joy
to Him as well as you. He knows that Heaven
is richer made by each one you accept.
And God rejoices as His Son receives
what loving justice knows to be his due.
For love and justice are not different.
*Because* they are the same does mercy stand
at God's right Hand, and gives the Son of God
the power to forgive himself of sin.

To him who merits everything,
how can it be
that anything be kept from him? For that
would be injustice, and unfair indeed
to all the holiness that is in him,
however much he recognize it not.
God knows of no injustice. He would not
allow His Son be judged by those who seek

his death, and could not see his worth at all. What honest witnesses could they call forth to speak on his behalf? And who would come to plead for him, and not against his life? No justice would be given him by you. Yet God ensured that justice would be done unto the Son He loves, and would protect from all unfairness you might seek to offer, believing vengeance is his proper due.

As specialness cares not who pays the cost of sin, so it be paid, the Holy Spirit heeds not who looks on innocence at last, provided it is seen and recognized. For just *one* witness is enough, if he sees truly. Simple justice asks no more. Of each one does the Holy Spirit ask if he will be that one, so justice may return to love and there be satisfied. Each special function He allots is but for this; that each one learn that love and justice are not separate. And both are strengthened by their union with each other. Without love is justice prejudiced and weak. And love without justice is impossible. For love is fair, and cannot chasten without cause. What cause can be to warrant an attack upon the innocent? In justice, then, does love correct mistakes, but not in vengeance. For that would be unjust to innocence.

You can be perfect witness to the power of love and justice, if you understand it is impossible the Son of God could merit vengeance. You need not perceive, in every circumstance, that this is true. Nor need you look to your experience within the world, which is but shadows of all that is really happening within yourself. The understanding that you need comes not of you, but from a larger Self, so great and holy that He could not doubt His innocence.
Your special function is a call to Him, that He may smile on you whose sinlessness He shares. His understanding will be yours. And so the Holy Spirit's special function has been fulfilled. God's Son has found a witness unto his sinlessness and not his sins. How little need you give the Holy Spirit that simple justice may be given you.

Without impartiality there is no justice. How can specialness be just? Judge not because you cannot, not because you are a miserable sinner too. How can the special really understand that justice is the same for everyone? To take from one to give another must be an injustice to them both, since they are equal in the Holy Spirit's sight. Their Father gave the same inheritance to both. Who would have more or less is not aware that he has everything. He is no judge of what must be another's due, because he thinks he is deprived. And so must he be envious, and try to take away from whom he judges. He is not impartial, and cannot fairly see another's rights because his own have been obscured to him.

You have the right to all the universe; to perfect peace, complete deliverance from all effects of sin, and to the life eternal, joyous and complete in every way, as God appointed for His holy Son. This is the only justice Heaven knows, and all the Holy Spirit brings to earth. Your special function shows you nothing else but perfect justice can prevail for you. And you are safe from vengeance in all forms. The world deceives, but it cannot replace God's justice with a version of its own. For only love is just, and can perceive what justice must accord the Son of God. Let love decide, and never fear that you, in your unfairness, will deprive yourself of what God's justice has allotted you.

## The Justice of Heaven

What can it be but arrogance to think your little errors cannot be undone by Heaven's justice? And what could this mean except that they are sins and not mistakes, forever uncorrectable, and to be met with vengeance, not with justice? Are you willing to be released from all effects of sin? You cannot answer this until you see all that the answer must entail. For if you answer "yes" it means you will forego all values of this world in favor of the peace of Heaven. Not one sin would you retain. And not one doubt that this is possible will you hold dear that sin be kept in place. You mean that truth has greater value now than all illusions. And you recognize that truth must be revealed to you, because you know not what it is.

To give reluctantly is not to gain the gift, because you are reluctant to accept it. It is saved for you until reluctance to receive it disappears, and you are willing it be given you. God's justice warrants gratitude, not fear. Nothing you give is lost to you or anyone, but cherished and preserved in Heaven, where all of the treasures given to God's Son are kept for him, and offered anyone who but holds out his hand in willingness they be received. Nor is the treasure less as it is given out. Each gift but adds to the supply. For God is fair. He does not fight against His Son's reluctance to perceive salvation as a gift from Him. Yet would His justice not be satisfied until it is received by everyone.

Be certain any answer to a problem the Holy Spirit solves will always be one in which no one loses. And this must be true, because He asks no sacrifice of anyone. An answer which demands the slightest loss to anyone has not resolved the problem, but has added to it and made it greater, harder to resolve and more unfair. It is impossible the Holy Spirit could see unfairness as a resolution. To Him, what is unfair must be corrected *because* it is unfair. And every error is a perception in which one, at least, is seen unfairly. Thus is justice not accorded to the Son of God. When anyone is seen as losing, he has been condemned. And punishment becomes his due instead of justice.

The sight of innocence makes punishment impossible, and justice sure. The Holy Spirit's perception leaves no ground for an attack. Only a loss could justify attack, and loss of any kind He cannot see. The world solves problems in another way. It sees a resolution as a state in which it is decided who shall win and who shall lose; how much the one shall take, and how much can the loser still defend. Yet does the problem still remain unsolved, for only justice can set up a state in which there is no loser; no one left unfairly treated and deprived, and thus with grounds for vengeance. Problem solving cannot be vengeance, which at best can bring another problem added to the first, in which the murder is not obvious.

The Holy Spirit's problem solving is the way in which the problem ends. It has been solved because it has been met with justice. Until it has it will recur, because it has not yet been solved. The principle that justice means no one can lose is crucial to this course. For miracles depend on justice. Not as it is seen through this world's eyes, but as God knows it and as knowledge is reflected in the sight the Holy Spirit gives.

No one deserves to lose. And what would be unjust to him cannot occur. Healing must be for everyone, because he does not merit an attack of any kind. What order can there be in miracles, unless someone deserves to suffer more and others less? And is this justice to the wholly innocent? A miracle *is* justice. It is not a special gift to some, to be withheld from others as less worthy, more condemned, and thus apart from healing. Who is there who can be separate from salvation, if its purpose is the end of specialness? Where is salvation's justice if some errors are unforgivable, and warrant vengeance in place of healing and return of peace?

Salvation cannot seek to help God's Son be more unfair than he has sought to be. If miracles, the Holy Spirit's gift, were given specially to an elect and special group, and kept apart from others as less deserving, then is He ally to specialness. What He cannot perceive He bears no witness to. And everyone is equally entitled to His gift of healing and deliverance and peace. To give a problem to the Holy Spirit to solve for you means that you want it solved. To keep it for yourself to solve without His help is to decide it should remain unsettled, unresolved, and lasting in its power of injustice and attack. No one can be unjust to you, unless you have decided first to *be* unjust. And then must problems rise to block your way, and peace be scattered by the winds of hate.

Unless you think that all your brothers have an equal right to miracles with you, you will not claim your right to them because you were unjust to one with equal rights. Seek to deny and you will feel denied. Seek to deprive, and you have been deprived. A miracle can never be received because another could receive it not. Only forgiveness offers miracles. And pardon must be just to everyone.

The little problems that you keep and hide become your secret sins, because you did not choose to let them be removed for you. And so they gather dust and grow, until they cover everything that you perceive and leave you fair to no one. Not one right do you believe you have. And bitterness, with vengeance justified and mercy lost, condemns you as unworthy of forgiveness. The unforgiven have no mercy to bestow upon another. That is why your sole responsibility must be to take forgiveness for yourself.

The miracle that you receive, you give. Each one becomes an illustration of the law on which salvation rests; that justice must be done to all, if anyone is to be healed. No one can lose, and everyone must benefit. Each miracle is an example of what justice can accomplish when it is offered to everyone alike. It is received and given equally. It is awareness that giving and receiving are the same. Because it does not make the same unlike, it sees no differences where none exists. And thus it is the same for everyone, because it sees no differences in them. Its offering is universal, and it teaches but one message:

*What is God's belongs to everyone, and is his due.*

# Chapter 26
# THE TRANSITION

## The "Sacrifice" of Oneness

In the "dynamics" of attack is sacrifice a key idea. It is the pivot upon which all compromise, all desperate attempts to strike a bargain, and all conflicts achieve a seeming balance. It is the symbol of the central theme that *somebody must lose*. Its focus on the body is apparent, for it is always an attempt to limit loss. The body is itself a sacrifice; a giving up of power in the name of saving just a little for yourself. To see a brother in another body, separate from yours, is the expression of a wish to see a little part of him and sacrifice the rest. Look at the world, and you will see nothing attached to anything beyond itself. All seeming entities can come a little nearer, or go a little farther off, but cannot join.

The little that the body fences off becomes the self, preserved through sacrifice of all the rest. And all the rest must lose this little part, remaining incomplete to keep its own identity intact. In this perception of yourself the body's loss would be a sacrifice indeed. For sight of bodies becomes the sign that sacrifice is limited, and something still remains for you alone. And for this little to belong to you are limits placed on everything outside, just as they are on everything you think is yours. For giving and receiving are the same. And to accept the limits of a body is to impose these limits on each brother whom you see. For you must see him as you see yourself.

The body *is* a loss, and *can* be made to sacrifice. And while you see your brother as a body, apart from you and separate in his cell, you are demanding sacrifice of him and you. What greater sacrifice could be demanded than that God's Son perceive himself without his Father? And his Father be without His Son? Yet every sacrifice demands that they be separate and without the other. The memory of God must be denied if any sacrifice is asked of anyone. What witness to the wholeness of God's Son is seen within a world of separate bodies, however much he witnesses to truth? He is invisible in such a world. Nor can his song of union and of love be heard at all. Yet is it given him to make the world recede before his song, and sight of him replace the body's eyes.

Those who would see the witnesses to truth
instead of to illusion merely ask
that they might see a purpose in the world
that gives it sense and makes it meaningful.
Without your special function has this world
no meaning for you. Yet it can become
a treasure house as rich and limitless
as Heaven itself. No instant passes here
in which your brother's holiness cannot
be seen, to add a limitless supply
to every meager scrap and tiny crumb
of happiness that you allot yourself.

You can lose sight of oneness, but can not
make sacrifice of its reality.
Nor can you lose what you would sacrifice,
nor keep the Holy Spirit from His task
of showing you that it has not been lost.
Hear, then, the song your brother sings to you,
and let the world recede, and take the rest
his witness offers on behalf of peace.
But judge him not, for you will hear no song
of liberation for yourself, nor see
what it is given him to witness to,
that you may see it and rejoice with him.
Make not his holiness a sacrifice
to your belief in sin. You sacrifice
your innocence with his, and die each time
you see in him a sin deserving death.

Yet every instant can you be reborn,
and given life again. His holiness
gives life to you, who cannot die
because his sinlessness is known to God;
and can no more be sacrificed by you
than can the light in you be blotted out
because he sees it not.

You who would make a sacrifice of life,

and make your eyes and ears bear witness to
the death of God and of His holy Son,
think not that you have power to make of Them
what God willed not They be. In Heaven, God's Son
is not imprisoned in a body, nor
is sacrificed in solitude to sin.
And as he is in Heaven, so must he be
eternally and everywhere. He is
the same forever. Born again each instant,
untouched by time, and far beyond the reach
of any sacrifice of life or death.
For neither did he make, and only one
was given him by One Who knows His gifts
can never suffer sacrifice and loss.

God's justice rests in gentleness upon
His Son, and keeps him safe from all injustice
the world would lay upon him. Could it be
that you could make his sins reality,
and sacrifice his Father's Will for him?
Condemn him not by seeing him within
the rotting prison where he sees himself.
It is your special function to ensure
the door be opened, that he may come forth
to shine on you, and give you back the gift
of freedom by receiving it of you.
What is the Holy Spirit's special function
but to release the holy Son of God
from the imprisonment he made to keep
himself from justice? Could your function be
a task apart and separate from His Own?

### Many Forms; One Correction

It is not difficult to understand the reasons why you do not ask the Holy Spirit to solve all problems for you. He has not greater difficulty in resolving some than others. Every problem is the same to Him, because each one is solved in just the same respect and through the same approach. The aspects that need solving do not change, whatever form the problem seems to take. A problem can appear in many forms, and it will do so while the problem lasts. It serves no purpose to attempt to solve it in a special form. It will recur and then recur again and yet again, until it has been answered for all time and will not rise again in any form. And only then are you released from it.

The Holy Spirit offers you release
from every problem that you think you have.
They are the same to Him because each one,
regardless of the form it seems to take,
is a demand that someone suffer loss
and make a sacrifice that you might gain.
And when the situation is worked out
so no one loses is the problem gone,
because it was an error in perception
that now has been corrected. One mistake
is not more difficult for Him to bring
to truth than is another. For there *is*
but one mistake; the whole idea that loss
is possible, and could result in gain
for anyone. If this were true, then God
would be unfair; sin would be possible,
attack be justified and vengeance fair.

This one mistake, in any form,
has one correction. There is
no loss; to think there is, is a mistake.
You have no problems, though you think you have.

And yet you could not think so if you saw
them vanish one by one, without regard
to size, complexity, or place and time,
or any attribute which you perceive
that makes each one seem different from the rest.
Think not the limits you impose on what
you see can limit God in any way.

The miracle of justice can correct
all errors. Every problem is an error.
It does injustice to the Son of God,
and therefore is not true. The Holy Spirit
does not evaluate injustices
as great or small, or more or less. They have
no properties to Him. They are mistakes
from which the Son of God is suffering,
but needlessly. And so He takes the thorns
and nails away. He does not pause to judge
whether the hurt be large or little. He
makes but one judgment; that to hurt God's Son
must be unfair and therefore is not so.

You who believe it safe to give but some mistakes to be corrected while you keep the others to yourself, remember this: Justice is total. There is no such thing as partial justice. If the Son of God is guilty then is he condemned, and he deserves no mercy from the God of justice. But ask not God to punish him because *you* find him guilty and would have him die. God offers you the means to see his innocence. Would it be fair to punish him because you will not look at what is there to see? Each time you keep a problem for yourself to solve, or judge that it is one that has no resolution, you have made it great, and past the hope of healing. You deny the miracle of justice *can* be fair.

If God is just, then can there be no problems that justice cannot solve. But you believe that some injustices are fair and good, and necessary to preserve yourself. It is these problems that you think are great and cannot be resolved. For there are those you want to suffer loss, and no one whom you wish to be preserved from sacrifice entirely. Consider once again your special function. One is given you to see in him his perfect sinlessness. And you will ask no sacrifice of him because you could not will he suffer loss. The miracle of justice you call forth will rest on you as surely as on him. Nor will the Holy Spirit be content until it is received by everyone. For what you give to Him is everyone's, and by your giving it can He ensure that everyone receives it equally.

Think, then, how great your own release will be when you are willing to receive correction for all your problems. You will not keep one, for pain in any form you will not want. And you will see each little hurt resolved before the Holy Spirit's gentle sight. For all of them *are* little in His sight, and worth no more than just a tiny sigh before they disappear, to be forever undone and unremembered. What seemed once to be a special problem, a mistake without a remedy, or an affliction without a cure, has been transformed into a universal blessing. Sacrifice is gone. And in its place the Love of God can be remembered, and will shine away all memory of sacrifice and loss.

God cannot be remembered until justice is loved instead of feared. He cannot be unjust to anyone or anything, because He knows that everything that is belongs to Him, and will forever be as He created it. Nothing He loves but must be sinless and beyond attack. Your special function opens wide the door beyond which is the memory of His Love kept perfectly intact and undefiled. And all you need to do is but to wish that Heaven be given you instead of hell, and every bolt and barrier that seems to hold the door securely barred and locked will merely fall away and disappear. For it is not your Father's Will that you should offer or receive less than He gave, when He created you in perfect love.

## The Borderland

Complexity is not of God. How could it be, when all He knows is one? He knows of one creation, one reality, one truth and but one Son. Nothing conflicts with oneness. How, then, could there be complexity in Him? What is there to decide? For it is conflict that makes choice possible. The truth is simple; it is one, without an opposite. And how could strife enter in its simple presence, and bring complexity where oneness is? The truth makes no decisions, for there is nothing to decide *between.* And only if there were could choosing be a necessary step in the advance toward oneness. What is everything leaves room for nothing else. Yet is this magnitude beyond the scope of this curriculum. Nor is it necessary we dwell on anything that cannot be immediately grasped.

There is a borderland of thought that stands between this world and Heaven. It is not a place, and when you reach it is apart from time. Here is the meeting place where thoughts are brought together; where conflicting values meet and all illusions are laid down beside the truth, where they are judged to be untrue. This borderland is just beyond the gate of Heaven. Here is every thought made pure and wholly simple. Here is sin denied, and everything that *is* received instead.

This is the journey's end. We have referred to it as the real world. And yet there is a contradiction here, in that the words imply a limited reality,
a partial truth,
a segment of the universe made true.
This is because knowledge makes no attack upon perception. They are brought together, and only one continues past the gate where Oneness is. Salvation is
a borderland where place and time and choice have meaning still, and yet it can be seen that they are temporary, out of place, and every choice has been already made.

Nothing the Son of God believes can be destroyed. But what is truth to him must be brought to the last comparison that he will ever make; the last evaluation that will be possible, the final judgment upon this world. It is the judgment of the truth upon illusion,
of knowledge on perception:
"It has no meaning, and does not exist."
This is not your decision. It is but
a simple statement of a simple fact.
But in this world there are no simple facts, because what is the same and what is different remain unclear. The one essential thing to make a choice at all is this distinction. And herein lies the difference between the worlds. In this one, choice is made impossible. In the real world is choosing simplified.

Salvation stops just short of Heaven, for only perception needs salvation. Heaven was never lost, and so cannot be saved.

Yet who can make a choice between the wish for Heaven and the wish for hell unless he recognizes they are not the same? This difference is the learning goal this course has set. It will not go beyond this aim. Its only purpose is to teach what is the same and what is different, leaving room to make the only choice that can be made.

There is no basis for a choice in this complex and over-complicated world. For no one understands what is the same, and seems to choose where no choice really is. The real world is the area of choice made real, not in the outcome, but in the perception of alternatives for choice. That there is choice is an illusion. Yet within this one lies the undoing of every illusion, not excepting this.

Is not this like your special function, where the separation is undone by change of purpose in what once was specialness, and now is union?
All illusions are but one.
And in the recognition this is so
lies the ability to give up all
attempts to choose between them, and to make them different. How simple is the choice between two things so clearly unalike. There is no conflict here. No sacrifice is possible in the relinquishment of an illusion recognized as such.
Where all reality has been withdrawn from what was never true, can it be hard to give it up, and choose what *must* be true?

### Where Sin Has Left

Forgiveness is this world's equivalent of Heaven's justice. It translates the world of sin into a simple world, where justice can be reflected from beyond the gate behind which total lack of limits lies. Nothing in boundless love could need forgiveness. And what is charity within the world gives way to simple justice past the gate that opens into Heaven. No one forgives unless he has believed in sin, and still

believes that he has much to be forgiven.
Forgiveness thus becomes the means by which
he learns he has done nothing to forgive.
Forgiveness always rests upon the one
who offers it, until he sees himself
as needing it no more. And thus is he
returned to his real function of creating,
which his forgiveness offers him again.

Forgiveness turns the world of sin into
a world of glory, wonderful to see.
Each flower shines in light, and every bird
sings of the joy of Heaven. There is
no sadness and there is no parting here,
for everything is totally forgiven.
And what has been forgiven must join,
for nothing stands between to keep them separate
and apart. The sinless must perceive
that they are one, for nothing stands between
to push the other off. And in the space
that sin left vacant do they join as one,
in gladness recognizing what is part of them
has not been kept apart and separate.

The holy place on which you stand is but
the space that sin has left. And here you see
the face of Christ, arising in its place.
Who could behold the face of Christ and not
recall His Father as He really is?
Who could fear love, and stand upon the ground
where sin has left a place for Heaven's altar
to rise and tower far above the world,
and reach beyond the universe to touch
the Heart of all creation? What is Heaven
but a song of gratitude and love and praise
by everything created to the Source
of its creation? The holiest of altars
is set where once sin was believed to be.
And here does every light of Heaven come,
to be rekindled and increased in joy.
For here is what was lost restored to them,
and all their radiance made whole again.

Forgiveness brings no little miracles
to lay before the gate of Heaven. Here
the Son of God Himself comes to receive
each gift that brings him nearer to his home.
Not one is lost, and none is cherished more
than any other. Each reminds him of

his Father's Love as surely as the rest.
And each one teaches him that what he feared
he loves the most. What but a miracle
could change his mind, so that he understands
that love cannot be feared? What other miracle
is there but this? And what else need there be
to make the space between you disappear?

Where sin once was perceived will rise a world
that will become an altar to the truth,
and you will join the lights of Heaven there,
and sing their song of gratitude and praise.
And as they come to you to be complete,
so will you go with them. For no one hears
the song of Heaven and remains without
a voice that adds its power to the song,
and makes it sweeter still. And each one joins
the singing at the altar that was raised
within the tiny spot that sin proclaimed
to be its own. And what was tiny then
has soared into a magnitude of song
in which the universe has joined
with but a single voice.

This tiny spot of sin that stands between
you and your brother still is holding back
the happy opening of Heaven's gate.
How little is the hindrance that withholds
the wealth of Heaven from you. And how great
will be the joy in Heaven when you join
the mighty chorus to the Love of God!

### The Little Hindrance

A little hindrance can seem large indeed
to those who do not understand that miracles
are all the same. Yet teaching that is what
this course is for. This is its only purpose,
for only that is all there is to learn.
And you can learn it in many different ways.
All learning is a help or hindrance to
the gate of Heaven. Nothing in between
is possible. There are two teachers only,
who point in different ways. And you will go
along the way your chosen teacher leads.
There are but two directions you can take,
while time remains and choice is meaningful.
For never will another road be made
except the way to Heaven. You but choose
whether to go toward Heaven, or away

to nowhere. There is nothing else to choose.

Nothing is ever lost but time, which in
the end is meaningless. For it is but
a little hindrance to eternity,
quite meaningless to the real Teacher of
the world. Yet since you do believe in it,
why should you waste it going nowhere, when
it can be used to reach a goal as high
as learning can achieve? Think not the way
to Heaven's gate is difficult at all.
Nothing you undertake with certain purpose
and high resolve and happy confidence,
holding your brother's hand and keeping step
to Heaven's song, is difficult to do.
But it is hard indeed to wander off,
alone and miserable, down a road
that leads to nothing and that has no purpose.

God gave His Teacher to replace
the one you made, not to conflict with it.
And what He would replace has been replaced.
Time lasted but an instant in your mind,
with no effect upon eternity.
And so is all time past, and everything
exactly as it was before the way
to nothingness was made. The tiny tick
of time in which the first mistake was made,
and all of them within that one mistake,
held also the Correction for that one,
and all of them that came within the first.
And in that tiny instant time was gone,
for that was all it ever was. What God
gave answer to is answered and is gone.

To you who still believe you live in time
and know not it is gone, the Holy Spirit
still guides you through the infinitely small
and senseless maze you still perceive in time,
though it has long since gone. You think you live
in what is past. Each thing you look upon
you saw but for an instant, long ago,
before its unreality gave way
to truth. Not one illusion still remains
unanswered in your mind. Uncertainty
was brought to certainty so long ago
that it is hard indeed to hold it to
your heart, as if it were before you still.

The tiny instant you would keep and make
eternal, passed away in Heaven too soon
for anything to notice it had come.
What disappeared too quickly to affect
the simple knowledge of the Son of God
can hardly still be there, for you to choose
to be your teacher. Only in the past,
- an ancient past, too short to make a world
in answer to creation, - did this world
appear to rise. So very long ago,
for such a tiny interval of time,
that not one note in Heaven's song was missed.
Yet in each unforgiving act or thought,
in every judgment and in all belief
in sin, is that one instant still called back,
as if it could be made again in time.
You keep an ancient memory before
your eyes. And he who lives in memories
alone is unaware of where he is.

Forgiveness is the great release from time.
It is the key to learning that the past
is over. Madness speaks no more. There *is*
no other teacher and no other way.
For what has been undone no longer is.
And who can stand upon a distant shore,
and dream himself across an ocean, to
a place and time that have long since gone by?
How real a hindrance can this dream be
to where he really is? For this is fact,
and does not change whatever dreams he has.
Yet can he still imagine he is elsewhere,
and in another time. In the extreme,
he can delude himself that this is true,
and pass from mere imagining into
belief and into madness, quite convinced
that where he would prefer to be, he *is*.

Is this a hindrance to the place whereon
he stands? Is any echo from the past
that he may hear a fact in what is there
to hear where he is now? And how much can
his own illusions about time and place
effect a change in where he really is?

The unforgiven is a voice that calls
from out a past forevermore gone by.
And everything that points to it as real
is but a wish that what is gone could be
made real again and seen as here and now,

in place of what is *really* now and here.
Is this a hindrance to the truth the past
is gone, and cannot be returned to you?
And do you want that fearful instant kept,
when Heaven seemed to disappear and God
was feared and made a symbol of your hate?

Forget the time of terror that has been
so long ago corrected and undone.
Can sin withstand the Will of God?
Can it be up to you to see the past
and put it in the present? You can *not*
go back. And everything that points the way
in the direction of the past but sets
you on a mission whose accomplishment
can only be unreal. Such is the justice
your All-Loving Father has ensured
must come to you.
And from your own unfairness to yourself
has He protected you. You cannot lose
your way because there is no way but His,
and nowhere can you go except to Him.

Would God allow His Son to lose his way
along a road long since a memory
of time gone by?
This course will teach you only what is now.
A dreadful instant in a distant past,
now perfectly corrected, is of no
concern nor value. Let the dead and gone
be peacefully forgotten. Resurrection
has come to take its place. And now you are
a part of resurrection, not of death.
No past illusions have the power to keep
you in a place of death, a vault God's Son
entered an instant, to be instantly
restored unto his Father's perfect Love.
And how can he be kept in chains long since
removed and gone forever from his mind?

The Son whom God created is as free
as God created him. He was reborn
the instant that he chose to die instead
of live. And will you not forgive him now,
because he made an error in the past
that God remembers not, and is not there?
Now you are shifting back and forth between
the past and present.
Sometimes the past seems real, as if it *were*
the present. Voices from the past are heard
and then are doubted. You are like to one
who still hallucinates,
but lacks conviction in what he perceives.
This is the borderland between the worlds,
the bridge between the past and present. Here
the shadow of the past remains, but still
a present light is dimly recognized.
Once it is seen, this light can never be
forgotten. It must draw you from the past
into the present, where you really are.

The shadow voices do not change the laws
of time nor of eternity. They come
from what is past and gone, and hinder not
the true existence of the here and now.
The real world is the second part of the
hallucination time and death are real,
and have existence that can be perceived.
This terrible illusion was denied
in but the time it took for God to give
His Answer to illusion for all time
and every circumstance. And then it was
no more to be experienced as there.

Each day, and every minute in each day,
and every instant that each minute holds,
you but relive the single instant when
the time of terror took the place of love.
And so you die each day to live again,
until you cross the gap between the past
and present, which is not a gap at all.
Such is each life; a seeming interval
from birth to death and on to life again,
a repetition of an instant gone
by long ago that cannot be relived.
And all of time is but the mad belief
that what is over is still here and now.

Forgive the past and let it go, for it
*is* gone. You stand no longer on the ground
that lies between the worlds. You have gone on,
and reached the world that lies at Heaven's gate.
There is no hindrance to the Will of God,
nor any need that you repeat again
a journey that was over long ago.
Look gently on your brother, and behold
the world in which perception of your hate
has been transformed into a world of love.

### The Appointed Friend

Anything in this world that you believe
is good and valuable and worth striving for
can hurt you, and will do so. Not because
it has the power to hurt, but just because
you have denied it is but an illusion,
and made it real. And it is real to you.
It is not nothing. And through its perceived
reality has entered all the world
of sick illusions. All belief in sin,
in power of attack, in hurt and harm,
in sacrifice and death, has come to you.
For no one can make one illusion real,
and still escape the rest. For who can choose
to keep the ones that he prefers, and find
the safety that the truth alone can give?
Who can believe illusions are the same,
and still maintain that even one is best?

Lead not your little life in solitude,
with one illusion as your only friend.
This is no friendship worthy of God's Son,
nor one with which he could remain content.
Yet God has given him a better Friend,
in Whom all power in earth and Heaven rests.
The one illusion that you think is friend
obscures His grace and majesty from you,
and keeps His friendship and forgiveness from
your welcoming embrace. Without Him you
are friendless. Seek not another friend
to take His place. There *is* no other friend.
What God appointed has no substitute,
for what illusion can replace the truth?

Who dwells with shadows is alone indeed,
and loneliness is not the Will of God.
Would you allow one shadow to usurp
the throne that God appointed for your Friend,
if you but realized its emptiness
has left yours empty and unoccupied?
Make no illusion friend, for if you do,
it can but take the place of Him Whom God
has called your Friend. And it is He Who is
your only Friend in truth. He brings you gifts
that are not of this world, and only He
to Whom they have been given can make sure
that you receive them. He will place them on
your throne, when you make room for Him on His.

### The Laws of Healing

This is a course in miracles. As such, the laws of healing must be understood before the purpose of the course can be accomplished. Let us review the principles that we have covered, and arrange them in a way that summarizes all that must occur for healing to be possible. For when it once is possible it must occur.

All sickness comes from separation. When
the separation is denied, it goes.
For it is gone as soon as the idea
that brought it has been healed, and been replaced
by sanity. Sickness and sin are seen
as consequence and cause, in a relationship
kept hidden from awareness that it may
be carefully preserved from reason's light.

Guilt asks for punishment, and its request
is granted. Not in truth, but in the world
of shadows and illusions built on sin.
The Son of God perceived what he would see
because perception is a wish fulfilled.
Perception changes, made to take the place
of changeless knowledge. Yet is truth unchanged.

It cannot be perceived, but only known.
What is perceived takes many forms, but none
has meaning. Brought to truth, its senselessness
is quite apparent. Kept apart from truth,
it seems to have a meaning and be real.

Perception's laws are opposite to truth,
and what is true of knowledge is not true
of anything that is apart from it.
Yet has God given answer to the world
of sickness, which applies to all its forms.
God's answer is eternal, though it works
in time, where it is needed. Yet because
it is of God, the laws of time do not
affect its workings. It is in this world,
but not a part of it. For it is real,

and dwells where all reality must be.
Ideas leave not their source, and their effects
but seem to be apart from them. Ideas
are of the mind. What is projected out,
and seems to be external to the mind,
is not outside at all, but an effect
of what is in, and has not left its source.

God's answer lies where the belief in sin
must be, for only there can its effects
be utterly undone and without cause.
Perception's laws must be reversed, because
they *are* reversals of the laws of truth.
The laws of truth forever will be true,
and cannot be reversed; yet can be seen
as upside down. And this must be corrected
where the illusion of reversal lies.

It is impossible that one illusion
be less amenable to truth than are
the rest. But it is possible that some
are given greater value, and less willingly
offered to truth for healing and for help.
No illusion has any truth in it.
Yet it appears some are more true than others,
although this clearly makes no sense at all.
All that a hierarchy of illusions
can show is preference, not reality.
What relevance has preference to the truth?
Illusions are illusions and are false.
Your preference gives them no reality.
Not one is true in any way, and all
must yield with equal ease to what God gave
as answer to them all. God's Will is one.
And any wish that seems to go against
His Will has no foundation in the truth.

Sin is not error, for it goes beyond
correction to impossibility.
Yet the belief that it is real has made
some errors seem forever past the hope
of healing, and the lasting grounds for hell.
If this were so, would Heaven be opposed
by its own opposite, as real as it.
Then would God's Will be split in two, and all
creation be subjected to the laws
of two opposing powers, until God
becomes impatient, splits the world apart,
and relegates attack unto Himself.

Thus has He lost His Mind, proclaiming sin
has taken His reality from Him
and brought His Love at last to vengeance's heels.
For such an insane picture an insane
defense can be expected, but can not
establish that the picture must be true.

Nothing gives meaning where no meaning is.
And truth needs no defense to make it true.
Illusions have no witnesses and no
effects. Who looks on them is but deceived.
Forgiveness is the only function here,
and serves to bring the joy this world denies
to every aspect of God's Son where sin
was thought to rule. Perhaps you do not see
the role forgiveness plays in ending death
and all beliefs that rise from mists of guilt.
Sins are beliefs that you impose between
your brother and yourself. They limit you
to time and place, and give a little space
to you, another little space to him.
This separating off is symbolized,
in your perception, by a body which
is clearly separate and a thing apart.
Yet what this symbol represents is but
your wish to *be* apart and separate.

Forgiveness takes away what stands between
your brother and yourself. It is the wish
that you be joined with him, and not apart.
We call it "wish" because it still conceives
of other choices, and has not yet reached
beyond the world of choice entirely.
Yet is this wish in line with Heaven's state,
and not in opposition to God's Will.
Although it falls far short of giving you
your full inheritance, it does remove
the obstacles that you have placed between
the Heaven where you are, and recognition
of where and what you are. Facts are unchanged.
Yet facts can be denied and thus unknown,
though they were known before they were denied.

Salvation, perfect and complete, asks but
a little wish that what is true be true;
a little willingness to overlook
what is not there; a little sigh that speaks
for Heaven as a preference to this world
that death and desolation seem to rule.

In joyous answer will creation rise
within you, to replace the world you see
with Heaven, wholly perfect and complete.
What is forgiveness but a willingness
that truth be true? What can remain unhealed
and broken from a Unity Which holds
all things within Itself? There is no sin.
And every miracle is possible
the instant that the Son of God perceives
his wishes and the Will of God are one.

What is the Will of God? He wills His Son
have everything. And this He guaranteed
when He created him *as* everything.
It is impossible that anything
be lost, if what you *have* is what you *are*.
This is the miracle by which creation
became your function, sharing it with God.
It is not understood apart from Him,
and therefore has no meaning in this world.
Here does the Son of God ask not too much,
but far too little. He would sacrifice
his own identity with everything,
to find a little treasure of his own.
And this he cannot do without a sense
of isolation, loss and loneliness.
This is the treasure he has sought to find.
And he could only be afraid of it.
Is fear a treasure? Can uncertainty
be what you want? Or is it a mistake
about your will, and what you really are?

Let us consider what the error is,
so it can be corrected, not protected.
Sin is belief attack can be projected
outside the mind where the belief arose.
Here is the firm conviction that ideas
can leave their source made real and meaningful.
And from this error does the world of sin
and sacrifice arise. This world is an
attempt to prove your innocence, while cherishing
attack. Its failure lies in that you still
feel guilty, though without understanding why.
Effects are seen as separate from their source,
and seem to be beyond you to control
or to prevent. What is thus kept apart
can never join.

Cause and effect are one, not separate.
God wills you learn what always has been true:
That He created you as part of Him,
and this must still be true because ideas
leave not their source. Such is creation's law;
that each idea the mind conceives but adds
to its abundance, never takes away.
This is as true of what is idly wished
as what is truly willed, because the mind
can wish to be deceived, but cannot make
it be what it is not. And to believe
ideas can leave their source is to invite
illusions to be true, without success.
For never will success be possible
in trying to deceive the Son of God.

The miracle is possible when cause
and consequence are brought together, not
kept separate. The healing of effect
without the cause can merely shift effects
to other forms. And this is not release.
God's Son could never be content with less
than full salvation and escape from guilt.
For otherwise he still demands that he
must make some sacrifice, and thus denies
that everything is his, unlimited
by loss of any kind. A tiny sacrifice
is just the same in its effects as is
the whole idea of sacrifice. If loss
in any form is possible, then is
God's Son made incomplete and not himself.
Nor will he know himself,
nor recognize his will.
He has forsworn his Father and himself,
and made Them both his enemies in hate.

Illusions serve the purpose they were made
to serve. And from their purpose they derive
whatever meaning that they seem to have.
God gave to all illusions that were made
another purpose that would justify
a miracle whatever form they took.
In every miracle all healing lies,
for God gave answer to them all as one.
And what is one to Him must be the same.
If you believe what is the same is different
you but deceive yourself. What God calls one
will be forever one, not separate.

His Kingdom is united; thus it was
created, and thus will it ever be.

The miracle but calls your ancient Name,
which you will recognize because the truth
is in your memory. And to this Name
your brother calls for his release and yours.
Heaven is shining on the Son of God.
Deny him not, that you may be released.
Each instant is the Son of God reborn
until he chooses not to die again.
In every wish to hurt he chooses death
instead of what his Father wills for him.
Yet every instant offers life to him
because his Father wills that he should live.

In crucifixion is redemption laid,
for healing is not needed where there is
no pain or suffering. Forgiveness is
the answer to attack of any kind.
So is attack deprived of its effects,
and hate is answered in the name of love.
To you to whom it has been given to save
the Son of God from crucifixion and
from hell and death, all glory be forever.
For you have power to save the Son of God
because his Father willed that it be so.
And in your hands does all salvation lie,
to be both offered and received as one.

To use the power God has given you
as He would have it used is natural.
It is not arrogant to be as He
created you, nor to make use of what
He gave to answer all His Son's mistakes
and set him free. But it is arrogant
to lay aside the power that He gave,
and choose a little senseless wish instead
of what He wills. The gift of God to you
is limitless. There is no circumstance
it cannot answer, and no problem which
is not resolved within its gracious light.

Abide in peace, where God would have you be.
And be the means whereby your brother finds
the peace in which your wishes are fulfilled.
Let us unite in bringing blessing to
the world of sin and death. For what can save
each one of us can save us all. There is
no difference among the Sons of God.

The unity that specialness denies
will save them all, for what is one can have
no specialness. And everything belongs
to each of them. No wishes lie between
a brother and his own. To get from one
is to deprive them all. And yet to bless
but one gives blessing to them all as one.

Your ancient Name belongs to everyone,
as theirs to you. Call on your brother's name
and God will answer, for on Him you call.
Could He refuse to answer when He has
already answered all who call on Him?
A miracle can make no change at all.
But it can make what always has been true
be recognized by those who know it not;
and by this little gift of truth but let
to be itself, the Son of God allowed
to be himself, and all creation freed
to call upon the Name of God as one.

### The Immediacy of Salvation

The one remaining problem that you have
is that you see an interval between
the time when you forgive, and will receive
the benefits of trusting in your brother.
This but reflects the little you would keep
between you and your brother, that you
and he might be a little separate.
For time and space are one illusion, which
takes different forms. If it has been projected
beyond your mind you think of it as time.
The nearer it is brought to where it is,
the more you think of it in terms of space.

There is a distance you would keep apart
from your brother, and this space you
perceive as time because you still believe
you are external to him. This makes trust
impossible. And you cannot believe
that trust would settle every problem now.
Thus do you think it safer to remain
a little careful and a little watchful
of interests perceived as separate.
From this perception you cannot conceive
of gaining what forgiveness offers *now*.
The interval you think lies in between
the giving and receiving of the gift

seems to be one in which you sacrifice
and suffer loss. You see eventual
salvation, not immediate results.

Salvation *is* immediate. Unless
you so perceive it, you will be afraid
of it, believing that the risk of loss
is great between the time its purpose is
made yours and its effects will come to you.
In this form is the error still obscured
that is the source of fear. Salvation *would*
wipe out the space you see between you still,
and let you instantly become as one.
And it is here you fear the loss would lie.
Do not project this fear to time, for time
is not the enemy that you perceive.
Time is as neutral as the body is,
except in terms of what you see it for.
If you would keep a little space between
you and your brother still, you then would want
a little time in which forgiveness is
withheld a little while. And this but makes
the interval between the time in which
forgiveness is withheld from you and given
seem dangerous, with terror justified.

Yet space between you and your brother is
apparent only in the present, *now*,
and cannot be perceived in future time.
No more can it be overlooked except
within the present. Future loss is not
your fear. But present joining is your dread.
Who can feel desolation except now?
A future cause as yet has no effects.
And therefore must it be that if you fear,
there is a present cause. And it is *this*
that needs correction, not a future state.

The plans you make for safety all are laid
within the future, where you cannot plan.
No purpose has been given it as yet,
and what will happen has as yet no cause.
Who can predict effects without a cause?
And who could fear effects unless he thought
they had been caused, and judged disastrous *now*?
Belief in sin arouses fear, and like
its cause, is looking forward, looking back,
but overlooking what is here and now.
Yet only here and now its cause must be,
if its effects already have been judged
as fearful. And in overlooking this,
is it protected and kept separate
from healing. For a miracle is *now*.
It stands already here, in present grace,
within the only interval of time
that sin and fear have overlooked, but which
is all there is to time.

The working out
of all correction takes no time at all.
Yet the acceptance of the working out
can seem to take forever. The change of
purpose the Holy Spirit brought to your
relationship has in it all effects
that you will see.
They can be looked at *now*.
Why wait till they unfold in time and fear
they may not come, although already there?
You have been told that everything brings good
that comes from God. And yet it seems as if
this is not so. Good in disaster's form
is difficult to credit in advance.
Nor is there really sense in this idea.

Why should the good appear in evil's form?
And is it not deception if it does?
Its cause is here, if it appears at all.
Why are not its effects apparent, then?
Why in the future? And you seek to be
content with sighing, and with "reasoning"
you do not understand it now, but will
some day. And then its meaning will be clear.
This is not reason, for it is unjust,
and clearly hints at punishment until
the time of liberation is at hand.
Given a change of purpose for the good,
there is no reason for an interval
in which disaster strikes, to be perceived
as "good" some day but now in form of pain.
This is a sacrifice of *now*, which could
not be the cost the Holy Spirit asks
for what He gave without a cost at all.

Yet this illusion has a cause which, though
untrue, must be already in your mind.
And this illusion is but one effect
that it engenders, and one form in which
its outcome is perceived. This interval

in time, when retribution is perceived
to be the form in which the "good" appears,
is but one aspect of the little space
that lies between you, unforgiven still.

Be not content with future happiness.
It has no meaning, and is not your just
reward. For you have cause for freedom *now*.
What profits freedom in a prisoner's form?
Why should deliverance be disguised as death?
Delay is senseless, and the "reasoning"
that would maintain effects of present cause
must be delayed until a future time,
is merely a denial of the fact
that consequence and cause must come as one.
Look not to time, but to the little space
between you still, to be delivered from.
And do not let it be disguised as time,
and so preserved because its form is changed
and what it is cannot be recognized.
The Holy Spirit's purpose now is yours.
Should not His happiness be yours as well?

## For They Have Come

Think but how holy you must be from whom
the Voice for God calls lovingly unto
your brother, that you may awake in him
the Voice that answers to your call! And think
how holy he must be when in him sleeps
your own salvation, with his freedom joined!
However much you wish he be condemned,
God is in him. And never will you know
He is in you as well while you attack
His chosen home, and battle with His host.
Regard him gently. Look with loving eyes
on him who carries Christ within him, that
you may behold his glory and rejoice
that Heaven is not separate from you.

Is it too much to ask a little trust
for him who carries Christ to you, that you
may be forgiven all your sins, and left
without a single one you cherish still?
Forget not that a shadow held between
your brother and yourself obscures
the face of Christ and memory of God.
And would you trade Them for an ancient hate?
The ground whereon you stand is holy ground
because of Them Who, standing there with you,
have blessed it with Their innocence and peace.

The blood of hatred fades to let the grass
grow green again, and let the flowers be
all white and sparkling in the summer sun.
What was a place of death has now become
a living temple in a world of light.
Because of Them. It is Their Presence which
has lifted holiness again to take
its ancient place upon an ancient throne.
Because of Them have miracles sprung up
as grass and flowers on the barren ground
that hate had scorched and rendered desolate.
What hate has wrought have They undone. And now
you stand on ground so holy Heaven leans
to join with it, and make it like itself.
The shadow of an ancient hate has gone,
and all the blight and withering have passed
forever from the land where They have come.

What is a hundred or a thousand years
to Them, or tens of thousands? When They come,
time's purpose is fulfilled. What never was
passes to nothingness when They have come.
What hatred claimed is given up to love,
and freedom lights up every living thing
and lifts it into Heaven, where the lights
grow ever brighter as each one comes home.
The incomplete is made complete again,
and Heaven's joy has been increased because
what is its own has been restored to it.
The bloodied earth is cleansed, and the insane
have shed their garments of insanity
to join Them on the ground whereon you stand.

Heaven is grateful for this gift of what
has been withheld so long. For They have come
to gather in Their Own. What has been locked
is opened; what was held apart from light
is given up, that light may shine on it
and leave no space nor distance lingering
between the light of Heaven and the world.

The holiest of all the spots on earth
is where an ancient hatred has become
a present love. And They come quickly to
the living temple, where a home for Them
has been set up.
There is no place in Heaven holier.

And They have come
to dwell within the temple offered Them,
to be Their resting place as well as yours.
What hatred has released to love becomes
the brightest light in Heaven's radiance.
And all the lights in Heaven brighter grow,
in gratitude for what has been restored.

Around you angels hover lovingly,
to keep away all darkened thoughts of sin,
and keep the light where it has entered in.
Your footprints lighten up the world, for where
you walk forgiveness gladly goes with you.
No one on earth but offers thanks to one
who has restored his home, and sheltered him
from bitter winter and the freezing cold.
And shall the Lord of Heaven and His Son
give less in gratitude for so much more?

Now is the temple of the living God
rebuilt as host again to Him by Whom
it was created. Where He dwells, His Son
dwells with Him, never separate. And They
give thanks that They are welcome made at last.
Where stood a cross stands now the risen Christ,
and ancient scars are healed within His sight.
An ancient miracle has come to bless
and to replace an ancient enmity
that came to kill. In gentle gratitude
do God the Father and the Son return
to what is Theirs, and will forever be.
Now is the Holy Spirit's purpose done.
For They have come! For They have come at last!

### The End of Injustice

What, then, remains to be undone for you
to realize Their Presence? Only this;
you have a differential view of when
attack is justified, and when you think
it is unfair and not to be allowed.
When you perceive it as unfair, you think
that a response of anger now is just.
And thus you see what is the same as different.
Confusion is not limited. If it
occurs at all it will be total. And
its presence, in whatever form, will hide
Their Presence. They are known with clarity
or not at all. Confused perception will
block knowledge. It is not a question of
the size of the confusion, or how much
it interferes. Its simple presence shuts
the door to Theirs, and keeps Them there unknown.

What does it mean if you perceive attack
in certain forms to be unfair to you?
It means that there must be some forms in which
you think it fair. For otherwise, how could
some be evaluated as unfair?
Some, then, are given meaning and perceived
as sensible. And only some are seen
as meaningless. And this denies the fact
that *all* are senseless, equally without
a cause or consequence, and cannot have
effects of any kind. Their Presence is
obscured by any veil that stands between
Their shining innocence, and your awareness
that it is your own and equally belongs
to every living thing along with you.
God limits not. And what is limited
cannot be Heaven. So it must be hell.

Unfairness and attack are one mistake,
so firmly joined that where one is perceived
the other must be seen. You cannot be
unfairly treated. The belief you are
is but another form of the idea
you are deprived by someone not yourself.
Projection of the cause of sacrifice
is at the root of everything perceived
to be unfair and not your just deserts.
Yet it is you who ask this of yourself,
in deep injustice to the Son of God.
You have no enemy except yourself,
and you are enemy indeed to him
because you do not know him *as* yourself.
What could be more unjust than that he be
deprived of what he is, denied the right
to be himself, and asked to sacrifice
his Father's Love and yours as not his due?

Beware of the temptation to perceive
yourself unfairly treated. In this view,
you seek to find an innocence that is
not Theirs but yours alone, and at the cost
of someone else's guilt. Can innocence
be purchased by the giving of your guilt
to someone else? And *is* it innocence

that your attack on him attempts to get?
Is it not retribution for your own
attack upon the Son of God you seek?
Is it not safer to believe that you
are innocent of this, and victimized
despite your innocence? Whatever way
the game of guilt is played, there must be loss.
Someone must lose his innocence
that someone else
can take it from him, making it his own.

You think your brother is unfair to you
because you think that one must be unfair
to make the other innocent. And in
this game do you perceive one purpose for
your whole relationship. And this you seek
to add unto the purpose given it.
The Holy Spirit's purpose is to let
the Presence of your holy Guests be known
to you. And to this purpose nothing can
be added, for the world is purposeless
except for this. To add or take away
from this one goal is but to take away
all purpose from the world and from yourself.

And each unfairness that the world appears
to lay upon you, you have laid on it
by rendering it purposeless, without
the function that the Holy Spirit sees.
And simple justice has been thus denied
to every living thing upon the earth.

What this injustice does to you who judge
unfairly, and who see as you have judged,
you cannot calculate. The world grows dim
and threatening, not a trace of all
the happy sparkle that salvation brings
can you perceive to lighten up your way.
And so you see yourself deprived of light,
abandoned to the dark, unfairly left
without a purpose in a futile world.
The world is fair because the Holy Spirit
has brought injustice to the light within,
and there has all unfairness been resolved
and been replaced with justice and with love.
If you perceive injustice anywhere,
you need but say:

*By this do I deny*
*the Presence of the Father and the Son.*
*And I would rather know of Them than see*
*injustice, which Their Presence shines away.*

# Chapter 27
## THE HEALING OF THE DREAM

### The Picture of Crucifixion

The wish to be unfairly treated is a compromise attempt that would combine attack and innocence. Who can combine the wholly incompatible, and make a unity of what can never join? Walk you the gentle way, and you will fear no evil and no shadows in the night. But place no terror symbols on your path, or you will weave a crown of thorns from which your brother and yourself will not escape. You cannot crucify yourself alone. And if you are unfairly treated, he must suffer the unfairness that you see. You cannot sacrifice yourself alone. For sacrifice is total. If it could occur at all it would entail the whole of God's creation, and the Father with the sacrifice of His beloved Son.

In your release from sacrifice is his made manifest, and shown to be his own. But every pain you suffer do you see as proof that he is guilty of attack. Thus would you make yourself to be the sign that he has lost his innocence, and need but look on you to realize that he has been condemned. And what to you has been unfair will come to him in righteousness. The unjust vengeance that you suffer now belongs to him, and when it rests on him are you set free. Wish not to make yourself a living symbol of his guilt, for you will not escape the death you made for him. But in his innocence you find your own.

Whenever you consent to suffer pain, to be deprived, unfairly treated or in need of anything, you but accuse your brother of attack upon God's Son. You hold a picture of your crucifixion before his eyes, that he may see his sins are writ in Heaven in your blood and death, and go before him, closing off the gate and damning him to hell. Yet this is writ in hell and not in Heaven, where you are beyond attack and prove his innocence. The picture of yourself you offer him you show yourself, and give it all your faith. The Holy Spirit offers you, to give to him, a picture of yourself in which there is no pain and no reproach at all. And what was martyred to his guilt becomes the perfect witness to his innocence.

The power of witness is beyond belief because it brings conviction in its wake. The witness is believed because he points beyond himself to what he represents. A sick and suffering you but represents your brother's guilt; the witness that you send lest he forget the injuries he gave, from which you swear he never will escape. This sick and sorry picture *you* accept, if only it can serve to punish him. The sick are merciless to everyone, and in contagion do they seek to kill. Death seems an easy price, if they can say, "Behold me, brother, at your hand I die." For sickness is the witness to his guilt, and death would prove his errors must be sins. Sickness is but a "little" death; a form of vengeance not yet total. Yet it speaks with certainty for what it represents. The bleak and bitter picture you have sent your brother *you* have looked upon in grief. And everything that it has shown to him have you believed, because it witnessed to the guilt in him which you perceived and loved.

Now in the hands made gentle by His touch, the Holy Spirit lays a picture of a different you. It is a picture of a body still, for what you really are cannot be seen nor pictured. Yet this one has not been used for purpose of attack, and therefore never suffered pain at all. It witnesses to the eternal truth that you cannot be hurt, and points beyond

itself to both your innocence and his.
Show this unto your brother, who will see
that every scar is healed, and every tear
is wiped away in laughter and in love.
And he will look on his forgiveness there,
and with healed eyes will look beyond it to
the innocence that he beholds in you.
Here is the proof that he has never sinned;
that nothing which his madness bid him do
was ever done, or ever had effects
of any kind. That no reproach he laid
upon his heart was ever justified,
and no attack can ever touch him with
the poisoned and relentless sting of fear.

Attest his innocence and not his guilt.
Your healing is his comfort and his health
because it proves illusions are not true.
It is not will for life but wish for death
that is the motivation for this world.
Its only purpose is to prove guilt real.
No worldly thought or act or feeling has
a motivation other than this one.
These are the witnesses that are called forth
to be believed, and lend conviction to
the system they speak for and represent.
And each has many voices, speaking to
your brother and yourself in different tongues.
And yet to both the message is the same.
Adornment of the body seeks to show
how lovely are the witnesses for guilt.
Concerns about the body demonstrate
how frail and vulnerable is your life;
how easily destroyed is what you love.
Depression speaks of death, and vanity
of real concern with anything at all.

The strongest witness to futility,
that bolsters all the rest and helps them paint
the picture in which sin is justified,
is sickness in whatever form it takes.
The sick have reason for each one of their
unnatural desires and strange needs.
For who could live a life so soon cut short
and not esteem the worth of passing joys?
What pleasures could there be that will endure?
Are not the frail entitled to believe
that every stolen scrap of pleasure is
their righteous payment for their little lives?
Their death will pay the price for all of them,
if they enjoy their benefits or not.
The end of life must come, whatever way
that life be spent. And so take pleasure in
the quickly passing and ephemeral.

These are not sins, but witnesses unto
the strange belief that sin and death are real,
and innocence and sin will end alike
within the termination of the grave.
If this were true, there would be reason to
remain content to seek for passing joys
and cherish little pleasures where you can.
Yet in this picture is the body not
perceived as neutral and without a goal
inherent in itself. For it becomes
the symbol of reproach, the sign of guilt
whose consequences still are there to see,
so that the cause can never be denied.

Your function is to show your brother sin
can have no cause. How futile must it be
to see yourself a picture of the proof
that what your function is can never be!
The Holy Spirit's picture changes not
the body into something it is not.
It only takes away from it all signs
of accusation and of blamefulness.
Pictured without a purpose, it is seen
as neither sick nor well, nor bad nor good.
No grounds are offered that it may be judged
in any way at all. It has no life,
but neither is it dead. It stands apart
from all experience of love or fear.
For now it witnesses to nothing yet,
its purpose being open, and the mind
made free again to choose what it is for.
Now is it not condemned, but waiting for
a purpose to be given, that it may
fulfill the function that it will receive.

Into this empty space, from which the goal
of sin has been removed, is Heaven free
to be remembered. Here its peace can come,
and perfect healing take the place of death.
The body can become a sign of life,
a promise of redemption, and a breath
of immortality to those grown sick

of breathing in the fetid scent of death.
Let it have healing as its purpose. Then
will it send forth the message it received,
and by its health and loveliness proclaim
the truth and value that it represents.
Let it receive the power to represent
an endless life, forever unattacked.
And to your brother let its message be,
"Behold me, brother, at your hand I live."

The simple way to let this be achieved
is merely this; to let the body have
no purpose from the past, when you were sure
you knew its purpose was to foster guilt.
For this insists your crippled picture is
a lasting sign of what it represents.
This leaves no space in which a different view,
another purpose, can be given it.
You do *not* know its purpose. You but gave
illusions of a purpose to a thing
you made to hide your function from yourself.
This thing without a purpose cannot hide
the function that the Holy Spirit gave.
Let, then, its purpose and your function both
be reconciled at last and seen as one.

## The Fear of Healing

Is healing frightening? To many, yes.
For accusation is a bar to love,
and damaged bodies are accusers. They
stand firmly in the way of trust and peace,
proclaiming that the frail can have no trust
and that the damaged have no grounds for peace.
Who has been injured by his brother, and
could love and trust him still? He has attacked
and will attack again. Protect him not,
because your damaged body shows that *you*
must be protected from him. To forgive
may be an act of charity, but not
his due. He may be pitied for his guilt,
but not exonerated. And if you
forgive him his transgressions, you but add
to all the guilt that he has really earned.

The unhealed cannot pardon. For they are
the witnesses that pardon is unfair.
They would retain the consequences of
the guilt they overlook. Yet no one can
forgive a sin that he believes is real.
And what has consequences must be real,
because what it has done is there to see.
Forgiveness is not pity, which but seeks
to pardon what it thinks to be the truth.
Good cannot *be* returned for evil, for
forgiveness does not first establish sin
and then forgive it. Who can say and mean,
"My brother, you have injured me, and yet,
because I am the better of the two,
I pardon you my hurt." His pardon and
your hurt cannot exist together. One
denies the other and must make it false.

To witness sin and yet forgive it is
a paradox that reason cannot see.
For it maintains what has been done to you
deserves no pardon. And by giving it,
you grant your brother mercy but retain
the proof he is not really innocent.
The sick remain accusers. They cannot
forgive their brothers and themselves as well.
For no one in whom true forgiveness rests
can suffer. He holds not the proof of sin
before his brother's eyes. And thus he must
have overlooked it and removed it from
his own. Forgiveness cannot be for one
and not the other. Who forgives is healed.
And in his healing lies the proof that he
has truly pardoned, and retains no trace
of condemnation that he still would hold
against himself or any living thing.

Forgiveness is not real unless it brings
a healing to your brother and yourself.
You must attest his sins have no effect
on you to demonstrate they are not real.
How else could he be guiltless? And how could
his innocence be justified unless
his sins have no effect to warrant guilt?
Sins are beyond forgiveness just because
they would entail effects that cannot be
undone and overlooked entirely.
In their undoing lies the proof that they
are merely errors. Let yourself be healed
that you may be forgiving, offering
salvation to your brother and yourself.

A broken body shows the mind has not
been healed. A miracle of healing proves
that separation is without effect.
What you would prove to him you will believe.
The power of witness comes from your belief.
And everything you say or do or think
but testifies to what you teach to him.
Your body can be means to teach that it
has never suffered pain because of him.
And in its healing can it offer him
mute testimony of his innocence.
It is this testimony that can speak
with power greater than a thousand tongues.
For here is his forgiveness proved to him.

A miracle can offer nothing less
to him than it has given unto you.
So does your healing show your mind is healed,
and has forgiven what he did not do.
And so is he convinced his innocence
was never lost, and healed along with you.
Thus does the miracle undo all things
the world attests can never be undone.
And hopelessness and death must disappear
before the ancient clarion call of life.
This call has power far beyond the weak
and miserable cry of death and guilt.
The ancient calling of the Father to
His Son, and of the Son unto his own,
will yet be the last trumpet that the world
will ever hear. Brother, there is no death.
And this you learn when you but wish to show
your brother that you had no hurt of him.
He thinks your blood is on his hands, and so
he stands condemned. Yet it is given you
to show him, by your healing, that his guilt
is but the fabric of a senseless dream.

How just are miracles! For they bestow
an equal gift of full deliverance
from guilt upon your brother and yourself.
Your healing saves him pain as well as you,
and you are healed because you wished him well.
This is the law the miracle obeys;
that healing sees no specialness at all.
It does not come from pity but from love.
And love would prove all suffering is but
a vain imagining, a foolish wish
with no effects. Your health is a result
of your desire to see your brother with
no blood upon his hands, nor guilt upon
his heart made heavy with the proof of sin.
And what you wish is given you to see.

The "cost" of your serenity is his.
This is the "price" the Holy Spirit and
the world interpret differently. The world
perceives it as a statement of the "fact"
that your salvation sacrifices his.
The Holy Spirit knows your healing is
the witness unto his, and cannot be
apart from his at all. As long as he
consents to suffer, you will be unhealed.
Yet you can show him that his suffering
is purposeless and wholly without cause.
Show him your healing, and he will consent
no more to suffer. For his innocence
has been established in your sight and his.
And laughter will replace your sighs, because
God's Son remembered that he *is* God's Son.

Who, then, fears healing? Only those to whom
their brother's sacrifice and pain are seen
to represent their own serenity.
Their helplessness and weakness represent
the grounds on which they justify his pain.
The constant sting of guilt he suffers serves
to prove that he is slave, but they are free.
The constant pain they suffer demonstrates
that they are free *because* they hold him bound.
And sickness is desired to prevent
a shift of balance in the sacrifice.
How could the Holy Spirit be deterred
an instant, even less, to reason with
an argument for sickness such as this?
And need your healing be delayed because
you pause to listen to insanity?

Correction is not your function. It belongs
to One Who knows of fairness, not of guilt.
If you assume correction's role, you lose
the function of forgiveness. No one can
forgive until he learns correction is
but to forgive, and never to accuse.
Alone, you cannot see they are the same,
and therefore is correction not of you.
Identity and function are the same,

and by your function do you know yourself.
And thus, if you confuse your function with
the function of Another, you must be
confused about yourself and who you are.
What is the separation but a wish
to take God's function from Him
and deny that it is His?
Yet if it is not His it is not yours,
for you must lose what you would take away.

In a split mind, identity must seem
to be divided. Nor can anyone
perceive a function unified which has
conflicting purposes and different ends.
Correction, to a mind so split, must be
a way to punish sins you think are yours
in someone else. And thus does he become
your victim, not your brother, different
from you in that he is more guilty, thus
in need of your correction, as the one
more innocent than he.
This splits his function off
from yours, and gives you both a different role.
And so you cannot be perceived as one,
and with a single function that would mean
a shared identity with but one end.

Correction *you* would do must separate,
because that is the function given it
*by* you. When you perceive correction is
the same as pardon, then you also know
the Holy Spirit's Mind and yours are one.
And so your own Identity is found.
Yet must He work with what is given Him,
and you allow Him only half your mind.
And thus He represents the other half,
and seems to have a different purpose from
the one you cherish, and you think is yours.
Thus does your function seem divided, with
a half in opposition to a half.
And these two halves appear to represent
a split within a self perceived as two.

Consider how this self-perception must
extend, and do not overlook the fact
that every thought extends because that is
its purpose, being what it really is.
From an idea of self as two, there comes
a necessary view of function split
between the two. And what you would correct
is only half the error, which you think
is all of it. Your brother's sins become
the central target for correction, lest
your errors and his own be seen as one.
Yours are mistakes, but his are sins and not
the same as yours. His merit punishment,
while yours, in fairness, should be overlooked.

In this interpretation of correction,
your own mistakes you will not even see.
The focus of correction has been placed
outside yourself, on one who cannot be
a part of you while this perception lasts.
What is condemned can never be returned
to its accuser, who had hated it,
and hates it still as symbol of his fear.
This is your brother, focus of your hate,
unworthy to be part of you and thus
outside yourself; the other half, which is
denied. And only what is left without
his presence is perceived as all of you.
To this remaining half the Holy Spirit
must represent the other half until
you recognize it *is* the other half.
And this He does by giving you and him
a function that is one, not different.

Correction is the function given both,
but neither one alone. And when it is
fulfilled as shared, it must correct mistakes
in you and him. It cannot leave mistakes
in one unhealed and set the other free.
That is divided purpose, which can not
be shared, and so it cannot be the goal
in which the Holy Spirit sees His Own.
And you can rest assured that He will not
fulfill a function that He does not see
and recognize as His. For only thus
can He keep yours preserved intact, despite
Your separate views of what your function is.
If He upheld divided function, you
were lost indeed. His inability
to see His goal divided and distinct
for you and him, preserves yourself from the
awareness of a function not your own.
And thus is healing given you and him.

Correction must be left to One Who knows

correction and forgiveness are the same.
With half a mind this is not understood.
Leave, then, correction to the Mind that is
united, functioning as one because
it is not split in purpose, and conceives
a single function as its only one.
Here is the function given it conceived

to be its own, and not apart from that
its Giver keeps *because* it has been shared.
In His acceptance of this function lies
the means whereby your mind is unified.
His single purpose unifies the halves
of you that you perceive as separate.
And each forgives the other, that he may
accept his other half as part of him.

## Beyond All Symbols

Power cannot oppose. For opposition would weaken it, and weakened power is a contradiction in ideas. Weak strength is meaningless, and power used to weaken is employed to limit. And therefore it must be limited and weak, because that is its purpose. Power is unopposed, to be itself. No weakness can intrude on it without changing it into something it is not. To weaken is to limit, and impose an opposite that contradicts the concept that it attacks. And by this does it join to the idea a something it is not, and make it unintelligible. Who can understand a double concept, such as "weakened-power" or "hateful-love"?

You have decided that your brother is a symbol for a "hateful-love," a "weakened-power," and above all, a "living-death." And so he has no meaning to you, for he stands for what is meaningless. He represents a double thought, where half is cancelled out by the remaining half. Yet even this is quickly contradicted by the half it cancelled out, and so they both are gone. And now he stands for nothing. Symbols which but represent ideas that cannot be must stand for empty space and nothingness. Yet nothingness and empty space can not be interference. What can interfere with the awareness of reality is the belief that there is something there.

The picture of your brother that you see
means nothing. There is nothing to attack
or to deny; to love or hate, or to
endow with power or to see as weak.
The picture has been wholly cancelled out,
because it symbolized a contradiction
that cancelled out the thought it represents.
And thus the picture has no cause at all.
Who can perceive effect without a cause?
What can the causeless be but nothingness?
The picture of your brother that you see
is wholly absent and has never been.
Let, then, the empty space it occupies
be recognized as vacant, and the time
devoted to its seeing be perceived
as idly spent, a time unoccupied.

An empty space that is not seen as filled,
an unused interval of time not seen
as spent and fully occupied, become
a silent invitation to the truth
to enter, and to make itself at home.
No preparation can be made that would

enhance the invitation's real appeal.
For what you leave as vacant God will fill,
and where He is there must the truth abide.
Unweakened power, with no opposite,
is what creation is. For this there are
no symbols. Nothing points beyond the truth,
for what can stand for more than everything?
Yet true undoing must be kind. And so
the first replacement for your picture is
another picture of another kind.

As nothingness cannot be pictured, so
there is no symbol for totality.
Reality is ultimately known
without a form, unpictured and unseen.
Forgiveness is not yet a power known
as wholly free of limits. Yet it sets
no limits you have chosen to impose.
Forgiveness is the means by which the truth
is represented temporarily.
It lets the Holy Spirit make exchange
of pictures possible, until the time
when aids are meaningless and learning done.

No learning aid has use that can extend
beyond the goal of learning. When its aim
has been accomplished it is functionless.
Yet in the learning interval it has
a use that now you fear, but yet will love.

The picture of your brother given you
to occupy the space so lately left
unoccupied and vacant will not need
defense of any kind. For you will give
it overwhelming preference. Nor delay
an instant in deciding that it is
the only one you want. It does not stand
for double concepts. Though it is but half
the picture and is incomplete, within
itself it is the same. The other half
of what it represents remains unknown,
but is not cancelled out. And thus is God
left free to take the final step Himself.
For this you need no pictures and no learning aids.
And what will ultimately take the place
of every learning aid will merely *be*.

Forgiveness vanishes and symbols fade,
and nothing that the eyes have ever seen
or ears have heard remains to be perceived.
A Power wholly limitless has come,
not to destroy, but to receive Its Own.
There is no choice of function anywhere.
The choice you fear to lose you never had.
Yet only this appears to interfere
with power unlimited and single thoughts,
complete and happy, without opposite.
You do not know the peace of power that
opposes nothing. Yet no other kind
can be at all. Give welcome to the Power
beyond forgiveness, and beyond the world
of symbols and of limitations. He
would merely be, and so He merely is.

### The Quiet Answer

In quietness are all things answered, and
is every problem quietly resolved.
In conflict there can be no answer and
no resolution, for its purpose is
to make no resolution possible,
and to ensure no answer will be plain.
A problem set in conflict has no answer,
for it is seen in different ways. And what
would be an answer from one point of view
is not an answer in another light.
You *are* in conflict. Thus it must be clear
you cannot answer anything at all,
for conflict has no limited effects.
Yet if God gave an answer there must be
a way in which your problems are resolved,
for what He wills already has been done.

Thus it must be that time is not involved
and every problem can be answered *now*.
Yet it must also be that, in your state
of mind, solution is impossible.
Therefore, God must have given you a way
of reaching to another state of mind
in which the answer is already there.
Such is the holy instant. It is here
that all your problems should be brought and left.
Here they belong, for here their answer is.
And where its answer is, a problem must
be simple and be easily resolved.
It must be pointless to attempt to solve
a problem where the answer cannot be.
Yet just as surely it must be resolved,
if it is brought to where the answer is.

Attempt to solve no problems but within
the holy instant's surety. For there
the problem *will* be answered and resolved.
Outside there will be no solution, for
there is no answer there that could be found.
Nowhere outside a single, simple question
is ever asked. The world can only ask
a double question. One with many answers
can have no answers. None of them will do.
It does not ask a question to be answered,
but only to restate its point of view.

All questions asked within this world are but
a way of looking, not a question asked.
A question asked in hate cannot be answered,
because it is an answer in itself.
A double question asks and answers, both
attesting the same thing in different form.
The world asks but one question. It is this:
"Of these illusions, which of them *is* true?
Which ones establish peace and offer joy?
And which can bring escape from all the pain

of which this world is made?" Whatever form
the question takes, its purpose is the same.
It asks but to establish sin is real,
and answers in the form of preference.
"Which sin do you prefer? That is the one
that you should choose. The others are not true.
What can the body get that you would want
the most of all? It is your servant and
also your friend. But tell it what you want,
and it will serve you lovingly and well."
And this is not a question, for it tells
you what you want and where to go for it.
It leaves no room to question its beliefs,
except that what it states takes question's form.

A pseudo-question has no answer. It
dictates the answer even as it asks.
Thus is all questioning within the world
a form of propaganda for itself.
Just as the body's witnesses are but
the senses from within itself, so are
the answers to the questions of the world
contained within the questions that are asked.
Where answers represent the questions, they
add nothing new and nothing has been learned.
An honest question is a learning tool
that asks for something that you do not know.
It does not set conditions for response,
but merely asks what the response should be.
But no one in a conflict state is free
to ask this question, for he does not *want*
an honest answer where the conflict ends.

Only within the holy instant can
an honest question honestly be asked.
And from the meaning of the question does
the meaningfulness of the answer come.
Here is it possible to separate
your wishes from the answer, so it can
be given you and also be received.
The answer is provided everywhere.
Yet it is only here it can be heard.
An honest answer asks no sacrifice
because it answers questions truly asked.
The questions of the world but ask of whom
is sacrifice demanded, asking not
if sacrifice is meaningful at all.
And so, unless the answer tells "of whom,"
it will remain unrecognized, unheard,
and thus the question is preserved intact
because it gave the answer to itself.
The holy instant is the interval
in which the mind is still enough to hear
an answer that is not entailed within
the question asked. It offers something new
and different from the question. How could it
be answered if it but repeats itself?

Therefore, attempt to solve no problems in
a world from which the answer has been barred.
But bring the problem to the only place
that holds the answer lovingly for you.
Here are the answers that will solve your problems
because they stand apart from them, and see
what can be answered; what the question *is*.
Within the world the answers merely raise
another question, though they leave the first
unanswered. In the holy instant, you
can bring the question to the answer, and
receive the answer that was made for you.

### The Healing Example

The only way to heal is to be healed.
The miracle extends without your help,
but you are needed that it can begin.
Accept the miracle of healing, and
it will go forth because of what it is.
It is its nature to extend itself
the instant it is born. And it is born
the instant it is offered and received.
No one can ask another to be healed.
But he can let *himself* be healed, and thus
offer the other what he has received.
Who can bestow upon another what
he does not have? And who can share what he
denies himself? The Holy Spirit speaks
to *you*. He does not speak to someone else.
Yet by your listening His Voice extends,
because you have accepted what He says.

Health is the witness unto health. As long
as it is unattested, it remains
without conviction. Only when it has
been demonstrated is it proved, and must
provide a witness that compels belief.
No one is healed through double messages.

If you wish only to be healed, you heal.
Your single purpose makes this possible.
But if you are afraid of healing, then
it cannot come through you. The only thing
that is required for a healing is
a lack of fear. The fearful are not healed,
and cannot heal.
This does not mean the conflict must be gone
forever from your mind to heal. For if
it were, there were no need for healing then.
But it does mean, if only for an instant,
you love without attack. An instant is
sufficient. Miracles wait not on time.

The holy instant is the miracle's
abiding place. From there, each one is born
into this world as witness to a state
of mind that has transcended conflict, and
has reached to peace. It carries comfort from
the place of peace into the battleground,
and demonstrates that war has no effects.
For all the hurt that war has sought to bring,
the broken bodies and the shattered limbs,
the screaming dying and the silent dead,
are gently lifted up and comforted.

There is no sadness where a miracle
has come to heal. And nothing more than just
one instant of your love without attack
is necessary that all this occur.
In that one instant you are healed, and in
that single instant is all healing done.
What stands apart from you, when you accept
the blessing that the holy instant brings?
Be not afraid of blessing, for the One
Who blesses you loves all the world, and leaves
nothing within the world that could be feared.
But if you shrink from blessing, will the world
indeed seem fearful, for you have withheld
its peace and comfort, leaving it to die.

Would not a world so bitterly bereft
be looked on as a condemnation by
the one who could have saved it, but stepped back
because he was afraid of being healed?
The eyes of all the dying bring reproach,
and suffering whispers, "What is there to fear?"
Consider well its question. It is asked
of you on your behalf. A dying world
asks only that you rest an instant from
attack upon yourself, that it be healed.

Come to the holy instant and be healed,
for nothing that is there received is left
behind on your returning to the world.
And being blessed you will bring blessing. Life
is given you to give the dying world.
And suffering eyes no longer will accuse,
but shine in thanks to you who blessing gave.
The holy instant's radiance will light
your eyes, and give them sight to see beyond
all suffering and see Christ's face instead.
Healing replaces suffering. Who looks
on one cannot perceive the other, for
they cannot both be there. And what you see
the world will witness, and will witness to.

Thus is your healing everything the world
requires, that it may be healed. It needs
one lesson that has perfectly been learned.
And then, when you forget it, will the world
remind you gently of what you have taught.
No reinforcement will its thanks withhold
from you who let yourself be healed that it
might live. It will call forth its witnesses
to show the face of Christ to you who brought
the sight to them, by which they witnessed it.
The world of accusation is replaced
by one in which all eyes look lovingly
upon the Friend who brought them their release.
And happily your brother will perceive
the many friends he thought were enemies.

Problems are not specific but they take
specific forms, and these specific shapes
make up the world. And no one understands
the nature of his problem. If he did,
it would be there no more for him to see.
Its very nature is that it is *not*.
And thus, while he perceives it he can not
perceive it as it is. But healing is
apparent in specific instances,
and generalizes to include them all.
This is because they really are the same,
despite their different forms. All learning aims
at transfer, which becomes complete within
two situations that are seen as one,
for only common elements are there.

Yet this can only be attained by One
Who does not see the differences you see.
The total transfer of your learning is
not made by you. But that it has been made
in spite of all the differences you see,
convinces you that they could not be real.

Your healing will extend, and will be brought
to problems that you thought were not your own.
And it will also be apparent that
your many different problems will be solved
as any one of them has been escaped.
It cannot be their differences which made
this possible, for learning does not jump
from situations to their opposites
and bring the same results. All healing must
proceed in lawful manner, in accord
with laws that have been properly perceived
but never violated. Fear you not
the way that you perceive them. You are wrong,
but there is One within you Who is right.

Leave, then, the transfer of your learning to
the One Who really understands its laws,
and Who will guarantee that they remain
unviolated and unlimited.
Your part is merely to apply what He
has taught you to yourself, and He will do
the rest. And it is thus the power of
your learning will be proved to you by all
the many different witnesses it finds.
Your brother first among them will be seen,
but thousands stand behind him, and beyond
each one of them there are a thousand more.
Each one may seem to have a problem that
is different from the rest. Yet they are solved
together. And their common answer shows
the questions could not have been separate.

Peace be to you to whom is healing offered.
And you will learn that peace is given you
when you accept the healing for yourself.
Its total value need not be appraised
by you to let you understand that you
have benefited from it. What occurred
within the instant that love entered in
without attack will stay with you forever.
Your healing will be one of its effects,
as will your brother's. Everywhere you go,
will you behold its multiplied effects.
Yet all the witnesses that you behold
will be far less than all there really are.
Infinity cannot be understood
by merely counting up its separate parts.
God thanks you for your healing, for He knows
it is a gift of love unto His Son,
and therefore is it given unto Him.

### The Witnesses to Sin

Pain demonstrates the body must be real.
It is a loud, obscuring voice whose shrieks
would silence what the Holy Spirit says,
and keep His words from your awareness. Pain
compels attention, drawing it away
from Him and focusing upon itself.
Its purpose is the same as pleasure, for
they both are means to make the body real.
What shares a common purpose is the same.
This is the law of purpose, which unites
all those who share in it within itself.
Pleasure and pain are equally unreal,
because their purpose cannot be achieved.
Thus are they means for nothing, for they have
a goal without a meaning. And they share
the lack of meaning which their purpose has.

Sin shifts from pain to pleasure, and again
to pain. For either witness is the same,
and carries but one message: "You are here,
within this body, and you can be hurt.
You can have pleasure, too, but only at
the cost of pain." These witnesses are joined
by many more. Each one seems different
because it has a different name, and so
it seems to answer to a different sound.
Except for this, the witnesses of sin
are all alike. Call pleasure pain, and it
will hurt. Call pain a pleasure, and the pain
behind the pleasure will be felt no more.
Sin's witnesses but shift from name to name,
as one steps forward and another back.
Yet which is foremost makes no difference.
Sin's witnesses hear but the call of death.

This body, purposeless within itself,
holds all your memories and all your hopes.
You use its eyes to see, its ears to hear,

and let it tell you what it is it feels.
*It does not know*. It tells you but the names
you gave to it to use, when you call forth
the witnesses to its reality.
You cannot choose among them which are real,
for any one you choose is like the rest.
This name or that, but nothing more, you choose.
You do not make a witness true because
you called him by truth's name. The truth is found
in him if it is truth he represents.
And otherwise he lies, if you should call
him by the holy Name of God Himself.

God's Witness sees no witnesses against
the body. Neither does He harken to
the witnesses by other names that speak
in other ways for its reality.
He knows it is not real. For nothing could
contain what you believe it holds within.
Nor could it tell a part of God Himself
what it should feel and what its function is.
Yet must He love whatever you hold dear.
And for each witness to the body's death
He sends a witness to your life in Him
Who knows no death. Each miracle He brings
is witness that the body is not real.
Its pains and pleasures does He heal alike,
for all sin's witnesses do His replace.

The miracle makes no distinctions in
the names by which sin's witnesses are called.
It merely proves that what they represent
has no effects. And this it proves because
its own effects have come to take their place.
It matters not the name by which you called
your suffering. It is no longer there.
The One Who brings the miracle perceives
them all as one, and called by name of fear.
As fear is witness unto death, so is
the miracle the witness unto life.
It is a witness no one can deny,
for it is the effects of life it brings.
The dying live, the dead arise, and pain
has vanished. Yet a miracle speaks not
but for itself, but what it represents.

Love, too, has symbols in a world of sin.
The miracle forgives because it stands
for what is past forgiveness and is true.

How foolish and insane it is to think
a miracle is bound by laws that it
came solely to undo! The laws of sin
have different witnesses with different strengths.
And they attest to different sufferings.
Yet to the One Who sends forth miracles
to bless the world, a tiny stab of pain,
a little worldly pleasure, and the throes
of death itself are but a single sound;
a call for healing, and a plaintive cry
for help within a world of misery.
It is their sameness that the miracle
attests. It is their sameness that it proves.
The laws that call them different are dissolved,
and shown as powerless. The purpose of
a miracle is to accomplish this.
And God Himself has guaranteed the strength
of miracles for what they witness to.

Be you then witness to the miracle,
and not the laws of sin. There is no need
to suffer any more. But there *is* need
that you be healed, because the suffering
and sorrow of the world have made it deaf
to its salvation and deliverance.

The resurrection of the world awaits
your healing and your happiness, that you
may demonstrate the healing of the world.
The holy instant will replace all sin
if you but carry its effects with you.
And no one will elect to suffer more.
What better function could you serve than this?
Be healed that you may heal, and suffer not
the laws of sin to be applied to you.
And truth will be revealed to you who chose
to let love's symbols take the place of sin.

### The Dreamer of the Dream

Suffering is an emphasis upon
all that the world has done to injure you.
Here is the world's demented version of
salvation clearly shown. Like to a dream
of punishment, in which the dreamer is
unconscious of what brought on the attack
against himself, he sees himself attacked
unjustly and by something not himself.
He is the victim of this "something else,"

a thing outside himself, for which he has
no reason to be held responsible.
He must be innocent because he knows
not what he does, but what is done to him.
Yet is his own attack upon himself
apparent still, for it is he who bears
the suffering. And he cannot escape
because its source is seen outside himself.

Now you are being shown you *can* escape.
All that is needed is you look upon
the problem as it is, and not the way
that you have set it up. How could there be
another way to solve a problem that
is very simple, but has been obscured
by heavy clouds of complication, which
were made to keep the problem unresolved?
Without the clouds the problem will emerge
in all its primitive simplicity.
The choice will not be difficult, because
the problem is absurd when clearly seen.
No one has difficulty making up
his mind to let a simple problem be
resolved if it is seen as hurting him,
and also very easily removed.

The "reasoning" by which the world is made,
on which it rests, by which it is maintained,
is simply this: "*You* are the cause of what
I do. Your presence justifies my wrath,
and you exist and think apart from me.
While you attack I must be innocent.
And what I suffer from is your attack."
No one who looks upon this "reasoning"
exactly as it is could fail to see
it does not follow and it makes no sense.
Yet it seems sensible, because it looks
as if the world were hurting you. And so
it seems as if there is no need to go
beyond the obvious in terms of cause.

There is indeed a need. The world's escape
from condemnation is a need which those
within the world are joined in sharing. Yet
they do not recognize their common need.
For each one thinks that if he does his part,
the condemnation of the world will rest
on him. And it is this that he perceives
to *be* his part in its deliverance.

Vengeance must have a focus. Otherwise
is the avenger's knife in his own hand,
and pointed to himself. And he must see
it in another's hand, if he would be
a victim of attack he did not choose.
And thus he suffers from the wounds a knife
he does not hold has made upon himself.

This is the purpose of the world he sees.
And looked at thus, the world provides the means
by which this purpose seems to be fulfilled.
The means attest the purpose, but are not
themselves a cause. Nor will the cause be changed
by seeing it apart from its effects.
The cause produces the effects, which then
bear witness to the cause, and not themselves.
Look, then, beyond effects. It is not here
the cause of suffering and sin must lie.
And dwell not on the suffering and sin,
for they are but reflections of their cause.

The part you play in salvaging the world
from condemnation is your own escape.
Forget not that the witness to the world
of evil cannot speak except for what
has seen a need for evil in the world.
And this is where your guilt was first beheld.
In separation from your brother was
the first attack upon yourself begun.
And it is this the world bears witness to.
Seek not another cause, nor look among
the mighty legions of its witnesses
for its undoing. They support its claim
on your allegiance. What conceals the truth
is not where you should look to *find* the truth.

The witnesses to sin all stand within
one little space. And it is here you find
the cause of your perspective on the world.
Once you were unaware of what the cause
of everything the world appeared to thrust
upon you, uninvited and unasked,
must really be. Of one thing you were sure:
Of all the many causes you perceived
as bringing pain and suffering to you,
your guilt was not among them. Nor did you
in any way request them for yourself.
This is how all illusions came about.
The one who makes them does not see himself

as making them, and their reality
does not depend on him. Whatever cause
they have is something quite apart from him,
and what he sees is separate from his mind.
He cannot doubt his dreams' reality,
because he does not see the part he plays
in making them and making them seem real.

No one can waken from a dream the world
is dreaming for him. He becomes a part
of someone else's dream. He cannot choose
to waken from a dream he did not make.
Helpless he stands, a victim to a dream
conceived and cherished by a separate mind.
Careless indeed of him this mind must be,
as thoughtless of his peace and happiness
as is the weather or the time of day.
It loves him not, but casts him as it will
in any role that satisfies its dream.
So little is his worth that he is but
a dancing shadow, leaping up and down
according to a senseless plot conceived
within the idle dreaming of the world.

This is the only picture you can see;
the one alternative that you can choose,
the other possibility of cause,
if you be not the dreamer of your dreams.
And this is what you choose if you deny
the cause of suffering is in your mind.
Be glad indeed it is, for thus are you
the one decider of your destiny
in time. The choice is yours to make between
a sleeping death and dreams of evil or
a happy wakening and joy of life.

What could you choose between but life or death,
waking or sleeping, peace or war, your dreams
or your reality? There is a risk
of thinking death is peace, because the world
equates the body with the Self Which God
created. Yet a thing can never be
its opposite. And death is opposite
to peace, because it is the opposite
of life. And life is peace. Awaken and
forget all thoughts of death, and you will find
you have the peace of God. Yet if the choice
is really given you, then you must see
the causes of the things you choose between
exactly as they are and where they are.

What choices can be made between two states,
but one of which is clearly recognized?
Who could be free to choose between effects,
when only one is seen as up to him?
An honest choice could never be perceived
as one in which the choice is split between
a tiny you and an enormous world,
with different dreams about the truth in you.
The gap between reality and dreams
lies not between the dreaming of the world
and what you dream in secret. They are one.
The dreaming of the world is but a part
of your own dream you gave away, and saw
as if it were its start and ending, both.
Yet was it started by your secret dream,
which you do not perceive although it caused
the part you see and do not doubt is real.
How could you doubt it while you lie asleep,
and dream in secret that its cause is real?

A brother separated from yourself,
an ancient enemy, a murderer
who stalks you in the night and plots your death,
yet plans that it be lingering and slow;
of this you dream. Yet underneath this dream
is yet another, in which you become
the murderer, the secret enemy,
the scavenger and the destroyer of
your brother and the world alike. Here is
the cause of suffering, the space between
your little dreams and your reality.
The little gap you do not even see,
the birthplace of illusions and of fear,
the time of terror and of ancient hate,
the instant of disaster, all are here.
Here is the cause of unreality.
And it is here that it will be undone.

You are the dreamer of the world of dreams.
No other cause it has, nor ever will.
Nothing more fearful than an idle dream
has terrified God's Son, and made him think
that he has lost his innocence, denied
his Father, and made war upon himself.
So fearful is the dream, so seeming real,
he could not waken to reality
without the sweat of terror and a scream

of mortal fear, unless a gentler dream
preceded his awaking, and allowed
his calmer mind to welcome, not to fear,
the Voice That calls with love to waken him;
a gentler dream, in which his suffering
was healed and where his brother was his friend.
God willed he waken gently and with joy,
and gave him means to waken without fear.

Accept the dream He gave instead of yours.
It is not difficult to change a dream
when once the dreamer has been recognized.
Rest in the Holy Spirit, and allow
His gentle dreams to take the place of those
you dreamed in terror and in fear of death.
He brings forgiving dreams, in which the choice
is not who is the murderer and who
shall be the victim. In the dreams He brings
there is no murder and there is no death.
The dream of guilt is fading from your sight,
although your eyes are closed. A smile has come
to lighten up your sleeping face. The sleep
is peaceful now, for these are happy dreams.

Dream softly of your sinless brother, who
unites with you in holy innocence.
And from this dream the Lord of Heaven will
Himself awaken His beloved Son.
Dream of your brother's kindnesses instead
of dwelling in your dreams on his mistakes.
Select his thoughtfulness to dream about
instead of counting up the hurts he gave.
Forgive him his illusions, and give thanks
to him for all the helpfulness he gave.
And do not brush aside his many gifts
because he is not perfect in your dreams.
He represents his Father, Whom you see
as offering both life and death to you.

Brother, He gives but life. Yet what you see
as gifts your brother offers represent
the gifts you dream your Father gives to you.
Let all your brother's gifts be seen in light
of charity and kindness offered you.
And let no pain disturb your dream of deep
appreciation for his gifts to you.

**The "Hero" of the Dream**

The body is the central figure in
the dreaming of the world. There is no dream
without it, nor does it exist without
the dream in which it acts as if it were
a person to be seen and be believed.
It takes the central place in every dream,
which tells the story of how it was made
by other bodies, born into the world
outside the body, lives a little while
and dies, to be united in the dust
with other bodies dying like itself.
In the brief time allotted it to live,
it seeks for other bodies as its friends
and enemies. Its safety is its main
concern. Its comfort is its guiding rule.
It tries to look for pleasure, and avoid
the things that would be hurtful. Above all,
it tries to teach itself its pains and joys
are different and can be told apart.

The dreaming of the world takes many forms,
because the body seeks in many ways
to prove it is autonomous and real.
It puts things on itself that it has bought
with little metal discs or paper strips
the world proclaims as valuable and real.
It works to get them, doing senseless things,
and tosses them away for senseless things
it does not need and does not even want.
It hires other bodies, that they may
protect it and collect more senseless things
that it can call its own. It looks about
for special bodies that can share its dream.
Sometimes it dreams it is a conqueror
of bodies weaker than itself. But in
some phases of the dream, it is the slave
of bodies that would hurt and torture it.

The body's serial adventures, from
the time of birth to dying are the theme
of every dream the world has ever had.
The "hero" of this dream will never change,
nor will its purpose. Though the dream itself
takes many forms, and seems to show a great
variety of places and events
wherein its "hero" finds itself, the dream
has but one purpose, taught in many ways.
This single lesson does it try to teach
again, and still again, and yet once more;

that it is cause and not effect. And you
are its effect, and cannot be its cause.

Thus are you not the dreamer, but the dream.
And so you wander idly in and out
of places and events that it contrives.
That this is all the body does is true,
for it is but a figure in a dream.
But who reacts to figures in a dream
unless he sees them as if they were real?
The instant that he sees them as they are
they have no more effects on him, because
he understands he gave them their effects
by causing them and making them seem real.

How willing are you to escape effects
of all the dreams the world has ever had?
Is it your wish to let no dream appear
to be the cause of what it is you do?
Then let us merely look upon the dream's
beginning, for the part you see is but
the second part, whose cause lies in the first.
No one asleep and dreaming in the world
remembers his attack upon himself.
No one believes there really was a time
when he knew nothing of a body, and
could never have conceived this world as real.
He would have seen at once that these ideas
are one illusion, too ridiculous
for anything but to be laughed away.
How serious they now appear to be!
And no one can remember when they would
have met with laughter and with disbelief.
We can remember this, if we but look
directly at their cause. And we will see
the grounds for laughter, not a cause for fear.

Let us return the dream he gave away
unto the dreamer, who perceives the dream
as separate from himself and done to him.
Into eternity, where all is one,
there crept a tiny, mad idea, at which
the Son of God remembered not to laugh.
In his forgetting did the thought become
a serious idea, and possible
of both accomplishment and real effects.
Together, we can laugh them both away,
and understand that time cannot intrude
upon eternity. It is a joke
to think that time can come to circumvent
eternity, which *means* there is no time.

A timelessness in which is time made real;
a part of God that can attack itself;
a separate brother as an enemy;
a mind within a body all are forms
of circularity whose ending starts
at its beginning, ending at its cause.
The world you see depicts exactly what
you thought you did. Except that now you think
that what you did is being done to you.
The guilt for what you thought is being placed
outside yourself, and on a guilty world
that dreams your dreams
and thinks your thoughts instead
of you. It brings its vengeance, not your own.
It keeps you narrowly confined within
a body, which it punishes because
of all the sinful things the body does
within its dream. You have no power to make
the body stop its evil deeds because
you did not make it, and cannot control
its actions nor its purpose nor its fate.

The world but demonstrates an ancient truth;
you will believe that others do to you
exactly what you think you did to them.
But once deluded into blaming them
you will not see the cause of what they do,
because you *want* the guilt to rest on them.
How childish is the petulant device
to keep your innocence by pushing guilt
outside yourself, but never letting go!
It is not easy to perceive the jest
when all around you do your eyes behold
its heavy consequences, but without
their trifling cause. Without the cause do its
effects seem serious and sad indeed.
Yet they but follow. And it is their cause
that follows nothing and is but a jest.

In gentle laughter does the Holy Spirit
perceive the cause, and looks not to effects.
How else could He correct your error, who
have overlooked the cause entirely?
He bids you bring each terrible effect
to Him that you may look together on
its foolish cause and laugh with Him a while.

*You* judge effects, but *He* has judged their cause. And by His judgment are effects removed. Perhaps you come in tears. But hear Him say, "My brother, holy Son of God, behold your idle dream, in which this could occur." And you will leave the holy instant with your laughter and your brother's joined with His.

The secret of salvation is but this: That you are doing this unto yourself. No matter what the form of the attack, this still is true. Whoever takes the role of enemy and of attacker, still is this the truth. Whatever seems to be the cause of any pain and suffering you feel, this is still true. For you would not react at all to figures in a dream you knew that you were dreaming. Let them be as hateful and as vicious as they may, they could have no effect on you unless you failed to recognize it is your dream.

This single lesson learned will set you free from suffering, whatever form it takes. The Holy Spirit will repeat this one inclusive lesson of deliverance until it has been learned, regardless of the form of suffering that brings you pain. Whatever hurt you bring to Him He will make answer with this very simple truth. For this one answer takes away the cause of every form of sorrow and of pain. The form affects His answer not at all, for He would teach you but the single cause of all of them, no matter what their form. And you will understand that miracles reflect the simple statement, "*I* have done this thing, and it is this I would undo."

Bring, then, all forms of suffering to Him Who knows that every one is like the rest. He sees no differences where none exists, and He will teach you how each one is caused. None has a different cause from all the rest, and all of them are easily undone by but a single lesson truly learned. Salvation is a secret you have kept but from yourself. The universe proclaims it so. Yet to its witnesses you pay no heed at all. For they attest the thing you do not want to know. They seem to keep it secret from you. Yet you need but learn you chose but not to listen, not to see.

How differently will you perceive the world when this is recognized! When you forgive the world your guilt, you will be free of it. Its innocence does not demand your guilt, nor does your guiltlessness rest on its sins. This is the obvious; a secret kept from no one but yourself. And it is this that has maintained you separate from the world, and kept your brother separate from you. Now need you but to learn that both of you are innocent or guilty. The one thing that is impossible is that you be unlike each other; that they both be true. This is the only secret yet to learn. And it will be no secret you are healed.

# Chapter 28
## THE UNDOING OF FEAR

**The Present Memory**

The miracle does nothing. All it does
is to undo. And thus it cancels out
the interference to what has been done.
It does not add, but merely takes away.
And what it takes away is long since gone,
but being kept in memory appears
to have immediate effects. This world
was over long ago. The thoughts that made
it are no longer in the mind that thought
of them and loved them for a little while.
The miracle but shows the past is gone,
and what has truly gone has no effects.
Remembering a cause can but produce
illusions of its presence, not effects.

All the effects of guilt are here no more.
For guilt is over. In its passing went
its consequences, left without a cause.
Why would you cling to it in memory
if you did not desire its effects?
Remembering is as selective as
perception, being its past tense. It is
perception of the past as if it were
occurring now, and still were there to see.
Memory, like perception, is a skill
made up by you to take the place of what
God gave in your creation. And like all
the things you made, it can be used to serve
another purpose, and to be the means
for something else. It can be used to heal
and not to hurt, if you so wish it be.

Nothing employed for healing represents
an effort to do anything at all.
It is a recognition that you have
no needs which mean that something must be done.
It is an unselective memory,
that is not used to interfere with truth.
All things the Holy Spirit can employ
for healing have been given Him, without
the content and the purposes for which
they have been made. They are but skills without
an application. They await their use.
They have no dedication and no aim.

The Holy Spirit can indeed make use
of memory, for God Himself is there.
Yet this is not a memory of past
events, but only of a present state.
You are so long accustomed to believe
that memory holds only what is past,
that it is hard for you to realize
it is a skill that can remember *now*.
The limitations on remembering
the world imposes on it are as vast
as those you let the world impose on you.
There is no link of memory to the past.
If you would have it there, then there it is.
But only your desire made the link,
and only you have held it to a part
of time where guilt appears to linger still.

The Holy Spirit's use of memory
is quite apart from time. He does not seek
to use it as a means to keep the past,
but rather as a way to let it go.
Memory holds the message it receives,
and does what it is given it to do.
It does not write the message, nor appoint
what it is for. Like to the body, it
is purposeless within itself. And if
it seems to serve to cherish ancient hate,
and gives you pictures of injustices
and hurts that you were saving, this is what
you asked its message be and that it is.
Committed to its vaults, the history
of all the body's past is hidden there.
All of the strange associations made
to keep the past alive, the present dead,
are stored within it, waiting your command
that they be brought to you, and lived again.
And thus do their effects appear to be
increased by time, which took away their cause.

Yet time is but another phase of what
does nothing. It works hand in hand with all
the other attributes with which you seek
to keep concealed the truth about yourself.
Time neither takes away nor can restore.

And yet you make strange use of it, as if
the past had caused the present, which is but
a consequence in which no change can be
made possible because its cause has gone.
Yet change must have a cause that will endure,
or else it will not last. No change can be
made in the present if its cause is past.
Only the past is held in memory
as you make use of it, and so it is
a way to hold the past against the now.

Remember nothing that you taught yourself,
for you were badly taught. And who would keep
a senseless lesson in his mind, when he
can learn and can preserve a better one?
When ancient memories of hate appear,
remember that their cause is gone. And so
you cannot understand what they are for.
Let not the cause that you would give them now
be what it was that made them what they were,
or seemed to be. Be glad that it is gone,
for this is what you would be pardoned from.
And see, instead, the new effects of cause
accepted *now*, with consequences *here*.
They will surprise you with their loveliness.
The ancient new ideas they bring will be
the happy consequences of a Cause
so ancient that it far exceeds the span
of memory which your perception sees.

This is the Cause the Holy Spirit has
remembered for you, when you would forget.
It is not past because He let It not
be unremembered. It has never changed,
because there never was a time in which
He did not keep It safely in your mind.
Its consequences will indeed seem new,
because you thought that you remembered not
their Cause. Yet was It never absent from
your mind, for it was not your Father's Will
that He be unremembered by His Son.

What *you* remember never was. It came
from causelessness which you confused with cause.
It can deserve but laughter, when you learn
you have remembered consequences that
were causeless and could never be effects.
The miracle reminds you of a Cause
forever present, perfectly untouched
by time and interference. Never changed
from what It is. And you are Its effect,
as changeless and as perfect as Itself.
Its memory does not lie in the past,
nor waits the future. It is not revealed
in miracles. They but remind you that
It has not gone. When you forgive It for
your sins, It will no longer be denied.

You who have sought to lay a judgment on
your own Creator cannot understand
it is not He Who laid a judgment on
His Son. You would deny Him His Effects,
yet have They never been denied. There was
no time in which His Son could be condemned
for what was causeless and against His Will.
What your remembering would witness to
is but the fear of God. He has not done
the thing you fear. No more have you. And so
your innocence has not been lost. You need
no healing to be healed. In quietness,
see in the miracle a lesson in
allowing Cause to have Its Own Effects,
and doing nothing that would interfere.

The miracle comes quietly into
the mind that stops an instant and is still.
It reaches gently from that quiet time,
and from the mind it healed in quiet then,
to other minds to share its quietness.
And they will join in doing nothing to
prevent its radiant extension back
into the Mind Which caused all minds to be.
Born out of sharing, there can be no pause
in time to cause the miracle delay
in hastening to all unquiet minds,
and bringing them an instant's stillness, when
the memory of God returns to them.
Their own remembering is quiet now,
and what has come to take its place will not
be wholly unremembered afterwards.

He to Whom time is given offers thanks
for every quiet instant given Him.
For in that instant is God's memory
allowed to offer all its treasures to
the Son of God, for whom they have been kept.
How gladly does He offer them unto
the one for whom He has been given them!

And His Creator shares His thanks, because
He would not be deprived of His Effects.
The instant's silence that His Son accepts
gives welcome to eternity and Him,
and lets Them enter where They would abide.
For in that instant does the Son of God
do nothing that would make himself afraid.

How instantly the memory of God
arises in the mind that has no fear
to keep the memory away! Its own
remembering has gone. There is no past
to keep its fearful image in the way
of glad awakening to present peace.
The trumpets of eternity resound
throughout the stillness, yet disturb it not.
And what is now remembered is not fear,
but rather is the Cause that fear was made
to render unremembered and undone.
The stillness speaks in gentle sounds of love
the Son of God remembers from before
his own remembering came in between
the present and the past, to shut them out.

Now is the Son of God at last aware
of present Cause and Its benign Effects.
Now does he understand what he has made
is causeless, having no effects at all.
He has done nothing. And in seeing this,
he understands he never had a need
for doing anything, and never did.
His Cause *is* Its Effects. There never was
a cause beside It that could generate
a different past or future. Its Effects
are changelessly eternal, beyond fear,
and past the world of sin entirely.

What has been lost, to see the causeless not?
And where is sacrifice, when memory
of God has come to take the place of loss?
What better way to close the little gap
between illusions and reality
than to allow the memory of God
to flow across it, making it a bridge
an instant will suffice to reach beyond?
For God has closed it with Himself. His memory
has not gone by, and left a stranded Son
forever on a shore where he can glimpse
another shore that he can never reach.

His Father wills that he be lifted up
and gently carried over. He has built
the bridge, and it is He Who will transport
His Son across it. Have no fear that He
will fail in what He wills. Nor that you be
excluded from the Will that is for you.

### Reversing Effect and Cause

Without a cause there can be no effects,
and yet without effects there is no cause.
The cause a cause is *made* by its effects;
the Father *is* a Father by His Son.
Effects do not create their cause, but they
establish its causation. Thus, the Son
gives Fatherhood to his Creator, and
receives the gift that he has given Him.
It is *because* he is God's Son that he
must also be a father, who creates
as God created him. The circle of
creation has no end. Its starting and
its ending are the same. But in itself
it holds the universe of all creation,
without beginning and without an end.

Fatherhood *is* creation. Love must be
extended. Purity is not confined.
It is the nature of the innocent
to be forever uncontained, without
a barrier or limitation. Thus
is purity not of the body. Nor
can it be found where limitation is.
The body can be healed by its effects,
which are as limitless as is itself.
Yet must all healing come about because
the mind is recognized as not within
the body, and its innocence is quite
apart from it, and where all healing is.
Where, then, is healing? Only where its cause
is given its effects. For sickness is
a meaningless attempt to give effects
to causelessness, and make it be a cause.

Always in sickness does the Son of God
attempt to make himself his cause, and not
allow himself to be his Father's Son.
For this impossible desire, he
does not believe that he is Love's effect,
and must be cause because of what he is.

The cause of healing is the only Cause
of everything. It has but *one* effect.
And in that recognition, causelessness
is given no effects and none is seen.
A mind within a body and a world
of other bodies, each with separate minds,
are your "creations," you the "other" mind,
creating with effects unlike yourself.
And as their "father," you must be like them.

Nothing at all has happened but that you
have put yourself to sleep, and dreamed a dream
in which you were an alien to yourself,
and but a part of someone else's dream.
The miracle does not awaken you,
but merely shows you who the dreamer is.
It teaches you there is a choice of dreams
while you are still asleep, depending on
the purpose of your dreaming. Do you wish
for dreams of healing, or for dreams of death?
A dream is like a memory in that
it pictures what you wanted shown to you.

An empty storehouse, with an open door,
holds all your shreds of memories and dreams.
Yet if you are the dreamer, you perceive
this much at least: That you have caused the dream,
and can accept another dream as well.
But for this change in content of the dream,
it must be realized that it is you
who dreamed the dreaming that you do not like.
It is but an effect that *you* have caused,
and you would not be cause of this effect.
In dreams of murder and attack are you
the victim in a dying body slain.
But in forgiving dreams is no one asked
to be the victim and the sufferer.
These are the happy dreams the miracle
exchanges for your own. It does not ask
you make another; only that you see
you made the one you would exchange for this.

This world is causeless, as is every dream
that anyone has dreamed within the world.
No plans are possible, and no design
exists that could be found and understood.
What else could be expected from a thing
that has no cause? Yet if it has no cause,
it has no purpose. You may cause a dream,
but never will you give it real effects.
For that would change its cause, and it is this
you cannot do. The dreamer of a dream
is not awake, but does not know he sleeps.
He sees illusions of himself as sick
or well, depressed or happy, but without
a stable cause with guaranteed effects.

The miracle establishes you dream
a dream, and that its content is not true.
This is a crucial step in dealing with
illusions. No one is afraid of them
when he perceives he made them up. The fear
was held in place because he did not see
that he was author of the dream, and not
a figure in the dream. He gives himself
the consequences that he dreams he gave
his brother. And it is but this the dream
has put together and has offered him,
to show him that his wishes have been done.
Thus does he fear his own attack, but sees
it at another's hands. As victim, he
is suffering from its effects, but not
their cause. He authored not his own attack,
and he is innocent of what he caused.
The miracle does nothing but to show
him that he has done nothing. What he fears
is cause without the consequences that
would make it cause. And so it never was.

The separation started with the dream
the Father was deprived of His Effects,
and powerless to keep them since He was
no longer their Creator. In the dream,
the dreamer made himself. But what he made
has turned against him, taking on the role
of its creator, as the dreamer had.
And as he hated his Creator, so
the figures in the dream have hated him.
His body is their slave, which they abuse
because the motives he has given it
have they adopted as their own. And hate
it for the vengeance it would offer them.
It is their vengeance on the body which
appears to prove the dreamer could not be
the maker of the dream. Effect and cause
are first split off, and then reversed, so that
effect becomes a cause; the cause, effect.

This is the separation's final step,
with which salvation, which proceeds to go
the other way, begins. This final step
is an effect of what has gone before,
appearing as a cause. The miracle
is the first step in giving back to cause
the function of causation, not effect.
For this confusion has produced the dream,
and while it lasts will wakening be feared.
Nor will the call to wakening be heard,
because it seems to be the call to fear.

Like every lesson that the Holy Spirit
requests you learn, the miracle is clear.
It demonstrates what He would have you learn,
and shows you its effects are what you want.
In His forgiving dreams are the effects
of yours undone, and hated enemies
perceived as friends with merciful intent.
Their enmity is seen as causeless now,
because they did not make it. And you can
accept the role of maker of their hate,
because you see that it has no effects.
Now are you freed from this much of the dream;
the world is neutral, and the bodies that
still seem to move about as separate things
need not be feared. And so they are not sick.

The miracle returns the cause of fear
to you who made it. But it also shows
that, having no effects, it is not cause,
because the function of causation is
to have effects. And where effects are gone,
there is no cause. Thus is the body healed
by miracles because they show the mind
made sickness, and employed the body to
be victim, or effect, of what it made.
Yet half the lesson will not teach the whole.
The miracle is useless if you learn
but that the body can be healed, for this
is not the lesson it was sent to teach.
The lesson is the *mind* was sick that thought
the body could be sick; projecting out
its guilt caused nothing, and had no effects.

This world is full of miracles. They stand
in shining silence next to every dream
of pain and suffering, of sin and guilt.
They are the dream's alternative, the choice
to be the dreamer, rather than deny
the active role in making up the dream.
They are the glad effects of taking back
the consequence of sickness to its cause.
The body is released because the mind
acknowledges "this is not done to me,
but *I* am doing this." And thus the mind
is free to make another choice instead.
Beginning here, salvation will proceed
to change the course of every step in the
descent to separation, until all
the steps have been retraced, the ladder gone,
and all the dreaming of the world undone.

### The Agreement to Join

What waits in perfect certainty beyond
salvation is not our concern. For you
have barely started to allow your first,
uncertain steps to be directed up
the ladder separation led you down.
The miracle alone is your concern
at present. Here is where we must begin.
And having started, will the way be made
serene and simple in the rising up
to waking and the ending of the dream.
When you accept a miracle, you do
not add your dream of fear to one that is
already being dreamed. Without support,
the dream will fade away without effects.
For it is your support that strengthens it.

No mind is sick until another mind
agrees that they are separate. And thus
it is their joint decision to be sick.
If you withhold agreement and accept
the part you play in making sickness real,
the other mind cannot project its guilt
without your aid in letting it perceive
itself as separate and apart from you.
Thus is the body not perceived as sick
by both your minds from separate points of view.
Uniting with a brother's mind prevents
the cause of sickness and perceived effects.
Healing is the effect of minds that join,
as sickness comes from minds that separate.

The miracle does nothing just *because*
the minds are joined, and cannot separate.

Yet in the dreaming has this been reversed,
and separate minds are seen as bodies, which
are separated and which cannot join.
Do not allow your brother to be sick,
for if he is, have you abandoned him
to his own dream by sharing it with him.
He has not seen the cause of sickness where
it is, and you have overlooked the gap
between you, where the sickness has been bred.
Thus are you joined in sickness, to preserve
the little gap unhealed, where sickness is
kept carefully protected, cherished, and
upheld by firm belief, lest God should come
to bridge the little gap that leads to Him.
Fight not His coming with illusions, for
it is His coming that you want above
all things that seem to glisten in the dream.

The end of dreaming is the end of fear,
and love was never in the world of dreams.
The gap *is* little. Yet it holds the seeds
of pestilence and every form of ill,
because it is a wish to keep apart
and not to join. And thus it seems to give
a cause to sickness which is not its cause.
The purpose of the gap is all the cause
that sickness has. For it was made to keep
you separated, in a body which
you see as if it were the cause of pain.

The cause of pain is separation, not
the body, which is only its effect.
Yet separation is but empty space,
enclosing nothing, doing nothing, and
as unsubstantial as the empty place
between the ripples that a ship has made
in passing by. And covered just as fast,
as water rushes in to close the gap,
and as the waves in joining cover it.
Where is the gap between the waves when they
have joined, and covered up the space which seemed
to keep them separate for a little while?
Where are the grounds for sickness when the minds
have joined to close the little gap between
them, where the seeds of sickness seemed to grow?

God builds the bridge, but only in the space
left clean and vacant by the miracle.
The seeds of sickness and the shame of guilt
He cannot bridge, for He can not destroy
the alien will that He created not.
Let its effects be gone and clutch them not
with eager hands, to keep them for yourself.
The miracle will brush them all aside,
and thus make room for Him Who wills to come
and bridge His Son's returning to Himself.

Count, then, the silver miracles and golden dreams
of happiness as all the treasures you
would keep within the storehouse of the world.
The door is open, not to thieves, but to
your starving brothers, who mistook for gold
the shining of a pebble, and who stored
a heap of snow that shone like silver. They
have nothing left behind the open door.
What is the world except a little gap
perceived to tear eternity apart,
and break it into days and months and years?
And what are you who live within the world
except a picture of the Son of God
in broken pieces, each concealed within
a separate and uncertain bit of clay?

Be not afraid, my child, but let your world
be gently lit by miracles. And where
the little gap was seen to stand between
you and your brother, join him there. And so
sickness will now be seen without a cause.
The dream of healing in forgiveness lies,
and gently shows you that you never sinned.
The miracle would leave no proof of guilt
to bring you witness to what never was.
And in your storehouse it will make a place
of welcome for your Father and your Self.
The door is open, that all those may come
who would no longer starve, and would enjoy
the feast of plenty set before them there.
And they will meet with your invited Guests
the miracle has asked to come to you.

This is a feast unlike indeed to those
the dreaming of the world has shown. For here,
the more that anyone receives, the more
is left for all the rest to share. The Guests
have brought unlimited supply with Them.
And no one is deprived or can deprive.
Here is a feast the Father lays before
His Son, and shares it equally with him.

And in Their sharing there can be no gap
in which abundance falters and grows thin.
Here can the lean years enter not, for time
waits not upon this feast, which has no end.
For Love has set its table in the space
that seemed to keep your Guests apart from you.

### The Greater Joining

Accepting the Atonement for yourself
means not to give support to someone's dream
of sickness and of death. It means that you
share not his wish to separate, and let
him turn illusions on himself. Nor do
you wish that they be turned, instead, on you.
Thus have they no effects. And you are free
of dreams of pain because you let him be.
Unless you help him, you will suffer pain
with him because that is your wish. And you
become a figure in his dream of pain,
as he in yours.
So do you and your brother both become
illusions, and without identity.
You could be anyone or anything,
depending on whose evil dream you share.
You can be sure of just one thing; that you
are evil, for you share in dreams of fear.

There is a way of finding certainty
right here and now. Refuse to be a part
of fearful dreams whatever form they take,
for you will lose identity in them.
You find yourself by not accepting them
as causing you, and giving you effects.
You stand apart from them, but not apart
from him who dreams them. Thus you separate
the dreamer from the dream, and join in one,
but let the other go. The dream is but
illusion in the mind. And with the mind
you would unite, but never with the dream.
It is the dream you fear, and not the mind.
You see them as the same, because you think
that *you* are but a dream. And what is real
and what is but illusion in yourself
you do not know and cannot tell apart.

Like you, your brother thinks he is a dream.
Share not in his illusion of himself,
for your identity depends on his

reality. Think, rather, of him as
a mind in which illusions still persist,
but as a mind which brother is to you.
He is not brother made by what he dreams,
nor is his body, "hero" of the dream,
your brother. It is his reality
that is your brother, as is yours to him.
Your mind and his are joined in brotherhood.
His body and his dreams but seem to make
a little gap, where yours have joined with his.

And yet, between your minds there is no gap.
To join his dreams is thus to meet him not,
because his dreams would separate from you.
Therefore release him, merely by your claim
on brotherhood, and not on dreams of fear.
Let him acknowledge who he is, by not
supporting his illusions by your faith,
for if you do, you will have faith in yours.
With faith in yours, he will not be released,
and you are kept in bondage to his dreams.
And dreams of fear will haunt the little gap,
inhabited but by illusions which
you have supported in your brother's mind.

Be certain, if you do your part, he will
do his, for he will join you where you stand.
Call not to him to meet you in the gap
between you, or you must believe that it
is your reality as well as his.
You cannot do his part, but this you *do*
when you become a passive figure in
his dreams, instead of dreamer of your own.
Identity in dreams is meaningless
because the dreamer and the dream are one.
Who shares a dream must be the dream he shares,
because by sharing is a cause produced.

You share confusion and you are confused,
for in the gap no stable self exists.
What is the same seems different, because
what is the same appears to be unlike.
His dreams are yours because you let them be.
But if you took your own away would he
be free of them, and of his own as well.
Your dreams are witnesses to his, and his
attest the truth of yours. Yet if you see
there is no truth in yours, his dreams will go,
and he will understand what made the dream.

The Holy Spirit is in both your minds,
and He is One because there is no gap
that separates His Oneness from Itself.
The gap between your bodies matters not,
for what is joined in Him is always one.
No one is sick if someone else accepts
his union with him. His desire to be
a sick and separated mind can not
remain without a witness or a cause.
And both are gone if someone wills to be
united with him. He has dreams that he
was separated from his brother who,
by sharing not his dream, has left the space
between them vacant. And the Father comes
to join His Son the Holy Spirit joined.

The Holy Spirit's function is to take
the broken picture of the Son of God
and put the pieces into place again.
This holy picture, healed entirely,
does He hold out to every separate piece
that thinks it is a picture in itself.
To each He offers his Identity,
Which the whole picture represents, instead
of just a little, broken bit that he
insisted was himself. And when he sees
this picture he will recognize himself.
If you share not your brother's evil dream,
this is the picture that the miracle
will place within the little gap, left clean
of all the seeds of sickness and of sin.
And here the Father will receive His Son,
because His Son was gracious to himself.

I thank You, Father, knowing You will come
to close each little gap that lies between
the broken pieces of Your holy Son.
Your holiness, complete and perfect, lies
in every one of them. And they are joined
because what is in one is in them all.
How holy is the smallest grain of sand,
when it is recognized as being part
of the completed picture of God's Son!
The forms the broken pieces seem to take
mean nothing. For the whole is in each one.
And every aspect of the Son of God
is just the same as every other part.

Join not your brother's dreams but join with him,
and where you join His Son the Father is.
Who seeks for substitutes when he perceives
he has lost nothing? Who would want to have
the "benefits" of sickness when he has
received the simple happiness of health?
What God has given cannot be a loss,
and what is not of Him has no effects.
What, then, would you perceive within the gap?
The seeds of sickness come from the belief
that there is joy in separation, and
its giving up would be a sacrifice.
But miracles are the result when you
do not insist on seeing in the gap
what is not there. Your willingness to let
illusions go is all the Healer of
God's Son requires. He will place the miracle
of healing where the seeds of sickness were.
And there will be no loss, but only gain.

### The Alternate to Dreams of Fear

What is a sense of sickness but a sense
of limitation? Of a splitting *off*
and separating *from*? A gap that is
perceived between you and your brother, and
what is now seen as health? And so the good
is seen to be outside; the evil, in.
And thus is sickness separating off
the self from good, and keeping evil in.
God is the Alternate to dreams of fear.
Who shares in them can never share in Him.
But who withdraws his mind from sharing them
*is* sharing Him. There is no other choice.
Except you share it, nothing can exist.
And you exist because God shared His Will
with you, that His creation might create.

It is the sharing of the evil dreams
of hate and malice, bitterness and death,
of sin and suffering and pain and loss,
that makes them real. Unshared, they are perceived
as meaningless. The fear is gone from them
because you did not give them your support.
Where fear has gone there love must come, because
there are but these alternatives. Where one
appears, the other disappears. And which
you share becomes the only one you have.
You have the one that you accept, because
it is the only one you wish to have.

You share no evil dreams if you forgive
the dreamer, and perceive that he is not
the dream he made. And so he cannot be
a part of yours, from which you both are free.
Forgiveness separates the dreamer from
the evil dream, and thus releases him.
Remember if you share an evil dream,
you will believe you are the dream you share.
And fearing it, you will not want to know
your own Identity, because you think
that It is fearful. And you will deny
your Self, and walk upon an alien ground
which your Creator did not make, and where
you seem to be a something you are not.
You will make war upon your Self, Which seems
to be your enemy; and will attack
your brother, as a part of what you hate.
There is no compromise. You are your Self
or an illusion. What can be between
illusion and the truth? A middle ground,
where you can be a thing that is not you,
must be a dream and cannot be the truth.

You have conceived a little gap between
illusions and the truth to be the place
where all your safety lies, and where your Self
is safely hidden by what you have made.
Here is a world established that is sick,
and this the world the body's eyes perceive.
Here are the sounds it hears; the voices that
its ears were made to hear. Yet sights and sounds
the body can perceive are meaningless.
It cannot see nor hear. It does not know
what seeing *is*; what listening is *for*.
It is as little able to perceive
as it can judge or understand or know.
Its eyes are blind; its ears are deaf. It can
not think, and so it cannot have effects.

What is there God created to be sick?
And what that He created not can be?
Let not your eyes behold a dream; your ears
bear witness to illusion. They were made
to look upon a world that is not there;
to hear the voices that can make no sound.
Yet are there other sounds and other sights
that *can* be seen and heard and understood.
For eyes and ears are senses without sense,
and what they see and hear they but report.
It is not they that hear and see, but you,
who put together every jagged piece,
each senseless scrap and shred of evidence,
and make a witness to the world you want.
Let not the body's ears and eyes perceive
these countless fragments seen within the gap
that you imagined, and let them persuade
their maker his imaginings are real.

Creation proves reality because
it shares the function all creation shares.
It is not made of little bits of glass,
a piece of wood, a thread or two, perhaps,
all put together to attest its truth.
Reality does not depend on this.
There is no gap that separates the truth
from dreams and from illusions. Truth has left
no room for them in any place or time.
For it fills every place and every time,
and makes them wholly indivisible.

You who believe there is a little gap
between you and your brother, do not see
that it is here you are as prisoners in
a world perceived to be existing here.
The world you see does not exist, because
the place where you perceive it is not real.
The gap is carefully concealed in fog,
and misty pictures rise to cover it
with vague uncertain forms and changing shapes,
forever unsubstantial and unsure.
Yet in the gap is nothing. And there are
no awesome secrets and no darkened tombs
where terror rises from the bones of death.
Look at the little gap, and you behold
the innocence and emptiness of sin
that you will see within yourself, when you
have lost the fear of recognizing love.

### The Secret Vows

Who punishes the body is insane.
For here the little gap is seen, and yet
it is not here. It has not judged itself,
nor made itself to be what it is not.
It does not seek to make of pain a joy
and look for lasting pleasure in the dust.
It does not tell you what its purpose is

and cannot understand what it is for.
It does not victimize, because it has
no will, no preferences and no doubts.
It does not wonder what it is. And so
it has no need to be competitive.
It can be victimized, but cannot feel
itself as victim. It accepts no role,
but does what it is told, without attack.

It is indeed a senseless point of view
to hold responsible for sight a thing
that cannot see, and blame it for the sounds
you do not like, although it cannot hear.
It suffers not the punishment you give
because it has no feeling. It behaves
in ways you want, but never makes the choice.
It is not born and does not die. It can
but follow aimlessly the path on which
it has been set. And if that path is changed,
it walks as easily another way.
It takes no sides and judges not the road
it travels. It perceives no gap, because
it does not hate. It can be used for hate,
but it cannot be hateful made thereby.

The thing you hate and fear and loathe and want,
the body does not know. You send it forth
to seek for separation and be separate.
And then you hate it, not for what it is,
but for the uses you have made of it.
You shrink from what it sees and what it hears,
and hate its frailty and littleness.
And you despise its acts, but not your own.
It sees and acts for *you*. It hears your voice.
And it is frail and little by your wish.
It seems to punish you, and thus deserve
your hatred for the limitations that
it brings to you. Yet you have made of it
a symbol for the limitations that
you want your mind to have and see and keep.

The body represents the gap between
the little bit of mind you call your own
and all the rest of what is really yours.
You hate it, yet you think it is your self,
and that, without it, would your self be lost.
This is the secret vow that you have made
with every brother who would walk apart.
This is the secret oath you take again,
whenever you perceive yourself attacked.
No one can suffer if he does not see
himself attacked, and losing by attack.
Unstated and unheard in consciousness
is every pledge to sickness. Yet it is
a promise to another to be hurt
by him, and to attack him in return.

Sickness is anger taken out upon
the body, so that it will suffer pain.
It is the obvious effect of what
was made in secret, in agreement with
another's secret wish to be apart
from you, as you would be apart from him.
Unless you both agree that is your wish,
it can have no effects. Whoever says,
"There is no gap between my mind and yours"
has kept God's promise, not his tiny oath
to be forever faithful unto death.
And by his healing is his brother healed.

Let this be your agreement with each one;
that you be one with him and not apart.
And he will keep the promise that you make
with him, because it is the one that he
has made to God, as God has made to him.
God keeps His promises; His Son keeps his.
In his creation did his Father say,
"You are beloved of Me and I of you
forever. Be you perfect as Myself,
for you can never be apart from Me."
His Son remembers not that he replied
"I will," though in that promise he was born.
Yet God reminds him of it every time
he does not share a promise to be sick,
but lets his mind be healed and unified.
His secret vows are powerless before
the Will of God, Whose promises he shares.
And what he substitutes is not his will,
who has made promise of himself to God.

### The Ark of Safety

God asks for nothing, and His Son, like Him,
need ask for nothing. For there is no lack
in him. An empty space, a little gap,
would be a lack. And it is only there
that he could want for something he has not.
A space where God is not, a gap between

the Father and the Son is not the Will
of Either, Who have promised to be one.
God's promise is a promise to Himself,
and there is no one who could be untrue
to what He wills as part of what He is.
The promise that there is no gap between
Himself and what He is cannot be false.
What will can come between what must be one,
and in Whose Wholeness there can be no gap?

The beautiful relationship you have
with all your brothers is a part of you
because it is a part of God Himself.
Are you not sick, if you deny yourself
your wholeness and your health, the Source of help,
the Call to healing and the Call to heal?
Your savior waits for healing, and the world
waits with him. Nor are you apart from it.
For healing will be one or not at all,
its oneness being where the healing is.
What could correct for separation but
its opposite? There is no middle ground
in any aspect of salvation. You
accept it wholly or accept it not.
What is unseparated must be joined.
And what is joined cannot be separate.

Either there is a gap between you and
your brother, or you are as one. There is
no in between, no other choice, and no
allegiance to be split between the two.
A split allegiance is but faithlessness
to both, and merely sets you spinning round,
to grasp uncertainly at any straw
that seems to hold some promise of relief.
Yet who can build his home upon a straw,
and count on it as shelter from the wind?
The body can be made a home like this,
because it lacks foundation in the truth.
And yet, because it does, it can be seen
as not your home, but merely as an aid
to help you reach the Home where God abides.

With *this* as purpose is the body healed.
It is not used to witness to the dream
of separation and disease. Nor is
it idly blamed for what it did not do.
It serves to help the healing of God's Son,
and for this purpose it cannot be sick.

It will not join a purpose not your own,
and you have chosen that it not be sick.
All miracles are based upon this choice,
and given you the instant it is made.
No forms of sickness are immune, because
the choice cannot be made in terms of form.
The choice of sickness seems to be of form,
yet it is one, as is its opposite.
And you are sick or well, accordingly.

But never you alone. This world is but
the dream that you can be alone, and think
without affecting those apart from you.
To be alone must mean you are apart,
and if you are, you cannot but be sick.
This seems to prove that you must be apart.
Yet all it means is that you tried to keep
a promise to be true to faithlessness.
Yet faithlessness is sickness. It is like
the house set upon straw. It seems to be
quite solid and substantial in itself.
Yet its stability cannot be judged
apart from its foundation. If it rests
on straw, there is no need to bar the door
and lock the windows and make fast the bolts.
The wind will topple it, and rain will come
and carry it into oblivion.

What is the sense in seeking to be safe
in what was made for danger and for fear?
Why burden it with further locks and chains
and heavy anchors, when its weakness lies,
not in itself, but in the frailty of
the little gap of nothingness whereon
it stands? What can be safe that rests upon
a shadow? Would you build your home upon
what will collapse beneath a feather's weight?

Your home is built upon your brother's health,
upon his happiness, his sinlessness,
and everything his Father promised him.
No secret promise you have made instead
has shaken the Foundation of his home.
The winds will blow upon it and the rain
will beat against it, but with no effect.
The world will wash away and yet this house
will stand forever, for its strength lies not
within itself alone. It is an ark
of safety, resting on God's promise that

His Son is safe forever in Himself.
What gap can interpose itself between
the safety of this shelter and its Source?
From here the body can be seen as what
it is, and neither less nor more in worth
than the extent to which it can be used
to liberate God's Son unto his home.
And with this holy purpose is it made
a home of holiness a little while,
because it shares your Father's Will with you.

# Chapter 29
## THE AWAKENING

### The Closing of the Gap

There is no time, no place, no state where God is absent. There is nothing to be feared. There is no way in which a gap could be conceived of in the Wholeness that is His. The compromise the least and littlest gap would represent in His eternal Love is quite impossible. For it would mean His Love could harbor just a hint of hate, His gentleness turn sometimes to attack, and His eternal patience sometimes fail. All this do you believe, when you perceive a gap between your brother and yourself. How could you trust Him, then? For He must be deceptive in His Love. Be wary, then; let Him not come too close, and leave a gap between you and His Love, through which you can escape if there be need for you to flee.

Here is the fear of God most plainly seen. For love *is* treacherous to those who fear, since fear and hate can never be apart. No one who hates but is afraid of love, and therefore must he be afraid of God. Certain it is he knows not what love means. He fears to love and loves to hate, and so he thinks that love is fearful; hate is love. This is the consequence the little gap must bring to those who cherish it, and think that it is their salvation and their hope.

The fear of God! The greatest obstacle that peace must flow across has not yet gone. The rest are past, but this one still remains to block your path, and make the way to light seem dark and fearful, perilous and bleak. You had decided that your brother is your enemy. Sometimes a friend, perhaps, provided that your separate interests made your friendship possible a little while. But not without a gap perceived between you and him, lest he turn again into an enemy. Let him come close to you, and you jumped back; as you approached, did he but instantly withdraw. A cautious friendship, and limited in scope and carefully restricted in amount, became the treaty that you had made with him. Thus you and your brother but shared a qualified entente, in which a clause of separation was a point you both agreed to keep intact. And violating this was thought to be a breach of treaty not to be allowed.

The gap between you and your brother is not one of space between two separate bodies. And this but seems to be dividing off your separate minds. It is the symbol of a promise made to meet when you prefer, and separate till you and he elect to meet again. And then your bodies seem to get in touch, and thereby signify a meeting place to join. But always is it possible for you and him to go your separate ways. Conditional upon the "right" to separate will you and he agree to meet from time to time, and keep apart in intervals of separation, which do protect you from the "sacrifice" of love. The body saves you, for it gets away from total sacrifice and gives to you the time in which to build again your separate self, which you truly believe diminishes as you and your brother meet.

The body could not separate your mind from your brother's unless you wanted it to be a cause of separation and of distance seen between you and him. Thus do you endow it with a power that lies not within itself. And herein lies its power over you. For now you think that it determines when your brother and you meet, and limits your ability to make communion with your brother's mind. And now it tells you where to go and how to go there, what is feasible for you to undertake, and what you cannot do. It dictates what its health can tolerate, and what will tire it and make it sick. And its "inherent" weaknesses set up

the limitations on what you would do,
and keep your purpose limited and weak.

The body will accommodate to this,
if you would have it so. It will allow
but limited indulgences in "love,"
with intervals of hatred in between.
And it will take command of when to "love,"
and when to shrink more safely into fear.
It will be sick because you do not know
what loving means. And so you must misuse
each circumstance and everyone you meet,
and see in them a purpose not your own.

It is not love that asks a sacrifice.
But fear demands the sacrifice of love,
for in love's presence fear cannot abide.
For hate to be maintained, love must be feared;
and only sometimes present, sometimes gone.
Thus is love seen as treacherous, because
it seems to come and go uncertainly,
and offer no stability to you.
You do not see how limited and weak
is your allegiance, and how frequently
you have demanded that love go away,
and leave you quietly alone in "peace."

The body, innocent of goals, is your
excuse for variable goals you hold,
and force the body to maintain. You do
not fear its weakness, but its lack of strength
or weakness. Would you know that nothing stands
between you and your brother? Would you know
there is no gap behind which you can hide?
There is a shock that comes to those who learn
their savior is their enemy no more.
There is a wariness that is aroused
by learning that the body is not real.
And there are overtones of seeming fear
around the happy message, "God is Love."

Yet all that happens when the gap is gone
is peace eternal. Nothing more than that,
and nothing less. Without the fear of God,
what could induce you to abandon Him?
What toys or trinkets in the gap could serve
to hold you back an instant from His Love?
Would you allow the body to say "no"
to Heaven's calling, were you not afraid
to find a loss of self in finding God?

Yet can your self be lost by being found?

**The Coming of the Guest**

Why would you not perceive it as release
from suffering to learn that you are free?
Why would you not acclaim the truth instead
of looking on it as an enemy?
Why does an easy path, so clearly marked
it is impossible to lose the way,
seem thorny, rough and far too difficult
for you to follow? Is it not because
you see it as the road to hell instead
of looking on it as a simple way,
without a sacrifice or any loss,
to find yourself in Heaven and in God?
Until you realize you give up nothing,
until you understand there is no loss,
you will have some regrets about the way
that you have chosen. And you will not see
the many gains your choice has offered you.
Yet though you do not see them, they are there.
Their cause has been effected, and they must
be present where their cause has entered in.

You have accepted healing's cause, and so
it must be you are healed. And being healed,
the power to heal must also now be yours.
The miracle is not a separate thing
that happens suddenly, as an effect
without a cause. Nor is it, in itself,
a cause. But where its cause is must it be.
Now is it caused, though not as yet perceived.
And its effects are there, though not yet seen.
Look inward now, and you will not behold
a reason for regret, but cause indeed
for glad rejoicing and for hope of peace.

It has been hopeless to attempt to find
the hope of peace upon a battleground.
It has been futile to demand escape
from sin and pain of what was made to serve
the function of retaining sin and pain.
For pain and sin are one illusion, as
are hate and fear, attack and guilt but one.
Where they are causeless their effects are gone,
and love must come wherever they are not.
Why are you not rejoicing? You are free
of pain and sickness, misery and loss,
and all effects of hatred and attack.

No more is pain your friend and guilt your god,
and you should welcome the effects of love.

Your Guest has come.
You asked Him, and He came.
You did not hear Him enter, for you did
not wholly welcome Him. And yet His gifts
came with Him. He has laid them at your feet,
and asks you now that you will look on them
and take them for your own. He needs your help
in giving them to all who walk apart,
believing they are separate and alone.
They will be healed when you accept your gifts,
because your Guest will welcome everyone
whose feet have touched the holy ground whereon
you stand, and where His gifts for them are laid.

You do not see how much you now can give,
because of everything you have received.
Yet He Who entered in but waits for you
to come where you invited Him to be.
There is no other place where He can find
His host, nor where His host can meet with Him.
And nowhere else His gifts of peace and joy,
and all the happiness His Presence brings,
can be obtained. For they are where He is
Who brought them with Him,
that they might be yours.
You cannot see your Guest, but you can see
the gifts He brought. And when you look on them,
you will believe His Presence must be there.
For what you now can do could not be done
without the love and grace His Presence holds.

Such is the promise of the living God;
His Son have life and every living thing
be part of him, and nothing else have life.
What you have given "life" is not alive,
and symbolizes but your wish to be
alive apart from life, alive in death,
with death perceived as life, and living, death.
Confusion follows on confusion here,
for on confusion has this world been based,
and there is nothing else it rests upon.
Its basis does not change, although it seems
to be in constant change. Yet what is that
except the state confusion really means?
Stability to those who are confused
is meaningless, and shift and change become
the law on which they predicate their lives.

The body does not change. It represents
the larger dream that change is possible.
To change is to attain a state unlike
the one in which you found yourself before.
There is no change in immortality,
and Heaven knows it not. Yet here on earth
it has a double purpose, for it can
be made to teach opposing things. And they
reflect the teacher who is teaching them.
The body can appear to change with time,
with sickness or with health, and with events
that seem to alter it. Yet this but means
the mind remains unchanged in its belief
of what the purpose of the body is.

Sickness is a demand the body be
a thing that it is not. Its nothingness
is guarantee that it can *not* be sick.
In your demand that it be more than this
lies the idea of sickness. For it asks
that God be less than all He really is.
What, then, becomes of you, for it is you
of whom the sacrifice is asked? For He
is told that part of Him belongs to Him
no longer. He must sacrifice your self,
and in His sacrifice are you made more
and He is lessened by the loss of you.
And what is gone from Him becomes your god,
protecting you from being part of Him.

The body that is asked to be a god
will be attacked, because its nothingness
has not been recognized. And so it seems
to be a thing with power in itself.
As something, it can be perceived and thought
to feel and act, and hold you in its grasp
as prisoner to itself. And it can fail
to be what you demanded that it be.
And you will hate it for its littleness,
unmindful that the failure does not lie
in that it is not more than it should be,
but only in your failure to perceive
that it is nothing. Yet its nothingness
is your salvation, from which you would flee.

As "something" is the body asked to be
God's enemy, replacing what He is
with littleness and limit and despair.

It is His loss you celebrate when you
behold the body as a thing you love,
or look upon it as a thing you hate.
For if He be the Sum of everything,
then what is not in Him does not exist,
and His completion is its nothingness.
Your savior is not dead, nor does he dwell
in what was built as temple unto death.
He lives in God, and it is this that makes
him savior unto you, and only this.
His body's nothingness releases yours
from sickness and from death. For what is yours
cannot be more or less than what is his.

### God's Witnesses

Condemn your savior not because he thinks
he is a body. For beyond his dreams
is his reality. But he must learn
he is a savior first, before he can
remember what he is. And he must save
who would be saved. On saving you depends
his happiness. For who is savior but
the one who gives salvation? Thus he learns
it must be his to give. Unless he gives
he will not know he has, for giving is
the proof of having. Only those who think
that God is lessened by their strength could fail
to understand this must be so. For who
could give unless he has, and who could lose
by giving what must be increased thereby?

Think you the Father lost Himself when He
created you? Was He made weak because
He shared His Love? Was He made incomplete
by your perfection? Or are you the proof
that He is perfect and complete? Deny
Him not His witness in the dream His Son
prefers to his reality. He must
be savior from the dream he made, that he
be free of it. He must see someone else
as not a body, one with him without
the wall the world has built to keep apart
all living things who know not that they live.

Within the dream of bodies and of death
is yet one theme of truth; no more, perhaps,
than just a tiny spark, a space of light
created in the dark, where God still shines.

You cannot wake yourself. Yet you can let
yourself be wakened. You can overlook
your brother's dreams. So perfectly can you
forgive him his illusions he becomes
your savior from your dreams. And as you see
him shining in the space of light where God
abides within the darkness, you will see
that God Himself is where his body is.
Before this light the body disappears,
as heavy shadows must give way to light.
The darkness cannot choose that it remain.
The coming of the light means it is gone.
In glory will you see your brother then,
and understand what really fills the gap
so long perceived as keeping you apart.
There, in its place, God's witness has set forth
the gentle way of kindness to God's Son.
Whom you forgive is given power to
forgive you your illusions. By your gift
of freedom is it given unto you.

Make way for love, which you did not create,
but which you can extend. On earth this means
forgive your brother, that the darkness may
be lifted from your mind. When light has come
to him through your forgiveness, he will not
forget his savior, leaving him unsaved.
For it was in your face he saw the light
that he would keep beside him, as he walks
through darkness to the everlasting Light.

How holy are you, that the Son of God
can be your savior in the midst of dreams
of desolation and disaster. See
how eagerly he comes, and steps aside
from heavy shadows that have hidden him,
and shines on you in gratitude and love.
He is himself, but not himself alone.
And as his Father lost not part of him
in your creation, so the light in him
is brighter still because you gave your light
to him, to save him from the dark. And now
the light in you must be as bright as shines
in him. This is the spark that shines within
the dream; that you can help him waken, and
be sure his waking eyes will rest on you.
And in his glad salvation you are saved.

**Dream Roles**

Do you believe that truth can be but some
illusions? They are dreams *because* they are
not true. Their equal lack of truth becomes
the basis for the miracle, which means
that you have understood that dreams are dreams;
and that escape depends, not on the dream,
but only on awaking. Could it be
some dreams are kept, and others wakened from?
The choice is not between which dreams to keep,
but only if you want to live in dreams
or to awaken from them. Thus it is
the miracle does not select some dreams
to leave untouched by its beneficence.
You cannot dream some dreams
and wake from some,
for you are either sleeping or awake.
And dreaming goes with only one of these.

The dreams you think you likewould hold you back
as much as those in which the fear is seen.
For every dream is but a dream of fear,
no matter what the form it seems to take.
The fear is seen within, without, or both.
Or it can be disguised in pleasant form.
But never is it absent from the dream,
for fear is the material of dreams,
from which they all are made.
Their form can change,
but they cannot be made of something else.
The miracle were treacherous indeed
if it allowed you still to be afraid
because you did not recognize the fear.
You would not then be willing to awake,
for which the miracle prepares the way.

In simplest form, it can be said attack
is a response to function unfulfilled
as you perceive the function. It can be
in you or someone else, but where it is
perceived it will be there it is attacked.
Depression or assault must be the theme
of every dream, for they are made of fear.
The thin disguise of pleasure and of joy
in which they may be wrapped but slightly veils
the heavy lump of fear that is their core.
And it is this the miracle perceives,
and not the wrappings in which it is bound.

When you are angry, is it not because
someone has failed to fill the function you
allotted him? And does not this become
the "reason" your attack is justified?
The dreams you think you like are those in which
the functions you have given have been filled;
the needs which you ascribe to you are met.
It does not matter if they be fulfilled
or merely wanted. It is the idea
that they exist from which the fears arise.
Dreams are not wanted more or less. They are
desired or not. And each one represents
some function that you have assigned; some goal
which an event, or body, or a thing
*should* represent, and *should* achieve for you.
If it succeeds you think you like the dream.
If it should fail you think the dream is sad.
But whether it succeeds or fails is not
its core, but just the flimsy covering.

How happy would your dreams become if you
were not the one who gave the "proper" role
to every figure which the dream contains.
No one can fail but your idea of him,
and there is no betrayal but of this.
The core of dreams the Holy Spirit gives
is never one of fear. The coverings
may not appear to change, but what they mean
has changed because they cover something else.
Perceptions are determined by their purpose,
in that they seem to be what they are for.
A shadow figure who attacks becomes
a brother giving you a chance to help,
if this becomes the function of the dream.
And dreams of sadness thus are turned to joy.

What is your brother for? You do not know,
because your function is obscure to you.
Do not ascribe a role to him that you
imagine would bring happiness to you.
And do not try to hurt him when he fails
to take the part that you assigned to him,
in what you dream your life was meant to be.
He asks for help in every dream he has,
and you have help to give him if you see
the function of the dream as He perceives
its function, Who can utilize all dreams
as means to serve the function given Him.

Because He loves the dreamer, not the dream,
each dream becomes an offering of love.
For at its center is His Love for you,
which lights whatever form it takes with love.

### The Changeless Dwelling Place

There is a place in you where this whole world
has been forgotten; where no memory
of sin and of illusion lingers still.
There is a place in you which time has left,
and echoes of eternity are heard.
There is a resting place so still no sound
except a hymn to Heaven rises up
to gladden God the Father and the Son.
Where Both abide are They remembered, Both.
And where They are is Heaven and is peace.

Think not that you can change Their dwelling place.
For your Identity abides in Them,
and where They are, forever must you be.
The changelessness of Heaven is in you,
so deep within that nothing in this world
but passes by, unnoticed and unseen.
The still infinity of endless peace
surrounds you gently in its soft embrace,
so strong and quiet, tranquil in the might
of its Creator, nothing can intrude
upon the sacred Son of God within.

Here is the role the Holy Spirit gives
to you who wait upon the Son of God,
and would behold him waken and be glad.
He is a part of you and you of him,
because he is his Father's Son, and not
for any purpose you may see in him.
Nothing is asked of you but to accept
the changeless and eternal that abide
in him, for your Identity is there.
The peace in you can but be found in him.
And every thought of love you offer him
but brings you nearer to your wakening
to peace eternal and to endless joy.

This sacred Son of God is like yourself;
the mirror of his Father's Love for you,
the soft reminder of his Father's Love
by which he was created and which still
abides in him as it abides in you.
Be very still and hear God's Voice in him,
and let It tell you what his function is.
He was created that you might be whole,
for only the complete can be a part
of God's completion, which created you.

There is no gift the Father asks of you
but that you see in all creation but
the shining glory of His gift to you.
Behold His Son, His perfect gift, in whom
his Father shines forever, and to whom
is all creation given as his own.
Because he has it is it given you,
and where it lies in him behold your peace.
The quiet that surrounds you dwells in him,
and from this quiet come the happy dreams
in which your hands are joined in innocence.
These are not hands that grasp in dreams of pain.
They hold no sword, for they have left their hold
on every vain illusion of the world.
And being empty they receive, instead,
a brother's hand in which completion lies.

If you but knew the glorious goal that lies
beyond forgiveness, you would not keep hold
on any thought, however light the touch
of evil on it may appear to be.
For you would understand how great the cost
of holding anything God did not give
in minds that can direct the hand to bless,
and lead God's Son unto his Father's house.
Would you not want to be a friend to him,
created by his Father as His home?
If God esteems him worthy of Himself,
would you attack him with the hands of hate?
Who would lay bloody hands on Heaven itself,
and hope to find its peace? Your brother thinks
he holds the hand of death. Believe him not.
But learn, instead, how blessed are you who can
release him, just by offering him yours.

A dream is given you in which he is
your savior, not your enemy in hate.
A dream is given you in which you have
forgiven him for all his dreams of death;
a dream of hope you share with him, instead
of dreaming evil separate dreams of hate.
Why does it seem so hard to share this dream?
Because unless the Holy Spirit gives
the dream its function, it was made for hate,

and will continue in death's services.
Each form it takes in some way calls for death.
And those who serve the lord of death have come
to worship in a separated world,
each with his tiny spear and rusted sword,
to keep his ancient promises to die.

Such is the core of fear in every dream
that has been kept apart from use by Him
Who sees a different function for a dream.
When dreams are shared they lose the function of
attack and separation, even though
it was for this that every dream was made.
Yet nothing in the world of dreams remains
without the hope of change and betterment,
for here is not where changelessness is found.
Let us be glad indeed that this is so,
and seek not the eternal in this world.
Forgiving dreams are means to step aside
from dreaming of a world outside yourself.
And leading finally beyond all dreams,
unto the peace of everlasting life.

### Forgiveness and the End of Time

How willing are you to forgive your brother?
How much do you desire peace instead
of endless strife and misery and pain?
These questions are the same, in different form.
Forgiveness is your peace, for herein lies
the end of separation and the dream
of danger and destruction, sin and death;
of madness and of murder, grief and loss.
This is the "sacrifice" salvation asks,
and gladly offers peace instead of this.

Swear not to die, you holy Son of God!
You make a bargain that you cannot keep.
The Son of Life cannot be killed. He is
immortal as his Father. What he is
cannot be changed. He is the only thing
in all the universe that must be one.
What *seems* eternal all will have an end.
The stars will disappear, and night and day
will be no more. All things that come and go,
the tides, the seasons and the lives of men;
all things that change with time and bloom and fade
will not return. Where time has set an end
is not where the eternal is. God's Son
can never change by what men made of him.
He will be as he was and as he is,
for time appointed not his destiny,
nor set the hour of his birth and death.
Forgiveness will not change him. Yet time waits
upon forgiveness that the things of time
may disappear because they have no use.

Nothing survives its purpose. If it be
conceived to die, then die it must unless
it does not take this purpose as its own.
Change is the only thing that can be made
a blessing here, where purpose is not fixed,
however changeless it appears to be.
Think not that you can set a goal unlike
God's purpose for you, and establish it
as changeless and eternal. You can give
yourself a purpose that you do not have.
But you can not remove the power to change
your mind, and see another purpose there.

Change is the greatest gift God gave to all
that you would make eternal, to ensure
that only Heaven would not pass away.
You were not born to die. You cannot change,
because your function has been fixed by God.
All other goals are set in time and change
that time might be preserved, excepting one.
Forgiveness does not aim at keeping time,
but at its ending, when it has no use.
Its purpose ended, it is gone. And where
it once held seeming sway is now restored
the function God established for His Son
in full awareness. Time can set no end
to its fulfillment nor its changelessness.
There is no death because the living share
the function their Creator gave to them.
Life's function cannot be to die. It must
be life's extension, that it be as one
forever and forever, without end.

This world will bind your feet and tie your hands
and kill your body only if you think
that it was made to crucify God's Son.
For even though it was a dream of death,
you need not let it stand for this to you.
Let *this* be changed, and nothing in the world
but must be changed as well. For nothing here
but is defined as what you see it for.

How lovely is the world whose purpose is
forgiveness of God's Son! How free from fear,
how filled with blessing and with happiness!
And what a joyous thing it is to dwell
a little while in such a happy place!
Nor can it be forgot, in such a world,
it *is* a little while till timelessness
comes quietly to take the place of time.

### Seek Not Outside Yourself

Seek not outside yourself. For it will fail,
and you will weep each time an idol falls.
Heaven cannot be found where it is not,
and there can be no peace excepting there.
Each idol that you worship when God calls
will never answer in His place. There is
no other answer you can substitute,
and find the happiness His answer brings.
Seek not outside yourself. For all your pain
comes simply from a futile search for what
you want, insisting where it must be found.
What if it is not there? Do you prefer
that you be right or happy? Be you glad
that you are told where happiness abides,
and seek no longer elsewhere. You will fail.
But it is given you to know the truth,
and not to seek for it outside yourself.

No one who comes here but must still have hope,
some lingering illusion, or some dream
that there is something outside of himself
that will bring happiness and peace to him.
If everything is in him this cannot
be so. And therefore by his coming, he
denies the truth about himself, and seeks
for something more than everything, as if
a part of it were separated off
and found where all the rest of it is not.
This is the purpose he bestows upon
the body; that it seek for what he lacks,
and give him what would make himself complete.
And thus he wanders aimlessly about,
in search of something that he cannot find,
believing that he is what he is not.

The lingering illusion will impel
him to seek out a thousand idols, and
to seek beyond them for a thousand more.

And each will fail him, all excepting one;
for he will die, and does not understand
the idol that he seeks *is* but his death.
Its form appears to be outside himself.
Yet does he seek to kill God's Son within,
and prove that he is victor over him.
This is the purpose every idol has,
for this the role that is assigned to it,
and this the role that cannot be fulfilled.

Whenever you attempt to reach a goal
in which the body's betterment is cast
as major beneficiary, you try
to bring about your death. For you believe
that you can suffer lack, and lack *is* death.
To sacrifice is to give up, and thus
to be without and to have suffered loss.
And by this giving up is life renounced.
Seek not outside yourself. The search implies
you are not whole within and fear to look
upon your devastation, but prefer
to seek outside yourself for what you are.

Idols must fall *because* they have no life,
and what is lifeless is a sign of death.
You came to die, and what would you expect
but to perceive the signs of death you seek?
No sadness and no suffering proclaim
a message other than an idol found
that represents a parody of life
which, in its lifelessness, is really death,
conceived as real and given living form.
Yet each must fail and crumble and decay,
because a form of death cannot be life,
and what is sacrificed cannot be whole.

All idols of this world were made to keep
the truth within from being known to you,
and to maintain allegiance to the dream
that you must find what is outside yourself
to be complete and happy. It is vain
to worship idols in the hope of peace.
God dwells within, and your completion lies
in Him. No idol takes His place. Look not
to idols. Do not seek outside yourself.

Let us forget the purpose of the world
the past has given it. For otherwise,
the future will be like the past, and but
a series of depressing dreams, in which

all idols fail you, one by one, and you
see death and disappointment everywhere.

To change all this, and open up a road
of hope and of release in what appeared
to be an endless circle of despair,
you need but to decide you do not know
the purpose of the world. You give it goals
it does not have, and thus do you decide
what it is for. You try to see in it
a place of idols found outside yourself,
with power to make complete what is within
by splitting what you are between the two.
You choose your dreams, for they are what you wish,
perceived as if it had been given you.
Your idols do what you would have them do,
and have the power you ascribe to them.
And you pursue them vainly in the dream,
because you want their power as your own.

Yet where are dreams but in a mind asleep?
And can a dream succeed in making real
the picture it projects outside itself?
Save time, my brother; learn what time is for.
And speed the end of idols in a world
made sad and sick by seeing idols there.
Your holy mind is altar unto God,
and where He is no idols can abide.
The fear of God is but the fear of loss
of idols. It is not the fear of loss
of your reality. But you have made
of your reality an idol, which
you must protect against the light of truth.
And all the world becomes the means by which
this idol can be saved. Salvation thus
appears to threaten life and offer death.

It is not so. Salvation seeks to prove
there is no death, and only life exists.
The sacrifice of death is nothing lost.
An idol cannot take the place of God.
Let Him remind you of His Love for you,
and do not seek to drown His Voice in chants
of deep despair to idols of yourself.
Seek not outside your Father for your hope.
For hope of happiness is *not* despair.

## The Anti-Christ

What is an idol? Do you think you know?
For idols are unrecognized as such,
and never seen for what they really are.
That is the only power that they have.
Their purpose is obscure, and they are feared
and worshipped, both, *because* you do not know
what they are for, and why they have been made.
An idol is an image of your brother
that you would value more than what he is.
Idols are made that he may be replaced,
no matter what their form. And it is this
that never is perceived and recognized.
Be it a body or a thing, a place,
a situation or a circumstance,
an object owned or wanted, or a right
demanded or achieved, it is the same.

Let not their form deceive you. Idols are
but substitutes for your reality.
In some way, you believe they will complete
your little self, for safety in a world
perceived as dangerous, with forces massed
against your confidence and peace of mind.
They have the power to supply your lacks,
and add the value that you do not have.
No one believes in idols who has not
enslaved himself to littleness and loss.
And thus must seek beyond his little self
for strength to raise his head, and stand apart
from all the misery the world reflects.
This is the penalty for looking not
within for certainty and quiet calm
that liberates you from the world, and lets
you stand apart, in quiet and in peace.

An idol is a false impression, or
a false belief; some form of anti-Christ,
that constitutes a gap between the Christ
and what you see. An idol is a wish,
made tangible and given form, and thus
perceived as real and seen outside the mind.
Yet it is still a thought, and cannot leave
the mind that is its source. Nor is its form
apart from the idea it represents.
All forms of anti-Christ oppose the Christ.
And fall before His face like a dark veil
that seems to shut you off from Him, alone

in darkness. Yet the light is there. A cloud
does not put out the sun. No more a veil
can banish what it seems to separate,
nor darken by one whit the light itself.

This world of idols *is* a veil across
the face of Christ, because its purpose is
to separate your brother from yourself.
A dark and fearful purpose, yet a thought
without the power to change one blade of grass
from something living to a sign of death.
Its form is nowhere, for its source abides
within your mind where God abideth not.
Where is this place where what is everywhere
has been excluded and been kept apart?
What hand could be held up to block God's way?
Whose voice could make demand He enter not?
The "more-than-everything" is not a thing
to make you tremble and to quail in fear.
Christ's enemy is nowhere. He can take
no form in which he ever will be real.

What is an idol? Nothing! It must be
believed before it seems to come to life,
and given power that it may be feared.
Its life and power are its believer's gift,
and this is what the miracle restores
to what *has* life and power worthy of
the gift of Heaven and eternal peace.
The miracle does not restore the truth,
the light the veil between has not put out.
It merely lifts the veil, and lets the truth
shine unencumbered, being what it is.
It does not need belief to be itself,
for it has been created; so it *is*.

An idol is established by belief,
and when it is withdrawn the idol "dies."
This is the anti-Christ; the strange idea
there is a power past omnipotence,
a place beyond the infinite, a time
transcending the eternal. Here the world
of idols has been set by the idea
this power and place and time are given form,
and shape the world where the impossible
has happened. Here the deathless come to die,
the all-encompassing to suffer loss,
the timeless to be made the slaves of time.
Here does the changeless change; the peace of God,
forever given to all living things,
give way to chaos. And the Son of God,
as perfect, sinless and as loving as
his Father, come to hate a little while;
to suffer pain and finally to die.

Where is an idol? Nowhere! Can there be
a gap in what is infinite, a place
where time can interrupt eternity?
A place of darkness set where all is light,
a dismal alcove separated off
from what is endless, *has* no place to be.
An idol is beyond where God has set
all things forever, and has left no room
for anything to be except His Will.
Nothing and nowhere must an idol be,
while God is everything and everywhere.

What purpose has an idol, then? What is
it for? This is the only question that
has many answers, each depending on
the one of whom the question has been asked.
The world believes in idols. No one comes
unless he worshipped them, and still attempts
to seek for one that yet might offer him
a gift reality does not contain.
Each worshipper of idols harbors hope
his special deities will give him more
than other men possess. It must be more.
It does not really matter more of what;
more beauty, more intelligence, more wealth,
or even more affliction and more pain.
But more of something is an idol for.
And when one fails another takes its place,
with hope of finding more of something else.
Be not deceived by forms the "something" takes.
An idol is a means for getting more.
And it is this that is against God's Will.

God has not many sons, but only one.
Who can have more, and who be given less?
In Heaven would the Son of God but laugh,
if idols could intrude upon his peace.
It is for him the Holy Spirit speaks,
and tells you idols have no purpose here.
For more than Heaven can you never have.
If Heaven is within, why would you seek
for idols that would make of Heaven less,
to give you more than God bestowed upon

your brother and on you, as one with Him?
God gave you all there is. And to be sure
you could not lose it, did He also give
the same to every living thing as well.
And thus is every living thing a part
of you, as of Himself. No idol can
establish you as more than God. But you
will never be content with being less.

## The Forgiving Dream

The slave of idols is a willing slave.
For willing he must be to let himself
bow down in worship to what has no life,
and seek for power in the powerless.
What happened to the holy Son of God
that this could be his wish; to let himself
fall lower than the stones upon the ground,
and look to idols that they raise him up?
Hear, then, your story in the dream you made,
and ask yourself if it be not the truth
that you believe that it is not a dream.

A dream of judgment came into the mind
that God created perfect as Himself.
And in that dream was Heaven changed to hell,
and God made enemy unto His Son.
How can God's Son awaken from the dream?
It is a dream of judgment. So must he
judge not, and he will waken. For the dream
will seem to last while he is part of it.
Judge not, for he who judges will have need
of idols, which will hold the judgment off
from resting on himself. Nor can he know
the Self he has condemned. Judge not, because
you make yourself a part of evil dreams,
where idols are your "true" identity,
and your salvation from the judgment laid
in terror and in guilt upon yourself.

All figures in the dream are idols, made
to save you from the dream. Yet they are part
of what they have been made to save you *from*.
Thus does an idol keep the dream alive
and terrible, for who could wish for one
unless he were in terror and despair?
And this the idol represents, and so
its worship is the worship of despair
and terror, and the dream from which they come.

Judgment is an injustice to God's Son,
and it *is* justice that who judges him
will not escape the penalty he laid
upon himself within the dream he made.
God knows of justice, not of penalty.
But in the dream of judgment you attack
and are condemned; and wish to be the slave
of idols, which are interposed between
your judgment and the penalty it brings.

There can be no salvation in the dream
as you are dreaming it. For idols must
be part of it, to save you from what you
believe you have accomplished, and have done
to make you sinful and put out the light
within you. Little child, the light is there.
You do but dream, and idols are the toys
you dream you play with. Who has need of toys
but children? They pretend they rule the world,
and give their toys the power to move about,
and talk and think and feel and speak for them.
Yet everything their toys appear to do
is in the minds of those who play with them.
But they are eager to forget that they
made up the dream in which their toys are real,
nor recognize their wishes are their own.

Nightmares are childish dreams. The toys have turned
against the child who thought he made them real.
Yet can a dream attack? Or can a toy
grow large and dangerous and fierce and wild?
This does the child believe, because he fears
his thoughts and gives them to the toys instead.
And their reality becomes his own,
because they seem to save him from his thoughts.
Yet do they keep his thoughts alive and real,
but seen outside himself, where they can turn
against him for his treachery to them.
He thinks he needs them that he may escape
his thoughts, because he thinks the thoughts are real.
And so he makes of anything a toy,
to make his world remain outside himself,
and play that he is but a part of it.

There is a time when childhood should be passed
and gone forever. Seek not to retain
the toys of children. Put them all away,
for you have need of them no more. The dream

of judgment is a children's game, in which
the child becomes the father, powerful,
but with the little wisdom of a child.
What hurts him is destroyed; what helps him, blessed.
Except he judges this as does a child,
who does not know what hurts and what will heal.
And bad things seem to happen, and he is
afraid of all the chaos in a world
he thinks is governed by the laws he made.
Yet is the real world unaffected by
the world he thinks is real. Nor have its laws
been changed because he does not understand.

The real world still is but a dream. Except
the figures have been changed. They are not seen
as idols which betray. It is a dream
in which no one is used to substitute
for something else, nor interposed between
the thoughts the mind conceives and what it sees.
No one is used for something he is not,
for childish things have all been put away.
And what was once a dream of judgment now
has changed into a dream where all is joy,
because that is the purpose that it has.
Only forgiving dreams can enter here,
for time is almost over. And the forms
that enter in the dream are now perceived
as brothers, not in judgment, but in love.

Forgiving dreams have little need to last.
They are not made to separate the mind
from what it thinks. They do not seek to prove
the dream is being dreamed by someone else.
And in these dreams a melody is heard
that everyone remembers, though he has
not heard it since before all time began.
Forgiveness, once complete, brings timelessness
so close the song of Heaven can be heard,
not with the ears, but with the holiness
that never left the altar that abides
forever deep within the Son of God.
And when he hears this song again, he knows
he never heard it not. And where is time,
when dreams of judgment have been put away?

Whenever you feel fear in any form, –
and you *are* fearful if you do not feel
a deep content, a certainty of help,
a calm assurance Heaven goes with you, –
be sure you made an idol, and believe
it will betray you. For beneath your hope
that it will save you lie the guilt and pain
of self-betrayal and uncertainty,
so deep and bitter that the dream cannot
conceal completely all your sense of doom.
Your self-betrayal must result in fear,
for fear *is* judgment, leading surely to
the frantic search for idols and for death.

Forgiving dreams remind you that you live
in safety and have not attacked yourself.
So do your childish terrors melt away,
and dreams become a sign that you have made
a new beginning, not another try
to worship idols and to keep attack.
Forgiving dreams are kind to everyone
who figures in the dream. And so they bring
the dreamer full release from dreams of fear.
He does not fear his judgment for he has
judged no one, nor has sought to be released
through judgment from what judgment must impose.
And all the while he is remembering
what he forgot, when judgment seemed to be
the way to save him from its penalty.

# Chapter 30
## THE NEW BEGINNING

### Introduction

The new beginning now becomes the focus of the curriculum. The goal is clear, but now you need specific methods for attaining it. The speed by which it can be reached depends on this one thing alone; your willingness to practice every step. Each one will help a little, every time it is attempted. And together will these steps lead you from dreams of judgment to forgiving dreams and out of pain and fear. They are not new to you, but they are more ideas than rules of thought to you as yet. So now we need to practice them awhile, until they are the rules by which you live. We seek to make them habits now, so you will have them ready for whatever need.

### Rules for Decision

Decisions are continuous. You do not always know when you are making them. But with a little practice with the ones you recognize, a set begins to form which sees you through the rest. It is not wise to let yourself become preoccupied with every step you take. The proper set, adopted consciously each time you wake, will put you well ahead. And if you find resistance strong and dedication weak, you are not ready. *Do not fight yourself.* But think about the kind of day you want, and tell yourself there is a way in which this very day can happen just like that. Then try again to have the day you want.

The outlook starts with this:

*Today I will make no decisions by myself.*

This means that you are choosing not to be the judge of what to do. But it must also mean you will not judge the situations where you will be called upon to make response. For if you judge them, you have set the rules for how you should react to them. And then another answer cannot but produce confusion and uncertainty and fear.

This is your major problem now. You still make up your mind, and *then* decide to ask what you should do. And what you hear may not resolve the problem as you saw it first. This leads to fear, because it contradicts what you perceive and so you feel attacked. And therefore angry. There are rules by which this will not happen. But it does occur at first, while you are learning how to hear.

Throughout the day, at any time you think of it and have a quiet moment for reflection, tell yourself again the kind of day you want; the feelings you would have, the things you want to happen to you, and the things you would experience, and say:

*If I make no decisions by myself, this is the day that will be given me.*

These two procedures, practiced well, will serve to let you be directed without fear, for opposition will not first arise and then become a problem in itself.

But there will still be times when you have judged already. Now the answer will provoke attack, unless you quickly straighten out your mind to want an answer that will work. Be certain this has happened if you feel yourself unwilling to sit by and ask to have the answer given you. This means you have decided by yourself, and can not see the question. Now you need a quick restorative before you ask again.

Remember once again the day you want, and recognize that something has occurred that is not part of it. Then realize that you have asked a question by yourself, and must have set an answer in your terms. Then say:

*I have no question. I forgot what to decide.*

This cancels out the terms

that you have set, and lets the answer show
you what the question must have really been.

Try to observe this rule without delay,
despite your opposition. For you have
already gotten angry. And your fear
of being answered in a different way
from what your version of the question asks
will gain momentum, until you believe
the day you want is one in which you get
*your* answer to *your* question. And you will
not get it, for it would destroy the day
by robbing you of what you really want.
This can be very hard to realize,
when once you have decided by yourself
the rules that promise you a happy day.
Yet this decision still can be undone,
by simple methods that you can accept.

If you are so unwilling to receive
you cannot even let your question go,
you can begin to change your mind with this:
*At least I can decide I do not like
what I feel now.*
This much is obvious,
and paves the way for the next easy step.

Having decided that you do not like
the way you feel, what could be easier
than to continue with:

*And so I hope I have been wrong.*

This works against the sense
of opposition, and reminds you that
help is not being thrust upon you but
is something that you want and that you need,
because you do not like the way you feel.
This tiny opening will be enough
to let you go ahead with just a few
more steps you need to let yourself be helped.

Now you have reached the turning point, because
it has occurred to you that you will gain
if what you have decided is not so.
Until this point is reached, you will believe
your happiness depends on being right.
But this much reason have you now attained;
you would be better off if you were wrong.

This tiny grain of wisdom will suffice
to take you further. You are not coerced,
but merely hope to get a thing you want.
And you can say in perfect honesty:

*I want another way to look at this.*

Now you have changed your mind about the day,
and have remembered what you really want.
Its purpose has no longer been obscured
by the insane belief you want it for
the goal of being right when you are wrong.
Thus is the readiness for asking brought
to your awareness, for you cannot be
in conflict when you ask for what you want,
and see that it is this for which you ask.

This final step is but acknowledgment
of lack of opposition to be helped.
It is a statement of an open mind,
not certain yet, but willing to be shown:

*Perhaps there is another way to look
at this. What can I lose by asking?*

Thus
you now can ask a question that makes sense,
and so the answer will make sense as well.
Nor will you fight against it, for you see
that it is you who will be helped by it.

It must be clear that it is easier
to have a happy day if you prevent
unhappiness from entering at all.
But this takes practice in the rules that will
protect you from the ravages of fear.
When this has been achieved, the sorry dream
of judgment has forever been undone.
But meanwhile, you have need for practicing
the rules for its undoing. Let us, then,
consider once again the very first
of the decisions which are offered here.

We said you can begin a happy day
with the determination not to make
decisions by yourself. This seems to be
a real decision in itself. And yet,
you *cannot* make decisions by yourself.
The only question really is with what
you choose to make them. That is really all.
The first rule, then, is not coercion, but
a simple statement of a simple fact.
You will not make decisions by yourself
whatever you decide. For they are made

with idols or with God. And you ask help
of anti-Christ or Christ, and which you choose
will join with you and tell you what to do.

Your day is not at random. It is set
by what you choose to live it with, and how
the friend whose counsel you have sought perceives
your happiness. You always ask advice
before you can decide on anything.
Let this be understood, and you can see
there cannot be coercion here, nor grounds
for opposition that you may be free.
There is no freedom from what must occur.
And if you think there is, you must be wrong.

The second rule as well is but a fact.
For you and your adviser must agree
on what you want before it can occur.
It is but this agreement that permits
all things to happen. Nothing can be caused
without some form of union, be it with
a dream of judgment or the Voice for God.
Decisions cause results *because* they are
not made in isolation. They are made
by you and your adviser, for yourself
and for the world as well. The day you want
you offer to the world, for it will be
what you have asked for, and will reinforce
the rule of your adviser in the world.
Whose kingdom is the world for you today?
What kind of day will you decide to have?

It needs but two who would have happiness
this day to promise it to all the world.
It needs but two to understand that they
cannot decide alone, to guarantee
the joy they asked for will be wholly shared.
For they have understood the basic law
that makes decision powerful, and gives
it all effects that it will ever have.
It needs but two. These two are joined before
there can be a decision. Let this be
the one reminder that you keep in mind,
and you will have the day you want, and give
it to the world by having it yourself.
Your judgment has been lifted from the world
by your decision for a happy day.
And as you have received, so must you give.

**Freedom of Will**

Do you not understand that to oppose
the Holy Spirit is to fight *yourself*?
He tells you but your will; He speaks for you.
In His Divinity is but your own.
And all He knows is but your knowledge, saved
for you that you may do your will through Him.
God *asks* you do your will. He joins with *you*.
He did not set His Kingdom up alone.
And Heaven itself but represents your will,
where everything created is for you.
No spark of life but was created with
your glad consent, as you would have it be.
And not one Thought that God has ever had
but waited for your blessing to be born.
God is no enemy to you. He asks
no more than that He hear you call Him "Friend."

How wonderful it is to do your will!
For that is freedom. There is nothing else
that ever should be called by freedom's name.
Unless you do your will you are not free.
And would God leave His Son without what he
has chosen for himself? God but ensured
that you would never lose your will when He
gave you His perfect Answer. Hear It now,
that you may be reminded of His Love
and learn your will. God would not have His Son
made prisoner to what he does not want.
He joins with you in willing you be free.
And to oppose Him is to make a choice
against yourself, and choose that you be bound.

Look once again upon your enemy,
the one you chose to hate instead of love.
For thus was hatred born into the world,
and thus the rule of fear established there.
Now hear God speak to you, through Him Who is
His Voice and yours as well, reminding you
that it is not your will to hate and be
a prisoner to fear, a slave to death,
a little creature with a little life.
Your will is boundless; it is not your will
that it be bound. What lies in you has joined
with God Himself in all creation's birth.
Remember Him Who has created you,
and through your will created everything.
Not one created thing but gives you thanks,

for it is by your will that it was born.
No light of Heaven shines except for you,
for it was set in Heaven by your will.

What cause have you for anger in a world
that merely waits your blessing to be free?
If you be prisoner, then God Himself
could not be free. For what is done to him
whom God so loves is done to God Himself.
Think not He wills to bind you, Who has made
you co-creator of the universe
along with Him. He would but keep your will
forever and forever limitless.
This world awaits the freedom you will give
when you have recognized that you are free.
But you will not forgive the world until
you have forgiven Him Who gave your will
to you. For it is by your will the world
is given freedom. Nor can you be free
apart from Him Whose holy Will you share.

God turns to you to ask the world be saved,
for by your own salvation is it healed.
And no one walks upon the earth but must
depend on your decision, that he learn
death has no power over him, because
he shares your freedom as he shares your will.
It *is* your will to heal him, and because
you have decided with him, he is healed.
And now is God forgiven, for you chose
to look upon your brother as a friend.

### Beyond All Idols

Idols are quite specific. But your will
is universal, being limitless.
And so it has no form, nor is content
for its expression in the terms of form.
Idols are limits. They are the belief
that there are forms that will bring happiness,
and that, by limiting, is all attained.
It is as if you said, "I have no need
of everything. This little thing I want,
and it will be as everything to me."
And this must fail to satisfy, because
it is your will that everything be yours.
Decide for idols and you ask for loss.
Decide for truth and everything is yours.

It is not form you seek. What form can be
a substitute for God the Father's Love?
What form can take the place of all the love
in the Divinity of God the Son?
What idol can make two of what is one?
And can the limitless be limited?
You do not want an idol. It is not
your will to have one. It will not bestow
on you the gift you seek. When you decide
upon the form of what you want, you lose
the understanding of its purpose. So
you see your will within the idol, thus
reducing it to a specific form.
Yet this could never be your will, because
what shares in all creation cannot be
content with small ideas and little things.

Behind the search for every idol lies
the yearning for completion. Wholeness has
no form because it is unlimited.
To seek a special person or a thing
to add to you to make yourself complete,
can only mean that you believe some form
is missing. And by finding this, you will
achieve completion in a form you like.
This is the purpose of an idol; that
you will not look beyond it, to the source
of the belief that you are incomplete.
Only if you had sinned could this be so.
For sin is the idea you are alone
and separated off from what is whole.
And thus it would be necessary for
the search for wholeness to be made beyond
the boundaries of limits on yourself.

It never is the idol that you want.
But what you think it offers you, you want
indeed and have the right to ask for. Nor
could it be possible it be denied.
Your will to be complete is but God's Will,
and this is given you by being His.
God knows not form. He cannot answer you
in terms that have no meaning. And your will
could not be satisfied with empty forms,
made but to fill a gap that is not there.
It is not this you want. Creation gives
no separate person and no separate thing
the power to complete the Son of God.
What idol can be called upon to give

the Son of God what he already has?

Completion is the *function* of God's Son.
He has no need to seek for it at all.
Beyond all idols stands his holy will
to be but what he is. For more than whole
is meaningless. If there were change in him,
if he could be reduced to any form
and limited to what is not in him,
he would not be as God created him.
What idol can he need to be himself?
For can he give a part of him away?
What is not whole cannot make whole. But what
is really asked for cannot be denied.
Your will *is* granted. Not in any form
that would content you not, but in the whole
completely lovely Thought God holds of you.

Nothing that God knows not exists. And what
He knows exists forever, changelessly.
For thoughts endure as long as does the mind
that thought of them. And in the Mind of God
there is no ending, nor a time in which
His Thoughts were absent or could suffer change.
Thoughts are not born and cannot die. They share
the attributes of their creator, nor
have they a separate life apart from his.
The thoughts you think are in your mind, as you
are in the Mind Which thought of you. And so
there are no separate parts in what exists
within God's Mind. It is forever one,
eternally united and at peace.

Thoughts seem to come and go. Yet all this means
is that you are sometimes aware of them,
and sometimes not. An unremembered thought
is born again to you when it returns
to your awareness. Yet it did not die
when you forgot it. It was always there,
but you were unaware of it. The Thought
God holds of you is perfectly unchanged
by your forgetting. It will always be
exactly as it was before the time
when you forgot, and will be just the same
when you remember. And it is the same
within the interval when you forgot.

The Thoughts of God are far beyond all change,
and shine forever. They await not birth.
They wait for welcome and remembering.

The Thought God holds of you is like a star,
unchangeable in an eternal sky.
So high in Heaven is it set that those
outside of Heaven know not it is there.
Yet still and white and lovely will it shine
through all eternity. There was no time
it was not there; no instant when its light
grew dimmer or less perfect ever was.

Who knows the Father knows this light, for He
is the eternal sky that holds it safe,
forever lifted up and anchored sure.
Its perfect purity does not depend
on whether it is seen on earth or not.
The sky embraces it and softly holds
it in its perfect place, which is as far
from earth as earth from Heaven. It is not
the distance nor the time that keeps this star
invisible to earth. But those who seek
for idols cannot know the star is there.

Beyond all idols is the Thought God holds
of you. Completely unaffected by
the turmoil and the terror of the world,
the dreams of birth and death
that here are dreamed,
the myriad of forms that fear can take;
quite undisturbed, the Thought God holds of you
remains exactly as it always was.
Surrounded by a stillness so complete
no sound of battle comes remotely near,
it rests in certainty and perfect peace.
Here is your one reality kept safe,
completely unaware of all the world
that worships idols, and that knows not God.
In perfect sureness of its changelessness
and of its rest in its eternal home,
the Thought God holds of you has never left
the Mind of its Creator, Whom it knows
as its Creator knows that it is there.

Where could the Thought God holds of you exist
but where you are? Is your reality
a thing apart from you, and in a world
which your reality knows nothing of?
Outside you there is no eternal sky,
no changeless star and no reality.
The mind of Heaven's Son in Heaven is,
for there the Mind of Father and of Son

joined in creation which can have no end.
You have not two realities, but one.
Nor can you be aware of more than one.
An idol *or* the Thought God holds of you
is your reality. Forget not, then,
that idols must keep hidden what you are,
not from the Mind of God, but from your own.
The star shines still; the sky has never changed.
But you, the holy Son of God Himself,
are unaware of your reality.

### The Truth behind Illusions

You will attack what does not satisfy,
and thus you will not see you made it up.
You always fight illusions. For the truth
behind them is so lovely and so still
in loving gentleness, were you aware
of it you would forget defensiveness
entirely, and rush to its embrace.
The truth could never be attacked. And this
you knew when you made idols. They were made
that this might be forgotten. You attack
but false ideas, and never truthful ones.
All idols are the false ideas you made
to fill the gap you think arose between
yourself and what is true. And you attack
them for the things you think they represent.
What lies beyond them cannot be attacked.

The wearying, dissatisfying gods
you made are blown-up children's toys. A child
is frightened when a wooden head springs up
as a closed box is opened suddenly,
or when a soft and silent woolly bear
begins to squeak as he takes hold of it.
The rules he made for boxes and for bears
have failed him, and have broken his "control"
of what surrounds him. And he is afraid,
because he thought the rules protected him.
Now must he learn the boxes and the bears.
did not deceive him, broke no rules, nor mean
his world is made chaotic and unsafe.
He was mistaken. He misunderstood
what made him safe, and thought that it had left.

The gap that is not there is filled with toys
in countless forms. And each one seems to break
the rules you set for it. It never was
the thing you thought. It must appear to break
your rules for safety, since the rules were wrong.
But *you* are not endangered. You can laugh
at popping heads and squeaking toys, as does
the child who learns they are no threat to him.
Yet while he likes to play with them, he still
perceives them as obeying rules he made
for his enjoyment. So there still are rules
that they can seem to break and frighten him.
Yet *is* he at the mercy of his toys?
And *can* they represent a threat to him?

Reality observes the laws of God,
and not the rules you set. It is His laws
that guarantee your safety. All illusions
that you believe about yourself obey
no laws. They seem to dance a little while,
according to the rules you set for them.
But then they fall and cannot rise again.
They are but toys, my child, so do not grieve
for them. Their dancing never brought you joy.
But neither were they things to frighten you,
nor make you safe if they obeyed your rules.
They must be neither cherished nor attacked,
but merely looked upon as children's toys
without a single meaning of their own.
See one in them and you will see them all.
See none in them and they will touch you not.

Appearances deceive *because* they are
appearances and not reality.
Dwell not on them in any form. They but
obscure reality, and they bring fear
*because* they hide the truth. Do not attack
what you have made to let you be deceived,
for thus you prove that you have been deceived.
Attack has power to make illusions real.
Yet what it makes is nothing. Who could be
made fearful by a power that can have
no real effects at all? What could it be
but an illusion, making things appear
like to itself? Look calmly at its toys,
and understand that they are idols which
but dance to vain desires. Give them not
your worship, for they are not there. Yet this
is equally forgotten in attack.
God's Son needs no defense against his dreams.
His idols do not threaten him at all.

His one mistake is that he thinks them real.
What can the power of illusions do?

Appearances can but deceive the mind
that wants to be deceived. And you can make
a simple choice that will forever place
you far beyond deception. You need not
concern yourself with how this will be done,
for this you cannot understand. But you
will understand that mighty changes have
been quickly brought about, when you decide
one very simple thing; you do not want
whatever you believe an idol gives.
For thus the Son of God declares that he
is free of idols. And thus *is* he free.

Salvation is a paradox indeed!
What could it be except a happy dream?
It asks you but that you forgive all things
that no one ever did; to overlook
what is not there, and not to look upon
the unreal as reality. You are
but asked to let your will be done, and seek
no longer for the things you do not want.
And you are asked to let yourself be free
of all the dreams of what you never were,
and seek no more to substitute the strength
of idle wishes for the Will of God.

Here does the dream of separation start
to fade and disappear. For here the gap
that is not there begins to be perceived
without the toys of terror that you made.
No more than this is asked. Be glad indeed
salvation asks so little, not so much.
It asks for nothing in reality.
And even in illusions it but asks
forgiveness be the substitute for fear.
Such is the only rule for happy dreams.
The gap is emptied of the toys of fear,
and then its unreality is plain.
Dreams are for nothing. And the Son of God
can have no need of them. They offer him
no single thing that he could ever want.
He is delivered from illusions by
his will, and but restored to what he is.
What could God's plan for his salvation be,
except a means to give him to Himself?

## The Only Purpose

The real world is the state of mind in which
the only purpose of the world is seen
to be forgiveness. Fear is not its goal,
for the escape from guilt becomes its aim.
The value of forgiveness is perceived
and takes the place of idols, which are sought
no longer, for their "gifts" are not held dear.
No rules are idly set, and no demands
are made of anyone or anything
to twist and fit into the dream of fear.
Instead, there is a wish to understand
all things created as they really are.
And it is recognized that all things must
be first forgiven, and *then* understood.

Here, it is thought that understanding is
acquired by attack. There, it is clear
that by attack is understanding lost.
The folly of pursuing guilt as goal
is fully recognized. And idols are
not wanted there, for guilt is understood
as the sole cause of pain in any form.
No one is tempted by its vain appeal,
for suffering and death have been perceived
as things not wanted and not striven for.
The possibility of freedom has
been grasped and welcomed, and the means by which
it can be gained can now be understood.
The world becomes a place of hope, because
its only purpose is to be a place
where hope of happiness can be fulfilled.
And no one stands outside this hope, because
the world has been united in belief
the purpose of the world is one which all
must share, if hope be more than just a dream.

Not yet is Heaven quite remembered, for
the purpose of forgiveness still remains.
Yet everyone is certain he will go
beyond forgiveness, and he but remains
until it is made perfect in himself.
He has no wish for anything but this.
And fear has dropped away, because he is
united in his purpose with himself.
There is a hope of happiness in him
so sure and constant he can barely stay
and wait a little longer, with his feet

still touching earth. Yet is he glad to wait
till every hand is joined, and every heart
made ready to arise and go with him.
For thus is he made ready for the step
in which is all forgiveness left behind.

The final step is God's, because it is
but God Who could create a perfect Son
and share His Fatherhood with him. No one
outside of Heaven knows how this can be,
for understanding this is Heaven itself.
Even the real world has a purpose still
beneath creation and eternity.
But fear is gone because its purpose is
forgiveness, not idolatry. And so
is Heaven's Son prepared to be himself,
and to remember that the Son of God
knows everything his Father understands,
and understands it perfectly with Him.

The real world still falls short of this, for this
is God's Own purpose; only His, and yet
completely shared and perfectly fulfilled.
The real world is a state in which the mind
has learned how easily do idols go
when they are still perceived but wanted not.
How willingly the mind can let them go
when it has understood that idols are
nothing and nowhere, and are purposeless.
For only then can guilt and sin be seen
without a purpose, and as meaningless.

Thus is the real world's purpose gently brought
into awareness, to replace the goal
of sin and guilt. And all that stood between
your image of yourself and what you are,
forgiveness washes joyfully away.
Yet God need not create His Son again,
that what is his be given back to him.
The gap between your brother and yourself
was never there. And what the Son of God
knew in creation he must know again.

When brothers join in purpose in the world
of fear, they stand already at the edge
of the real world. Perhaps they still look back,
and think they see an idol that they want.
Yet has their path been surely set away
from idols toward reality. For when
they joined their hands it was Christ's hand they took,
and they will look on Him Whose hand they hold.
The face of Christ is looked upon before
the Father is remembered. For He must
be unremembered till His Son has reached
beyond forgiveness to the Love of God.
Yet is the Love of Christ accepted first.
And then will come the knowledge They are one.

How light and easy is the step across
the narrow boundaries of the world of fear
when you have recognized Whose hand you hold!
Within your hand is everything you need
to walk with perfect confidence away
from fear forever, and to go straight on,
and quickly reach the gate of Heaven itself.
For He Whose hand you hold was waiting but
for you to join Him. Now that you have come,
would He delay in showing you the way
that He must walk with you? His blessing lies
on you as surely as His Father's Love
rests upon Him. His gratitude to you
is past your understanding, for you have
enabled Him to rise from chains and go
with you, together, to His Father's house.

An ancient hate is passing from the world.
And with it goes all hatred and all fear.
Look back no longer, for what lies ahead
is all you ever wanted in your heart.
Give up the world! But not to sacrifice.
You never wanted it. What happiness
have you sought here that did not bring you pain?
What moment of content has not been bought
at fearful price in coins of suffering?
Joy has no cost. It is your sacred right,
and what you pay for is not happiness.
Be speeded on your way by honesty,
and let not your experiences here
deceive in retrospect. They were not free
from bitter cost and joyless consequence.

Do not look back except in honesty.
And when an idol tempts you, think of this:

*There never was a time an idol brought
you anything except the "gift" of guilt.
Not one was bought except at cost of pain,
nor was it ever paid by you alone.*

Be merciful unto your brother, then.

And do not choose an idol thoughtlessly,
remembering that he will pay the cost
as well as you. For he will be delayed
when you look back, and you will not perceive
Whose loving hand you hold. Look forward, then;
in confidence walk with a happy heart
that beats in hope and does not pound in fear.

The Will of God forever lies in those
whose hands are joined. Until they joined, they thought
He was their enemy. But when they joined
and shared a purpose, they were free to learn
their will is one. And thus the Will of God
must reach to their awareness. Nor can they
forget for long that it is but their own.

### The Justification for Forgiveness

Anger is *never* justified. Attack
has *no* foundation. It is here escape
from fear begins, and will be made complete.
Here is the real world given in exchange
for dreams of terror. For it is on this
forgiveness rests, and is but natural.
You are not asked to offer pardon where
attack is due, and would be justified.
For that would mean that you forgive a sin
by overlooking what is really there.
This is not pardon. For it would assume
that, by responding in a way which is
not justified, your pardon will become
the answer to attack that has been made.
And thus is pardon inappropriate,
by being granted where it is not due.

Pardon is *always* justified. It has
a sure foundation. You do not forgive
the unforgivable, nor overlook
a real attack that calls for punishment.
Salvation does not lie in being asked
to make unnatural responses which
are inappropriate to what is real.
Instead, it merely asks that you respond
appropriately to what is not real
by not perceiving what has not occurred.
If pardon were unjustified, you would
be asked to sacrifice your rights when you
return forgiveness for attack. But you
are merely asked to see forgiveness as
the natural reaction to distress
that rests on error, and thus calls for help.
Forgiveness is the only sane response.
It *keeps* your rights from being sacrificed.

This understanding is the only change
that lets the real world rise to take the place
of dreams of terror. Fear cannot arise
unless attack is justified, and if
it had a real foundation pardon would
have none. The real world is achieved when you
perceive the basis of forgiveness is
quite real and fully justified. While you
regard it as a gift unwarranted,
it must uphold the guilt you would "forgive."
Unjustified forgiveness is attack.
And this is all the world can ever give.
It pardons "sinners" sometimes, but remains
aware that they have sinned. And so they do
not merit the forgiveness that it gives.

This is the false forgiveness which the world
employs to keep the sense of sin alive.
And recognizing God is just, it seems
impossible His pardon could be real.
Thus is the fear of God the sure result
of seeing pardon as unmerited.
No one who sees himself as guilty can
avoid the fear of God. But he is saved
from this dilemma if he can forgive.
The mind must think of its Creator as
it looks upon itself. If you can see
your brother merits pardon, you have learned
forgiveness is your right as much as his.
Nor will you think that God intends for you
a fearful judgment that your brother does
not merit. For it is the truth that you
can merit neither more nor less than he.

Forgiveness recognized as merited
will heal. It gives the miracle its strength
to overlook illusions. This is how
you learn that you must be forgiven too.
There can be no appearance that can not
be overlooked. For if there were, it would
be necessary first there be some sin
that stands beyond forgiveness. There would be
an error that is more than a mistake;
a special form of error that remains

unchangeable, eternal, and beyond
correction or escape. There would be one
mistake that had the power to undo
creation, and to make a world that could
replace it and destroy the Will of God.
Only if this were possible could there
be some appearances that could withstand
the miracle, and not be healed by it.

There is no surer proof idolatry
is what you wish than a belief there are
some forms of sickness and of joylessness
forgiveness cannot heal. This means that you
prefer to keep some idols, and are not
prepared, as yet, to let all idols go.
And thus you think that some appearances
are real and not appearances at all.
Be not deceived about the meaning of
a fixed belief that some appearances
are harder to look past than others are.
It always means you think forgiveness must
be limited. And you have set a goal
of partial pardon and a limited
escape from guilt for you. What can this be
except a false forgiveness of yourself,
and everyone who seems apart from you?

It must be true the miracle can heal
all forms of sickness, or it cannot heal.
Its purpose cannot be to judge which forms
are real, and which appearances are true.
If one appearance must remain apart
from healing, one illusion must be part
of truth. And you could not escape all guilt,
but only some of it. You must forgive
God's Son entirely. Or you will keep
an image of yourself that is not whole,
and will remain afraid to look within
and find escape from every idol there.
Salvation rests on faith there cannot be
some forms of guilt that you cannot forgive.
And so there cannot be appearances
that have replaced the truth about God's Son.

Look on your brother with the willingness
to see him as he is. And do not keep
a part of him outside your willingness
that he be healed. To heal is to make whole.
And what is whole can have no missing parts
that have been kept outside. Forgiveness rests
on recognizing this, and being glad
there cannot be some forms of sickness which
the miracle must lack the power to heal.

God's Son is perfect, or he cannot be
God's Son. Nor will you know him, if you think
he does not merit the escape from guilt
in all its consequences and its forms.
There is no way to think of him but this,
if you would know the truth about yourself.

*I thank You, Father, for Your perfect Son,
and in his glory will I see my own.*

Here is the joyful statement that there are
no forms of evil that can overcome
the Will of God; the glad acknowledgment
that guilt has not succeeded by your wish
to make illusions real. And what is this
except a simple statement of the truth?

Look on your brother with this hope in you,
and you will understand he could not make
an error that could change the truth in him.
It is not difficult to overlook
mistakes that have been given no effects.
But what you see as having power to make
an idol of the Son of God you will
not pardon. For he has become to you
a graven image and a sign of death.
Is this your savior? Is his Father wrong
about His Son? Or have you been deceived
in him who has been given you to heal,
for your salvation and deliverance?

### The New Interpretation

Would God have left the meaning of the world
to your interpretation? If He had,
it *has* no meaning. For it cannot be
that meaning changes constantly, and yet
is true. The Holy Spirit looks upon
the world as with one purpose, changelessly
established. And no situation can
affect its aim, but must be in accord
with it. For only if its aim could change
with every situation could each one
be open to interpretation which
is different every time you think of it.
You add an element into the script

you write for every minute in the day,
and all that happens now means something else.
You take away another element,
and every meaning shifts accordingly.

What do your scripts reflect except your plans
for what the day *should* be? And thus you judge
disaster and success, advance, retreat,
and gain and loss. These judgments all are made
according to the roles the script assigns.
The fact they have no meaning in themselves
is demonstrated by the ease with which
these labels change with other judgments, made
on different aspects of experience.
And then, in looking back, you think you see
another meaning in what went before.
What have you really done, except to show
there was no meaning there? But you assigned
a meaning in the light of goals that change,
with every meaning shifting as they change.

Only a constant purpose can endow
events with stable meaning. But it must
accord *one* meaning to them all. If they
are given different meanings, it must be
that they reflect but different purposes.
And this is all the meaning that they have.
Can this be meaning? Can confusion be
what meaning means? Perception cannot be
in constant flux, and make allowance for
stability of meaning anywhere.
Fear is a judgment never justified.
Its presence has no meaning but to show
you wrote a fearful script, and are afraid
accordingly. But not because the thing
you fear has fearful meaning in itself.

A common purpose is the only means
whereby perception can be stabilized,
and one interpretation given to
the world and all experiences here.
In this shared purpose is one judgment shared
by everyone and everything you see.
You do not have to judge, for you have learned
one meaning has been given everything,
and you are glad to see it everywhere.
It cannot change *because* you would perceive
it everywhere, unchanged by circumstance.
And so you offer it to all events,
and let them offer you stability.

Escape from judgment simply lies in this;
all things have but one purpose, which you share
with all the world. And nothing in the world
can be opposed to it, for it belongs
to everything, as it belongs to you.
In single purpose is the end of all
ideas of sacrifice, which must assume
a different purpose for the one who gains
and him who loses. There could be no thought
of sacrifice apart from this idea.
And it is this idea of different goals
that makes perception shift and meaning change.
In one united goal does this become
impossible,for your agreement makes
interpretation stabilize and last.

How can communication really be
established while the symbols that are used
mean different things? The Holy Spirit's goal
gives one interpretation, meaningful
to you and to your brother. Thus can you
communicate with him, and he with you.
In symbols that you both can understand
the sacrifice of meaning is undone.
All sacrifice entails the loss of your
ability to see relationships
among events. And looked at separately
they have no meaning. For there is no light
by which they can be seen and understood.
They have no purpose. And what they are for
cannot be seen. In any thought of loss
there is no meaning. No one has agreed
with you on what it means. It is a part
of a distorted script, which cannot be
interpreted with meaning. It must be
forever unintelligible. This
is not communication. Your dark dreams
are but the senseless, isolated scripts
you write in sleep. Look not to separate dreams
for meaning. Only dreams of pardon can
be shared. They mean the same to both of you.

Do not interpret out of solitude,
for what you see means nothing. It will shift
in what it stands for, and you will believe
the world is an uncertain place, in which
you walk in danger and uncertainty.

It is but your interpretations which
are lacking in stability, for they
are not in line with what you really are.
This is a state so seemingly unsafe
that fear must rise. Do not continue thus,
my brother. We have one Interpreter.
And through His use of symbols are we joined,
so that they mean the same to all of us.
Our common language lets us speak to all
our brothers, and to understand with them
forgiveness has been given to us all,
and thus we can communicate again.

### Changeless Reality

Appearances deceive, but can be changed.
Reality is changeless. It does not
deceive at all, and if you fail to see
beyond appearances you *are* deceived.
For everything you see will change, and yet
you thought it real before, and now you think
it real again. Reality is thus
reduced to form, and capable of change.
Reality is changeless. It is this
that makes it real, and keeps it separate
from all appearances. It must transcend
all form to be itself. It cannot change.

The miracle is means to demonstrate
that all appearances can change because
they *are* appearances, and cannot have
the changelessness reality entails.
The miracle attests salvation from
appearances by showing they can change.
Your brother has a changelessness in him
beyond appearance and deception, both.
It is obscured by changing views of him
that you perceive as his reality.
The happy dream about him takes the form
of the appearance of his perfect health,
his perfect freedom from all forms of lack,
and safety from disaster of all kinds.
The miracle is proof he is not bound
by loss or suffering in any form,
because it can so easily be changed.
This demonstrates that it was never real,
and could not stem from his reality.
For that is changeless, and has no effects
that anything in Heaven or on earth
could ever alter. But appearances
are shown to be unreal *because* they change.

What is temptation but a wish to make
illusions real? It does not seem to be
the wish that no reality be so.
Yet it is an assertion that some forms
of idols have a powerful appeal
that makes them harder to resist than those
you would not want to have reality.
Temptation, then, is nothing more than this;
a prayer the miracle touch not some dreams,
but keep their unreality obscure
and give to them reality instead.
And Heaven gives no answer to the prayer,
nor can a miracle be given you
to heal appearances you do not like.
You have established limits. What you ask
*is* given you, but not of God Who knows
no limits. You have limited yourself.

Reality is changeless. Miracles
but show what you have interposed between
reality and your awareness is
unreal, and does not interfere at all.
The cost of the belief there must be some
appearances beyond the hope of change
is that the miracle cannot come forth
from you consistently. For you have asked
it be withheld from power to heal all dreams.
There is no miracle you cannot have
when you desire healing. But there is
no miracle that can be given you
unless you want it. Choose what you would heal,
and He Who gives all miracles has not
been given freedom to bestow His gifts
upon God's Son. When he is tempted, he
denies reality. And he becomes
the willing slave of what he chose instead.

*Because* reality is changeless is
a miracle already there to heal
all things that change, and offer them to you
to see in happy form, devoid of fear.
It will be given you to look upon
your brother thus. But not while you would have
it otherwise in some respects. For this
but means you would not have him
healed and whole.

The Christ in him is perfect. Is it this
that you would look upon? Then let there be
no dreams about him that you would prefer
to seeing this. And you will see the Christ
in him because you let Him come to you.
And when He has appeared to you, you will
be certain you are like Him, for He is
the changeless in your brother and in you.

This will you look upon when you decide
there is not one appearance you would hold
in place of what your brother really is.
Let no temptation to prefer a dream
allow uncertainty to enter here.
Be not made guilty and afraid when you
are tempted by a dream of what he is.
But do not give it power to replace
the changeless in him in your sight of him.
There is no false appearance but will fade,
if you request a miracle instead.
There is no pain from which he is not free,
if you would have him be but what he is.
Why should you fear to see the Christ in him?
You but behold yourself in what you see.
As he is healed are you made free of guilt,
for his appearance is your own to you.

# Chapter 31
# THE FINAL VISION

## The Simplicity of Salvation

How simple is salvation! All it says
is what was never true is not true now,
and never will be. The impossible
has not occurred, and can have no effects.
And that is all. Can this be hard to learn
by anyone who wants it to be true?
Only unwillingness to learn it could
make such an easy lesson difficult.
How hard is it to see that what is false
can not be true, and what is true can not
be false? You can no longer say that you
perceive no differences in false and true.
You have been told exactly how to tell
one from the other, and just what to do
if you become confused. Why, then, do you
persist in learning not such simple things?

There is a reason. But confuse it not
with difficulty in the simple things
salvation asks you learn. It teaches but
the very obvious. It merely goes
from one apparent lesson to the next,
in easy steps that lead you gently from
one to another, with no strain at all.
This cannot be confusing, yet you are
confused. For somehow you believe that what
is totally confused is easier
to learn and understand. What you have taught
yourself is such a giant learning feat
it is indeed incredible. But you
accomplished it because you wanted to,
and did not pause in diligence to judge
it hard to learn or too complex to grasp.

No one who understands what you have learned,
how carefully you learned it, and the pains
to which you went to practice and repeat
the lessons endlessly, in every form
you could conceive of them, could ever doubt
the power of your learning skill. There is
no greater power in the world. The world
was made by it, and even now depends
on nothing else. The lessons you have taught
yourself have been so overlearned and fixed
they rise like heavy curtains to obscure
the simple and the obvious. Say not
you cannot learn them. For your power to
learn is strong enough to teach you that your will
is not your own, your thoughts do not belong
to you, and even you are someone else.

Who could maintain that lessons such as these
are easy? Yet you have learned more than this.
You have continued, taking every step,
however difficult, without complaint,
until a world was built that suited you.
And every lesson that makes up the world
arises from the first accomplishment
of learning; an enormity so great
the Holy Spirit's Voice seems small and still
before its magnitude. The world began
with one strange lesson, powerful enough
to render God forgotten, and His Son
an alien to himself, in exile from
the home where God Himself established him.
You who have taught yourself the Son of God
is guilty, say not that you cannot learn
the simple things salvation teaches you!

Learning is an ability you made
and gave yourself. It was not made to do
the Will of God, but to uphold a wish
that it could be opposed, and that a will
apart from it was yet more real than it.
And this has learning sought to demonstrate,
and you have learned what it was made to teach.
Now does your ancient overlearning stand
implacable before the Voice of truth,
and teach you that Its lessons are not true;
too hard to learn, too difficult to see,
and too opposed to what is really true.
Yet you will learn them, for their learning is
the only purpose for your learning skill
the Holy Spirit sees in all the world.
His simple lessons in forgiveness have
a power mightier than yours, because
they call from God and from your Self to you.

Is this a little Voice, so small and still
It cannot rise above the senseless noise

of sounds that have no meaning? God willed not His Son forget Him. And the power of His Will is in the Voice That speaks for Him. Which lesson will you learn? What outcome is inevitable, sure as God, and far beyond all doubt and question? Can it be your little learning, strange in outcome and incredible in difficulty will withstand the simple lessons being taught to you in every moment of each day, since time began and learning had been made?

The lessons to be learned are only two. Each has its outcome in a different world. And each world follows surely from its source. The certain outcome of the lesson that God's Son is guilty is the world you see. It is a world of terror and despair. Nor is there hope of happiness in it. There is no plan for safety you can make that ever will succeed. There is no joy that you can seek for here and hope to find. Yet this is not the only outcome which your learning can produce. However much you may have overlearned your chosen task, the lesson that reflects the Love of God is stronger still. And you will learn God's Son is innocent, and see another world.

The outcome of the lesson that God's Son is guiltless is a world in which there is no fear, and everything is lit with hope and sparkles with a gentle friendliness. Nothing but calls to you in soft appeal to be your friend, and let it join with you. And never does a call remain unheard, misunderstood, nor left unanswered in the selfsame tongue in which the call was made. And you will understand it was this call that everyone and everything within the world has always made, but you had not perceived it as it was. And now you see you were mistaken. You had been deceived by forms the call was hidden in. And so you did not hear it, and had lost a friend who always wanted to be part of you. The soft eternal calling of each part of God's creation to the whole is heard throughout the world this second lesson brings.

There is no living thing that does not share the universal Will that it be whole, and that you do not leave its call unheard. Without your answer is it left to die, as it is saved from death when you have heard its calling as the ancient call to life, and understood that it is but your own. The Christ in you remembers God with all the certainty with which He knows His Love. But only if His Son is innocent can He be Love. For God were fear indeed if he whom He created innocent could be a slave to guilt. God's perfect Son remembers his creation. But in guilt he has forgotten what he really is.

The fear of God results as surely from the lesson that His Son is guilty as God's Love must be remembered when he learns his innocence. For hate must father fear, and look upon its father as itself. How wrong are you who fail to hear the call that echoes past each seeming call to death, that sings behind each murderous attack and pleads that love restore the dying world. You do not understand Who calls to you beyond each form of hate; each call to war. Yet you will recognize Him as you give Him answer in the language that He calls. He will appear when you have answered Him, and you will know in Him that God is Love.

What is temptation but a wish to make the wrong decision on what you would learn, and have an outcome that you do not want? It is the recognition that it is a state of mind unwanted that becomes the means whereby the choice is reassessed; another outcome seen to be preferred. You are deceived if you believe you want disaster and disunity and pain. Hear not the call for this within yourself. But listen, rather, to the deeper call beyond it that appeals for peace and joy. And all the world will give you joy and peace. For as you hear, you answer. And behold! Your answer is the proof of what you learned.

Its outcome is the world you look upon.

Let us be still an instant, and forget
all things we ever learned, all thoughts we had,
and every preconception that we hold
of what things mean and what their purpose is.
Let us remember not our own ideas
of what the world is for. We do not know.
Let every image held of everyone
be loosened from our minds and swept away.

Be innocent of judgment, unaware
of any thoughts of evil or of good
that ever crossed your mind of anyone.
Now do you know him not. But you are free
to learn of him, and learn of him anew.
Now is he born again to you, and you
are born again to him, without the past
that sentenced him to die, and you with him.
Now is he free to live as you are free,
because an ancient learning passed away,
and left a place for truth to be reborn.

### Walking with Christ

An ancient lesson is not overcome
by the opposing of the new and old.
It is not vanquished that the truth be known,
nor fought against to lose to truth's appeal.
There is no battle that must be prepared;
no time to be expended, and no plans
that need be laid for bringing in the new.
There *is* an ancient battle being waged
against the truth, but truth does not respond.
Who could be hurt in such a war, unless
he hurts himself? He has no enemy
in truth. And can he be assailed by dreams?

Let us review again what seems to stand
between you and the truth of what you are.
For there are steps in its relinquishment.
The first is a decision that you make.
But afterwards, the truth is given you.
You would establish truth. And by your wish
you set two choices to be made, each time
you think you must decide on anything.
Neither is true. Nor are they different.
Yet must we see them both, before you can
look past them to the one alternative
that *is* a different choice. But not in dreams
you made, that this might be obscured to you.

What you would choose between is not a choice
and gives but the illusion it is free,
for it will have one outcome either way.
Thus is it really not a choice at all.
The leader and the follower emerge
as separate roles, each seeming to possess
advantages you would not want to lose.
So in their fusion there appears to be
the hope of satisfaction and of peace.
You see yourself divided into both
these roles, forever split between the two.
And every friend or enemy becomes
a means to help you save yourself from this.

Perhaps you call it love. Perhaps you think
that it is murder justified at last.
You hate the one you gave the leader's role
when you would have it, and you hate as well
his not assuming it at times you want
to let the follower in you arise,
and give away the role of leadership.
And this is what you made your brother for,
and learned to think that this his purpose is.
Unless he serves it, he has not fulfilled
the function that was given him by you.
And thus he merits death, because he has
no purpose and no usefulness to you.

And what of him? What does he want of you?
What could he want, but what you want of him?
Herein is life as easily as death,
for what you choose you choose as well for him.
Two calls you make to him, as he to you.
Between these two *is* choice, because from them
there is a different outcome. If he be
the leader or the follower to you
it matters not, for you have chosen death.
But if he calls for death or calls for life,
for hate or for forgiveness and for help,
is not the same in outcome. Hear the one,
and you are separate from him and are lost.
But hear the other, and you join with him
and in your answer is salvation found.
The voice you hear in him is but your own.
What does he ask you for? And listen well!
For he is asking what will come to you,
because you see an image of yourself

and hear your voice requesting what you want.

Before you answer, pause to think of this:

*The answer that I give my brother is
what I am asking for. And what I learn
of him is what I learn about myself.*

Then let us wait an instant and be still,
forgetting everything we thought we heard;
remembering how much we do not know.
This brother neither leads nor follows us,
but walks beside us on the selfsame road.
He is like us, as near or far away
from what we want as we will let him be.
We make no gains he does not make with us,
and we fall back if he does not advance.
Take not his hand in anger but in love,
for in his progress do you count your own.
And we go separately along the way
unless you keep him safely by your side.

Because he is your equal in God's Love,
you will be saved from all appearances
and answer to the Christ Who calls to you.
Be still and listen. Think not ancient thoughts.
Forget the dismal lessons that you learned
about this Son of God who calls to you.
Christ calls to all with equal tenderness,
seeing no leaders and no followers,
and hearing but one answer to them all.
Because He hears one Voice, He cannot hear
a different answer from the one He gave
when God appointed Him His only Son.

Be very still an instant. Come without
all thought of what you ever learned before,
and put aside all images you made.
The old will fall away before the new
without your opposition or intent.
There will be no attack upon the things
you thought were precious and in need of care.
There will be no assault upon your wish
to hear a call that never has been made.
Nothing will hurt you in this holy place,
to which you come to listen silently
and learn the truth of what you really want.
No more than this will you be asked to learn.
But as you hear it, you will understand
you need but come away without the thoughts
you did not want, and that were never true.

Forgive your brother all appearances,
that are but ancient lessons you have taught
yourself about the sinfulness in you.
Hear but his call for mercy and release
from all the fearful images he holds
of what he is and of what you must be.
He is afraid to walk with you, and thinks
perhaps a bit behind, a bit ahead
would be a safer place for him to be.
Can you make progress if you think the same,
advancing only when he would step back,
and falling back when he would go ahead?
For so do you forget the journey's goal,
which is but to decide to walk with him,
so neither leads nor follows. Thus it is
a way you go together, not alone.
And in this choice is learning's outcome changed,
for Christ has been reborn to both of you.

An instant spent without your old ideas
of who your great companion is and what
he should be asking for, will be enough
to let this happen. And you will perceive
his purpose is the same as yours. He asks
for what you want, and needs the same as you.
It takes, perhaps, a different form in him,
but it is not the form you answer to.
He asks and you receive, for you have come
with but one purpose; that you learn you love
your brother with a brother's love. And as
a brother, must his Father be the same
as yours, as he is like yourself in truth.

Together is your joint inheritance
remembered and accepted by you both.
Alone it is denied to both of you.
Is it not clear that while you still insist
on leading or on following, you think
you walk alone, with no one by your side?
This is the road to nowhere, for the light
cannot be given while you walk alone,
and so you cannot see which way you go.
And thus there is confusion, and a sense
of endless doubting as you stagger back
and forward in the darkness and alone.
Yet these are but appearances of what
the journey is, and how it must be made.

For next to you is One Who holds the light
before you, so that every step is made
in certainty and sureness of the road.
A blindfold can indeed obscure your sight,
but cannot make the way itself grow dark.
And He Who travels with you *has* the light.

**The Self-Accused**

Only the self-accused condemn. As you
prepare to make a choice that will result
in different outcomes, there is first one thing
that must be overlearned. It must become
a habit of response so typical
of everything you do that it becomes
your first response to all temptation, and
to every situation that occurs.
Learn this, and learn it well, for it is here
delay of happiness is shortened by
a span of time you cannot realize.
You never hate your brother for his sins,
but only for your own. Whatever form
his sins appear to take, it but obscures
the fact that you believe them to be yours,
and therefore meriting a "just" attack.

Why should his sins be sins, if you did not
believe they could not be forgiven in you?
Why are they real in him, if you did not
believe that they are your reality?
And why do you attack them everywhere
except you hate yourself? Are *you* a sin?
You answer "yes" whenever you attack,
for by attack do you assert that you
are guilty, and must give as you deserve.
And what can you deserve but what you are?
If you did not believe that you deserved
attack, it never would occur to you
to give attack to anyone at all.
Why should you? What would be the gain to you?
What could the outcome be that you would want?
And how could murder bring you benefit?

Sins are in bodies. They are not perceived
in minds. They are not seen as purposes,
but actions. Bodies act, and minds do not.
And therefore must the body be at fault
for what it does. It is not seen to be
a passive thing, obeying your commands,
and doing nothing of itself at all.
If you are sin you *are* a body, for
the mind acts not. And purpose must be in
the body, not the mind. The body must
act on its own, and motivate itself.
If you are sin you lock the mind within
the body, and you give its purpose to
its prison house, which acts instead of it.
A jailer does not follow orders, but
enforces orders on the prisoner.

Yet is the *body* prisoner, and not
the mind. The body thinks no thoughts. It has
no power to learn, to pardon, nor enslave.
It gives no orders that the mind need serve,
nor sets conditions that it must obey.
It holds in prison but the willing mind
that would abide in it. It sickens at
the bidding of the mind that would become
its prisoner. And it grows old and dies,
because that mind is sick within itself.
Learning is all that causes change. And so
the body, where no learning can occur,
could never change unless the mind preferred
the body change in its appearances,
to suit the purpose given by the mind.
For mind can learn, and there is all change made.

The mind that thinks it is a sin has but
one purpose; that the body be the source
of sin, to keep it in the prison house
it chose and guards and holds itself at bay,
a sleeping prisoner to the snarling dogs
of hate and evil, sickness and attack;
of pain and age, of grief and suffering.
Here are the thoughts of sacrifice preserved,
for here guilt rules, and orders that the world
be like itself; a place where nothing can
find mercy, nor survive the ravages
of fear except in murder and in death.
For here are you made sin, and sin cannot
abide the joyous and the free, for they
are enemies which sin must kill. In death
is sin preserved, and those who think that they
are sin must die for what they think they are.

Let us be glad that you will see what you
believe, and that it has been given you
to change what you believe. The body will

but follow. It can never lead you where
you would not be. It does not guard your sleep,
nor interfere with your awakening.
Release your body from imprisonment,
and you will see no one as prisoner
to what you have escaped. You will not want
to hold in guilt your chosen enemies,
nor keep in chains, to the illusion of
a changing love, the ones you think are friends.

The innocent release in gratitude
for their release. And what they see upholds
their freedom from imprisonment and death.
Open your mind to change, and there will be
no ancient penalty exacted from
your brother or yourself. For God has said
there *is* no sacrifice that can be asked;
there *is* no sacrifice that can be made.

### The Real Alternative

There is a tendency to think the world
can offer consolation and escape
from problems that its purpose is to keep.
Why should this be? Because it is a place
where choice among illusions seems to be
the only choice. And you are in control
of outcomes of your choosing. Thus you think,
within the narrow band from birth to death,
a little time is given you to use
for you alone; a time when everyone
conflicts with you, but you can choose which road
will lead you out of conflict, and away
from difficulties that concern you not.
Yet they *are* your concern. How, then, can you
escape from them by leaving them behind?
What must go with you, you will take with you
whatever road you choose to walk along.

Real choice is no illusion. But the world
has none to offer. All its roads but lead
to disappointment, nothingness and death.
There is no choice in its alternatives.
Seek not escape from problems here. The world
was made that problems could not *be* escaped.
Be not deceived by all the different names
its roads are given. They have but one end.
And each is but the means to gain that end,
for it is here that all its roads will lead,
however differently they seem to start;
however differently they seem to go.
Their end is certain, for there is no choice
among them. All of them will lead to death.
On some you travel gaily for a while,
before the bleakness enters. And on some
the thorns are felt at once. The choice is not
what will the ending be, but when it comes.

There is no choice where every end is sure.
Perhaps you would prefer to try them all,
before you really learn they are but one.
The roads this world can offer seem to be
quite large in number, but the time must come
when everyone begins to see how like
they are to one another. Men have died
on seeing this, because they saw no way
except the pathways offered by the world.
And learning they led nowhere, lost their hope.
And yet this was the time they could have learned
their greatest lesson. All must reach this point,
and go beyond it. It is true indeed
there is no choice at all within the world.
But this is not the lesson in itself.
The lesson has a purpose, and in this
you come to understand what it is for.

Why would you seek to try another road,
another person or another place,
when you have learned the way the lesson starts,
but do not yet perceive what it is for?
Its purpose is the answer to the search
that all must undertake who still believe
there is another answer to be found.
Learn now, without despair, there is no hope
of answer in the world. But do not judge
the lesson that is but begun with this.
Seek not another signpost in the world
that seems to point to still another road.
No longer look for hope where there is none.
Make fast your learning now, and understand
you but waste time unless you go beyond
what you have learned to what is yet to learn.
For from this lowest point will learning lead
to heights of happiness, in which you see
the purpose of the lesson shining clear,
and perfectly within your learning grasp.

Who would be willing to be turned away

from all the roadways of the world, unless
he understood their real futility?
Is it not needful that he should begin
with this, to seek another way instead?
For while he sees a choice where there is none,
what power of decision can he use?
The great release of power must begin
with learning where it really has a use.
And what decision has power if it be
applied in situations without choice?

The learning that the world can offer but
one choice, no matter what its form may be,
is the beginning of acceptance that
there is a real alternative instead.
To fight against this step is to defeat
your purpose here. You did not come to learn
to find a road the world does not contain.
The search for different pathways in the world
is but the search for different forms of truth.
And this would *keep* the truth from being reached.

Think not that happiness is ever found
by following a road away from it.
This makes no sense, and cannot be the way.
To you who seem to find this course to be
too difficult to learn, let me repeat
that to achieve a goal you must proceed
in its direction, not away from it.
And every road that leads the other way
will not advance the purpose to be found.
If this be difficult to understand,
then is this course impossible to learn.
But only then. For otherwise, it is
a simple teaching in the obvious.

There *is* a choice that you have power to make
when you have seen the real alternatives.
Until that point is reached you have no choice,
and you can but decide how you would choose
the better to deceive yourself again.
This course attempts to teach no more than that
the power of decision cannot lie
in choosing different forms of what is still
the same illusion and the same mistake.
All choices in the world depend on this;
you choose between your brother and yourself,
and you will gain as much as he will lose,
and what you lose is what is given him.

How utterly opposed to truth is this,
when all the lesson's purpose is to teach
that what your brother loses *you* have lost,
and what he gains is what is given *you*.

He has not left His Thoughts! But you forgot
His Presence and remembered not His Love.
No pathway in the world can lead to Him,
nor any worldly goal be one with His.
What road in all the world will lead within,
when every road was made to separate
the journey from the purpose it must have
unless it be but futile wandering?
All roads that lead away from what you are
will lead you to confusion and despair.
Yet has He never left His Thoughts to die,
without their Source forever in themselves.

He has not left His Thoughts! He could no more
depart from them than they could keep Him out.
In unity with Him do they abide,
and in their oneness Both are kept complete.
There is no road that leads away from Him.
A journey from yourself does not exist.
How foolish and insane it is to think
that there could be a road with such an aim!
Where could it go? And how could you be made
to travel on it, walking there without
your own reality at one with you?

Forgive yourself your madness, and forget
all senseless journeys and all goal-less aims.
They have no meaning. You can not escape
from what you are. For God is merciful,
and did not let His Son abandon Him.
For what He is be thankful, for in that
is your escape from madness and from death.
Nowhere but where He is can you be found.
There *is* no path that does not lead to Him.

### Self-Concept versus Self

The learning of the world is built upon
a concept of the self adjusted to
the world's reality. It fits it well.
For this an image is that suits a world
of shadows and illusions. Here it walks
at home, where what it sees is one with it.
The building of a concept of the self
is what the learning of the world is for.

This is its purpose; that you come without
a self, and make one as you go along.
And by the time you reach "maturity"
you have perfected it, to meet the world
on equal terms, at one with its demands.

A concept of the self is made by you.
It bears no likeness to yourself at all.
It is an idol, made to take the place
of your reality as Son of God.
The concept of the self the world would teach
is not the thing that it appears to be.
For it is made to serve two purposes,
but one of which the mind can recognize.
The first presents the face of innocence,
the aspect acted on. It is this face
that smiles and charms and even seems to love.
It searches for companions and it looks,
at times with pity, on the suffering,
and sometimes offers solace. It believes
that it is good within an evil world.

This aspect can grow angry, for the world
is wicked and unable to provide
the love and shelter innocence deserves.
And so this face is often wet with tears
at the injustices the world accords
to those who would be generous and good.
This aspect never makes the first attack.
But every day a hundred little things
make small assaults upon its innocence,
provoking it to irritation, and
at last to open insult and abuse.

The face of innocence the concept of
the self so proudly wears can tolerate
attack in self-defense, for is it not
a well-known fact the world deals harshly with
defenseless innocence? No one who makes
a picture of himself omits this face,
for he has need of it. The other side
he does not want to see. Yet it is here
the learning of the world has set its sights,
for it is here the world's "reality"
is set, to see to it the idol lasts.

Beneath the face of innocence there is
a lesson that the concept of the self
was made to teach. It is a lesson in
a terrible displacement, and a fear
so devastating that the face that smiles
above it must forever look away,
lest it perceive the treachery it hides.
The lesson teaches this: "I am the thing
you made of me, and as you look on me,
you stand condemned because of what I am."
On this conception of the self the world
smiles with approval, for it guarantees
the pathways of the world are safely kept,
and those who walk on them will not escape.

Here is the central lesson that ensures
your brother is condemned eternally.
For what you are has now become his sin.
For this is no forgiveness possible.
No longer does it matter what he does,
for your accusing finger points to him,
unwavering and deadly in its aim.
It points to you as well, but this is kept
still deeper in the mists below the face
of innocence. And in these shrouded vaults
are all his sins and yours preserved and kept
in darkness, where they cannot be perceived
as errors, which the light would surely show.
You can be neither blamed for what you are,
nor can you change the things it makes you do.
Your brother then is symbol of your sins
to you who are but silently, and yet
with ceaseless urgency, condemning still
your brother for the hated thing you are.

Concepts are learned. They are not natural.
Apart from learning they do not exist.
They are not given, so they must be made.
Not one of them is true, and many come
from feverish imaginations, hot
with hatred and distortions born of fear.
What is a concept but a thought to which
its maker gives a meaning of his own?
Concepts maintain the world. But they can not
be used to demonstrate the world is real.
For all of them are made within the world,
born in its shadow, growing in its ways
and finally "maturing" in its thought.
They are ideas of idols, painted with
the brushes of the world, which cannot make
a single picture representing truth.

A concept of the self is meaningless,

for no one here can see what it is for,
and therefore cannot picture what it is.
Yet is all learning that the world directs
begun and ended with the single aim
of teaching you this concept of yourself,
that you will choose to follow this world's laws,
and never seek to go beyond its roads
nor realize the way you see yourself.
Now must the Holy Spirit find a way
to help you see this concept of the self
must be undone, if any peace of mind
is to be given you. Nor can it be
unlearned except by lessons aimed to teach
that you are something else. For otherwise,
you would be asked to make exchange of what
you now believe for total loss of self,
and greater terror would arise in you.

Thus are the Holy Spirit's lesson plans
arranged in easy steps, that though there be
some lack of ease at times and some distress,
there is no shattering of what was learned,
but just a re-translation of what seems
to be the evidence on its behalf.
Let us consider, then, what proof there is
that you are what your brother made of you.
For even though you do not yet perceive
that this is what you think, you surely learned
by now that you behave as if it were.
Does he react for you? And does he know
exactly what would happen? Can he see
your future and ordain, before it comes,
what you should do in every circumstance?
He must have made the world as well as you
to have such prescience in the things to come.

That you are what your brother made of you
seems most unlikely. Even if he did,
who gave the face of innocence to you?
Is this your contribution? Who is, then,
the "you" who made it? And who is deceived
by all your goodness, and attacks it so?
Let us forget the concept's foolishness,
and merely think of this; there are two parts
to what you think yourself to be. If one
were generated by your brother, who
was there to make the other? And from whom
must something be kept hidden? If the world
be evil, there is still no need to hide
what you are made of. Who is there to see?
And what but is attacked could need defense?

Perhaps the reason why this concept must
be kept in darkness is that, in the light,
the one who would not think it true is you.
And what would happen to the world you see,
if all its underpinnings were removed?
Your concept of the world depends upon
this concept of the self. And both would go,
if either one were ever raised to doubt.
The Holy Spirit does not seek to throw
you into panic. So He merely asks
if just a little question might be raised.

There are alternatives about the thing
that you must be. You might, for instance, be
the thing you chose to have your brother be.
This shifts the concept of the self from what
is wholly passive, and at least makes way
for active choice, and some acknowledgment
that interaction must have entered in.
There is some understanding that you chose
for both of you, and what he represents
has meaning that was given it by you.
It also shows some glimmering of sight
into perception's law that what you see
reflects the state of the perceiver's mind.
Yet who was it that did the choosing first?
If you are what you chose your brother be,
alternatives were there to choose among,
and someone must have first decided on
the one to choose, and let the other go.

Although this step has gains, it does not yet
approach a basic question. Something must
have gone before these concepts of the self.
And something must have done the learning which
gave rise to them. Nor can this be explained
by either view. The main advantage of
the shifting to the second from the first
is that you somehow entered in the choice
by your decision. But this gain is paid
in almost equal loss, for now you stand
accused of guilt for what your brother is.
And you must share his guilt, because you chose
it for him in the image of your own.
While only he was treacherous before,

now must you be condemned along with him.

The concept of the self has always been
the great preoccupation of the world.
And everyone believes that he must find
the answer to the riddle of himself.
Salvation can be seen as nothing more
than the escape from concepts. It does not
concern itself with content of the mind,
but with the simple statement that it thinks.
And what can think has choice, and can be shown
that different thoughts have different consequence.
So it can learn that everything it thinks
reflects the deep confusion that it feels
about how it was made and what it is.
And vaguely does the concept of the self
appear to answer what it does not know.

Seek not your Self in symbols. There can be
no concept that can stand for what you are.
What matters it which concept you accept
while you perceive a self that interacts
with evil, and reacts to wicked things?
Your concept of yourself will still remain
quite meaningless. And you will not perceive
that you can interact but with yourself.
To see a guilty world is but the sign
your learning has been guided by the world,
and you behold it as you see yourself.
The concept of the self embraces all
you look upon, and nothing is outside
of this perception. If you can be hurt
by anything, you see a picture of
your secret wishes. Nothing more than this.
And in your suffering of any kind
you see your own concealed desire to kill.

You will make many concepts of the self
as learning goes along. Each one will show
the changes in your own relationships,
as your perception of yourself is changed.
There will be some confusion every time
there is a shift, but be you thankful that
the learning of the world is loosening
its grasp upon your mind. And be you sure
and happy in the confidence that it
will go at last, and leave your mind at peace.
The role of the accuser will appear
in many places and in many forms.
And each will seem to be accusing you.
Yet have no fear it will not be undone.

The world can teach no images of you
unless you want to learn them. There will come
a time when images have all gone by,
and you will see you know not what you are.
It is to this unsealed and open mind
that truth returns, unhindered and unbound.
Where concepts of the self have been laid by
is truth revealed exactly as it is.
When every concept has been raised to doubt
and question, and been recognized as made
on no assumptions that would stand the light,
then is the truth left free to enter in
its sanctuary, clean and free of guilt.
There is no statement that the world is more
afraid to hear than this:

*I do not know
the thing I am, and therefore do not know
what I am doing, where I am, or how
to look upon the world or on myself.*

Yet in this learning is salvation born.
And What you are will tell you of Itself.

### Recognizing the Spirit

You see the flesh or recognize the spirit.
There is no compromise between the two.
If one is real the other must be false,
for what is real denies its opposite.
There is no choice in vision but this one.
What you decide in this determines all
you see and think is real and hold as true.
On this one choice does all your world depend,
for here have you established what you are,
as flesh or spirit in your own belief.
If you choose flesh, you never will escape
the body as your own reality,
for you have chosen that you want it so.
But choose the spirit, and all Heaven bends
to touch your eyes and bless your holy sight,
that you may see the world of flesh no more
except to heal and comfort and to bless.

Salvation is undoing. If you choose
to see the body, you behold a world
of separation, unrelated things,
and happenings that make no sense at all.

This one appears and disappears in death;
that one is doomed to suffering and loss.
And no one is exactly as he was
an instant previous, nor will he be
the same as he is now an instant hence.
Who could have trust where so much change is seen,
for who is worthy if he be but dust?
Salvation is undoing of all this.
For constancy arises in the sight
of those whose eyes salvation has released
from looking at the cost of keeping guilt,
because they chose to let it go instead.

Salvation does not ask that you behold
the spirit and perceive the body not.
It merely asks that this should be your choice.
For you can see the body without help,
but do not understand how to behold
a world apart from it. It is your world
salvation will undo, and let you see
another world your eyes could never find.
Be not concerned how this could ever be.
You do not understand how what you see
arose to meet your sight. For if you did,
it would be gone. The veil of ignorance
is drawn across the evil and the good,
and must be passed that both may disappear,
so that perception finds no hiding place.
How is this done? It is not done at all.
What could there be within the universe
that God created that must still be done?

Only in arrogance could you conceive
that you must make the way to Heaven plain.
The means are given you by which to see
the world that will replace the one you made.
Your will be done! In Heaven as on earth
this is forever true. It matters not
where you believe you are, nor what you think
the truth about yourself must really be.
It makes no difference what you look upon,
nor what you choose to feel or think or wish.
For God Himself has said, "Your will be done."
And it is done to you accordingly.

You who believe that you can choose to see
the Son of God as you would have him be,
forget not that no concept of yourself
will stand against the truth of what you are.

Undoing truth would be impossible.
But concepts are not difficult to change.
One vision, clearly seen, that does not fit
the picture as it was perceived before
will change the world for eyes that learn to see,
because the concept of the self has changed.

Are you invulnerable? Then the world
is harmless in your sight. Do you forgive?
Then is the world forgiving, for you have
forgiven it its trespasses, and so
it looks on you with eyes that see as yours.
Are you a body? So is all the world
perceived as treacherous, and out to kill.
Are you a spirit, deathless, and without
the promise of corruption and the stain
of sin upon you? So the world is seen
as stable, fully worthy of your trust;
a happy place to rest in for a while,
where nothing need be feared, but only loved.
Who is unwelcome to the kind in heart?
And what could hurt the truly innocent?

Your will be done, you holy child of God.
It does not matter if you think you are
in earth or Heaven. What your Father wills
of you can never change. The truth in you
remains as radiant as a star, as pure
as light, as innocent as love itself.
And you *are* worthy that your will be done!

### The Savior's Vision

Learning is change. Salvation does not seek
to use a means as yet too alien to
your thinking to be helpful, nor to make
the kinds of change you could not recognize.
Concepts are needed while perception lasts,
and changing concepts is salvation's task.
For it must deal in contrasts, not in truth,
which has no opposite and cannot change.
In this world's concepts are the guilty "bad";
the "good" are innocent. And no one here
but holds a concept of himself in which
he counts the "good" to pardon him the "bad."
Nor does he trust the "good" in anyone,
believing that the "bad" must lurk behind.
This concept emphasizes treachery,
and trust becomes impossible. Nor could

it change while you perceive the "bad" in you.

You could not recognize your "evil" thoughts
as long as you see value in attack.
You will perceive them sometimes, but will not
see them as meaningless. And so they come
in fearful form, with content still concealed,
to shake your sorry concept of yourself
and blacken it with still another "crime."
You cannot give yourself your innocence,
for you are too confused about yourself.
But should *one* brother dawn upon your sight
as wholly worthy of forgiveness, then
your concept of yourself is wholly changed.
Your "evil" thoughts have been forgiven with his,
because you let them all affect you not.
No longer do you choose that you should be
the sign of evil and of guilt in him.
And as you give your trust to what is good
in him, you give it to the good in you.

In terms of concepts, it is thus you see
him more than just a body, for the good
is never what the body seems to be.
The actions of the body are perceived
as coming from the "baser" part of you,
and thus of him as well. By focusing
upon the good in him, the body grows
decreasingly persistent in your sight,
and will at length be seen as little more
than just a shadow circling round the good.
And this will be your concept of yourself,
when you have reached the world beyond the sight
your eyes alone can offer you to see.
For you will not interpret what you see
without the Aid That God has given you.
And in His sight there *is* another world.

You live in that world just as much as this.
For both are concepts of yourself, which can
be interchanged but never jointly held.
The contrast is far greater than you think,
for you will love this concept of yourself,
because it was not made for you alone.
Born as a gift for someone not perceived
to be yourself, it has been given you.
For your forgiveness, offered unto him,
has been accepted now for both of you.

Have faith in him who walks with you,

so that your fearful concept of yourself may change.
And look upon the good in him, that you
may not be frightened by your "evil" thoughts
because they do not cloud your view of him.
And all this shift requires is that you
be willing that this happy change occur.
No more than this is asked. On its behalf,
remember what the concept of yourself
that now you hold has brought you in its wake,
and welcome the glad contrast offered you.
Hold out your hand, that you may have the gift
of kind forgiveness which you offer one
whose need for it is just the same as yours.
And let the cruel concept of yourself
be changed to one that brings the peace of God.

The concept of yourself that now you hold
would guarantee your function here remain
forever unaccomplished and undone.
And thus it dooms you to a bitter sense
of deep depression and futility.
Yet it need not be fixed, unless you choose
to hold it past the hope of change and keep
it static and concealed within your mind.
Give it instead to Him Who understands
the changes that it needs to let it serve
the function given you to bring you peace,
that you may offer peace to have it yours.
Alternatives are in your mind to use,
and you can see yourself another way.
Would you not rather look upon yourself
as needed for salvation of the world,
instead of as salvation's enemy?

The concept of the self stands like a shield,
a silent barricade before the truth,
and hides it from your sight. All things you see
are images, because you look on them
as through a barrier that dims your sight
and warps your vision, so that you behold
nothing with clarity. The light is kept
from everything you see. At most, you glimpse
a shadow of what lies beyond. At least,
you merely look on darkness, and perceive
the terrified imaginings that come
from guilty thoughts and concepts born of fear.
And what you see is hell, for fear *is* hell.
All that is given you is for release;

the sight, the vision and the inner Guide
all lead you out of hell with those you love
beside you, and the universe with them.

Behold your role within the universe!
To every part of true creation has
the Lord of Love and Life entrusted all
salvation from the misery of hell.
And to each one has He allowed the grace
to be a savior to the holy ones
especially entrusted to his care.
And this he learns when first he looks upon
one brother as he looks upon himself,
and sees the mirror of himself in him.
Thus is the concept of himself laid by,
for nothing stands between his sight and what
he looks upon, to judge what he beholds.
And in this single vision does he see
the face of Christ, and understands he looks
on everyone as he beholds this one.
For there is light where darkness was before,
and now the veil is lifted from his sight.

The veil across the face of Christ, the fear
of God and of salvation, and the love
of guilt and death, they all are different names
for just one error; that there is a space
between you and your brother, kept apart
by an illusion of yourself that holds
him off from you, and you away from him.
The sword of judgment is the weapon that
you give to the illusion of yourself,
that it may fight to keep the space that holds
your brother off unoccupied by love.
Yet while you hold this sword, you must perceive
the body as yourself, for you are bound
to separation from the sight of him
who holds the mirror to another view
of what he is, and thus what you must be.

What is temptation but the wish to stay
in hell and misery? And what could this
give rise to but an image of yourself
that can be miserable, and remain
in hell and torment? Who has learned to see
his brother not as this has saved himself,
and thus is he a savior to the rest.
To everyone has God entrusted all,
because a partial savior would be one
who is but partly saved. The holy ones
whom God has given you to save are but
everyone you meet or look upon,
not knowing who they are; all those you saw
an instant and forgot, and those you knew
a long while since, and those you will yet meet;
the unremembered and the not yet born.
For God has given you His Son to save
from every concept that he ever held.

Yet while you wish to stay in hell, how could
you be the savior of the Son of God?
How would you know his holiness while you
see him apart from yours? For holiness
is seen through holy eyes that look upon
the innocence within, and thus expect
to see it everywhere. And so they call
it forth in everyone they look upon,
that he may be what they expect of him.
This is the savior's vision; that he see
his innocence in all he looks upon,
and see his own salvation everywhere.
He holds no concept of himself between
his calm and open eyes and what he sees.
He brings the light to what he looks upon,
that he may see it as it really is.

Whatever form temptation seems to take,
it always but reflects a wish to be
a self that you are not. And from that wish
a concept rises, teaching that you are
the thing you wish to be. It will remain
your concept of yourself until the wish
that fathered it no longer is held dear.
But while you cherish it, you will behold
your brother in the likeness of the self
whose image has the wish begot of you.
For seeing can but represent a wish,
because it has no power to create.
Yet it can look with love or look with hate,
depending only on the simple choice
of whether you would join with what you see,
or keep yourself apart and separate.

The savior's vision is as innocent
of what your brother is as it is free
of any judgment made upon yourself.
It sees no past in anyone at all.
And thus it serves a wholly open mind,

uncloudedby old concepts, and prepared
to look on only what the present holds.
It cannot judge because it does not know.
And recognizing this, it merely asks,
"What is the meaning of what I behold?"
Then is the answer given. And the door
held open for the face of Christ to shine
upon the one who asks, in innocence,
to see beyond the veil of old ideas
and ancient concepts held so long and dear
against the vision of the Christ in you.

Be vigilant against temptation, then,
remembering that it is but a wish,
insane and meaningless, to make yourself
a thing that you are not. And think as well
upon the thing that you would be instead.
It is a thing of madness, pain and death;
a thing of treachery and black despair,
of failing dreams and no remaining hope
except to die, and end the dream of fear.
*This* is temptation; nothing more than this.
Can this be difficult to choose *against*?
Consider what temptation is, and see
the real alternatives you choose between.
There are but two. Be not deceived by what
appears as many choices. There is hell
or Heaven, and of these you choose but one.

Let not the world's light, given unto you,
be hidden from the world. It needs the light,
for it is dark indeed, and men despair
because the savior's vision is withheld
and what they see is death. Their savior stands,
unknowing and unknown, beholding them
with eyes unopened. And they cannot see
until he looks on them with seeing eyes,
and offers them forgiveness with his own.
Can you to whom God says, "Release My Son!"
be tempted not to listen, when you learn
that it is you for whom He asks release?
And what but this is what this course would teach?
And what but this is there for you to learn?

## Choose Once Again

Temptation has one lesson it would teach,
in all its forms, wherever it occurs.
It would persuade the holy Son of God
he is a body, born in what must die,
unable to escape its frailty,
and bound by what it orders him to feel.
It sets the limits on what he can do;
its power is the only strength he has;
his grasp cannot exceed its tiny reach.
Would you be this, if Christ appeared to you
in all His glory, asking you but this:

*Choose once again if you would take your place
among the saviors of the world, or would
remain in hell, and hold your brothers there.*

For He *has* come, and He *is* asking this.

How do you make the choice? How easily
is this explained! You always choose between
your weakness and the strength of Christ in you.
And what you choose is what you think is real.
Simply by never using weakness to
direct your actions, you have given it
no power. And the light of Christ in you
is given charge of everything you do.
For you have brought your weakness unto Him,
and He has given you His strength instead.

Trials are but lessons that you failed to learn
presented once again, so where you made
a faulty choice before you now can make
a better one, and thus escape all pain
that what you chose before has brought to you.
In every difficulty, all distress,
and each perplexity Christ calls to you
and gently says, "My brother, choose again."
He would not leave one source of pain unhealed,
nor any image left to veil the truth.
He would remove all misery from you
whom God created altar unto joy.
He would not leave you comfortless, alone
in dreams of hell, but would release your mind
from everything that hides His face from you.
His holiness is yours because He is
the only Power that is real in you.
His strength is yours because He is the Self
That God created as His only Son.

The images you make cannot prevail
against what God Himself would have you be.
Be never fearful of temptation, then,
but see it as it is; another chance

to choose again, and let Christ's strength prevail
in every circumstance and every place
you raised an image of yourself before.
For what appears to hide the face of Christ
is powerless before His majesty,
and disappears before His holy sight.
The saviors of the world, who see like Him,
are merely those who choose His strength instead
of their own weakness, seen apart from Him.
They will redeem the world, for they are joined
in all the power of the Will of God.
And what they will is only what He wills.

Learn, then, the happy habit of response
to all temptation to perceive yourself
as weak and miserable with these words:

*I am as God created me. His Son
can suffer nothing. And I am His Son.*

Thus is Christ's strength invited to prevail,
replacing all your weakness with the strength
that comes from God and that can never fail.
And thus are miracles as natural
as fear and agony appeared to be
before the choice for holiness was made.
For in that choice are false distinctions gone,
illusory alternatives laid by,
and nothing left to interfere with truth.

You *are* as God created you, and so
is every living thing you look upon,
regardless of the images you see.
What you behold as sickness and as pain,
as weakness and as suffering and loss,
is but temptation to perceive yourself
defenseless and in hell. Yield not to this,
and you will see all pain, in every form,
wherever it occurs, but disappear
as mists before the sun. A miracle
has come to heal God's Son, and close the door
upon his dreams of weakness, opening
the way to his salvation and release.
Choose once again what you would have him be,
remembering that every choice you make
establishes your own identity
as you will see it and believe it is.

Deny me not the little gift I ask,
when in exchange I lay before your feet

the peace of God, and power to bring this peace
to everyone who wanders in the world
uncertain, lonely, and in constant fear.
For it is given you to join with him,
and through the Christ in you unveil his eyes,
and let him look upon the Christ in him.

My brothers in salvation, do not fail
to hear my voice and listen to my words.
I ask for nothing but your own release.
There is no place for hell within a world
whose loveliness can yet be so intense
and so inclusive it is but a step
from there to Heaven. To your tired eyes
I bring a vision of a different world,
so new and clean and fresh you will forget
the pain and sorrow that you saw before.
Yet this a vision is which you must share
with everyone you see, for otherwise
you will behold it not. To give this gift
is how to make it yours. And God ordained,
in loving kindness, that it be for you.

Let us be glad that we can walk the world,
and find so many chances to perceive
another situation where God's gift
can once again be recognized as ours!
And thus will all the vestiges of hell,
the secret sins and hidden hates be gone.
And all the loveliness which they concealed
appear like lawns of Heaven to our sight,
to lift us high above the thorny roads
we travelled on before the Christ appeared.
Hear me, my brothers, hear and join with me.
God has ordained I cannot call in vain,
and in His certainty I rest content.
For you *will* hear, and you *will* choose again.
And in this choice is everyone made free.

I thank You, Father, for these holy ones
who are my brothers as they are Your Sons.
My faith in them is Yours. I am as sure
that they will come to me as You are sure
of what they are, and will forever be.
They will accept the gift I offer them,
because You gave it me on their behalf.
And as I would but do Your holy Will,
so will they choose. And I give thanks for them.
Salvation's song will echo through the world

with every choice they make. For we are one
in purpose, and the end of hell is near.

In joyous welcome is my hand outstretched
to every brother who would join with me
in reaching past temptation, and who looks
with fixed determination toward the light
that shines beyond in perfect constancy.
Give me my own, for they belong to You.
And can You fail in what is but Your Will?
I give You thanks for what my brothers are.
And as each one elects to join with me,
the song of thanks from earth to Heaven grows
from tiny scattered threads of melody
to one inclusive chorus from a world
redeemed from hell, and giving thanks to You.

And now we say "Amen." For Christ has come
to dwell in the abode You set for Him
before time was, in calm eternity.
The journey closes, ending at the place
where it began. No trace of it remains.
Not one illusion is accorded faith,
and not one spot of darkness still remains
to hide the face of Christ from anyone.
Thy Will is done, complete and perfectly,
and all creation recognizes You,
and knows You as the only Source it has.
Clear in Your likeness does the Light shine forth
from everything that lives and moves in You.
For we have reached where all of us are one,
and we are home, where You would have us be.

## LESSON 78

**Let miracles replace all grievances.**

Perhaps it is not yet quite clear to you
that each decision that you make is one
between a grievance and a miracle.
Each grievance stands like a dark shield of hate
before the miracle it would conceal.
And as you raise it up before your eyes,
you will not see the miracle beyond.
Yet all the while it waits for you in light,
but you behold your grievances instead.

Today we go beyond the grievances,
to look upon the miracle instead.
We will reverse the way you see by not
allowing sight to stop before it sees.
We will not wait before the shield of hate,
but lay it down and gently lift our eyes
in silence to behold the Son of God.

He waits for you behind your grievances,
and as you lay them down he will appear
in shining light where each one stood before.
For every grievance is a block to sight,
and as it lifts you see the Son of God
where he has always been. He stands in light,
but you were in the dark. Each grievance made
the darkness deeper, and you could not see.

Today we will attempt to see God's Son.
We will not let ourselves be blind to him;
we will not look upon our grievances.
So is the seeing of the world reversed,
as we look out toward truth, away from fear.
We will select one person you have used
as target for your grievances, and lay
the grievances aside and look at him.
Someone, perhaps, you fear and even hate;
someone you think you love who angered you;
someone you call a friend, but whom you see
as difficult at times or hard to please,
demanding, irritating or untrue
to the ideal he should accept as his,
according to the role you set for him.

You know the one to choose; his name has crossed
your mind already. He will be the one
of whom we ask God's Son be shown to you.
Through seeing him behind the grievances
that you have held against him, you will learn
that what lay hidden while you saw him not
is there in everyone, and can be seen.
He who was enemy is more than friend
when he is freed to take the holy role
the Holy Spirit has assigned to him.
Let him be savior unto you today.
Such is his role in God your Father's plan.

Our longer practice periods today
will see him in this role. You will attempt
to hold him in your mind, first as you now
consider him. You will review his faults,
the difficulties you have had with him,
the pain he caused you, his neglect, and all
the little and the larger hurts he gave.
You will regard his body with its flaws
and better points as well, and you will think
of his mistakes and even of his "sins."

Then let us ask of Him Who knows this Son
of God in his reality and truth,
that we may look on him a different way,
and see our savior shining in the light
of true forgiveness, given unto us.
We ask Him in the holy Name of God
and of His Son, as holy as Himself:

*Let me behold my savior in this one
You have appointed as the one for me
to ask to lead me to the holy light
in which he stands, that I may join with him.*

The body's eyes are closed, and as you think
of him who grieved you, let your mind be shown
the light in him beyond your grievances.

What you have asked for cannot be denied.
Your savior has been waiting long for this.
He would be free, and make his freedom yours.
The Holy Spirit leans from him to you,
seeing no separation in God's Son.
And what you see through Him will free you both.
Be very quiet now, and look upon

your shining savior. No dark grievances
obscure the sight of him. You have allowed
the Holy Spirit to express through him
the role God gave Him that you might be saved.

God thanks you for these quiet times today
in which you laid your images aside,
and looked upon the miracle of love
the Holy Spirit showed you in their place.
The world and Heaven join in thanking you,
for not one Thought of God but must rejoice
as you are saved, and all the world with you.

We will remember this throughout the day,
and take the role assigned to us as part
of God's salvation plan, and not our own.
Temptation falls away when we allow
each one we meet to save us, and refuse
to hide his light behind our grievances.
To everyone you meet, and to the ones
you think of or remember from the past,
allow the role of savior to be given,
that you may share it with him. For you both,
and all the sightless ones as well, we pray:

*Let miracles replace all grievances.*

# LESSON 91

### Miracles are seen in light.

It is important to remember that miracles and vision necessarily go together. This needs repeating, and frequent repeating. It is a central idea in your new thought system, and the perception that it produces. The miracle is always there. Its presence is not caused by your vision; its absence is not the result of your failure to see. It is only your awareness of miracles that is affected. You will see them in the light; you will not see them in the dark.

To you, then, light is crucial. While you remain in darkness, the miracle remains unseen. Thus you are convinced it is not there. This follows from the premises from which the darkness comes. Denial of light leads to failure to perceive it. Failure to perceive light is to perceive darkness. The light is useless to you then, even though it is there. You cannot use it because its presence is unknown to you. And the seeming reality of the darkness makes the idea of light meaningless.

To be told that what you do not see is there sounds like insanity. It is very difficult to become convinced that it is insanity not to see what is there, and to see what is not there instead. You do not doubt that the body's eyes can see. You do not doubt the images they show you are reality. Your faith lies in the darkness, not the light. How can this be reversed? For you it is impossible, but you are not alone in this.

Your efforts, however little they may be, have strong support. Did you but realize how great this strength, your doubts would vanish. Today we will devote ourselves to the attempt to let you feel this strength. When you have felt the strength in you, which makes all miracles within your easy reach, you will not doubt. The miracles your sense of weakness hides will leap into awareness as you feel the strength in you.

Three times today, set aside about ten minutes for a quiet time in which you try to leave your weakness behind. This is accomplished very simply, as you instruct yourself that you are not a body. Faith goes to what you want, and you instruct your mind accordingly. Your will remains your teacher, and your will has all the strength to do what it desires. You can escape the body if you choose. You can experience the strength in you.

Begin the longer practice periods with this statement of true cause and effect relationships:
*Miracles are seen in light.*
*The body's eyes do not perceive the light.*
*But I am not a body. What am I?*

The question with which this statement ends is needed for our exercises today. What you think you are is a belief to be undone. But what you really are must be revealed to you. The belief you are a body calls for correction, being a mistake. The truth of what you are calls on the strength in you to bring to your awareness what the mistake conceals.

If you are not a body, what are you? You need to be aware of what the Holy Spirit uses to replace the image of a body in your mind. You need to feel something to put your faith in, as you lift it from the body. You need a real experience of something else, something more solid and more sure; more worthy of your faith, and really there.

If you are not a body, what are you? Ask this in honesty, and then devote several minutes to allowing your mistaken thoughts about your attributes to be corrected, and their opposites to take their place. Say, for example:

*I am not weak, but strong.*
*I am not helpless, but all powerful.*

*I am not limited, but unlimited.*
*I am not doubtful, but certain.*
*I am not an illusion, but a reality.*
*I cannot see in darkness, but in light.*

In the second phase of the exercise period, try to experience these truths about yourself. Concentrate particularly on the experience of strength. Remember that all sense of weakness is associated with the belief you are a body, a belief that is mistaken and deserves no faith. Try to remove your faith from it, if only for a moment. You will be accustomed to keeping faith with the more worthy in you as we go along.

Relax for the rest of the practice period, confident that your efforts, however meager, are fully supported by the strength of God and all His Thoughts. It is from Them that your strength will come. It is through Their strong support that you will feel the strength in you. They are united with you in this practice period, in which you share a purpose like Their own. Theirs is the light in which you will see miracles, because Their strength is yours. Their strength becomes your eyes, that you may see.

Five or six times an hour, at reasonably regular intervals, remind yourself that miracles are seen in light. Also, be sure to meet temptation with today's idea. This form would be helpful for this special purpose:

*Miracles are seen in light. Let me not*
*close my eyes because of this.*

# LESSON 92

## Miracles are seen in light, and light and strength are one.

The idea for today is an extension of the previous one. You do not think of light in terms of strength, and darkness in terms of weakness. That is because your idea of what seeing means is tied up with the body and its eyes and brain. Thus you believe that you can change what you see by putting little bits of glass before your eyes. This is among the many magical beliefs that come from the conviction you are a body, and the body's eyes can see.

You also believe the body's brain can think. If you but understood the nature of thought, you could but laugh at this insane idea. It is as if you thought you held the match that lights the sun and gives it all its warmth; or that you held the world within your hand, securely bound until you let it go. Yet this is no more foolish than to believe the body's eyes can see; the brain can think.

It is God's strength in you that is the light in which you see, as it is His Mind with which you think. His strength denies your weakness. It is your weakness that sees through the body's eyes, peering about in darkness to behold the likeness of itself; the small, the weak, the sickly and the dying, those in need, the helpless and afraid, the sad, the poor, the starving and the joyless. These are seen through eyes that cannot see and cannot bless.

Strength overlooks these things by seeing past appearances. It keeps its steady gaze upon the light that lies beyond them. It unites with light, of which it is a part. It sees itself. It brings the light in which your Self appears. In darkness you perceive a self that is not there. Strength is the truth about you; weakness is an idol falsely worshipped and adored that strength may be dispelled, and darkness rule where God appointed that there should be light.

Strength comes from truth, and shines with light its Source has given it; weakness reflects the darkness of its maker. It is sick and looks on sickness, which is like itself. Truth is a savior and can only will for happiness and peace for everyone. It gives its strength to everyone who asks, in limitless supply. It sees that lack in anyone would be a lack in all. And so it gives its light that all may see and benefit as one. Its strength is shared, that it may bring to all the miracle in which they will unite in purpose and forgiveness and in love.

Weakness, which looks in darkness, cannot see a purpose in forgiveness and in love. It sees all others different from itself, and nothing in the world that it would share. It judges and condemns, but does not love. In darkness it remains to hide itself, and dreams that it is strong and conquering, a victor over limitations that but grow in darkness to enormous size.

It fears and it attacks and hates itself, and darkness covers everything it sees, leaving its dreams as fearful as itself. No miracles are here, but only hate. It separates itself from what it sees, while light and strength perceive themselves as one. The light of strength is not the light you see. It does not change and flicker and go out. It does not shift from night to day, and back to darkness till the morning comes again.

The light of strength is constant, sure as love, forever glad to give itself away, because it cannot give but to itself. No one can ask in vain to share its sight, and none who enters its abode can leave without a miracle before his eyes, and strength and light abiding in his heart.

The strength in you will offer you the light, and guide your seeing so you do not dwell on idle shadows that the body's eyes provide for self-deception. Strength and light unite in you, and where they meet, your Self stands ready to embrace you as Its Own. Such is the meeting place we try today to find and rest in, for the peace of God is where your Self, His Son, is waiting now to meet Itself again, and be as one.

Let us give twenty minutes twice today to join this meeting. Let yourself be brought unto your Self. Its strength will be the light in which the gift of sight is given you. Leave, then, the dark a little while today, and we will practice seeing in the light, closing the body's eyes and asking truth to show us how to find the meeting place of self and Self, where light and strength are one.

Morning and evening we will practice thus. After the morning meeting, we will use the day in preparation for the time at night when we will meet again in trust. Let us repeat as often as we can the idea for today, and recognize that we are being introduced to sight, and led away from darkness to the light where only miracles can be perceived.

# LESSON 93

**Light and joy and peace abide in me.**

You think you are the home of evil, darkness and sin. You think if anyone could see the truth about you he would be repelled, recoiling from you as if from a poisonous snake. You think if what is true about you were revealed to you, you would be struck with horror so intense that you would rush to death by your own hand, living on after seeing this being impossible.

These are beliefs so firmly fixed that it is difficult to help you see that they are based on nothing. That you have made mistakes is obvious. That you have sought salvation in strange ways; have been deceived, deceiving and afraid of foolish fantasies and savage dreams; and have bowed down to idols made of dust,– all this is true by what you now believe.

Today we question this, not from the point of view of what you think, but from a very different reference point, from which such idle thoughts are meaningless. These thoughts are not according to God's Will. These weird beliefs He does not share with you. This is enough to prove that they are wrong, but you do not perceive that this is so.

Why would you not be overjoyed to be assured that all the evil that you think you did was never done, that all your sins are nothing, that you are as pure and holy as you were created, and that light and joy and peace abide in you? Your image of yourself cannot withstand the Will of God. You think that this is death, but it is life. You think you are destroyed, but you are saved.

The self you made is not the Son of God. Therefore, this self does not exist at all. And anything it seems to do and think means nothing. It is neither bad nor good. It is unreal, and nothing more than that. It does not battle with the Son of God. It does not hurt him, nor attack his peace. It has not changed creation, nor reduced eternal sinlessness to sin, and love to hate. What power can this self you made possess, when it would contradict the Will of God?

Your sinlessness is guaranteed by God. Over and over this must be repeated, until it is accepted. It is true. Your sinlessness is guaranteed by God. Nothing can touch it, or change what God created as eternal. The self you made, evil and full of sin, is meaningless. Your sinlessness is guaranteed by God, and light and joy and peace abide in you.

Salvation requires the acceptance of but one thought; - you are as God created you, not what you made of yourself. Whatever evil you may think you did, you are as God created you. Whatever mistakes you made, the truth about you is unchanged. Creation is eternal and unalterable. Your sinlessness is guaranteed by God. You are and will forever be exactly as you were created. Light and joy and peace abide in you because God put them there.

In our longer exercise periods today, which would be most profitable if done for the first five minutes of every waking hour, begin by stating the truth about your creation:

*Light and joy and peace abide in me.*
*My sinlessness is guaranteed by God.*

Then put away your foolish self-images, and spend the rest of the practice period in trying to experience what God has given you, in place of what you have decreed for yourself.

You are what God created or what you made. One Self is true; the other is not there. Try to experience the unity of your one Self. Try to appreciate Its holiness and the Love from Which It was created. Try not to interfere with the Self Which God created as you, by hiding Its majesty behind the tiny idols of evil and sinfulness you have made to replace It. Let It come into Its Own. Here you are; This is You. And light and joy and peace abide in you because this is so.

You may not be willing or even able to use the first five minutes of each hour for these exercises. Try, however, to do so when you can. At least remember to repeat these thoughts each hour:

*Light and joy and peace abide in me.*
*My sinlessness is guaranteed by God.*

Then try to devote at least a minute or so to closing your eyes and realizing that this is a statement of the truth about you.

If a situation arises that seems to be disturbing, quickly dispel the illusion of fear by repeating these thoughts again. Should you be tempted to become angry with someone, tell him silently:

*Light and joy and peace abide in you.*
*Your sinlessness is guaranteed by God.*

You can do much for the world's salvation today. You can do much today to bring you closer to the part in salvation that God has assigned to you. And you can do much today to bring the conviction to your mind that the idea for the day is true indeed.

# LESSON 94

### I am as God created me.

Today we continue with the one idea which brings complete salvation; the one statement which makes all forms of temptation powerless; the one thought which renders the ego silent and entirely undone. You are as God created you. The sounds of this world are still, the sights of this world disappear, and all the thoughts that this world ever held are wiped away forever by this one idea. Here is salvation accomplished. Here is sanity restored.

True light is strength, and strength is sinlessness. If you remain as God created you, you must be strong and light must be in you. He Who ensured your sinlessness must be the guarantee of strength and light as well. You are as God created you. Darkness cannot obscure the glory of God's Son. You stand in light, strong in the sinlessness in which you were created, and in which you will remain throughout eternity.

Today we will again devote the first five minutes of each waking hour to the attempt to feel the truth in you. Begin these times of searching with these words:

*I am as God created me.*
*I am His Son eternally.*

Now try to reach the Son of God in you. This is the Self That never sinned, nor made an image to replace reality. This is the Self That never left Its home in God to walk the world uncertainly. This is the Self That knows no fear, nor could conceive of loss or suffering or death.

Nothing is required of you to reach this goal except to lay all idols and self-images aside; go past the list of attributes, both good and bad, you have ascribed to yourself; and wait in silent expectancy for the truth. God has Himself promised that it will be revealed to all who ask for it. You are asking now. You cannot fail because He cannot fail.

If you do not meet the requirement of practicing for the first five minutes of every hour, at least remind yourself hourly:

*I am as God created me.*
*I am His Son eternally.*

Tell yourself frequently today that you are as God created you. And be sure to respond to anyone who seems to irritate you with these words:

*You are as God created you.*
*You are His Son eternally.*

Make every effort to do the hourly exercises today. Each one you do will be a giant stride toward your release, and a milestone in learning the thought system which this course sets forth.

## LESSON 95

**I am one Self, united with my Creator.**

Today's idea accurately describes you as God created you. You are one within yourself, and one with Him. Yours is the unity of all creation. Your perfect unity makes change in you impossible. You do not accept this, and you fail to realize it must be so, only because you believe that you have changed yourself already.

You see yourself as a ridiculous parody on God's creation; weak, vicious, ugly and sinful, miserable and beset with pain. Such is your version of yourself; a self divided into many warring parts, separate from God, and tenuously held together by its erratic and capricious maker, to which you pray. It does not hear your prayers, for it is deaf. It does not see the oneness in you, for it is blind. It does not understand you are the Son of God, for it is senseless and understands nothing.

We will attempt today to be aware only of what can hear and see, and what makes perfect sense. We will again direct our exercises towards reaching your one Self, Which is united with Its Creator. In patience and in hope we try again today.

The use of the first five minutes of every waking hour for practicing the idea for the day has special advantages at the stage of learning in which you are at present. It is difficult at this point not to allow your mind to wander, if it undertakes extended practice. You have surely realized this by now. You have seen the extent of your lack of mental discipline, and of your need for mind training. It is necessary that you be aware of this, for it is indeed a hindrance to your advance.

Frequent but shorter practice periods have other advantages for you at this time. In addition to recognizing your difficulties with sustained attention, you must also have noticed that, unless you are reminded of your purpose frequently, you tend to forget about it for long periods of time. You often fail to remember the short applications of the idea for the day, and you have not yet formed the habit of using the idea as an automatic response to temptation.

Structure, then, is necessary for you at this time, planned to include frequent reminders of your goal and regular attempts to reach it. Regularity in terms of time is not the ideal requirement for the most beneficial form of practice in salvation. It is advantageous, however, for those whose motivation is inconsistent, and who remain heavily defended against learning.

We will, therefore, keep to the five-minutes-an-hour practice periods for a while, and urge you to omit as few as possible. Using the first five minutes of the hour will be particularly helpful, since it imposes firmer structure. Do not, however, use your lapses from this schedule as an excuse not to return to it again as soon as you can. There may well be a temptation to regard the day as lost because you have already failed to do what is required. This should, however, merely be recognized as what it is; a refusal to let your mistake be corrected, and an unwillingness to try again.

The Holy Spirit is not delayed in His teaching by your mistakes. He can be held back only by your unwillingness to let them go. Let us therefore be determined, particularly for the next week or so, to be willing to forgive ourselves for our lapses in diligence, and our failures to follow the instructions for practicing the day's idea. This tolerance for weakness will enable us to overlook it, rather than give it power to delay our learning. If we give it power to do this, we are regarding it as strength, and are confusing strength with weakness.

When you fail to comply with the requirements of this course, you have merely made a mistake. This calls for correction, and for nothing else. To allow a mistake to continue is to make additional mistakes, based on the first and reinforcing it. It is this process that must be laid aside, for it is but another way in which you would defend illusions against the truth.

Let all these errors go by recognizing them for what they are. They are attempts to keep you unaware you are one Self, united with your Creator, at one with every aspect of creation, and limitless in power and in peace. This is the truth, and nothing else is true. Today we will affirm this truth again, and try to reach the place in you in which there is no doubt that only this is true.

Begin the practice periods today
with this assurance, offered to your mind
with all the certainty that you can give:

*I am one Self, united with my Creator,*
*at one with every aspect of creation,*
*and limitless in power and in peace.*

Then close your eyes and tell yourself again,
slowly and thoughtfully, attempting to
allow the meaning of the words to sink
into your mind, replacing false ideas:

*I am one Self.*

Repeat this several times, and then attempt
to feel the meaning that the words convey.

You are one Self, united and secure in
light and joy and peace. You are God's Son,
one Self, with one Creator and one goal;
to bring awareness of this oneness to
all minds, that true creation may extend
the Allness and the Unity of God.
You are one Self, complete and healed and whole,
with power to lift the veil of darkness from
the world, and let the light in you come through
to teach the world the truth about yourself.

You are one Self, in perfect harmony
with all there is, and all that there will be.
You are one Self, the holy Son of God,
united with your brothers in that Self;
united with your Father in His Will.
Feel this one Self in you, and let It shine
away all your illusions and your doubts.
This is your Self, the Son of God Himself,
sinless as Its Creator, with His strength
within you and His Love forever yours.
You are one Self, and it is given you
to feel this Self within you, and to cast
all your illusions out of the one Mind
that is this Self, the holy truth in you.

Do not forget today. We need your help;
your little part in bringing happiness
to all the world. And Heaven looks to you
in confidence that you will try today.
Share, then, its surety, for it is yours.
Be vigilant. Do not forget today.
Throughout the day do not forget your goal.
Repeat today's idea as frequently
as possible, and understand each time
you do so, someone hears the voice of hope,
the stirring of the truth within his mind,
the gentle rustling of the wings of peace.

Your own acknowledgment you are one Self,
united with your Father, is a call
to all the world to be at one with you.
To everyone you meet today, be sure
to give the promise of today's idea
and tell him this:

*You are one Self with me,*
*united with our Creator in this Self.*
*I honor you because of What I am,*
*and What He is, Who loves us both as one.*

## LESSON 96

**Salvation comes from my one Self.**

Although you are one Self, you experience yourself as two; as both good and evil, loving and hating, mind and body. This sense of being split into opposites induces feelings of acute and constant conflict, and leads to frantic attempts to reconcile the contradictory aspects of this self-perception. You have sought many such solutions, and none of them has worked. The opposites you see in you will never be compatible. But one exists.

The fact that truth and illusion cannot be reconciled, no matter how you try, what means you use and where you see the problem, must be accepted if you would be saved. Until you have accepted this, you will attempt an endless list of goals you cannot reach; a senseless series of expenditures of time and effort, hopefulness and doubt, each one as futile as the one before, and failing as the next one surely will.

Problems that have no meaning cannot be resolved within the framework they are set. Two selves in conflict could not be resolved, and good and evil have no meeting place. The self you made can never be your Self, nor can your Self be split in two, and still be what It is and must forever be. A mind and body cannot both exist. Make no attempt to reconcile the two, for one denies the other can be real. If you are physical, your mind is gone from your self-concept, for it has no place in which it could be really part of you. If you are spirit, then the body must be meaningless to your reality.

Spirit makes use of mind as means to find its Self expression. And the mind which serves the spirit is at peace and filled with joy. Its power comes from spirit, and it is fulfilling happily its function here. Yet mind can also see itself divorced from spirit, and perceive itself within a body it confuses with itself. Without its function then it has no peace, and happiness is alien to its thoughts.

Yet mind apart from spirit cannot think. It has denied its Source of strength, and sees itself as helpless, limited and weak. Dissociated from its function now, it thinks it is alone and separate, attacked by armies massed against itself and hiding in the body's frail support. Now must it reconcile unlike with like, for this is what it thinks that it is for.

Waste no more time on this. Who can resolve the senseless conflicts which a dream presents? What could the resolution mean in truth? What purpose could it serve? What is it for? Salvation cannot make illusions real, nor solve a problem that does not exist. Perhaps you hope it can. Yet would you have God's plan for the release of His dear Son bring pain to him, and fail to set him free?

Your Self retains Its thoughts, and they remain within your mind and in the Mind of God. The Holy Spirit holds salvation in your mind, and offers it the way to peace. Salvation is a thought you share with God, because His Voice accepted it for you and answered in your name that it was done. Thus is salvation kept among the thoughts your Self holds dear and cherishes for you.

We will attempt today to find this thought, whose presence in your mind is guaranteed by Him Who speaks to you from your one Self. Our hourly five-minute practicing will be a search for Him within your mind. Salvation comes from this one Self through Him Who is the bridge between your mind and It. Wait patiently, and let Him speak to you about your Self, and what your mind can do, restored to It and free to serve Its Will.

Begin with saying this:

*Salvation comes from my one Self.*
*Its thoughts are mine to use.*

Then seek Its thoughts, and claim them as your own.
These are your own real thoughts you have denied,
and let your mind go wandering in a world
of dreams, to find illusions in their place.
Here are your thoughts, the only ones you have.
Salvation is among them; find it there.

If you succeed, the thoughts that come to you
will tell you you are saved, and that your mind
has found the function that it sought to lose.
Your Self will welcome it and give it peace.
Restored in strength, it will again flow out
from spirit to the spirit in all things
created by the Spirit as Itself.
Your mind will bless all things. Confusion done,
you are restored, for you have found your Self.

Your Self knows that you cannot fail today.

Perhaps your mind remains uncertain yet
a little while. Be not dismayed by this.
The joy your Self experiences It
will save for you, and it will yet be yours
in full awareness. Every time you spend
five minutes of the hour seeking Him
Who joins your mind and Self, you offer Him
another treasure to be kept for you.

Each time today you tell your frantic mind
salvation comes from your one Self, you lay
another treasure in your growing store.
And all of it is given everyone
who asks for it, and will accept the gift.
Think, then, how much is given unto you
to give this day, that it be given you!

## LESSON 97

**I am spirit.**

Today's idea identifies you with your one Self. It accepts no split identity, nor tries to weave opposing factors into unity. It simply states the truth. Practice this truth today as often as you can, for it will bring your mind from conflict to the quiet fields of peace. No chill of fear can enter, for your mind has been absolved from madness, letting go illusions of a split identity.

We state again the truth about your Self, the holy Son of God Who rests in you; Whose mind has been restored to sanity. You are the spirit lovingly endowed with all your Father's Love and peace and joy. You are the spirit which completes Himself, and shares His function as Creator. He is with you always, as you are with Him.

Today we try to bring reality still closer to your mind. Each time you practice, awareness is brought a little nearer at least; sometimes a thousand years or more are saved. The minutes which you give are multiplied over and over, for the miracle makes use of time, but is not ruled by it. Salvation is a miracle, the first and last; the first that is the last, for it is one.

You are the spirit in whose mind abides
the miracle in which all time stands still;
the miracle in which a minute spent
in using these ideas becomes a time
that has no limit and that has no end.
Give, then, these minutes willingly, and count
on Him Who promised to lay timelessness
beside them. He will offer all His strength
to every little effort that you make.
Give Him the minutes which He needs today,
to help you understand with Him you are
the spirit that abides in Him, and that
calls through His Voice to every living thing;
offers His sight to everyone who asks;
replaces error with the simple truth.

The Holy Spirit will be glad to take
five minutes of each hour from your hands,
and carry them around this aching world
where pain and misery appear to rule.
He will not overlook one open mind
that will accept the healing gifts they bring,
and He will lay them everywhere He knows
they will be welcome. And they will increase
in healing power each time someone accepts
them as his thoughts, and uses them to heal.

Thus will each gift to Him be multiplied
a thousandfold and tens of thousands more.
And when it is returned to you, it will
surpass in might the little gift you gave
as much as does the radiance of the sun
outshine the tiny gleam a firefly
makes an uncertain moment and goes out.
The steady brilliance of this light remains
and leads you out of darkness, nor will you
be able to forget the way again.

Begin these happy exercises with
the words the Holy Spirit speaks to you,
and let them echo round the world through Him:

*Spirit am I, a holy Son of God,*
*free of all limits, safe and healed and whole,*
*free to forgive, and free to save the world.*

Expressed through you, the Holy Spirit will
accept this gift that you received of Him,
increase its power and give it back to you.

Offer each practice period today
gladly to Him. And He will speak to you,
reminding you that you are spirit, one
with Him and God, your brothers and your Self.
Listen for His assurance every time
you speak the words He offers you today,
and let Him tell your mind that they are true.
Use them against temptation, and escape
its sorry consequences if you yield
to the belief that you are something else.
The Holy Spirit gives you peace today.
Receive His words, and offer them to Him.

# LESSON 98

**I will accept my part in God's plan for salvation.**

Today is a day of special dedication.
We take a stand on but one side today.
We side with truth and let illusions go.
We will not vacillate between the two,
but take a firm position with the One.
We dedicate ourselves to truth today,
and to salvation as God planned it be.
We will not argue it is something else.
We will not seek for it where it is not.
In gladness we accept it as it is,
and take the part assigned to us by God.

How happy to be certain! All our doubts
we lay aside today, and take our stand
with certainty of purpose, and with thanks
that doubt is gone and surety has come.
We have a mighty purpose to fulfill,
and have been given everything we need
with which to reach the goal. Not one mistake
stands in our way. For we have been absolved
from errors. All our sins are washed away
by realizing they were but mistakes.

The guiltless have no fear, for they are safe
and recognize their safety. They do not
appeal to magic, nor invent escapes
from fancied threats without reality.
They rest in quiet certainty that they
will do what it is given them to do.
They do not doubt their own ability
because they know their function will be filled
completely in the perfect time and place.
They took the stand which we will take today,
that we may share their certainty and thus
increase it by accepting it ourselves.

They will be with us; all who took the stand
we take today will gladly offer us
all that they learned and every gain they made.
Those still uncertain, too, will join with us,
and, borrowing our certainty, will make
it stronger still. While those as yet unborn
will hear the call we heard, and answer it
when they have come to make their choice again.
We do not choose but for ourselves today.

Is it not worth five minutes of your time
each hour to be able to accept
the happiness that God has given you?
Is it not worth five minutes hourly
to recognize your special function here?
Is not five minutes but a small request
to make in terms of gaining a reward
so great it has no measure? You have made
a thousand losing bargains at the least.

Here is an offer guaranteeing you
your full release from pain of every kind,
and joy the world does not contain. You can
exchange a little of your time for peace
of mind and certainty of purpose, with
the promise of complete success. And since
time has no meaning, you are being asked
for nothing in return for everything.
Here is a bargain that you cannot lose.
And what you gain is limitless indeed!

Each hour today give Him your tiny gift
of but five minutes. He will give the words
you use in practicing today's idea
the deep conviction and the certainty
you lack. His words will join with yours, and make
each repetition of today's idea
a total dedication, made in faith
as perfect and as sure as His in you.
His confidence in you will bring the light
to all the words you say, and you will go
beyond their sound to what they really mean.
Today you practice with Him, as you say:

*I will accept my part in God's plan for salvation.*

In each five minutes that you spend with Him,
He will accept your words and give them back
to you all bright with faith and confidence
so strong and steady they will light the world
with hope and gladness. Do not lose one chance
to be the glad receiver of His gifts,
that you may give them to the world today.

Give Him the words, and He will do the rest.
He will enable you to understand
your special function. He will open up

the way to happiness, and peace and trust
will be His gifts; His answer to your words.
He will respond with all His faith and joy
and certainty that what you say is true.
And you will have conviction then of Him
Who knows the function that you have on earth
as well as Heaven. He will be with you
each practice period you share with Him,
exchanging every instant of the time
you offer Him for timelessness and peace.

Throughout the hour, let your time be spent
in happy preparation for the next
five minutes you will spend again with Him.
Repeat today's idea while you wait
for the glad time to come to you again.
Repeat it often, and do not forget
each time you do so, you have let your mind
be readied for the happy time to come.

And when the hour goes and He is there
once more to spend a little time with you,
be thankful and lay down all earthly tasks,
all little thoughts and limited ideas,
and spend a happy time again with Him.
Tell Him once more that you accept the part
that He would have you take and help you fill,
and He will make you sure you want this choice,
which He has made with you and you with Him.

# LESSON 99

## Salvation is my only function here.

Salvation and forgiveness are the same. They both imply that something has gone wrong; something to be saved from, forgiven for; something amiss that needs corrective change; something apart or different from the Will of God. Thus do both terms imply a thing impossible but yet which has occurred, resulting in a state of conflict seen between what is and what could never be.

Truth and illusions both are equal now, for both have happened. The impossible becomes the thing you need forgiveness for, salvation from. Salvation now becomes the borderland between the truth and the illusion. It reflects the truth because it is the means by which you can escape illusions. Yet it is not yet the truth because it undoes what was never done.

How could there be a meeting place at all where earth and Heaven can be reconciled within a mind where both of them exist? The mind that sees illusions thinks them real. They have existence in that they are thoughts. And yet they are not real, because the mind that thinks these thoughts is separate from God.

What joins the separated mind and thoughts with Mind and Thought which are forever one? What plan could hold the truth inviolate, yet recognize the need illusions bring, and offer means by which they are undone without attack and with no touch of pain? What but a Thought of God could be this plan, by which the never done is overlooked, and sins forgotten which were never real?

The Holy Spirit holds this plan of God exactly as it was received of Him within the Mind of God and in your own. It is apart from time in that its Source is timeless. Yet it operates in time, because of your belief that time is real. Unshaken does the Holy Spirit look on what you see; on sin and pain and death, on grief and separation and on loss. Yet does He know one thing must still be true; God is still Love, and this is not His Will.

This is the Thought that brings illusions to the truth, and sees them as appearances behind which is the changeless and the sure. This is the Thought that saves and that forgives, because it lays no faith in what is not created by the only Source it knows. This is the Thought whose function is to save by giving you its function as your own. Salvation is your function, with the One to Whom the plan was given. Now are you entrusted with this plan, along with Him. He has one answer to appearances; regardless of their form, their size, their depth or any attribute they seem to have:

*Salvation is my only function here.*
*God still is Love, and this is not His Will.*

You who will yet work miracles, be sure you practice well the idea for today. Try to perceive the strength in what you say, for these are words in which your freedom lies. Your Father loves you. All the world of pain is not His Will. Forgive yourself the thought He wanted this for you. Then let the Thought with which He has replaced all your mistakes enter the darkened places of your mind that thought the thoughts that never were His Will.

This part belongs to God, as does the rest. It does not think its solitary thoughts, and make them real by hiding them from Him. Let in the light, and you will look upon no obstacle to what He wills for you. Open your secrets to His kindly light, and see how bright this light still shines in you.

Practice His Thought today, and let His light seek out and lighten up all darkened spots, and shine through them to join them to the rest. It is God's Will your mind be one with His.

It is God's Will that He has but one Son.
It is God's Will that His one Son is you.
Think of these things in practicing today,
and start the lesson that we learn today
with this instruction in the way of truth:

*Salvation is my only function here.*
*Salvation and forgiveness are the same.*

Then turn to Him Who shares your function here,
and let Him teach you what you need to learn
to lay all fear aside, and know your Self
as love which has no opposite in you.

Forgive all thoughts which would oppose the truth
of your completion, unity and peace.
You cannot lose the gifts your Father gave.
You do not want to be another self.
You have no function that is not of God.
Forgive yourself the one you think you made.
Forgiveness and salvation are the same.
Forgive what you have made and you are saved.

There is a special message for today
which has the power to remove all forms
of doubt and fear forever from your mind.
If you are tempted to believe them true,
remember that appearances can not
withstand the truth these mighty words contain:

*Salvation is my only function here.*
*God still is Love, and this is not His Will.*

Your only function tells you you are one.
Remind yourself of this between the times
you give five minutes to be shared with Him
Who shares God's plan with you. Remind yourself:

*Salvation is my only function here.*

Thus do you lay forgiveness on your mind
and let all fear be gently laid aside,
that love may find its rightful place in you
and show you that you are the Son of God.

# LESSON 100

**My part is essential to God's plan for salvation.**

Just as God's Son completes his Father, so your part in it completes your Father's plan. Salvation must reverse the mad belief in separate thoughts and separate bodies, which lead separate lives and go their separate ways. One function shared by separate minds unites them in one purpose, for each one of them is equally essential to them all.

God's Will for you is perfect happiness. Why should you choose to go against His Will? The part that He has saved for you to take in working out His plan is given you that you might be restored to what He wills. This part is as essential to His plan as to your happiness. Your joy must be complete to let His plan be understood by those to whom He sends you. They will see their function in your shining face, and hear God calling to them in your happy laugh.

You are indeed essential to God's plan. Without your joy, His joy is incomplete. Without your smile, the world cannot be saved. While you are sad, the light that God Himself appointed as the means to save the world is dim and lusterless, and no one laughs because all laughter can but echo yours.

You are indeed essential to God's plan. Just as your light increases every light that shines in Heaven, so your joy on earth calls to all minds to let their sorrows go, and take their place beside you in God's plan. God's messengers are joyous, and their joy heals sorrow and despair. They are the proof that God wills perfect happiness for all who will accept their Father's gifts as theirs.

We will not let ourselves be sad today. For if we do, we fail to take the part that is essential to God's plan, as well as to our vision. Sadness is the sign that you would play another part, instead of what has been assigned to you by God. Thus do you fail to show the world how great the happiness He wills for you. And so you do not recognize that it is yours.

Today we will attempt to understand joy is our function here. If you are sad, your part is unfulfilled, and all the world is thus deprived of joy, along with you. God asks you to be happy, so the world can see how much He loves His Son, and wills no sorrow rises to abate his joy; no fear besets him to disturb his peace. You are God's messenger today. You bring His happiness to all you look upon; His peace to everyone who looks on you and sees His message in your happy face.

We will prepare ourselves for this today, in our five-minute practice periods, by feeling happiness arise in us according to our Father's Will and ours. Begin the exercises with the thought today's idea contains. Then realize your part is to be happy. Only this is asked of you or anyone who wants to take his place among God's messengers. Think what this means. You have indeed been wrong in your belief that sacrifice is asked. You but receive according to God's plan, and never lose or sacrifice or die.

Now let us try to find that joy that proves to us and all the world God's Will for us. It is your function that you find it here, and that you find it now. For this you came. Let this one be the day that you succeed! Look deep within you, undismayed by all the little thoughts and foolish goals you pass as you ascend to meet the Christ in you.

He will be there. And you can reach Him now. What could you rather look upon in place of Him Who waits that you may look on Him? What little thought has power to hold you back? What foolish goal can keep you from success when He Who calls to you is God Himself?

He will be there. You are essential to

His plan. You are His messenger today.
And you must find what He would have you give.
Do not forget the idea for today
between your hourly practice periods.
It is your Self Who calls to you today.

And it is Him you answer, every time
you tell yourself you are essential to
God's plan for the salvation of the world.

# LESSON 101

**God's Will for me is perfect happiness.**

Today we will continue with the theme of happiness. This is a key idea in understanding what salvation means. You still believe it asks for suffering as penance for your "sins." This is not so. Yet you must think it so while you believe that sin is real, and that God's Son can sin.

If sin is real, then punishment is just and cannot be escaped. Salvation thus cannot be purchased but through suffering. If sin is real, then happiness must be illusion, for they cannot both be true. The sinful warrant only death and pain, and it is this they ask for. For they know it waits for them, and it will seek them out and find them somewhere, sometime, in some form that evens the account they owe to God. They would escape Him in their fear. And yet He will pursue, and they can not escape.

If sin is real, salvation must be pain. Pain is the cost of sin, and suffering can never be escaped, if sin is real. Salvation must be feared, for it will kill, but slowly, taking everything away before it grants the welcome boon of death to victims who are little more than bones before salvation is appeased. Its wrath is boundless, merciless, but wholly just.

Who would seek out such savage punishment? Who would not flee salvation, and attempt in every way he can to drown the Voice Which offers it to him? Why would he try to listen and accept Its offering? If sin is real, its offering is death, and meted out in cruel form to match the vicious wishes in which sin is born. If sin is real, salvation has become your bitter enemy, the curse of God upon you who have crucified His Son.

You need the practice periods today. The exercises teach sin is not real, and all that you believe must come from sin will never happen, for it has no cause. Accept Atonement with an open mind, which cherishes no lingering belief that you have made a devil of God's Son. There is no sin. We practice with this thought as often as we can today, because it is the basis for today's idea.

God's Will for you is perfect happiness because there is no sin, and suffering is causeless. Joy is just, and pain is but the sign you have misunderstood yourself. Fear not the Will of God. But turn to it in confidence that it will set you free from all the consequences sin has wrought in feverish imagination. Say:

*God's Will for me is perfect happiness.*
*There is no sin; it has no consequence.*

So should you start your practice periods, and then attempt again to find the joy these thoughts will introduce into your mind.

Give these five minutes gladly, to remove the heavy load you lay upon yourself with the insane belief that sin is real. Today escape from madness. You are set on freedom's road, and now today's idea brings wings to speed you on, and hope to go still faster to the waiting goal of peace. There is no sin. Remember this today, and tell yourself as often as you can:

*God's Will for me is perfect happiness.*
*This is the truth, because there is no sin.*

## LESSON 102

**I share God's Will for happiness for me.**

You do not want to suffer. You may think it buys you something, and may still believe a little that it buys you what you want. Yet this belief is surely shaken now, at least enough to let you question it, and to suspect it really makes no sense. It has not gone as yet, but lacks the roots that once secured it tightly to the dark and hidden secret places of your mind.

Today we try to loose its weakened hold still further, and to realize that pain is purposeless, without a cause and with no power to accomplish anything. It cannot purchase anything at all. It offers nothing, and does not exist. And everything you think it offers you is lacking in existence, like itself. You have been slave to nothing. Be you free today to join the happy Will of God.

For several days we will continue to devote our periods of practicing to exercises planned to help you reach the happiness God's Will has placed in you. Here is your home, and here your safety is. Here is your peace, and here there is no fear. Here is salvation. Here is rest at last.

Begin your practice periods today with this acceptance of God's Will for you:

*I share God's Will for happiness for me, and I accept it as my function now.*

Then seek this function deep within your mind, for it is there, awaiting but your choice. You cannot fail to find it when you learn it is your choice, and that you share God's Will.

Be happy, for your only function here is happiness. You have no need to be less loving to God's Son than He Whose Love created him as loving as Himself. Besides these hourly five-minute rests, pause frequently today, to tell yourself that you have now accepted happiness as your one function. And be sure that you are joining with God's Will in doing this.

# LESSON 103

### God, being Love, is also happiness.

Happiness is an attribute of love.
It cannot be apart from it. Nor can
it be experienced where love is not.
Love has no limits, being everywhere.
And therefore joy is everywhere as well.
Yet can the mind deny that this is so,
believing there are gaps in love where sin
can enter, bringing pain instead of joy.
This strange belief would limit happiness
by redefining love as limited,
and introducing opposition in
what has no limit and no opposite.

Fear is associated then with love,
and its results become the heritage
of minds that think what they have made is real.
These images, with no reality
in truth, bear witness to the fear of God,
forgetting being Love, He must be joy.
This basic error we will try again
to bring to truth today, and teach ourselves:

*God, being Love, is also happiness.*
*To fear Him is to be afraid of joy.*

Begin your periods of practicing
today with this association, which
corrects the false belief that God is fear.
It also emphasizes happiness
belongs to you, because of what He is

Allow this one correction to be placed
within your mind each waking hour today.
Then welcome all the happiness it brings
as truth replaces fear, and joy becomes
what you expect to take the place of pain.
God, being Love, it will be given you.
Bolster this expectation frequently
throughout the day, and quiet all your fears
with this assurance, kind and wholly true:

*God, being Love, is also happiness.*
*And it is happiness I seek today.*
*I cannot fail, because I seek the truth.*

# LESSON 104

**I seek but what belongs to me in truth.**

Today's idea continues with the thought
that joy and peace are not but idle dreams.
They are your right, because of what you are.
They come to you from God, Who cannot fail
to give you what He wills. Yet must there be
a place made ready to receive His gifts.
They are not welcomed gladly by a mind
that has instead received the gifts it made
where His belong, as substitutes for them.

Today we would remove all meaningless
and self-made gifts which we have placed upon
the holy altar where God's gifts belong.
His are the gifts that are our own in truth.
His are the gifts that we inherited
before time was, and that will still be ours
when time has passed into eternity.
His are the gifts that are within us now,
for they are timeless. And we need not wait
to have them. They belong to us today.

Therefore, we chooseto have them now, and know,
in choosing them in place of what we made,
we but unite our will with what God wills,
and recognize the same as being one.
Our longer practice periods today,
the hourly five minutes given truth
for your salvation, should begin with this:

*I seek but what belongs to me in truth,*
*And joy and peace are my inheritance.*

Then lay aside the conflicts of the world
that offer other gifts and other goals
made of illusions, witnessed to by them,
and sought for only in a world of dreams.

All this we lay aside, and seek instead
that which is truly ours, as we ask
to recognize what God has given us.
We clear a holy place within our minds
before His altar, where His gifts of peace
and joy are welcome, and to which we come
to find what has been given us by Him.
We come in confidence today, aware
that what belongs to us in truth is what
He gives. And we would wish for nothing else,
for nothing else belongs to us in truth.

So do we clear the way for Him today
by simply recognizing that His Will
is done already, and that joy and peace
belong to us as His eternal gifts.
We will not let ourselves lose sight of them
between the times we come to seek for them
where He has laid them. This reminder will
we bring to mind as often as we can:

*I seek but what belongs to me in truth.*
*God's gifts of joy and peace are all I want.*

# LESSON 105

### God's peace and joy are mine.

God's peace and joy are yours. Today we will
accept them, knowing they belong to us.
And we will try to understand these gifts
increase as we receive them. They are not
like to the gifts the world can give, in which
the giver loses as he gives the gift;
the taker is the richer by his loss.
Such are not gifts, but bargains made with guilt.
The truly given gift entails no loss.
It is impossible that one can gain
because another loses. This implies
a limit and an insufficiency.

No gift is given thus. Such "gifts" are but
a bid for a more valuable return;
a loan with interest to be paid in full;
a temporary lending, meant to be
a pledge of debt to be repaid with more
than was received by him who took the gift.
This strange distortion of what giving means
pervades all levels of the world you see.
It strips all meaning from the gifts you give,
and leaves you nothing in the ones you take.

A major learning goal this course has set
is to reverse your view of giving, so
you can receive. For giving has become
a source of fear, and so you would avoid
the only means by which you can receive.
Accept God's peace and joy, and you will learn
a different way of looking at a gift.
God's gifts will never lessen when they are
given away. They but increase thereby.

As Heaven's peace and joy intensify
when you accept them as God's gift to you,
so does the joy of your Creator grow
when you accept His joy and peace as yours.
True giving is creation. It extends
the limitless to the unlimited,
eternity to timelessness, and love
unto itself. It adds to all that is
complete already, not in simple terms
of adding more, for that implies that it
was less before. It adds by letting what
cannot contain itself fulfill its aim
of giving everything it has away,
securing it forever for itself.

Today accept God's peace and joy as yours.
Let Him complete Himself as He defines
completion. You will understand that what
completes Him must complete His Son as well.
He cannot give through loss. No more can you.
Receive His gift of joy and peace today,
and He will thank you for your gift to Him.

Today our practice periods will start
a little differently. Begin today
by thinking of those brothers who have been
denied by you the peace and joy that are
their right under the equal laws of God.
Here you denied them to yourself. And here
you must return to claim them as your own.

Think of your "enemies" a little while,
and tell each one, as he occurs to you:

*My brother, peace and joy I offer you,
That I may have God's peace and joy as mine.*

Thus you prepare yourself to recognize
God's gifts to you, and let your mind be free
of all that would prevent success today.
Now are you ready to accept the gift
of peace and joy that God has given you.
Now are you ready to experience
the joy and peace you have denied yourself.
Now you can say, "God's peace and joy are mine,"
for you have given what you would receive.

You must succeed today, if you prepare
your mind as we suggest. For you have let
all bars to peace and joy be lifted up,
and what is yours can come to you at last.
So tell yourself, "God's peace and joy are mine,"
and close your eyes a while, and let His Voice
assure you that the words you speak are true.

Spend your five minutes thus with Him each time
you can today, but do not think that less
is worthless when you cannot give Him more.
At least remember hourly to say

the words which call to Him to give you what
He wills to give, and wills you to receive.
Determine not to interfere today
with what He wills. And if a brother seems
to tempt you to deny God's gift to him,
see it as but another chance to let
yourself receive the gifts of God as yours.
Then bless your brother thankfully, and say:

*My brother, peace and joy I offer you,*
*That I may have God's peace and joy as mine.*

## LESSON 106

**Let me be still and listen to the truth.**

If you will lay aside the ego's voice, however loudly it may seem to call, if you will not accept its petty gifts that give you nothing that you really want; if you will listen with an open mind, that has not told you what salvation is; then you will hear the mighty Voice of truth, quiet in power, strong in stillness, and completely certain in Its messages.

Listen, and hear your Father speak to you through His appointed Voice, Which silences the thunder of the meaningless, and shows the way to peace to those who cannot see. Be still today and listen to the truth. Be not deceived by voices of the dead, which tell you they have found the source of life and offer it to you for your belief. Attend them not, but listen to the truth.

Be not afraid today to circumvent the voices of the world. Walk lightly past their meaningless persuasion. Hear them not. Be still today and listen to the truth. Go past all things which do not speak of Him Who holds your happiness within His hand, held out to you in welcome and in love. Hear only Him today, and do not wait to reach Him longer. Hear one Voice today.

Today the promise of God's Word is kept. Hear and be silent. He would speak to you. He comes with miracles a thousand times as happy and as wonderful as those you ever dreamed or wished for in your dreams. His miracles are true. They will not fade when dreaming ends. They end the dream instead; and last forever, for they come from God to His dear Son, whose other name is you. Prepare yourself for miracles today. Today allow your Father's ancient pledge to you and all your brothers to be kept.

Hear Him today, and listen to the Word which lifts the veil that lies upon the earth, and wakes all those who sleep and cannot see. God calls to them through you. He needs your voice to speak to them, for who could reach God's Son except his Father, calling through your Self? Hear Him today, and offer Him your voice to speak to all the multitude who wait to hear the Word that He will speak today.

Be ready for salvation. It is here, and will today be given unto you. And you will learn your function from the One Who chose it in your Father's Name for you. Listen today, and you will hear a Voice Which will resound throughout the world through you. The Bringer of all miracles has need that you receive them first, and thus become the joyous giver of what you received.

Thus does salvation start and thus it ends; when everything is yours and everything is given away, it will remain with you forever. And the lesson has been learned. Today we practice giving, not the way you understand it now, but as it is. Each hour's exercises should begin with this request for your enlightenment:

*I will be still and listen to the truth.*
*What does it mean to give and to receive?*

Ask and expect an answer. Your request is one whose answer has been waiting long to be received by you. It will begin the ministry for which you came, and which will free the world from thinking giving is a way to lose. And so the world becomes ready to understand and to receive.

Be still and listen to the truth today. For each five minutes spent in listening, a thousand minds are opened to the truth and they will hear the holy Word you hear. And when the hour is past, you will again release a thousand more who pause to ask that truth be given them, along with you.

Today the holy Word of God is kept through your receiving it to give away, so you can teach the world what giving means

by listening and learning it of Him.
Do not forget today to reinforce
your choice to hear and to receive the Word
by this reminder, given to yourself
as often as is possible today:

*Let me be still and listen to the truth.*
*I am the messenger of God today,*
*My voice is His, to give what I receive.*

# LESSON 107

## Truth will correct all errors in my mind.

What can correct illusions but the truth?
And what are errors but illusions that
remain unrecognized for what they are?
Where truth has entered errors disappear.
They merely vanish, leaving not a trace
by which to be remembered. They are gone
because, without belief, they have no life.
And so they disappear to nothingness,
returning whence they came. From dust to dust
they come and go, for only truth remains.

Can you imagine what a state of mind
without illusions is? How it would feel?
Try to remember when there was a time,
perhaps a minute, maybe even less
when nothing came to interrupt your peace;
when you were certain you were loved and safe.
Then try to picture what it would be like
to have that moment be extended to
the end of time and to eternity.
Then let the sense of quiet that you felt
be multiplied a hundred times, and then
be multiplied another hundred more.

And now you have a hint, not more than just
the faintest intimation of the state
your mind will rest in when the truth has come.
Without illusions there could be no fear,
no doubt and no attack. When truth has come
all pain is over, for there is no room
for transitory thoughts and dead ideas
to linger in your mind. Truth occupies
your mind completely, liberating you
from all beliefs in the ephemeral.
They have no place because the truth has come,
and they are nowhere. They can not be found,
for truth is everywhere forever, now.

When truth has come it does not stay a while,
to disappear or change to something else.
It does not shift and alter in its form,
nor come and go and go and come again.
It stays exactly as it always was,
to be depended on in every need,
and trusted with a perfect trust in all
the seeming difficulties and the doubts
that the appearances the world presents
engender. They will merely blow away,
when truth corrects the errors in your mind.

When truth has come it harbors in its wings
the gift of perfect constancy, and love
which does not falter in the face of pain,
but looks beyond it, steadily and sure.
Here is the gift of healing, for the truth
needs no defense, and therefore no attack
is possible. Illusions can be brought
to truth to be corrected. But the truth
stands far beyond illusions, and can not
be brought to them to turn them into truth.

Truth does not come and go nor shift nor change,
in this appearance now and then in that,
evading capture and escaping grasp.
It does not hide. It stands in open light,
in obvious accessibility.
It is impossible that anyone
could seek it truly, and would not succeed.
Today belongs to truth. Give truth its due,
and it will give you yours. You were not meant
to suffer and to die. Your Father wills
these dreams be gone. Let truth correct them all.

We do not ask for what we do not have.
We merely ask for what belongs to us,
that we may recognize it as our own.
Today we practice on the happy note
of certainty that has been born of truth.
The shaky and unsteady footsteps of
illusion are not our approach today.
We are as certain of success as we
are sure we live and hope and breathe and think.
We do not doubt we walk with truth today,
and count on it to enter into all
the exercises that we do this day.

Begin by asking Him Who goes with you
upon this undertaking that He be
in your awareness as you go with Him.
You are not made of flesh and blood and bone,
but were created by the selfsame Thought
which gave the gift of life to Him as well.
He is your Brother, and so like to you

your Father knows that you are both the same.
It is your Self you ask to go with you,
and how could He be absent where you are?

Truth will correct all errors in your mind
which tell you you could be apart from Him.
You speak to Him today, and make your pledge
to let His function be fulfilled through you.
To share His function is to share His joy.
His confidence is with you, as you say:

*Truth will correct all errors in my mind,*
*And I will rest in Him Who is my Self.*

Then let Him lead you gently to the truth,
which will envelop you and give you peace
so deep and tranquil that you will return
to the familiar world reluctantly.

And yet you will be glad to look again
upon this world. For you will bring with you
the promise of the changes which the truth
that goes with you will carry to the world.
They will increase with every gift you give
of five small minutes, and the errors that
surround the world will be corrected as
you let them be corrected in your mind.

Do not forget your function for today.
Each time you tell yourself with confidence,
"Truth will correct all errors in my mind,"
you speak for all the world and Him Who would
release the world, as He would set you free.

## LESSON 108

**To give and to receive are one in truth.**

Vision depends upon today's idea. The light is in it, for it reconciles all seeming opposites. And what is light except the resolution, born of peace, of all your conflicts and mistaken thoughts into one concept which is wholly true? Even that one will disappear, because the Thought behind it will appear instead to take its place. And now you are at peace forever, for the dream is over then.

True light that makes true vision possible is not the light the body's eyes behold. It is a state of mind that has become so unified that darkness cannot be perceived at all. And thus what is the same is seen as one, while what is not the same remains unnoticed, for it is not there.

This is the light that shows no opposites, and vision, being healed, has power to heal. This is the light that brings your peace of mind to other minds, to share it and be glad that they are one with you and with themselves. This is the light that heals because it brings single perception, based upon one frame of reference, from which one meaning comes.

Here are both giving and receiving seen as different aspects of one Thought whose truth does not depend on which is seen as first, nor which appears to be in second place. Here it is understood that both occur together, that the Thought remain complete. And in this understanding is the base on which all opposites are reconciled, because they are perceived from the same frame of reference which unifies this Thought.

One thought, completely unified, will serve to unify all thought. This is the same as saying one correction will suffice for all correction, or that to forgive one brother wholly is enough to bring salvation to all minds. For these are but some special cases of one law which holds for every kind of learning, if it be directed by the One Who knows the truth.

To learn that giving and receiving are the same has special usefulness, because it can be tried so easily and seen as true. And when this special case has proved it always works, in every circumstance where it is tried, the thought behind it can be generalized to other areas of doubt and double vision. And from there it will extend, and finally arrive at the one Thought which underlies them all.

Today we practice with the special case of giving and receiving. We will use this simple lesson in the obvious because it has results we cannot miss. To give is to receive. Today we will attempt to offer peace to everyone, and see how quickly peace returns to us. Light is tranquility, and in that peace is vision given us, and we can see.

So we begin the practice periods with the instruction for today, and say:

*To give and to receive are one in truth.*
*I will receive what I am giving now.*

Then close your eyes, and for five minutes think of what you would hold out to everyone, to have it yours. You might, for instance, say:

*To everyone I offer quietness.*
*To everyone I offer peace of mind.*
*To everyone I offer gentleness.*

Say each one slowly and then pause a while, expecting to receive the gift you gave. And it will come to you in the amount in which you gave it. You will find you have exact return, for that is what you asked. It might be helpful, too, to think of one to whom to give your gifts. He represents the others, and through him you give to all.

Our very simple lesson for today will teach you much. Effect and cause will be

far better understood from this time on,
and we will make much faster progress now.
Think of the exercises for today

as quick advances in your learning, made
still faster and more sure each time you say,
"To give and to receive are one in truth."

# LESSON 109

## I rest in God.

We ask for rest today, and quietness unshaken by the world's appearances. We ask for peace and stillness, in the midst of all the turmoil born of clashing dreams. We ask for safety and for happiness, although we seem to look on danger and on sorrow. And we have the thought that will answer our asking with what we request.

"I rest in God." This thought will bring to you the rest and quiet, peace and stillness, and the safety and the happiness you seek. "I rest in God." This thought has power to wake the sleeping truth in you, whose vision sees beyond appearances to that same truth in everyone and everything there is. Here is the end of suffering for all the world, and everyone who ever came and yet will come to linger for a while. Here is the thought in which the Son of God is born again, to recognize himself.

"I rest in God." Completely undismayed, this thought will carry you through storms and strife, past misery and pain, past loss and death, and onward to the certainty of God. There is no suffering it cannot heal. There is no problem that it cannot solve. And no appearance but will turn to truth before the eyes of you who rest in God.

This is the day of peace. You rest in God, and while the world is torn by winds of hate your rest remains completely undisturbed. Yours is the rest of truth. Appearances cannot intrude on you. You call to all to join you in your rest, and they will hear and come to you because you rest in God. They will not hear another voice than yours because you gave your voice to God, and now you rest in Him and let Him speak through you.

In Him you have no cares and no concerns, no burdens, no anxiety, no pain, no fear of future and no past regrets. In timelessness you rest, while time goes by without its touch upon you, for your rest can never change in any way at all. You rest today. And as you close your eyes, sink into stillness. Let these periods of rest and respite reassure your mind that all its frantic fantasies were but the dreams of fever that has passed away. Let it be still and thankfully accept its healing. No more fearful dreams will come, now that you rest in God. Take time today to slip away from dreams and into peace.

Each hour that you take your rest today, a tired mind is suddenly made glad, a bird with broken wings begins to sing, a stream long dry begins to flow again. The world is born again each time you rest, and hourly remember that you came to bring the peace of God into the world, that it might take its rest along with you.

With each five minutes that you rest today, the world is nearer waking. And the time when rest will be the only thing there is comes closer to all worn and tired minds, too weary now to go their way alone. And they will hear the bird begin to sing and see the stream begin to flow again, with hope reborn and energy restored to walk with lightened steps along the road that suddenly seems easy as they go.

You rest within the peace of God today, and call upon your brothers from your rest to draw them to their rest, along with you. You will be faithful to your trust today, forgetting no one, bringing everyone into the boundless circle of your peace, the holy sanctuary where you rest. Open the temple doors and let them come from far across the world, and near as well; your distant brothers and your closest friends; bid them all enter here and rest with you.

You rest within the peace of God today, quiet and unafraid. Each brother comes to take his rest, and offer it to you. We rest together here, for thus our rest

is made complete, and what we give today
we have received already. Time is not
the guardian of what we give today.
We give to those unborn and those passed by,
to every Thought of God, and to the Mind
in which these Thoughts were born
and where they rest.
And we remind them of their resting place
each time we tell ourselves, "I rest in God."

## LESSON 110

### I AM AS GOD CREATED ME.

We will repeat today's idea from time to time. For this one thought would be enough to save you and the world, if you believed that it is true. Its truth would mean that you have made no changes in yourself that have reality, nor changed the universe so that what God created was replaced by fear and evil, misery and death. If you remain as God created you fear has no meaning, evil is not real, and misery and death do not exist.

Today's idea is therefore all you need to let complete correction heal your mind, and give you perfect vision that will heal all the mistakes that any mind has made at any time or place. It is enough to heal the past and make the future free. It is enough to let the present be accepted as it is. It is enough to let time be the means for all the world to learn escape from time, and every change that time appears to bring in passing by.

If you remain as God created you, appearances cannot replace the truth, health cannot turn to sickness, nor can death be substitute for life, or fear for love. All this has not occurred, if you remain as God created you. You need no thought but just this one, to let redemption come to light the world and free it from the past.

In this one thought is all the past undone; the present saved to quietly extend into a timeless future. If you are as God created you, then there has been no separation of your mind from His, no split between your mind and other minds, and only unity within your own.

The healing power of today's idea is limitless. It is the birthplace of all miracles, the great restorer of the truth to the awareness of the world. Practice today's idea with gratitude. This is the truth that comes to set you free. This is the truth that God has promised you. This is the Word in which all sorrow ends.

For your five-minute practice periods, begin with this quotation from the text:

*I am as God created me. His Son can suffer nothing. And I am His Son.*

Then, with this statement firmly in your mind, try to discover in your mind the Self Who is the holy Son of God Himself.

Seek Him within you who is Christ in you, the Son of God and brother to the world; the Savior Who has been forever saved, with power to save whoever touches Him, however lightly, asking for the Word that tells him he is brother unto Him.

You are as God created you. Today honor your Self. Let graven images you made to be the Son of God instead of what he is be worshipped not today. Deep in your mind the holy Christ in you is waiting your acknowledgment as you. And you are lost and do not know yourself while He is unacknowledged and unknown.

Seek Him today, and find Him. He will be your Savior from all idols you have made. For when you find Him, you will understand how worthless are your idols, and how false the images which you believed were you. Today we make a great advance to truth by letting idols go, and opening our hands and hearts and minds to God today.

We will remember Him throughout the day
with thankful hearts and loving thoughts for all
who meet with us today. For it is thus
that we remember Him. And we will say,
that we may be reminded of His Son,
our holy Self, the Christ in each of us:

*I am as God created me.*

Let us declare this truth as often as we can.
This is the Word of God that sets you free.
This is the key that opens up the gate
of Heaven, and that lets you enter in
the peace of God and His eternity.

# REVIEW III

**Introduction**

Our next review begins today. We will review two recent lessons every day for ten successive days of practicing. We will observe a special format for these practice periods, that you are urged to follow just as closely as you can.

We understand, of course, that it may be impossible for you to undertake what is suggested here as optimal each day and every hour of the day. Learning will not be hampered when you miss a practice period because it is impossible at the appointed time. Nor is it necessary that you make excessive efforts to be sure that you catch up in terms of numbers. Rituals are not our aim, and would defeat our goal.

But learning will be hampered when you skip a practice period because you are unwilling to devote the time to it that you are asked to give. Do not deceive yourself in this. Unwillingness can be most carefully concealed behind a cloak of situations you cannot control. Learn to distinguish situations that are poorly suited to your practicing from those that you establish to uphold a camouflage for your unwillingness.

Those practice periods that you have lost because you did not want to do them, for whatever reason, should be done as soon as you have changed your mind about your goal. You are unwilling to cooperate in practicing salvation only if it interferes with goals you hold more dear. When you withdraw the value given them, allow your practice periods to be replacements for your litanies to them. They gave you nothing. But your practicing can offer everything to you. And so accept their offering and be at peace.

The format you should use for these reviews is this: Devote five minutes twice a day, or longer if you would prefer it, to considering the thoughts that are assigned. Read over the ideas and comments that are written down for each day's exercise. And then begin to think about them, while letting your mind relate them to your needs, your seeming problems and all your concerns.

Place the ideas within your mind, and let it use them as it chooses. Give it faith that it will use them wisely, being helped in its decisions by the One Who gave the thoughts to you. What can you trust but what is in your mind? Have faith, in these reviews, the means the Holy Spirit uses will not fail. The wisdom of your mind will come to your assistance. Give direction at the outset; then lean back in quiet faith, and let the mind employ the thoughts you gave as they were given you for it to use.

You have been given them in perfect trust; in perfect confidence that you would use them well; in perfect faith that you would see their messages and use them for yourself. Offer them to your mind in that same trust and confidence and faith. It will not fail. It is the Holy Spirit's chosen means for your salvation. Since it has His trust, His means must surely merit yours as well.

We emphasize the benefits to you if you devote the first five minutes of the day to your reviews, and also give the last five minutes of your waking day to them. If this cannot be done, at least try to divide them so you undertake one in the morning, and the other in the hour just before you go to sleep.

The exercises to be done throughout the day are equally important, and perhaps of even greater value. You have been inclined to practice only at appointed times, and then go on your way to other things, without applying what you learned to them. As a result, you have gained little reinforcement, and have not given your learning a fair chance to prove how great are its potential gifts to you. Here is another chance to use it well.

In these reviews, we stress the need to let your learning not lie idly by between your longer practice periods. Attempt to give your daily two ideas a brief but serious review each hour. Use one on the hour, and the other one a half an hour later. You need not give more than just a moment to each one. Repeat it, and allow your mind to rest a little time in silence and in peace. Then turn to other things, but try to keep the thought with you, and let it serve to help you keep your peace throughout the day as well.

If you are shaken, think of it again. These practice periods are planned to help you form the habit of applying what you learn each day to everything you do. Do not repeat the thought and lay it down. Its usefulness is limitless to you. And it is meant to serve you in all ways, all times and places, and whenever you need help of any kind. Try, then, to take it with you in the business of the day and make it holy, worthy of God's Son, acceptable to God and to your Self.

Each day's review assignments will conclude with a restatement of the thought to use each hour, and the one to be applied on each half hour as well. Forget them not. This second chance with each of these ideas will bring such large advances that we come from these reviews with learning gains so great we will continue on more solid ground, with firmer footsteps and with stronger faith.

*Do not forget how little you have learned.*
*Do not forget how much you can learn now.*
*Do not forget your Father's need of you,*
*As you review these thoughts He gave to you.*

# LESSON 111

### For morning and evening review:

**Miracles are seen in light.**

*I cannot see in darkness. Let the light
of holiness and truth light up my mind,
and let me see the innocence within.*

**Miracles are seen in light, and light and strength are one.**

*I see through strength, the gift of God to me.
My weakness is the dark His gift dispels,
by giving me His strength to take its place.*

On the hour:

**Miracles are seen in light.**

On the half hour:

**Miracles are seen in light, and light and strength are one.**


# LESSON 112

### For morning and evening review:

**Light and joy and peace abide in me.**

*I am the home of light and joy and peace.
I welcome them into the home I share
with God, because I am a part of Him.*

**I am as God created me.**

*I will remain forever as I was,
created by the Changeless like Himself.
And I am one with Him, and He with me.*

On the hour:

**Light and joy and peace abide in me.**

On the half hour:

**I am as God created me.**

# LESSON 113

### For morning and evening review:

**I am one Self, united with my Creator.**

*Serenity and perfect peace are mine,*
*because I am one Self, completely whole,*
*at one with all creation and with God.*

**Salvation comes from my one Self.**

*From my one Self, Whose knowledge still remains*
*within my mind, I see God's perfect plan*
*for my salvation perfectly fulfilled.*

On the hour:

**I am one Self, united with my Creator.**

On the half hour:

**Salvation comes from my one Self.**


# LESSON 114

### For morning and evening review:

**I am spirit.**

*I am the Son of God. No body can*
*contain my spirit, nor impose on me*
*a limitation God created not.*

**I will accept my part in God's plan for salvation.**

*What can my function be but to accept*
*the Word of God, Who has created me*
*for what I am and will forever be?*

On the hour:

**I am spirit.**

On the half hour:

**I will accept my part in God's plan for salvation.**

## LESSON 115

### For morning and evening review:

**Salvation is my only function here.**

*My function here is to forgive the world*
*for all the errors I have made. For thus*
*am I released from them with all the world.*

**My part is essential to God's plan for salvation.**

*I am essential to the plan of God*
*for the salvation of the world. For He*
*gave me His plan that I might save the world.*

On the hour:

**Salvation is my only function here.**

On the half hour:

**My part is essential to God's plan for salvation.**


## LESSON 116

### For morning and evening review:

**God's Will for me is perfect happiness.**

*God's Will is perfect happiness for me.*
*And I can suffer but from the belief*
*there is another will apart from His.*

**I share God's Will for happiness for me.**

*I share my Father's Will for me, His Son.*
*What He has given me is all I want.*
*What He has given me is all there is.*

On the hour:

**God's Will for me is perfect happiness.**

On the half hour:

**I share God's Will for happiness for me.**

## LESSON 117

**For morning and evening review:**

**God, being Love, is also happiness.**

*Let me remember love is happiness,*
*and nothing else brings joy. And so I choose*
*to entertain no substitutes for love.*

**I seek but what belongs to me in truth.**

*Love is my heritage, and with it joy.*
*These are the gifts my Father gave to me.*
*I would accept all that is mine in truth.*

On the hour:

**God, being Love, is also happiness.**

On the half hour:

**I seek but what belongs to me in truth.**


## LESSON 118

**For morning and evening review:**

**God's peace and joy are mine.**

*Today I will accept God's peace and joy,*
*in glad exchange for all the substitutes*
*that I have made for happiness and peace.*

**Let me be still and listen to the truth.**

*Let my own feeble voice be still, and let*
*me hear the mighty Voice for Truth Itself*
*assure me that I am God's perfect Son.*

On the hour:

**God's peace and joy are mine.**

On the half hour:

**Let me be still and listen to the truth.**

# LESSON 119

### For morning and evening review:

**Truth will correct all errors in my mind.**

*I am mistaken when I think I can
be hurt in any way. I am God's Son,
whose Self rests safely in the Mind of God.*

**To give and to receive are one in truth.**

*I will forgive all things today, that I
may learn how to accept the truth in me,
and come to recognize my sinlessness.*

On the hour:

**Truth will correct all errors in my mind.**

On the half hour:

**To give and to receive are one in truth.**

# LESSON 120

### For morning and evening review:

**I rest in God.**

*I rest in God today, and let Him work
in me and through me, while I rest in Him
in quiet and in perfect certainty.*

**I am as God created me.**

*I am God's Son. Today I lay aside
all sick illusions of myself, and let
my Father tell me Who I really am.*

On the hour:

**I rest in God.**

On the half hour:

**I am as God created me.**

# LESSON 121

**Forgiveness is the key to happiness.**

Here is the answer to your search for peace.
Here is the key to meaning in a world
that seems to make no sense. Here is the way
to safety in apparent dangers that
appear to threaten you at every turn,
and bring uncertainty to all your hopes
of ever finding quietness and peace.
Here are all questions answered; here the end
of all uncertainty ensured at last.

The unforgiving mind is full of fear,
and offers love no room to be itself;
no place where it can spread its wings in peace
and soar above the turmoil of the world.
The unforgiving mind is sad, without
the hope of respite and release from pain.
It suffers and abides in misery,
peering about in darkness, seeing not,
yet certain of the danger lurking there.

The unforgiving mind is torn with doubt,
confused about itself and all it sees;
afraid and angry, weak and blustering,
afraid to go ahead, afraid to stay,
afraid to waken or to go to sleep,
afraid of every sound, yet more afraid
of stillness; terrified of darkness, yet
more terrified at the approach of light.
What can the unforgiving mind perceive
but its damnation? What can it behold
except the proof that all its sins are real?

The unforgiving mind sees no mistakes,
but only sins. It looks upon the world
with sightless eyes, and shrieks as it beholds
its own projections rising to attack
its miserable parody of life.
It wants to live, yet wishes it were dead.
It wants forgiveness, yet it sees no hope.
It wants escape, yet can conceive of none
because it sees the sinful everywhere.

The unforgiving mind is in despair,
without the prospect of a future which
can offer anything but more despair.
Yet it regards its judgment of the world
as irreversible, and does not see
it has condemned itself to this despair.
It thinks it cannot change, for what it sees
bears witness that its judgment is correct.
It does not ask, because it thinks it knows.
It does not question, certain it is right.

Forgiveness is acquired. It is not
inherent in the mind, which cannot sin.
As sin is an idea you taught yourself,
forgiveness must be learned by you as well,
but from a Teacher other than yourself,
Who represents the other Self in you.
Through Him you learn how to forgive the self
you think you made, and let it disappear.
Thus you return your mind as one to Him
Who is your Self, and Who can never sin.

Each unforgiving mind presents you with
an opportunity to teach your own
how to forgive itself. Each one awaits
release from hell through you, and turns to you
imploringly for Heaven here and now.
It has no hope, but you become its hope.
And as its hope, do you become your own.
The unforgiving mind must learn through your
forgiveness that it has been saved from hell.
And as you teach salvation, you will learn.
Yet all your teaching and your learning will
be not of you, but of the Teacher Who
was given you to show the way to you.

Today we practice learning to forgive.
If you are willing, you can learn today
to take the key to happiness, and use
it on your own behalf. We will devote
ten minutes in the morning, and at night
another ten, to learning how to give
forgiveness and receive forgiveness, too.

The unforgiving mind does not believe
that giving and receiving are the same.
Yet we will try to learn today that they
are one through practicing forgiveness toward
one whom you think of as an enemy,
and one whom you consider as a friend.

And as you learn to see them both as one,
we will extend the lesson to yourself,
and see that their escape included yours.

Begin the longer practice periods
by thinking of someone you do not like,
who seems to irritate you, or to cause
regret in you if you should meet him; one
you actively despise, or merely try
to overlook. It does not matter what
the form your anger takes. You probably
have chosen him already. He will do.

Now close your eyes and see him in your mind,
and look at him a while. Try to perceive
some light in him somewhere; a little gleam
which you had never noticed. Try to find
some little spark of brightness shining through
the ugly picture that you hold of him.
Look at this picture till you see a light
somewhere within it, and then try to let
this light extend until it covers him,
and makes the picture beautiful and good.

Look at this changed perception for a while,
and turn your mind to one you call a friend.
Try to transfer the light you learned to see
around your former "enemy" to him.
Perceive him now as more than friend to you,
for in that light his holiness shows you
your savior, saved and saving, healed and whole.

Then let him offer you the light you see
in him, and let your "enemy" and friend
unite in blessing you with what you gave.
Now are you one with them, and they with you.
Now have you been forgiven by yourself.
Do not forget, throughout the day, the role
forgiveness plays in bringing happiness
to every unforgiving mind, with yours
among them. Every hour tell yourself:

*Forgiveness is the key to happiness.*
*I will awaken from the dream that I*
*am mortal, fallible and full of sin,*
*and know I am the perfect Son of God.*

## LESSON 122

### Forgiveness offers everything I want.

What could you want forgiveness cannot give?
Do you want peace? Forgiveness offers it.
Do you want happiness, a quiet mind,
a certainty of purpose, and a sense
of worth and beauty that transcends the world?
Do you want care and safety, and the warmth
of sure protection always? Do you want
a quietness that cannot be disturbed,
a gentleness that never can be hurt,
a deep, abiding comfort, and a rest
so perfect it can never be upset?

All this forgiveness offers you, and more.
It sparkles on your eyes as you awake,
and gives you joy with which to meet the day.
It soothes your forehead while you sleep, and rests
upon your eyelids so you see no dreams
of fear and evil, malice and attack.
And when you wake again, it offers you
another day of happiness and peace.
All this forgiveness offers you, and more.

Forgiveness lets the veil be lifted up
that hides the face of Christ from those who look
with unforgiving eyes upon the world.
It lets you recognize the Son of God,
and clears your memory of all dead thoughts
so that remembrance of your Father can
arise across the threshold of your mind.
What would you want forgiveness cannot give?
What gifts but these are worthy to be sought?
What fancied value, trivial effect
or transient promise, never to be kept,
can hold more hope than what forgiveness brings?

Why would you seek an answer other than
the answer that will answer everything?
Here is the perfect answer, given to
imperfect questions, meaningless requests,
half-hearted willingness to hear, and less
than halfway diligence and partial trust.
Here is the answer! Seek for it no more.
You will not find another one instead.

God's plan for your salvation cannot change,
nor can it fail. Be thankful it remains
exactly as He planned it. Changelessly
it stands before you like an open door,
with warmth and welcome calling from beyond
the doorway, bidding you to enter in
and make yourself at home, where you belong.

Here is the answer! Would you stand outside
while all of Heaven waits for you within?
Forgive and be forgiven. As you give
you will receive. There is no plan but this
for the salvation of the Son of God.
Let us today rejoice that this is so,
for here we have an answer, clear and plain,
beyond deceit in its simplicity.
All the complexities the world has spun
of fragile cobwebs disappear before
the power and the majesty of this
extremely simple statement of the truth.

Here is the answer! Do not turn away
in aimless wandering again. Accept
salvation now. It is the gift of God,
and not the world. The world can give no gifts
of any value to a mind that has
received what God has given as its own.
God wills salvation be received today,
and that the intricacies of your dreams
no longer hide their nothingness from you.

Open your eyes today and look upon
a happy world of safety and of peace.
Forgiveness is the means by which it comes
to take the place of hell. In quietness
it rises up to greet your open eyes,
and fill your heart with deep tranquility
as ancient truths, forever newly born,
arise in your awareness. What you will
remember then can never be described.
Yet your forgiveness offers it to you.

Remembering the gifts forgiveness gives,
we undertake our practicing today
with hope and faith that this will be the day
salvation will be ours. Earnestly
and gladly will we seek for it today,
aware we hold the key within our hands,

accepting Heaven's answer to the hell
we made, but where we would remain no more.

Morning and evening do we gladly give
a quarter of an hour to the search
in which the end of hell is guaranteed.
Begin in hopefulness, for we have reached
the turning point at which the road becomes
far easier. And now the way is short
that yet we travel. We are close indeed
to the appointed ending of the dream.

Sink into happiness as you begin
these practice periods, for they hold out
the sure rewards of questions answered and
what your acceptance of the answer brings.
Today it will be given you to feel
the peace forgiveness offers, and the joy
the lifting of the veil holds out to you.

Before the light you will receive today
the world will fade until it disappears,
and you will see another world arise
you have no words to picture. Now we walk
directly into light, and we receive
the gifts that have been held in store for us
since time began, kept waiting for today.

Forgiveness offers everything you want.
Today all things you want are given you.
Let not your gifts recede throughout the day,
as you return again to meet a world
of shifting change and bleak appearances.
Retain your gifts in clear awareness as
you see the changeless in the heart of change;
the light of truth behind appearances.

Be tempted not to let your gifts slip by
and drift into forgetfulness, but hold
them firmly in your mind by your attempts
to think of them at least a minute as
each quarter of an hour passes by.
Remind yourself how precious are these gifts
with this reminder, which has power to hold
your gifts in your awareness through the day:

*Forgiveness offers everything I want.*
*Today I have accepted this as true.*
*Today I have received the gifts of God.*

## LESSON 123

**I thank my Father for His gifts to me.**

Today let us be thankful. We have come
to gentler pathways and to smoother roads.
There is no thought of turning back, and no
implacable resistance to the truth.
A bit of wavering remains, some small
objections and a little hesitance,
but you can well be grateful for your gains,
which are far greater than you realize.

A day devoted now to gratitude
will add the benefit of some insight
into the real extent of all the gains
which you have made; the gifts you have received.
Be glad today, in loving thankfulness,
your Father has not left you to yourself,
nor let you wander in the dark alone.
Be grateful He has saved you from the self
you thought you made to take the place of Him
and His creation. Give Him thanks today.

Give thanks that He has not abandoned you,
and that His Love forever will remain
shining on you, forever without change.
Give thanks as well that you are changeless, for
the Son He loves is changeless as Himself.
Be grateful you are saved. Be glad you have
a function in salvation to fulfill.
Be thankful that your value far transcends
your meager gifts and petty judgments of
the one whom God established as His Son.

Today in gratitude we lift our hearts
above despair, and raise our thankful eyes,
no longer looking downward to the dust.
We sing the song of thankfulness today,
in honor of the Self That God has willed
to be our true Identity in Him.
Today we smile on everyone we see,
and walk with lightened footsteps as we go
to do what is appointed us to do.

We do not go alone. And we give thanks
that in our solitude a Friend has come
to speak the saving Word of God to us.
And thanks to you for listening to Him.
His Word is soundless if it be not heard.

In thanking Him the thanks are yours as well.
An unheard message will not save the world,
however mighty be the Voice that speaks,
however loving may the message be.

Thanks be to you who heard, for you become
the messenger who brings His Voice with you,
and lets It echo round and round the world.
Receive the thanks of God today, as you
give thanks to Him. For He would offer you
the thanks you give, since He receives your gifts
in loving gratitude, and gives them back
a thousand and a hundred thousand more
than they were given. He will bless your gifts
by sharing them with you. And so they grow
in power and in strength, until they fill
the world with gladness and with gratitude.

Receive His thanks and offer yours to Him
for fifteen minutes twice today. And you
will realize to Whom you offer thanks,
and Whom He thanks as you are thanking Him.
This holy half an hour given Him
will be returned to you in terms of years
for every second; power to save the world
eons more quickly for your thanks to Him.

Receive His thanks, and you will understand
how lovingly He holds you in His Mind,
how deep and limitless His care for you,
how perfect is His gratitude to you.
Remember hourly to think of Him,
and give Him thanks for everything He gave
His Son, that he might rise above the world
remembering his Father and his Self.

# LESSON 124

### Let me remember I am one with God.

Today we will again give thanks for our Identity in God. Our home is safe, protection guaranteed in all we do, power and strength available to us in all our undertakings. We can fail in nothing. Everything we touch takes on a shining light that blesses and that heals. At one with God and with the universe we go our way rejoicing, with the thought that God Himself goes everywhere with us.

How holy are our minds! And everything we see reflects the holiness within the mind at one with God and with itself. How easily do errors disappear, and death give place to everlasting life. Our shining footprints point the way to truth, for God is our Companion as we walk the world a little while. And those who come to follow us will recognize the way because the light we carry stays behind, yet still remains with us as we walk on.

What we receive is our eternal gift to those who follow after, and to those who went before or stayed with us a while. And God, Who loves us with the equal love in which we were created, smiles on us and offers us the happiness we gave.

Today we will not doubt His Love for us, nor question His protection and His care. No meaningless anxieties can come between our faith and our awareness of His Presence. We are one with Him today in recognition and remembrance. We feel Him in our hearts. Our minds contain His Thoughts; our eyes behold His loveliness in all we look upon. Today we see only the loving and the lovable.

We see it in appearances of pain, and pain gives way to peace. We see it in the frantic, in the sad and the distressed, the lonely and afraid, who are restored to the tranquility and peace of mind in which they were created. And we see it in the dying and the dead as well, restoring them to life. All this we see because we saw it first within ourselves.

No miracle can ever be denied to those who know that they are one with God. No thought of theirs but has the power to heal all forms of suffering in anyone, in times gone by and times as yet to come, as easily as in the ones who walk beside them now. Their thoughts are timeless, and apart from distance as apart from time.

We join in this awareness as we say that we are one with God. For in these words we say as well that we are saved and healed; that we can save and heal accordingly. We have accepted, and we now would give. For we would keep the gifts our Father gave. Today we would experience ourselves at one with Him, so that the world may share our recognition of reality. In our experience the world is freed. As we deny our separation from our Father, it is healed along with us.

Peace be to you today. Secure your peace by practicing awareness you are one with your Creator, as He is with you. Sometime today, whenever it seems best, devote a half an hour to the thought that you are one with God. This is our first attempt at an extended period for which we give no rules nor special words to guide your meditation. We will trust God's Voice to speak as He sees fit today, certain He will not fail. Abide with Him this half an hour. He will do the rest.

Your benefit will not be less if you believe that nothing happens. You may not be ready to accept the gain today. Yet sometime, somewhere, it will come to you, nor will you fail to recognize it when it dawns with certainty upon your mind.

This half an hour will be framed in gold,
with every minute like a diamond set
around the mirror that this exercise
will offer you. And you will see Christ's face
upon it, in reflection of your own.

Perhaps today, perhaps tomorrow, you
will see your own transfiguration in
the glass this holy half an hour will
hold out to you, to look upon yourself.
When you are ready you will find it there,
within your mind and waiting to be found.
You will remember then the thought to which
you gave this half an hour, thankfully
aware no time was ever better spent.

Perhaps today, perhaps tomorrow, you
will look into this glass, and understand
the sinless light you see belongs to you;
the loveliness you look on is your own.
Count this half hour as your gift to God,
in certainty that His return will be
a sense of love you cannot understand,
a joy too deep for you to comprehend,
a sight too holy for the body's eyes
to see. And yet you can be sure someday,
perhaps today, perhaps tomorrow, you
will understand and comprehend and see.

Add further jewels to the golden frame
that holds the mirror offered you today,
by hourly repeating to yourself:

*Let me remember I am one with God,
at one with all my brothers and my Self,
in everlasting holiness and peace.*

# LESSON 125

## In quiet I receive God's Word today.

Let this day be a day of stillness and of quiet listening. Your Father wills you hear His Word today. He calls to you from deep within your mind where He abides. Hear Him today. No peace is possible until His Word is heard around the world; until your mind, in quiet listening, accepts the message that the world must hear to usher in the quiet time of peace.

This world will change through you. No other means can save it, for God's plan is simply this: The Son of God is free to save himself, given the Word of God to be his Guide, forever in his mind and at his side to lead him surely to his Father's house by his own will, forever free as God's. He is not led by force, but only love. He is not judged, but only sanctified.

In stillness we will hear God's Voice today without intrusion of our petty thoughts, without our personal desires, and without all judgment of His holy Word. We will not judge ourselves today, for what we are can not be judged. We stand apart from all the judgments which the world has laid upon the Son of God. It knows him not. Today we will not listen to the world, but wait in silence for the Word of God.

Hear, holy Son of God, your Father speak. His Voice would give to you His holy Word, to spread across the world the tidings of salvation and the holy time of peace. We gather at the throne of God today, the quiet place within the mind where He abides forever, in the holiness that He created and will never leave.

He has not waited until you return your mind to Him to give His Word to you. He has not hid Himself from you, while you have wandered off a little while from Him. He does not cherish the illusions which you hold about yourself. He knows His Son, and wills that he remain as part of Him regardless of his dreams; regardless of his madness that his will is not his own.

Today He speaks to you. His Voice awaits your silence, for His Word can not be heard until your mind is quiet for a while, and meaningless desires have been stilled. Await His Word in quiet. There is peace within you to be called upon today, to help make ready your most holy mind to hear the Voice for its Creator speak.

Three times today, at times most suitable for silence, give ten minutes set apart from listening to the world, and choose instead a gentle listening to the Word of God. He speaks from nearer than your heart to you. His Voice is closer than your hand. His Love is everything you are and that He is; the same as you, and you the same as He.

It is your voice to which you listen as He speaks to you. It is your Word He speaks. It is the Word of freedom and of peace, of unity of will and purpose, with no separation nor division in the single Mind of Father and of Son. In quiet listen to your Self today, and let Him tell you God has never left His Son, and you have never left your Self.

Only be quiet. You will need no rule but this, to let your practicing today lift you above the thinking of the world, and free your vision from the body's eyes. Only be still and listen. You will hear the Word in which the Will of God the Son joins in his Father's Will, at one with it, with no illusions interposed between the wholly indivisible and true. As every hour passes by today, be still a moment and remind yourself you have a special purpose for this day; in quiet to receive the Word of God.

## LESSON 126

**All that I give is given to myself.**

Today's idea, completely alien to
the ego and the thinking of the world,
is crucial to the thought reversal that
this course will bring about. If you believed
this statement, there would be no problem in
complete forgiveness, certainty of goal,
and sure direction. You would understand
the means by which salvation comes to you,
and would not hesitate to use it now.

Let us consider what you do believe,
in place of this idea. It seems to you
that other people are apart from you,
and able to behave in ways which have no
bearing on your thoughts, nor yours on theirs.
Therefore, your attitudes have no effect
on them, and their appeals for help are not
in any way related to your own.
You further think that they can sin without
affecting your perception of yourself,
while you can judge their sin, and yet remain
apart from condemnation and at peace.

When you "forgive" a sin, there is no gain
to you directly. You give charity
to one unworthy, merely to point out
that you are better, on a higher plane
than he whom you forgive. He has not earned
your charitable tolerance, which you
bestow on one unworthy of the gift,
because his sins have lowered him beneath
a true equality with you. He has
no claim on your forgiveness. It holds out
a gift to him, but hardly to yourself.

Thus is forgiveness basically unsound;
a charitable whim, benevolent
yet undeserved, a gift bestowed at times,
at other times withheld. Unmerited,
withholding it is just, nor is it fair
that you should suffer when it is withheld.
The sin that you forgive is not your own.
Someone apart from you committed it.
And if you then are gracious unto him
by giving him what he does not deserve,
the gift is no more yours than was his sin.

If this be true, forgiveness has no grounds
on which to rest dependably and sure.
It is an eccentricity, in which
you sometimes choose to give indulgently
an undeserved reprieve. Yet it remains
your right to let the sinner not escape
the justified repayment for his sin.
Think you the Lord of Heaven would allow
the world's salvation to depend on this?
Would not His care for you be small indeed,
if your salvation rested on a whim?

You do not understand forgiveness. As
you see it, it is but a check upon
overt attack, without requiring
correction in your mind. It cannot give
you peace as you perceive it. It is not
a means for your release from what you see
in someone other than yourself. It has
no power to restore your unity
with him to your awareness. It is not
what God intended it to be for you.

Not having given Him the gift He asks
of you, you cannot recognize His gifts,
and think He has not given them to you.
Yet would He ask you for a gift unless
it was for you? Could He be satisfied
with empty gestures, and evaluate
such petty gifts as worthy of His Son?
Salvation is a better gift than this.
And true forgiveness, as the means by which
it is attained, must heal the mind that gives,
for giving is receiving. What remains
as unreceived has not been given, but
what has been given must have been received.

Today we try to understand the truth
that giver and receiver are the same.
You will need help to make this meaningful,
because it is so alien to the thoughts
to which you are accustomed. But the Help
you need is there. Give Him your faith today,
and ask Him that He share your practicing

in truth today. And if you only catch
a tiny glimpse of the release that lies
in the idea we practice for today,
this is a day of glory for the world.

Give fifteen minutes twice today to the
attempt to understand today's idea.
It is the thought by which forgiveness takes
its proper place in your priorities.
It is the thought that will release your mind
from every bar to what forgiveness means,
and let you realize its worth to you.

In silence, close your eyes upon the world
that does not understand forgiveness, and
seek sanctuary in the quiet place
where thoughts are changed and false beliefs laid by.
Repeat today's idea, and ask for help
in understanding what it really means.

Be willing to be taught. Be glad to hear
the Voice of truth and healing speak to you,
and you will understand the words He speaks,
and recognize He speaks your words to you.

As often as you can, remind yourself
you have a goal today; an aim which makes
this day of special value to yourself
and all your brothers. Do not let your mind
forget this goal for long, but tell yourself:

*All that I give is given to myself.*
*The Help I need to learn that this is true*
*is with me now. And I will trust in Him.*

Then spend a quiet moment, opening
your mind to His correction and His Love.
And what you hear of Him you will believe,
for what He gives will be received by you.

# LESSON 127

## There is no love but God's.

Perhaps you think that different kinds of love are possible. Perhaps you think there is a kind of love for this, a kind for that; a way of loving one, another way of loving still another. Love is one. It has no separate parts and no degrees; no kinds nor levels, no divergencies and no distinctions. It is like itself, unchanged throughout. It never alters with a person or a circumstance. It is the Heart of God, and also of His Son.

Love's meaning is obscure to anyone who thinks that love can change. He does not see that changing love must be impossible. And thus he thinks that he can love at times, and hate at other times. He also thinks that love can be bestowed on one, and yet remain itself although it is withheld from others. To believe these things of love is not to understand it. If it could make such distinctions, it would have to judge between the righteous and the sinner, and perceive the Son of God in separate parts.

Love cannot judge. As it is one itself, it looks on all as one. Its meaning lies in oneness. And it must elude the mind that thinks of it as partial or in part. There is no love but God's, and all of love is His. There is no other principle that rules where love is not. Love is a law without an opposite. Its wholeness is the power holding everything as one, the link between the Father and the Son which holds Them both forever as the same.

No course whose purpose is to teach you to remember what you really are could fail to emphasize that there can never be a difference in what you really are and what love is. Love's meaning is your own, and shared by God Himself. For what you are is what He is. There is no love but His, and what He is, is everything there is. There is no limit placed upon Himself, and so are you unlimited as well.

No law the world obeys can help you grasp love's meaning. What the world believes was made to hide love's meaning, and to keep it dark and secret. There is not one principle the world upholds but violates the truth of what love is, and what you are as well.

Seek not within the world to find your Self. Love is not found in darkness and in death. Yet it is perfectly apparent to the eyes that see and ears that hear love's Voice. Today we practice making free your mind of all the laws you think you must obey; of all the limits under which you live, and all the changes that you think are part of human destiny. Today we take the largest single step this course requests in your advance towards its established goal.

If you achieve the faintest glimmering of what love means today, you have advanced in distance without measure and in time beyond the count of years to your release. Let us together, then, be glad to give some time to God today, and understand there is no better use for time than this.

For fifteen minutes twice today escape from every law in which you now believe. Open your mind and rest. The world that seems to hold you prisoner can be escaped by anyone who does not hold it dear. Withdraw all value you have placed upon its meager offerings and senseless gifts, and let the gift of God replace them all.

Call to your Father, certain that His Voice will answer. He Himself has promised this. And He Himself will place a spark of truth within your mind wherever you give up a false belief, a dark illusion of

your own reality and what love means.
He will shine through your idle thoughts today,
and help you understand the truth of love.
In loving gentleness He will abide with you,
as you allow His Voice to teach
love's meaning to your clean and open mind.
And He will bless the lesson with His Love.

Today the legion of the future years
of waiting for salvation disappears
before the timelessness of what you learn.
Let us give thanks today that we are spared
a future like the past. Today we leave
the past behind us, nevermore to be
remembered. And we raise our eyes upon
a different present, where a future dawns
unlike the past in every attribute.

The world in infancy is newly born.
And we will watch it grow in health and strength,
to shed its blessing upon all who come
to learn to cast aside the world they thought
was made in hate to be love's enemy.
Now are they all made free, along with us.
Now are they all our brothers in God's Love.

We will remember them throughout the day,
because we cannot leave a part of us
outside our love if we would know our Self.
At least three times an hour think of one
who makes the journey with you, and who came
to learn what you must learn. And as he comes
to mind, give him this message from your Self:

*I bless you, brother, with the Love of God,
which I would share with you. For I would learn
the joyous lesson that there is no love
but God's and yours and mine and everyone's.*

# LESSON 128

## The world I see holds nothing that I want.

The world you see holds nothing that you need to offer you; nothing that you can use in any way, nor anything at all that serves to give you joy. Believe this thought, and you are saved from years of misery, from countless disappointments, and from hopes that turn to bitter ashes of despair. No one but must accept this thought as true, if he would leave the world behind and soar beyond its petty scope and little ways.

Each thing you value here is but a chain that binds you to the world, and it will serve no other end but this. For everything must serve the purpose you have given it, until you see a different purpose there. The only purpose worthy of your mind this world contains is that you pass it by, without delaying to perceive some hope where there is none. Be you deceived no more. The world you see holds nothing that you want.

Escape today the chains you place upon your mind when you perceive salvation here. For what you value you make part of you as you perceive yourself. All things you seek to make your value greater in your sight limit you further, hide your worth from you, and add another bar across the door that leads to true awareness of your Self.

Let nothing that relates to body thoughts delay your progress to salvation, nor permit temptation to believe the world holds anything you want to hold you back. Nothing is here to cherish. Nothing here is worth one instant of delay and pain; one moment of uncertainty and doubt. The worthless offer nothing. Certainty of worth can not be found in worthlessness.

Today we practice letting go all thought of values we have given to the world. We leave it free of purposes we gave its aspects and its phases and its dreams. We hold it purposeless within our minds, and loosen it from all we wish it were. Thus do we lift the chains that bar the door to freedom from the world, and go beyond all little values and diminished goals.

Pause and be still a little while, and see how far you rise above the world, when you release your mind from chains and let it seek the level where it finds itself at home. It will be grateful to be free a while. It knows where it belongs. But free its wings, and it will fly in sureness and in joy to join its holy purpose. Let it rest in its Creator, there to be restored to sanity, to freedom and to love.

Give it ten minutes rest three times today. And when your eyes are opened afterwards, you will not value anything you see as much as when you looked at it before. Your whole perspective on the world will shift by just a little, every time you let your mind escape its chains. The world is not where it belongs. And you belong where it would be, and where it goes to rest when you release it from the world. Your Guide is sure. Open your mind to Him. Be still and rest.

Protect your mind throughout the day as well. And when you think you see some value in an aspect or an image of the world, refuse to lay this chain upon your mind, but tell yourself with quiet certainty:

*This will not tempt me to delay myself.*
*The world I see holds nothing that I want.*

# LESSON 129

**Beyond this world there is a world I want.**

This is the thought that follows from the one we practiced yesterday. You cannot stop with the idea the world is worthless, for unless you see that there is something else to hope for, you will only be depressed. Our emphasis is not on giving up the world, but on exchanging it for what is far more satisfying, filled with joy, and capable of offering you peace. Think you this world can offer that to you?

It might be worth a little time to think once more about the value of this world. Perhaps you will concede there is no loss in letting go all thought of value here. The world you see is merciless indeed, unstable, cruel, unconcerned with you, quick to avenge and pitiless with hate. It gives but to rescind, and takes away all things that you have cherished for a while. No lasting love is found, for none is here. This is the world of time, where all things end.

Is it a loss to find a world instead where losing is impossible; where love endures forever, hate cannot exist and vengeance has no meaning? Is it loss to find all things you really want, and know they have no ending and they will remain exactly as you want them throughout time? Yet even they will be exchanged at last for what we cannot speak of, for you go from there to where words fail entirely, into a silence where the language is unspoken and yet surely understood.

Communication, unambiguous and plain as day, remains unlimited for all eternity. And God Himself speaks to His Son, as His Son speaks to Him. Their language has no words, for what They say cannot be symbolized. Their knowledge is direct and wholly shared and wholly one. How far away from this are you who stay bound to this world. And yet how near are you, when you exchange it for the world you want.

Now is the last step certain; now you stand an instant's space away from timelessness. Here can you but look forward, never back to see again the world you do not want. Here is the world that comes to take its place, as you unbind your mind from little things the world sets forth to keep you prisoner. Value them not, and they will disappear. Esteem them, and they will seem real to you.

Such is the choice. What loss can be for you in choosing not to value nothingness? This world holds nothing that you really want, but what you choose instead you want indeed! Let it be given you today. It waits but for your choosing it, to take the place of all the things you seek but do not want.

Practice your willingness to make this change ten minutes in the morning and at night, and once more in between. Begin with this:

*Beyond this world there is a world I want.*
*I choose to see that world instead of this,*
*for here is nothing that I really want.*

Then close your eyes upon the world you see, and in the silent darkness watch the lights that are not of this world light one by one, until where one begins another ends loses all meaning as they blend in one.

Today the lights of Heaven bend to you, to shine upon your eyelids as you rest beyond the world of darkness. Here is light your eyes can not behold. And yet your mind can see it plainly, and can understand. A day of grace is given you today, and we give thanks. This day we realize that what you feared to lose was only loss.

Now do we understand there is no loss. For we have seen its opposite at last, and we are grateful that the choice is made. Remember your decision hourly, and take a moment to confirm your choice by laying by whatever thoughts you have, and dwelling briefly only upon this:

*The world I see holds nothing that I want.*
*Beyond this world there is a world I want.*

# LESSON 130

**It is impossible to see two worlds.**

Perception is consistent. What you see reflects your thinking. And your thinking but reflects your choice of what you want to see. Your values are determiners of this, for what you value you must want to see, believing what you see is really there. No one can see a world his mind has not accorded value. And no one can fail to look upon what he believes he wants.

Yet who can really hate and love at once? Who can desire what he does not want to have reality? And who can choose to see a world of which he is afraid? Fear must make blind, for this its weapon is: That which you fear to see you cannot see. Love and perception thus go hand in hand, but fear obscures in darkness what is there.

What, then, can fear project upon the world? What can be seen in darkness that is real? Truth is eclipsed by fear, and what remains is but imagined. Yet what can be real in blind imaginings of panic born? What would you want that this is shown to you? What would you wish to keep in such a dream?

Fear has made everything you think you see. All separation, all distinctions, and the multitude of differences you believe make up the world. They are not there. Love's enemy has made them up. Yet love can have no enemy, and so they have no cause, no being and no consequence. They can be valued, but remain unreal. They can be sought, but they can not be found. Today we will not seek for them, nor waste this day in seeking what can not be found.

It is impossible to see two worlds which have no overlap of any kind. Seek for the one; the other disappears. But one remains. They are the range of choice beyond which your decision cannot go. The real and the unreal are all there are to choose between, and nothing more than these.

Today we will attempt no compromise where none is possible. The world you see is proof you have already made a choice as all-embracing as its opposite. What we would learn today is more than just the lesson that you cannot see two worlds. It also teaches that the one you see is quite consistent from the point of view from which you see it. It is all a piece because it stems from one emotion, and reflects its source in everything you see.

Six times today, in thanks and gratitude, we gladly give five minutes to the thought that ends all compromise and doubt, and go beyond them all as one. We will not make a thousand meaningless distinctions, nor attempt to bring with us a little part of unreality, as we devote our minds to finding only what is real.

Begin your searching for the other world by asking for a strength beyond your own, and recognizing what it is you seek. You do not want illusions. And you come to these five minutes emptying your hands of all the petty treasures of this world. You wait for God to help you, as you say:

*It is impossible to see two worlds.*
*Let me accept the strength God offers me*
*and see no value in this world, that I*
*may find my freedom and deliverance.*

God will be there. For you have called upon the great unfailing Power Which will take this giant step with you in gratitude. Nor will you fail to see His thanks expressed in tangible perception and in truth. You will not doubt what you will look upon, for though it is perception, it is not the kind of seeing that your eyes alone have ever seen before. And you will know God's strength upheld you as you made this choice.

Dismiss temptation easily today whenever it arises, merely by

remembering the limits of your choice.
The unreal or the real, the false or true
is what you see and only what you see.
Perception is consistent with your choice,
and hell or Heaven comes to you as one.

Accept a little part of hell as real,
and you have damned your eyes
and cursed your sight,
and what you will behold is hell indeed.

Yet the release of Heaven still remains
within your range of choice, to take the place
of everything that hell would show to you.
All you need say to any part of hell,
whatever form it takes, is simply this:

*It is impossible to see two worlds.*
*I seek my freedom and deliverance,*
*and this is not a part of what I want.*

## LESSON 131

**No one can fail who seeks to reach the truth.**

Failure is all about you while you seek for goals that cannot be achieved. You look for permanence in the impermanent, for love where there is none, for safety in the midst of danger; immortality within the darkness of the dream of death. Who could succeed where contradiction is the setting of his searching, and the place to which he comes to find stability?

Goals that are meaningless are not attained. There is no way to reach them, for the means by which you strive for them are meaningless as they are. Who can use such senseless means, and hope through them to gain in anything? Where can they lead? And what could they achieve that offers any hope of being real? Pursuit of the imagined leads to death because it is the search for nothingness, and while you seek for life you ask for death. You look for safety and security, while in your heart you pray for danger and protection for the little dream you made.

Yet searching is inevitable here. For this you came, and you will surely do the thing you came for. But the world can not dictate the goal for which you search, unless you give it power to do so. Otherwise, you still are free to choose a goal that lies beyond the world and every worldly thought, and one that comes to you from an idea relinquished yet remembered, old yet new; an echo of a heritage forgot, yet holding everything you really want.

Be glad that search you must. Be glad as well to learn you search for Heaven, and must find the goal you really want. No one can fail to want this goal and reach it in the end. God's Son can not seek vainly, though he try to force delay, deceive himself and think that it is hell he seeks. When he is wrong, he finds correction. When he wanders off, he is led back to his appointed task.

No one remains in hell, for no one can abandon his Creator, nor affect His perfect, timeless and unchanging Love. You will find Heaven. Everything you seek but this will fall away. Yet not because it has been taken from you. It will go because you do not want it. You will reach the goal you really want as certainly as God created you in sinlessness.

Why wait for Heaven? It is here today. Time is the great illusion it is past or in the future. Yet this cannot be, if it is where God wills His Son to be. How could the Will of God be in the past, or yet to happen? What He wills is now, without a past and wholly futureless. It is as far removed from time as is a tiny candle from a distant star, or what you chose from what you really want.

Heaven remains your one alternative to this strange world you made and all its ways; its shifting patterns and uncertain goals, its painful pleasures and its tragic joys. God made no contradictions. What denies its own existence and attacks itself is not of Him. He did not make two minds, with Heaven as the glad effect of one, and earth the other's sorry outcome which is Heaven's opposite in every way.

God does not suffer conflict. Nor is His creation split in two. How could it be His Son could be in hell, when God Himself established him in Heaven? Could he lose what the Eternal Will has given him to be his home forever? Let us not try longer to impose an alien will upon God's single purpose. He is here because He wills to be, and what He wills is present now, beyond the reach of time.

Today we will not choose a paradox in place of truth. How could the Son of God make time to take away the Will of God? He thus denies himself, and contradicts what has no opposite. He thinks he made

a hell opposing Heaven, and believes
that he abides in what does not exist,
while Heaven is the place he cannot find.

Leave foolish thoughts like these behind today,
and turn your mind to true ideas instead.
No one can fail who seeks to reach the truth,
and it is truth we seek to reach today.
We will devote ten minutes to this goal
three times today, and we will ask to see
the rising of the real world to replace
the foolish images that we hold dear,
with true ideas arising in the place
of thoughts that have no meaning, no effect,
and neither source nor substance in the truth.

This we acknowledge as we start upon
our practice periods. Begin with this:

*I ask to see a different world, and think
a different kind of thought from those I made.
The world I seek I did not make alone,
the thoughts I want to think are not my own.*

For several minutes watch your mind and see,
although your eyes are closed, the senseless world
you think is real. Review the thoughts as well
which are compatible with such a world,
and which you think are true. Then let them go,
and sink below them to the holy place
where they can enter not. There is a door
beneath them in your mind, which you could not
completely lock to hide what lies beyond.

Seek for that door and find it. But before
you try to open it, remind yourself
no one can fail who seeks to reach the truth.
And it is this request you make today.
Nothing but this has any meaning now;
no other goal is valued now nor sought,
nothing before this door you really want,
and only what lies past it do you seek.

Put out your hand, and see how easily
the door swings open with your one intent
to go beyond it. Angels light the way,
so that all darkness vanishes, and you
are standing in a light so bright and clear
that you can understand all things you see.
A tiny moment of surprise, perhaps,
will make you pause before you realize
the world you see before you in the light
reflects the truth you knew, and did not quite
forget in wandering away in dreams.

You cannot fail today. There walks with you
the Spirit Heaven sent you, that you might
approach this door some day, and through His aid
slip effortlessly past it, to the light.
Today that day has come. Today God keeps
His ancient promise to His holy Son,
as does His Son remember his to Him.
This is a day of gladness, for we come
to the appointed time and place where you
will find the goal of all your searching here,
and all the seeking of the world, which end
together as you pass beyond the door.

Remember often that today should be
a time of special gladness, and refrain
from dismal thoughts and meaningless laments.
Salvation's time has come. Today is set
by Heaven itself to be a time of grace
for you and for the world. If you forget
this happy fact, remind yourself with this:

*Today I seek and find all that I want.
My single purpose offers it to me.
No one can fail who seeks to reach the truth.*

## LESSON 132

**I loose the world from all I thought it was.**

What keeps the world in chains but your beliefs?
And what can save the world except your Self?
Belief is powerful indeed. The thoughts
you hold are mighty, and illusions are
as strong in their effects as is the truth.
A madman thinks the world he sees is real,
and does not doubt it. Nor can he be swayed
by questioning his thoughts' effects. It is
but when their source is raised to question that
the hope of freedom comes to him at last.

Yet is salvation easily achieved,
for anyone is free to change his mind,
and all his thoughts change with it. Now the source
of thought has shifted, for to change your mind
means you have changed the source of all ideas
you think or ever thought or yet will think.
You free the past from what you thought before.
You free the future from all ancient thoughts
of seeking what you do not want to find.

The present now remains the only time.
Here in the present is the world set free.
For as you let the past be lifted and
release the future from your ancient fears,
you find escape and give it to the world.
You have enslaved the world with all your fears,
your doubts and miseries, your pain and tears,
and all your sorrows press on it, and keep
the world a prisoner to your beliefs.
Death strikes it everywhere because you hold
the bitter thoughts of death within your mind.

The world is nothing in itself. Your mind
must give it meaning. And what you behold
upon it are your wishes, acted out
so you can look on them and think them real.
Perhaps you think you did not make the world,
but came unwillingly to what was made
already, hardly waiting for your thoughts
to give it meaning. Yet in truth you found
exactly what you looked for when you came.

There is no world apart from what you wish,
and herein lies your ultimate release.
Change but your mind on what you want to see,
and all the world must change accordingly.

Ideas leave not their source. This central theme
is often stated in the text, and must
be borne in mind if you would understand
the lesson for today. It is not pride
which tells you that you made the world you see,
and that it changes as you change your mind.

But it is pride that argues you have come
into a world quite separate from yourself,
impervious to what you think, and quite
apart from what you chance to think it is.
There is no world! This is the central thought
the course attempts to teach. Not everyone
is ready to accept it, and each one
must go as far as he can let himself
be led along the road to truth. He will
return and go still farther, or perhaps
step back a while and then return again.

But healing is the gift of those who are
prepared to learn there is no world, and can
accept the lesson now. Their readiness
will bring the lesson to them in some form
which they can understand and recognize.
Some see it suddenly on point of death,
and rise to teach it. Others find it in
experience that is not of this world,
which shows them that the world does not exist
because what they behold must be the truth,
and yet it clearly contradicts the world.

And some will find it in this course, and in
the exercises that we do today.
Today's idea is true because the world
does not exist. And if it is indeed
your own imagining, then you can loose
it from all things you ever thought it was
by merely changing all the thoughts that gave
it these appearances. The sick are healed
as you let go all thoughts of sickness, and
the dead arise when you let thoughts of life
replace all thoughts you ever held of death.

A lesson earlier repeated once
must now be stressed again, for it contains
the firm foundation for today's idea.
You are as God created you. There is

no place where you can suffer, and no time
that can bring change to your eternal state.
How can a world of time and place exist,
if you remain as God created you?

What is the lesson for today except
another way of saying that to know
your Self is the salvation of the world?
To free the world from every kind of pain
is but to change your mind about yourself.
There is no world apart from your ideas
because ideas leave not their source, and you
maintain the world within your mind in thought.

Yet if you are as God created you,
you cannot think apart from Him, nor make
what does not share His timelessness and Love.
Are these inherent in the world you see?
Does it create like Him? Unless it does,
it is not real, and cannot be at all.
If you are real the world you see is false,
for God's creation is unlike the world
in every way. And as it was His Thought
by which you were created, so it is
your thoughts which made it and must set it free,
that you may know the Thoughts you share with
God.

Release the world! Your real creations wait
for this release to give you fatherhood,
not of illusions, but as God in truth.
God shares His Fatherhood with you who are
His Son, for He makes no distinctions in
what is Himself and what is still Himself.
What He creates is not apart from Him,
and nowhere does the Father end, the Son
begin as something separate from Him.

There is no world because it is a thought
apart from God, and made to separate
the Father and the Son, and break away
a part of God Himself and thus destroy

His Wholeness. Can a world which comes from this
idea be real? Can it be anywhere?
Deny illusions, but accept the truth.
Deny you are a shadow briefly laid
upon a dying world. Release your mind,
and you will look upon a world released.

Today our purpose is to free the world
from all the idle thoughts we ever held
about it, and about all living things
we see upon it. They can not be there.
No more can we. For we are in the home
our Father set for us, along with them.
And we who are as He created us
would loose the world this day from every one
of our illusions, that we may be free.

Begin the fifteen-minute periods
in which we practice twice today with this:

*I who remain as God created me
would loose the world from all I thought it was.
For I am real because the world is not,
and I would know my own reality.*

Then merely rest, alert but with no strain,
and let your mind in quietness be changed
so that the world is freed, along with you.

You need not realize that healing comes
to many brothers far across the world,
as well as to the ones you see nearby,
as you send out these thoughts to bless the world.
But you will sense your own release, although
you may not fully understand as yet
that you could never be released alone.

Throughout the day, increase the freedom sent
through your ideas to all the world, and say
whenever you are tempted to deny
the power of your simple change of mind:

*I loose the world from all I thought it was,
and choose my own reality instead.*

## LESSON 133

**I will not value what is valueless.**

Sometimes in teaching there is benefit, particularly after you have gone through what seems theoretical and far from what the student has already learned, to bring him back to practical concerns. This we will do today. We will not speak of lofty, world-encompassing ideas, but dwell instead on benefits to you.

You do not ask too much of life, but far too little. When you let your mind be drawn to bodily concerns, to things you buy, to eminence as valued by the world, you ask for sorrow, not for happiness. This course does not attempt to take from you the little that you have. It does not try to substitute utopian ideas for satisfactions which the world contains. There are no satisfactions in the world.

Today we list the real criteria by which to test all things you think you want. Unless they meet these sound requirements, they are not worth desiring at all, for they can but replace what offers more. The laws that govern choice you cannot make, no more than you can make alternatives from which to choose. The choosing you can do; indeed, you must. But it is wise to learn the laws you set in motion when you choose, and what alternatives you choose between.

We have already stressed there are but two, however many there appear to be. The range is set, and this we cannot change. It would be most ungenerous to you to let alternatives be limitless, and thus delay your final choice until you had considered all of them in time; and not been brought so clearly to the place where there is but one choice that must be made.

Another kindly and related law is that there is no compromise in what your choice must bring. It cannot give you just a little, for there is no in between. Each choice you make brings everything to you or nothing. Therefore, if you learn the tests by which you can distinguish everything from nothing, you will make the better choice.

First, if you choose a thing that will not last forever, what you chose is valueless. A temporary value is without all value. Time can never take away a value that is real. What fades and dies was never there, and makes no offering to him who chooses it. He is deceived by nothing in a form he thinks he likes.

Next, if you choose to take a thing away from someone else, you will have nothing left. This is because, when you deny his right to everything, you have denied your own. You therefore will not recognize the things you really have, denying they are there. Who seeks to take away has been deceived by the illusion loss can offer gain. Yet loss must offer loss, and nothing more.

Your next consideration is the one on which the others rest. Why is the choice you make of value to you? What attracts your mind to it? What purpose does it serve? Here it is easiest of all to be deceived. For what the ego wants it fails to recognize. It does not even tell the truth as it perceives it, for it needs to keep the halo which it uses to protect its goals from tarnish and from rust, that you may see how "innocent" it is.

Yet is its camouflage a thin veneer, which could deceive but those who are content to be deceived. Its goals are obvious to anyone who cares to look for them. Here is deception doubled, for the one who is deceived will not perceive that he has merely failed to gain. He will believe that he has served the ego's hidden goals.

Yet though he tries to keep its halo clear within his vision, still must he perceive its tarnished edges and its rusted core.

His ineffectual mistakes appear
as sins to him, because he looks upon
the tarnish as his own; the rust a sign
of deep unworthiness within himself.
He who would still preserve the ego's goals
and serve them as his own makes no mistakes,
according to the dictates of his guide.
This guidance teaches it is error to
believe that sins are but mistakes, for who
would suffer for his sins if this were so?

And so we come to the criterion
for choice that is the hardest to believe,
because its obviousness is overlaid
with many levels of obscurity.
If you feel any guilt about your choice,
you have allowed the ego's goals to come
between the real alternatives. And thus
you do not realize there are but two,
and the alternative you think you chose
seems fearful, and too dangerous to be
the nothingness it actually is.

All things are valuable or valueless,
worthy or not of being sought at all,
entirely desirable or
not worth the slightest effort to obtain.
Choosing is easy just because of this.
Complexity is nothing but a screen
of smoke, which hides the very simple fact
that no decision can be difficult.
What is the gain to you in learning this?
It is far more than merely letting you
make choices easily and without pain.

Heaven itself is reached with empty hands
and open minds, which come with nothing to
find everything and claim it as their own.
We will attempt to reach this state today,
with self-deception laid aside, and with
an honest willingness to value
but the truly valuable and the real.
Our two extended practice periods
of fifteen minutes each begin with this:

*I will not value what is valueless,*
*and only what has value do I seek,*
*for only that do I desire to find.*

And then receive what waits for everyone
who reaches, unencumbered, to the gate
of Heaven, which swings open as he comes.
Should you begin to let yourself collect
some needless burdens, or believe you see
some difficult decisions facing you,
be quick to answer with this simple thought:

*I will not value what is valueless,*
*for what is valuable belongs to me.*

## LESSON 134

**Let me perceive forgiveness as it is.**

Let us review the meaning of "forgive,"
for it is apt to be distorted and
to be perceived as something that entails
an unfair sacrifice of righteous wrath,
a gift unjustified and undeserved,
and a complete denial of the truth.
In such a view, forgiveness must be seen
as mere eccentric folly, and this course
appear to rest salvation on a whim.

This twisted view of what forgiveness means
is easily corrected, when you can
accept the fact that pardon is not asked
for what is true. It must be limited
to what is false. It is irrelevant
to everything except illusions. Truth
is God's creation, and to pardon that
is meaningless. All truth belongs to Him,
reflects His laws and radiates His Love.
Does this need pardon? How can you forgive
the sinless and eternally benign?

The major difficulty that you find
in genuine forgiveness on your part
is that you still believe you must forgive
the truth, and not illusions. You conceive
of pardon as a vain attempt to look
past what is there; to overlook the truth,
in an unfounded effort to deceive
yourself by making an illusion true.
This twisted viewpoint but reflects the hold
that the idea of sin retains as yet
upon your mind, as you regard yourself.

Because you think your sins are real, you look
on pardon as deception. For it is
impossible to think of sin as true
and not believe forgiveness is a lie.
Thus is forgiveness really but a sin,
like all the rest. It says the truth is false,
and smiles on the corrupt as if they were
as blameless as the grass; as white as snow.
It is delusional in what it thinks
it can accomplish. It would see as right
the plainly wrong; the loathsome as the good.

Pardon is no escape in such a view.
It merely is a further sign that sin
is unforgivable, at best to be
concealed, denied or called another name,
for pardon is a treachery to truth.
Guilt cannot be forgiven. If you sin,
your guilt is everlasting. Those who are
forgiven from the view their sins are real
are pitifully mocked and twice condemned;
first, by themselves for what they think they did,
and once again by those who pardon them.

It is sin's unreality that makes
forgiveness natural and wholly sane,
a deep relief to those who offer it;
a quiet blessing where it is received.
It does not countenance illusions, but
collects them lightly, with a little laugh,
and gently lays them at the feet of truth.
And there they disappear entirely.

Forgiveness is the only thing that stands
for truth in the illusions of the world.
It sees their nothingness, and looks straight through
the thousand forms in which they may appear.
It looks on lies, but it is not deceived.
It does not heed the self-accusing shrieks
of sinners mad with guilt. It looks on them
with quiet eyes, and merely says to them,
"My brother, what you think is not the truth."

The strength of pardon is its honesty,
which is so uncorrupted that it sees
illusions as illusions, not as truth.
It is because of this that it becomes
the undeceiver in the face of lies;
the great restorer of the simple truth.
By its ability to overlook
what is not there, it opens up the way
to truth, which has been blocked by dreams of guilt.
Now are you free to follow in the way
your true forgiveness opens up to you.
For if one brother has received this
gift of you, the door is open to yourself.

There is a very simple way to find
the door to true forgiveness, and perceive
it open wide in welcome. When you feel

that you are tempted to accuse someone
of sin in any form, do not allow
your mind to dwell on what you think he did,
for that is self-deception. Ask instead,
"Would I accuse myself of doing this?"

Thus will you see alternatives for choice
in terms that render choosing meaningful,
and keep your mind as free of guilt and pain
as God Himself intended it to be,
and as it is in truth. It is but lies
that would condemn. In truth is innocence
the only thing there is. Forgiveness stands
between illusions and the truth; between
the world you see and that which lies beyond;
between the hell of guilt and Heaven's gate.

Across this bridge, as powerful as Love
which laid its blessing on it, are all dreams
of evil and of hatred and attack
brought silently to truth. They are not kept
to swell and bluster, and to terrify
the foolish dreamer who believes in them.
He has been gently wakened from his dream
by understanding what he thought he saw
was never there. And now he cannot feel
that all escape has been denied to him.

He does not have to fight to save himself.
He does not have to kill the dragons which
he thought pursued him. Nor need he erect
the heavy walls of stone and iron doors
he thought would make him safe. He can remove
the ponderous and useless armor made
to chain his mind to fear and misery.
His step is light, and as he lifts his foot
to stride ahead a star is left behind,
to point the way to those who follow him.

Forgiveness must be practiced, for the world
cannot perceive its meaning, nor provide
a guide to teach you its beneficence.
There is no thought in all the world that leads
to any understanding of the laws
it follows, nor the Thought that it reflects.
It is as alien to the world as is
your own reality. And yet it joins
your mind with the reality in you.

Today we practice true forgiveness, that
the time of joining be no more delayed.
For we would meet with our reality
in freedom and in peace. Our practicing
becomes the footsteps lighting up the way
for all our brothers, who will follow us
to the reality we share with them.
That this may be accomplished, let us give
a quarter of an hour twice today,
and spend it with the Guide Who understands
the meaning of forgiveness, and was sent
to us to teach it. Let us ask of Him:

*Let me perceive forgiveness as it is.*

Then choose one brother as He will direct,
and catalogue his "sins," as one by one
they cross your mind. Be certain not to dwell
on any one of them, but realize
that you are using his "offenses" but
to save the world from all ideas of sin.
Briefly consider all the evil things
you thought of him, and each time ask yourself,
"Would I condemn myself for doing this?"

Let him be freed from all the thoughts you had
of sin in him. And now you are prepared
for freedom. If you have been practicing
thus far in willingness and honesty,
you will begin to sense a lifting up,
a lightening of weight across your chest,
a deep and certain feeling of relief.
The time remaining should be given to
experiencing the escape from all
the heavy chains you sought to lay upon
your brother, but were laid upon yourself.

Forgiveness should be practiced through the day,
for there will still be many times when you
forget its meaning and attack yourself.
When this occurs, allow your mind to see
through this illusion as you tell yourself:

*Let me perceive forgiveness as it is.*
*Would I accuse myself of doing this?*
*I will not lay this chain upon myself.*

In everything you do remember this:

*No one is crucified alone, and yet*
*no one can enter Heaven by himself.*

# LESSON 135

## If I defend myself I am attacked.

Who would defend himself unless he thought
he were attacked, that the attack were real,
and that his own defense could save himself?
And herein lies the folly of defense;
it gives illusions full reality,
and then attempts to handle them as real.
It adds illusions to illusions, thus
making correction doubly difficult.
And it is this you do when you attempt
to plan the future, activate the past,
or organize the present as you wish.

You operate from the belief you must
protect yourself from what is happening
because it must contain what threatens you.
A sense of threat is an acknowledgment
of an inherent weakness; a belief
that there is danger which has power to call
on you to make appropriate defense.
The world is based on this insane belief.
And all its structures, all its thoughts and doubts,
its penalties and heavy armaments,
its legal definitions and its codes,
its ethics and its leaders and its gods,
all serve but to preserve its sense of threat.
For no one walks the world in armature
but must have terror striking at his heart.

Defense is frightening. It stems from fear,
increasing fear as each defense is made.
You think it offers safety. Yet it speaks
of fear made real and terror justified.
Is it not strange you do not pause to ask,
as you elaborate your plans and make
your armor thicker and your locks more tight,
what you defend, and how, and against what?

Let us consider first what you defend.
It must be something that is very weak
and easily assaulted. It must be
something made easy prey, unable to
protect itself and needing your defense.
What but the body has such frailty
that constant care and watchful, deep concern
are needful to protect its little life?
What but the body falters and must fail
to serve the Son of God as worthy host?

Yet it is not the body that can fear,
nor be a thing of fear. It has no needs
but those which you assign to it. It needs
no complicated structures of defense,
no health-inducing medicine, no care
and no concern at all. Defend its life,
or give it gifts to make it beautiful
or walls to make it safe, and you but say
your home is open to the thief of time,
corruptible and crumbling, so unsafe
it must be guarded with your very life.

Is not this picture fearful? Can you be
at peace with such a concept of your home?
Yet what endowed the body with the right
to serve you thus except your own belief?
It is your mind which gave the body all
the functions that you see in it, and set
its value far beyond a little pile
of dust and water. Who would make defense
of something that he recognized as this?

The body is in need of no defense.
This cannot be too often emphasized.
It will be strong and healthy if the mind
does not abuse it by assigning it
to roles it cannot fill, to purposes
beyond its scope, and to exalted aims
which it cannot accomplish. Such attempts,
ridiculous yet deeply cherished, are
the sources for the many mad attacks
you make upon it. For it seems to fail
your hopes, your needs, your values and your
dreams.

The "self" that needs protection is not real.
The body, valueless and hardly worth
the least defense, need merely be perceived
as quite apart from you, and it becomes
a healthy, serviceable instrument
through which the mind can operate until
its usefulness is over. Who would want
to keep it when its usefulness is done?

Defend the body and you have attacked

your mind. For you have seen in it the faults,
the weaknesses, the limits and the lacks
from which you think the body must be saved.
You will not see the mind as separate
from bodily conditions. And you will
impose upon the body all the pain
that comes from the conception of the mind
as limited and fragile, and apart
from other minds and separate from its Source.

These are the thoughts in need of healing, and
the body will respond with health when they
have been corrected and replaced with truth.
This is the body's only real defense.
Yet is this where you look for its defense?
You offer it protection of a kind
from which it gains no benefit at all,
but merely adds to your distress of mind.
You do not heal, but merely take away
the hope of healing, for you fail to see
where hope must lie if it be meaningful.

A healed mind does not plan. It carries out
the plans that it receives through listening
to Wisdom that is not its own. It waits
until it has been taught what should be done,
and then proceeds to do it. It does not
depend upon itself for anything
except its adequacy to fulfill
the plans assigned to it. It is secure
in certainty that obstacles can not
impede its progress to accomplishment
of any goal that serves the greater plan
established for the good of everyone.

A healed mind is relieved of the belief
that it must plan, although it cannot know
the outcome which is best, the means by which
it is achieved, nor how to recognize
the problem that the plan is made to solve.
It must misuse the body in its plans
until it recognizes this is so.
But when it has accepted this as true,
then is it healed, and lets the body go.

Enslavement of the body to the plans
the unhealed mind sets up to save itself
must make the body sick. It is not free
to be the means of helping in a plan
which far exceeds its own protection, and
which needs its service for a little while.

In this capacity is health assured.
For everything the mind employs for this
will function flawlessly, and with the strength
that has been given it and cannot fail.

It is, perhaps, not easy to perceive
that self-initiated plans are but
defenses, with the purpose all of them
were made to realize. They are the means
by which a frightened mind would undertake
its own protection, at the cost of truth.
This is not difficult to realize
in some forms which these self-deceptions take,
where the denial of reality
is very obvious. Yet planning is
not often recognized as a defense.

The mind engaged in planning for itself
is occupied in setting up control
of future happenings. It does not think
that it will be provided for, unless
it makes its own provisions. Time becomes
a future emphasis, to be controlled
by learning and experience obtained
from past events and previous beliefs.
It overlooks the present, for it rests
on the idea the past has taught enough
to let the mind direct its future course.

The mind that plans is thus refusing to
allow for change. What it has learned before
becomes the basis for its future goals.
Its past experience directs its choice
of what will happen. And it does not see
that here and now is everything it needs
to guarantee a future quite unlike
the past, without a continuity
of any old ideas and sick beliefs.
Anticipation plays no part at all,
for present confidence directs the way.

Defenses are the plans you undertake
to make against the truth. Their aim is to
select what you approve, and disregard
what you consider incompatible
with your beliefs of your reality.
Yet what remains is meaningless indeed.
For it is your reality that is
the "threat" which your defenses would attack,
obscure, and take apart and crucify.

What could you not accept, if you but knew
that everything that happens, all events,
past, present and to come, are gently planned
by One Whose only purpose is your good?
Perhaps you have misunderstood His plan,
for He would never offer pain to you.
But your defenses did not let you see
His loving blessing shine in every step
you ever took. While you made plans for death,
He led you gently to eternal life.

Your present trust in Him is the defense
that promises a future undisturbed,
without a trace of sorrow, and with joy
that constantly increases, as this life
becomes a holy instant, set in time,
but heeding only immortality.
Let no defenses but your present trust
direct the future, and this life becomes
a meaningful encounter with the truth
that only your defenses would conceal.

Without defenses, you become a light
which Heaven gratefully acknowledges
to be its own. And it will lead you on
in ways appointed for your happiness
according to the ancient plan, begun
when time was born. Your followers will join
their light with yours, and it will be increased
until the world is lighted up with joy.
And gladly will our brothers lay aside
their cumbersome defenses, which availed
them nothing and could only terrify.

We will anticipate that time today
with present confidence, for this is part
of what was planned for us. We will be sure
that everything we need is given us
for our accomplishment of this today.
We make no plans for how it will be done,
but realize that our defenselessness
is all that is required for the truth
to dawn upon our minds with certainty.

For fifteen minutes twice today we rest
from senseless planning, and from every thought
that blocks the truth from entering our minds.
Today we will receive instead of plan,
that we may give instead of organize.
And we are given truly, as we say:

*If I defend myself I am attacked.*
*But in defenselessness I will be strong,*
*and I will learn what my defenses hide.*

Nothing but that. If there are plans to make,
you will be told of them. They may not be
the plans you thought were needed, nor indeed
the answers to the problems which you thought
confronted you. But they are answers to
another kind of question, which remains
unanswered yet in need of answering
until the Answer comes to you at last.

All your defenses have been aimed at not
receiving what you will receive today.
And in the light and joy of simple trust,
you will but wonder why you ever thought
that you must be defended from release.
Heaven asks nothing. It is hell that makes
extravagant demands for sacrifice.
You give up nothing in these times today
when, undefended, you present yourself
to your Creator as you really are.

He has remembered you. Today we will
remember Him. For this is Eastertime
in your salvation. And you rise again
from what was seeming death and hopelessness.
Now is the light of hope reborn in you,
for now you come without defense, to learn
the part for you within the plan of God.
What little plans or magical beliefs
can still have value, when you have received
your function from the Voice for God Himself?

Try not to shape this day as you believe
would benefit you most. For you can not
conceive of all the happiness that comes
to you without your planning. Learn today.
And all the world will take this giant stride,
and celebrate your Eastertime with you.
Throughout the day, as foolish little things
appear to raise defensiveness in you
and tempt you to engage in weaving plans,
remind yourself this is a special day
for learning, and acknowledge it with this:

*This is my Eastertime. And I would keep*
*it holy. I will not defend myself,*
*because the Son of God needs no defense*
*against the truth of his reality.*

## LESSON 136

### Sickness is a defense against the truth.

No one can heal unless he understands what purpose sickness seems to serve. For then he understands as well its purpose has no meaning. Being causeless and without a meaningful intent of any kind, it cannot be at all. When this is seen, healing is automatic. It dispels this meaningless illusion by the same approach that carries all of them to truth, and merely leaves them there to disappear.

Sickness is not an accident. Like all defenses, it is an insane device for self-deception. And like all the rest, its purpose is to hide reality, attack it, change it, render it inept, distort it, twist it, or reduce it to a little pile of unassembled parts. The aim of all defenses is to keep the truth from being whole. The parts are seen as if each one were whole within itself.

Defenses are not unintentional, nor are they made without awareness. They are secret, magic wands you wave when truth appears to threaten what you would believe. They seem to be unconscious but because of the rapidity with which you choose to use them. In that second, even less, in which the choice is made, you recognize exactly what you would attempt to do, and then proceed to think that it is done.

Who but yourself evaluates a threat, decides escape is necessary, and sets up a series of defenses to reduce the threat that has been judged as real? All this cannot be done unconsciously. But afterwards, your plan requires that you must forget you made it, so it seems to be external to your own intent; a happening beyond your state of mind, an outcome with a real effect on you, instead of one effected by yourself.

It is this quick forgetting of the part you play in making your "reality" that makes defenses seem to be beyond your own control. But what you have forgot can be remembered, given willingness to reconsider the decision which is doubly shielded by oblivion. Your not remembering is but the sign that this decision still remains in force, as far as your desires are concerned. Mistake not this for fact. Defenses must make facts unrecognizable. They aim at doing this, and it is this they do.

Every defense takes fragments of the whole, assembles them without regard to all their true relationships, and thus constructs illusions of a whole that is not there. It is this process that imposes threat, and not whatever outcome may result. When parts are wrested from the whole and seen as separate and wholes within themselves, they become symbols standing for attack upon the whole; successful in effect, and never to be seen as whole again. And yet you have forgotten that they stand but for your own decision of what should be real, to take the place of what is real.

Sickness is a decision. It is not a thing that happens to you, quite unsought, which makes you weak and brings you suffering. It is a choice you make, a plan you lay, when for an instant truth arises in your own deluded mind, and all your world appears to totter and prepare to fall. Now are you sick, that truth may go away and threaten your establishments no more.

How do you think that sickness can succeed in shielding you from truth? Because it proves the body is not separate from you, and so you must be separate from the truth. You suffer pain because the body does, and in this pain are you made one with it. Thus is your "true" identity preserved, and the strange, haunting thought that you might be

something beyond this little pile of dust
silenced and stilled. For see, this dust can make
you suffer, twist your limbs and stop your heart,
commanding you to die and cease to be.

Thus is the body stronger than the truth,
which asks you live, but cannot overcome
your choice to die. And so the body is
more powerful than everlasting life,
Heaven more frail than hell, and God's design
for the salvation of His Son opposed
by a decision stronger than His Will.
His Son is dust, the Father incomplete,
and chaos sits in triumph on His throne.

Such is your planning for your own defense.
And you believe that Heaven quails before
such mad attacks as these, with God made blind
by your illusions, truth turned into lies,
and all the universe made slave to laws
which your defenses would impose on it.
Yet who believes illusions but the one
who made them up? Who else can see them and
react to them as if they were the truth?

God knows not of your plans to change His Will.
The universe remains unheeding of
the laws by which you thought to govern it.
And Heaven has not bowed to hell, nor life
to death. You can but choose to think you die,
or suffer sickness or distort the truth
in any way. What is created is
apart from all of this. Defenses are
plans to defeat what cannot be attacked.
What is unalterable cannot change.
And what is wholly sinless cannot sin.

Such is the simple truth. It does not make
appeal to might nor triumph. It does not
command obedience, nor seek to prove
how pitiful and futile your attempts
to plan defenses that would alter it.
Truth merely wants to give you happiness,
for such its purpose is. Perhaps it sighs
a little when you throw away its gifts,
and yet it knows, with perfect certainty,
that what God wills for you must be received.

It is this fact that demonstrates that time
is an illusion. For time lets you think

what God has given you is not the truth
right now, as it must be. The Thoughts of God
are quite apart from time. For time is but
another meaningless defense you made
against the truth. Yet what He wills is here,
and you remain as He created you.

Truth has a power far beyond defense,
for no illusions can remain where truth
has been allowed to enter. And it comes
to any mind that would lay down its arms,
and cease to play with folly. It is found
at any time; today, if you will choose
to practice giving welcome to the truth.

This is our aim today. And we will give
a quarter of an hour twice to ask
the truth to come to us and set us free.
And truth will come, for it has never been
apart from us. It merely waits for just
this invitation which we give today.
We introduce it with a healing prayer,
to help us rise above defensiveness,
and let truth be as it has always been:

*Sickness is a defense against the truth.*
*I will accept the truth of what I am,*
*and let my mind be wholly healed today.*

Healing will flash across your open mind,
as peace and truth arise to take the place
of war and vain imaginings. There will
be no dark corners sickness can conceal,
and keep defended from the light of truth.
There will be no dim figures from your dreams,
nor their obscure and meaningless pursuits
with double purposes insanely sought,
remaining in your mind. It will be healed
of all the sickly wishes that it tried
to authorize the body to obey.

Now is the body healed, because the source
of sickness has been opened to relief.
And you will recognize you practiced well
by this: The body should not feel at all.
If you have been successful, there will be
no sense of feeling ill or feeling well,
of pain or pleasure. No response at all
is in the mind to what the body does.
Its usefulness remains and nothing more.

Perhaps you do not realize that this
removes the limits you had placed upon
the body by the purposes you gave
to it. As these are laid aside, the strength
the body has will always be enough
to serve all truly useful purposes.
The body's health is fully guaranteed,
because it is not limited by time,
by weather or fatigue, by food and drink,
or any laws you made it serve before.
You need do nothing now to make it well,
for sickness has become impossible.

Yet this protection needs to be preserved
by careful watching. If you let your mind
harbor attack thoughts, yield to judgment or
make plans against uncertainties to come,
you have again misplaced yourself, and made
a bodily identity which will
attack the body, for the mind is sick.

Give instant remedy, should this occur,
by not allowing your defensiveness
to hurt you longer. Do not be confused
about what must be healed, but tell yourself:

*I have forgotten what I really am,*
*for I mistook my body for myself.*
*Sickness is a defense against the truth.*
*But I am not a body. And my mind*
*cannot attack. So I can not be sick.*

## LESSON 137

### When I am healed I am not healed alone.

Today's idea remains the central thought on which salvation rests. For healing is the opposite of all the world's ideas which dwell on sickness and on separate states. Sickness is a retreat from others, and a shutting off of joining. It becomes a door that closes on a separate self, and keeps it isolated and alone.

Sickness is isolation. For it seems to keep one self apart from all the rest, to suffer what the others do not feel. It gives the body final power to make the separation real, and keep the mind in solitary prison, split apart and held in pieces by a solid wall of sickened flesh, which it can not surmount.

The world obeys the laws that sickness serves, but healing operates apart from them. It is impossible that anyone be healed alone. In sickness must he be apart and separate. But healing is his own decision to be one again, and to accept his Self with all Its parts intact and unassailed. In sickness does his Self appear to be dismembered, and without the unity that gives It life. But healing is accomplished as he sees the body has no power to attack the universal oneness of God's Son.

Sickness would prove that lies must be the truth. But healing demonstrates that truth is true. The separation sickness would impose has never really happened. To be healed is merely to accept what always was the simple truth, and always will remain exactly as it has forever been. Yet eyes accustomed to illusions must be shown that what they look upon is false. So healing, never needed by the truth, must demonstrate that sickness is not real.

Healing might thus be called a counter-dream, which cancels out the dream of sickness in the name of truth, but not in truth itself.

Just as forgiveness overlooks all sins that never were accomplished, healing but removes illusions that have not occurred. Just as the real world will arise to take the place of what has never been at all, healing but offers restitution for imagined states and false ideas which dreams embroider into pictures of the truth.

Yet think not healing is unworthy of your function here. For anti-Christ becomes more powerful than Christ to those who dream the world is real. The body seems to be more solid and more stable than the mind. And love becomes a dream, while fear remains the one reality that can be seen and justified and fully understood.

Just as forgiveness shines away all sin and the real world will occupy the place of what you made, so healing must replace the fantasies of sickness which you hold before the simple truth. When sickness has been seen to disappear in spite of all the laws that hold it cannot but be real, then questions have been answered. And the laws can be no longer cherished nor obeyed.

Healing is freedom. For it demonstrates that dreams will not prevail against the truth. Healing is shared. And by this attribute it proves that laws unlike the ones which hold that sickness is inevitable are more potent than their sickly opposites. Healing is strength. For by its gentle hand is weakness overcome, and minds that were walled off within a body free to join with other minds, to be forever strong.

Healing, forgiveness, and the glad exchange of all the world of sorrow for a world where sadness cannot enter, are the means by which the Holy Spirit urges you to follow Him. His gentle lessons teach how easily salvation can be yours; how little practice you need undertake to let His laws replace the ones you made

to hold yourself a prisoner to death.
His life becomes your own, as you extend
the little help He asks in freeing you
from everything that ever caused you pain.

And as you let yourself be healed, you see
all those around you, or who cross your mind,
or whom you touch or those who seem to have
no contact with you, healed along with you.
Perhaps you will not recognize them all,
nor realize how great your offering
to all the world, when you let healing come
to you. But you are never healed alone.
And legions upon legions will receive
the gift that you receive when you are healed.

Those who are healed become the instruments
of healing. Nor does time elapse between
the instant they are healed, and all the grace
of healing it is given them to give.
What is opposed to God does not exist,
and who accepts it not within his mind
becomes a haven where the weary can
remain to rest. For here is truth bestowed,
and here are all illusions brought to truth.

Would you not offer shelter to God's Will?
You but invite your Self to be at home.
And can this invitation be refused?
Ask the inevitable to occur,
and you will never fail. The other choice
is but to ask what cannot be to be,
and this can not succeed. Today we ask
that only truth will occupy our minds;
that thoughts of healing will this day go forth
from what is healed to what must yet be healed,
aware that they will both occur as one.

We will remember, as the hour strikes,
our function is to let our minds be healed,
that we may carry healing to the world,
exchanging curse for blessing, pain for joy,
and separation for the peace of God.
Is not a minute of the hour worth
the giving to receive a gift like this?
Is not a little time a small expense
to offer for the gift of everything?

Yet must we be prepared for such a gift.
And so we will begin the day with this,
and give ten minutes to these thoughts with which
we will conclude today at night as well:

*When I am healed I am not healed alone.*
*And I would share my healing with the world,*
*that sickness may be banished from the mind*
*of God's one Son, Who is my only Self.*

Let healing be through you this very day.
And as you rest in quiet, be prepared
to give as you receive, to hold but what
you give, and to receive the Word of God
to take the place of all the foolish thoughts
that ever were imagined. Now we come
together to make well all that was sick,
and offer blessing where there was attack.
Nor will we let this function be forgot
as every hour of the day slips by,
remembering our purpose with this thought:

*When I am healed I am not healed alone.*
*And I would bless my brothers, for I would*
*be healed with them, as they are healed with me.*

# LESSON 138

### Heaven is the decision I must make.

In this world Heaven is a choice, because here we believe there are alternatives to choose between. We think that all things have an opposite, and what we want we choose. If Heaven exists there must be hell as well, for contradiction is the way we make what we perceive, and what we think is real.

Creation knows no opposite. But here is opposition part of being "real." It is this strange perception of the truth that makes the choice of Heaven seem to be the same as the relinquishment of hell. It is not really thus. Yet what is true in God's creation cannot enter here until it is reflected in some form the world can understand. Truth cannot come where it could only be perceived with fear. For this would be the error truth can be brought to illusions. Opposition makes the truth unwelcome, and it cannot come.

Choice is the obvious escape from what appears as opposites. Decision lets one of conflicting goals become the aim of effort and expenditure of time. Without decision, time is but a waste and effort dissipated. It is spent for nothing in return, and time goes by without results. There is no sense of gain, for nothing is accomplished; nothing learned.

You need to be reminded that you think a thousand choices are confronting you, when there is really only one to make. And even this but seems to be a choice. Do not confuse yourself with all the doubts that myriad decisions would induce. You make but one. And when that one is made, you will perceive it was no choice at all. For truth is true, and nothing else is true. There is no opposite to choose instead. There is no contradiction to the truth.

Choosing depends on learning. And the truth cannot be learned, but only recognized. In recognition its acceptance lies, and as it is accepted it is known. But knowledge is beyond the goals we seek to teach within the framework of this course. Ours are teaching goals, to be attained through learning how to reach them, what they are, and what they offer you. Decisions are the outcome of your learning, for they rest on what you have accepted as the truth of what you are, and what your needs must be.

In this insanely complicated world, Heaven appears to take the form of choice, rather than merely being what it is. Of all the choices you have tried to make this is the simplest, most definitive and prototype of all the rest, the one which settles all decisions. If you could decide the rest, this one remains unsolved. But when you solve this one, the others are resolved with it, for all decisions but conceal this one by taking different forms. Here is the final and the only choice in which is truth accepted or denied.

So we begin today considering the choice that time was made to help us make. Such is its holy purpose, now transformed from the intent you gave it; that it be a means for demonstrating hell is real, hope changes to despair, and life itself must in the end be overcome by death. In death alone are opposites resolved, for ending opposition is to die. And thus salvation must be seen as death, for life is seen as conflict. To resolve the conflict is to end your life as well.

These mad beliefs can gain unconscious hold of great intensity, and grip the mind with terror and anxiety so strong that it will not relinquish its ideas about its own protection. It must be saved from salvation, threatened to be safe, and magically armored against truth. And these decisions are made unaware, to keep them safely undisturbed; apart from question and from reason and from doubt.

Heaven is chosen consciously. The choice
cannot be made until alternatives
are accurately seen and understood.
All that is veiled in shadows must be raised
to understanding, to be judged again,
this time with Heaven's help. And all mistakes
in judgment that the mind had made before
are open to correction, as the truth
dismisses them as causeless. Now are they
without effects. They cannot be concealed,
because their nothingness is recognized.

The conscious choice of Heaven is as sure
as is the ending of the fear of hell,
when it is raised from its protective shield
of unawareness, and is brought to light.
Who can decide between the clearly seen
and the unrecognized? Yet who can fail
to make a choice between alternatives
when only one is seen as valuable;
the other as a wholly worthless thing,
a but imagined source of guilt and pain?
Who hesitates to make a choice like this?
And shall we hesitate to choose today?

We make the choice for Heaven as we wake,
and spend five minutes making sure that we
have made the one decision that is sane.
We recognize we make a conscious choice
between what has existence and what has
nothing but an appearance of the truth.
Its pseudo-being, brought to what is real,
is flimsy and transparent in the light.
It holds no terror now, for what was made
enormous, vengeful, pitiless with hate,
demands obscurity for fear to be
invested there. Now it is recognized
as but a foolish, trivial mistake.

Before we close our eyes in sleep tonight,
we reaffirm the choice that we have made
each hour in between. And now we give
the last five minutes of our waking day
to the decision with which we awoke.
As every hour passed, we have declared
our choice again, in a brief quiet time
devoted to maintaining sanity.
And finally, we close the day with this,
acknowledging we chose but what we want:

*Heaven is the decision I must make.*
*I make it now, and will not change my mind,*
*because it is the only thing I want.*

## LESSON 139

**I will accept Atonement for myself.**

Here is the end of choice. For here we come
to a decision to accept ourselves
as God created us. And what is choice
except uncertainty of what we are?
There is no doubt that is not rooted here.
There is no question but reflects this one.
There is no conflict that does not entail
the single, simple question, "What am I?"

Yet who could ask this question except one
who has refused to recognize himself?
Only refusal to accept yourself
could make the question seem to be sincere.
The only thing that can be surely known
by any living thing is what it is.
From this one point of certainty, it looks
on other things as certain as itself.

Uncertainty about what you must be
is self-deception on a scale so vast,
its magnitude can hardly be conceived.
To be alive and not to know yourself
is to believe that you are really dead.
For what is life except to be yourself,
and what but you can be alive instead?
Who is the doubter? What is it he doubts?
Whom does he question? Who can answer him?

He merely states that he is not himself,
and therefore, being something else, becomes
a questioner of what that something is.
Yet he could never be alive at all
unless he knew the answer. If he asks
as if he does not know, it merely shows
he does not want to be the thing he is.
He has accepted it because he lives;
has judged against it and denied its worth,
and has decided that he does not know
the only certainty by which he lives.

Thus he becomes uncertain of his life,
for what it is has been denied by him.
It is for this denial that you need
Atonement. Your denial made no change
in what you are. But you have split your mind
into what knows and does not know the truth.

You are yourself. There is no doubt of this.
And yet you doubt it. But you do not ask
what part of you can really doubt yourself.
It cannot really be a part of you
that asks this question. For it asks of one
who knows the answer. Were it part of you,
then certainty would be impossible.

Atonement remedies the strange idea
that it is possible to doubt yourself,
and be unsure of what you really are.
This is the depth of madness. Yet it is
the universal question of the world.
What does this mean except the world is mad?
Why share its madness in the sad belief
that what is universal here is true?

Nothing the world believes is true. It is
a place whose purpose is to be a home
where those who claim they do not know themselves
can come to question what it is they are.
And they will come again until the time
Atonement is accepted, and they learn
it is impossible to doubt yourself,
and not to be aware of what you are.

Only acceptance can be asked of you,
for what you are is certain. It is set
forever in the holy Mind of God,
and in your own. It is so far beyond
all doubt and question that to ask what it
must be is all the proof you need to show
that you believe the contradiction that
you know not what you cannot fail to know.
Is this a question, or a statement which
denies itself in statement? Let us not
allow our holy minds to occupy
themselves with senseless musings such as this.

We have a mission here. We did not come
to reinforce the madness that we once
believed in. Let us not forget the goal
that we accepted. It is more than just
our happiness alone we came to gain.
What we accept as what we are proclaims
what everyone must be, along with us.

Fail not your brothers, or you fail yourself.
Look lovingly on them, that they may know
that they are part of you, and you of them.

This does Atonement teach, and demonstrates
the oneness of God's Son is unassailed
by his belief he knows not what he is.
Today accept Atonement, not to change
reality, but merely to accept the
truth about yourself, and go your way
rejoicing in the endless Love of God.
It is but this that we are asked to do.
It is but this that we will do today.

Five minutes in the morning and at night
we will devote to dedicate our minds
to our assignment for today. We start
with this review of what our mission is:

*I will accept Atonement for myself,*
*For I remain as God created me.*

We have not lost the knowledge that God gave
to us when He created us like Him.
We can remember it for everyone,
for in creation are all minds as one.
And in our memory is the recall
how dear our brothers are to us in truth,
how much a part of us is every mind,
how faithful they have really been to us,
and how our Father's Love contains them all.

In thanks for all creation, in the Name
of its Creator and His Oneness with
all aspects of creation, we repeat
our dedication to our cause today
each hour, as we lay aside all thoughts
that would distract us from our holy aim.
For several minutes let your mind be cleared
of all the foolish cobwebs which the world
would weave around the holy Son of God.
And learn the fragile nature of the chains
that seem to keep the knowledge of yourself
apart from your awareness, as you say:

*I will accept Atonement for myself,*
*For I remain as God created me.*

## LESSON 140

**Only salvation can be said to cure.**

"Cure" is a word that cannot be applied to any remedy the world accepts as beneficial. What the world perceives as therapeutic is but what will make the body "better." When it tries to heal the mind, it sees no separation from the body, where it thinks the mind exists. Its forms of healing thus must substitute illusion for illusion. One belief in sickness takes another form, and so the patient now perceives himself as well.

He is not healed. He merely had a dream that he was sick, and in the dream he found a magic formula to make him well. Yet he has not awakened from the dream, and so his mind remains exactly as it was before. He has not seen the light that would awaken him and end the dream. What difference does the content of a dream make in reality? One either sleeps or wakens. There is nothing in between.

The happy dreams the Holy Spirit brings are different from the dreaming of the world, where one can merely dream he is awake. The dreams forgiveness lets the mind perceive do not induce another form of sleep, so that the dreamer dreams another dream. His happy dreams are heralds of the dawn of truth upon the mind. They lead from sleep to gentle waking, so that dreams are gone. And thus they cure for all eternity.

Atonement heals with certainty, and cures all sickness. For the mind which understands that sickness can be nothing but a dream is not deceived by forms the dream may take. Sickness where guilt is absent cannot come, for it is but another form of guilt. Atonement does not heal the sick, for that is not a cure. It takes away the guilt that makes the sickness possible. And that is cure indeed. For sickness now is gone, with nothing left to which it can return.

Peace be to you who have been cured in God, and not in idle dreams. For cure must come from holiness, and holiness can not be found where sin is cherished. God abides in holy temples. He is barred where sin has entered. Yet there is no place where He is not. And therefore sin can have no home in which to hide from His beneficence. There is no place where holiness is not, and nowhere sin and sickness can abide.

This is the thought that cures. It does not make distinctions among unrealities. Nor does it seek to heal what is not sick, unmindful where the need for healing is. This is no magic. It is merely an appeal to truth, which cannot fail to heal and heal forever. It is not a thought that judges an illusion by its size, its seeming gravity, or anything that is related to the form it takes. It merely focuses on what it is, and knows that no illusion can be real.

Let us not try today to seek to cure what cannot suffer sickness. Healing must be sought but where it is, and then applied to what is sick, so that it can be cured. There is no remedy the world provides that can effect a change in anything. The mind that brings illusions to the truth is really changed. There is no change but this. For how can one illusion differ from another but in attributes that have no substance, no reality, no core, and nothing that is truly different?

Today we seek to change our minds about the source of sickness, for we seek a cure for all illusions, not another shift among them. We will try today to find the source of healing, which is in our minds because our Father placed it there for us. It is not farther from us than ourselves. It is as near to us as our own thoughts; so close it is impossible to lose.

We need but seek it and it must be found.

We will not be misled today by what
appears to us as sick. We go beyond
appearances today and reach the source
of healing, from which nothing is exempt.
We will succeed to the extent to which
we realize that there can never be
a meaningful distinction made between
what is untrue and equally untrue.
Here there are no degrees, and no beliefs
that what does not exist is truer in
some forms than others. All of them are false,
and can be cured because they are not true.

So do we lay aside our amulets,
our charms and medicines, our chants and bits
of magic in whatever form they take.
We will be still and listen for the Voice
of healing, Which will cure all ills as one,
restoring saneness to the Son of God.
No voice but This can cure. Today we hear
a single Voice Which speaks to us of truth,
where all illusions end, and peace returns
to the eternal, quiet home of God.

We waken hearing Him, and let Him speak
to us five minutes as the day begins,
and end the day by listening again
five minutes more before we go to sleep.
Our only preparation is to let
our interfering thoughts be laid aside,
not separately, but all of them as one.
They are the same. We have no need to make
them different, and thus delay the time
when we can hear our Father speak to us.
We hear Him now. We come to Him today.

With nothing in our hands to which we cling,
with lifted hearts and listening minds we pray:

*Only salvation can be said to cure.*
*Speak to us, Father, that we may be healed.*

And we will feel salvation cover us
with soft protection, and with peace so deep
that no illusion can disturb our minds,
nor offer proof to us that it is real.
This will we learn today. And we will say
our prayer for healing hourly, and take
a minute as the hour strikes, to hear
the answer to our prayer be given us
as we attend in silence and in joy.
This is the day when healing comes to us.
This is the day when separation ends,
and we remember Who we really are.

# REVIEW IV

## Introduction

Now we review again, this time aware we are preparing for the second part of learning how the truth can be applied. Today we will begin to concentrate on readiness for what will follow next. Such is our aim for this review, and for the lessons following. Thus, we review the recent lessons and their central thoughts in such a way as will facilitate the readiness that we would now achieve.

There is a central theme that unifies each step in the review we undertake, which can be simply stated in these words:

*My mind holds only what I think with God.*

That is a fact, and represents the truth of What you are and What your Father is. It is this thought by which the Father gave creation to the Son, establishing the Son as co-creator with Himself. It is this thought that fully guarantees salvation to the Son. For in his mind no thoughts can dwell but those his Father shares. Lack of forgiveness blocks this thought from his awareness. Yet it is forever true.

Let us begin our preparation with some understanding of the many forms in which the lack of true forgiveness may be carefully concealed. Because they are illusions, they are not perceived to be but what they are; defenses that protect your unforgiving thoughts from being seen and recognized. Their purpose is to show you something else, and hold correction off through self-deceptions made to take its place.

And yet, your mind holds only what you think with God. Your self-deceptions cannot take the place of truth. No more than can a child who throws a stick into the ocean change the coming and the going of the tides, the warming of the water by the sun, the silver of the moon on it by night. So do we start each practice period in this review with readying our minds to understand the lessons that we read, and see the meaning that they offer us.

Begin each day with time devoted to the preparation of your mind to learn what each idea you will review that day can offer you in freedom and in peace. Open your mind, and clear it of all thoughts that would deceive, and let this thought alone engage it fully, and remove the rest:

*My mind holds only what I think with God.*

Five minutes with this thought will be enough to set the day along the lines which God appointed, and to place His Mind in charge of all the thoughts you will receive that day.

They will not come from you alone, for they will all be shared with Him. And so each one will bring the message of His Love to you, returning messages of yours to Him. So will communion with the Lord of Hosts be yours, as He Himself has willed it be. And as His Own completion joins with Him, so will He join with you who are complete as you unite with Him, and He with you.

After your preparation, merely read each of the two ideas assigned to you to be reviewed that day. Then close your eyes, and say them slowly to yourself. There is no hurry now, for you are using time for its intended purpose. Let each word shine with the meaning God has given it, as it was given to you through His Voice. Let each idea which you review that day give you the gift that He has laid in it for you to have of Him. And we will use no format for our practicing but this:

Each hour of the day, bring to your mind the thought with which the day began, and spend a quiet moment with it. Then repeat the two ideas you practice for the day unhurriedly, with time enough to see the gifts that they contain for you, and let them be received where they were meant to be.

We add no other thoughts, but let these be
the messages they are. We need no more
than this to give us happiness and rest,
and endless quiet, perfect certainty,
and all our Father wills that we receive
as the inheritance we have of Him.
Each day of practicing, as we review,
we close as we began, repeating first
the thought that made the day a special time
of blessing and of happiness for us;
and through our faithfulness restored the world
from darkness to the light, from grief to joy,
from pain to peace, from sin to holiness.

God offers thanks to you who practice thus
the keeping of His Word. And as you give
your mind to the ideas for the day
again before you sleep, His gratitude
surrounds you in the peace wherein He wills
you be forever, and are learning now
to claim again as your inheritance.

### LESSON 141

**My mind holds only what I think with God.**

Forgiveness is the key to happiness.

Forgiveness offers everything I want.

### LESSON 142

**My mind holds only what I think with God.**

I thank my Father for His gifts to me.

Let me remember I am one with God.

### LESSON 143

**My mind holds only what I think with God.**

In quiet I receive God's Word today.

All that I give is given to myself.

### LESSON 144

**My mind holds only what I think with God.**

There is no love but God's.

The world I see holds nothing that I want.

### LESSON 145

**My mind holds only what I think with God.**

Beyond this world there is a world I want.

It is impossible to see two worlds.

### LESSON 146

My mind holds only what I think with God.

No one can fail who seeks to reach the truth.

loose the world from all I thought it was.

### LESSON 147

My mind holds only what I think with God.

I will not value what is valueless.

Let me perceive forgiveness as it is.

### LESSON 148

My mind holds only what I think with God.

If I defend myself I am attacked.

Sickness is a defense against the truth.

### LESSON 149

My mind holds only what I think with God.

When I am healed I am not healed alone.

Heaven is the decision I must make.

### LESSON 150

**My mind holds only what I think with God.**

I will accept Atonement for myself.

Only salvation can be said to cure.

# LESSON 151

### All things are echoes of the Voice for God.

No one can judge on partial evidence.
That is not judgment. It is merely an
opinion based on ignorance and doubt.
Its seeming certainty is but a cloak
for the uncertainty it would conceal.
It needs irrational defense because
it is irrational. And its defense
seems strong, convincing, and without a doubt
because of all the doubting underneath.

You do not seem to doubt the world you see.
You do not really question what is shown
you through the body's eyes. Nor do you ask
why you believe it, even though you learned
a long while since your senses do deceive.
That you believe them to the last detail
which they report is even stranger, when
you pause to recollect how frequently
they have been faulty witnesses indeed!
Why would you trust them so implicitly?
Why but because of underlying doubt,
which you would hide with show of certainty?

How can you judge? Your judgment rests upon
the witness that your senses offer you.
Yet witness never falser was than this.
But how else do you judge the world you see?
You place pathetic faith in what your eyes
and ears report. You think your fingers touch
reality, and close upon the truth.
This is awareness that you understand,
and think more real than what is witnessed to
by the eternal Voice for God Himself.

Can this be judgment? You have often been
urged to refrain from judging, not because
it is a right to be withheld from you.
You cannot judge. You merely can believe
the ego's judgments, all of which are false.
It guides your senses carefully, to prove
how weak you are; how helpless and afraid,
how apprehensive of just punishment,
how black with sin, how wretched in your guilt.

This thing it speaks of, and would yet defend,
it tells you is yourself. And you believe
that this is so with stubborn certainty.
Yet underneath remains the hidden doubt
that what it shows you as reality
with such conviction it does not believe.
It is itself alone that it condemns.
It is within itself it sees the guilt.
It is its own despair it sees in you.

Hear not its voice. The witnesses it sends
to prove to you its evil is your own
are false, and speak with certainty of what
they do not know. Your faith in them is blind
because you would not share the doubts their lord
can not completely vanquish. You believe
to doubt his vassals is to doubt yourself.

Yet you must learn to doubt their evidence
will clear the way to recognize yourself,
and let the Voice for God alone be Judge
of what is worthy of your own belief.
He will not tell you that your brother should
be judged by what your eyes behold in him,
nor what his body's mouth says to your ears,
nor what your fingers' touch reports of him.
He passes by such idle witnesses,
which merely bear false witness to God's Son.
He recognizes only what God loves,
and in the holy light of what He sees
do all the ego's dreams of what you are
vanish before the splendor He beholds.

Let Him be Judge of what you are, for He
has certainty in which there is no doubt,
because it rests on Certainty so great
that doubt is meaningless before Its face.
Christ cannot doubt Himself. The Voice for God
can only honor Him, rejoicing in
His perfect, everlasting sinlessness.
Whom He has judged can only laugh at guilt,
unwilling now to play with toys of sin;
unheeding of the body's witnesses
before the rapture of Christ's holy face.

And thus He judges you. Accept His Word
for what you are, for He bears witness to
your beautiful creation, and the Mind

Whose Thought created your reality.
What can the body mean to Him Who knows
the glory of the Father and the Son?
What whispers of the ego can He hear?
What could convince Him that your sins are real?
Let Him be Judge as well of everything
that seems to happen to you in this world.
His lessons will enable you to bridge
the gap between illusions and the truth.

He will remove all faith that you have placed
in pain, disaster, suffering and loss.
He gives you vision which can look beyond
these grim appearances, and can behold
the gentle face of Christ in all of them.
You will no longer doubt that only good
can come to you who are beloved of God,
for He will judge all happenings, and teach
the single lesson that they all contain.

He will select the elements in them
which represent the truth, and disregard
those aspects which reflect but idle dreams.
And He will reinterpret all you see,
and all occurrences, each circumstance,
and every happening that seems to touch
on you in any way from His one frame
of reference, wholly unified and sure.
And you will see the love beyond the hate,
the constancy in change, the pure in sin,
and only Heaven's blessing on the world.

Such is your resurrection, for your life
is not a part of anything you see.
It stands beyond the body and the world,
past every witness for unholiness,
within the Holy, holy as Itself.
In everyone and everything His Voice
would speak to you of nothing but your Self
and your Creator, Who is one with Him.
So will you see the holy face of Christ
in everything, and hear in everything
no sound except the echo of God's Voice.

We practice wordlessly today, except
at the beginning of the time we spend
with God. We introduce these times with but
a single, slow repeating of the thought
with which the day begins. And then we watch
our thoughts, appealing silently to Him

Who sees the elements of truth in them.
Let Him evaluate each thought that comes
to mind, remove the elements of dreams,
and give them back again as clean ideas
that do not contradict the Will of God.

Give Him your thoughts, and He will give them back
as miracles which joyously proclaim
the wholeness and the happiness God wills
His Son, as proof of His eternal Love.
And as each thought is thus transformed, it takes
on healing power from the Mind Which saw
the truth in it, and failed to be deceived
by what was falsely added. All the threads
of fantasy are gone. And what remains
is unified into a perfect Thought
that offers its perfection everywhere.

Spend fifteen minutes thus when you awake,
and gladly give another fifteen more
before you go to sleep. Your ministry
begins as all your thoughts are purified.
So are you taught to teach the Son of God
the holy lesson of his sanctity.
No one can fail to listen, when you hear
the Voice for God give honor to God's Son.
And everyone will share the thoughts with you
which He has retranslated in your mind.

Such is your Eastertide. And so you lay
the gift of snow-white lilies on the world,
replacing witnesses to sin and death.
Through your transfiguration is the world
redeemed, and joyfully released from guilt.
Now do we lift our resurrected minds
in gladness and in gratitude to Him
Who has restored our sanity to us.

And we will hourly remember Him
Who is salvation and deliverance.
As we give thanks, the world unites with us
and happily accepts our holy thoughts,
which Heaven has corrected and made pure.
Now has our ministry begun at last,
to carry round the world the joyous news
that truth has no illusions, and the peace
of God, through us, belongs to everyone.

## LESSON 152

### The power of decision is my own.

No one can suffer loss unless it be
his own decision. No one suffers pain
except his choice elects this state for him.
No one can grieve nor fear nor think him sick
unless these are the outcomes that he wants.
And no one dies without his own consent.
Nothing occurs but represents your wish,
and nothing is omitted that you choose.
Here is your world, complete in all details.
Here is its whole reality for you.
And it is only here salvation is.

You may believe that this position is
extreme, and too inclusive to be true.
Yet can truth have exceptions? If you have
the gift of everything, can loss be real?
Can pain be part of peace, or grief of joy?
Can fear and sickness enter in a mind
where love and perfect holiness abide?
Truth must be all-inclusive, if it be
the truth at all. Accept no opposites
and no exceptions, for to do so is
to contradict the truth entirely.

Salvation is the recognition that
the truth is true, and nothing else is true.
This you have heard before, but may not yet
accept both parts of it. Without the first,
the second has no meaning. But without
the second, is the first no longer true.
Truth cannot have an opposite. This can
not be too often said and thought about.
For if what is not true is true as well
as what is true, then part of truth is false.
And truth has lost its meaning. Nothing but
the truth is true, and what is false is false.

This is the simplest of distinctions, yet
the most obscure. But not because it is
a difficult distinction to perceive.
It is concealed behind a vast array
of choices that do not appear to be
entirely your own. And thus the truth
appears to have some aspects that belie
consistency, but do not seem to be
but contradictions introduced by you.

As God created you, you must remain
unchangeable, with transitory states
by definition false. And that includes
all shifts in feeling, alterations in
conditions of the body and the mind;
in all awareness and in all response.
This is the all-inclusiveness which sets
the truth apart from falsehood, and the false
kept separate from the truth, as what it is.

Is it not strange that you believe to think
you made the world you see is arrogance?
God made it not. Of this you can be sure.
What can He know of the ephemeral,
the sinful and the guilty, the afraid,
the suffering and lonely, and the mind
that lives within a body that must die?
You but accuse Him of insanity,
to think He made a world where such things seem
to have reality. He is not mad.
Yet only madness makes a world like this.

To think that God made chaos, contradicts
His Will, invented opposites to truth,
and suffers death to triumph over life;
all this is arrogance. Humility
would see at once these things are not of Him.
And can you see what God created not?
To think you can is merely to believe
you can perceive what God willed not to be.
And what could be more arrogant than this?

Let us today be truly humble, and
accept what we have made as what it is.
The power of decision is our own.
Decide but to accept your rightful place
as co-creator of the universe,
and all you think you made will disappear.
What rises to awareness then will be
all that there ever was, eternally
as it is now. And it will take the place
of self-deceptions made but to usurp
the altar to the Father and the Son.

Today we practice true humility,
abandoning the false pretense by which
the ego seeks to prove it arrogant.

Only the ego can be arrogant.
But truth is humble in acknowledging
its mightiness, its changelessness and its
eternal wholeness, all-encompassing,
God's perfect gift to His beloved Son.
We lay aside the arrogance which says
that we are sinners, guilty and afraid,
ashamed of what we are; and lift our hearts
in true humility instead to Him
Who has created us immaculate,
like to Himself in power and in love.

The power of decision is our own.
And we accept of Him that which we are,
and humbly recognize the Son of God.
To recognize God's Son implies as well
that all self-concepts have been laid aside,
and recognized as false. Their arrogance
has been perceived. And in humility
the radiance of God's Son, his gentleness,
his perfect sinlessness, his Father's Love,
his right to Heaven and release from hell,
are joyously accepted as our own.

Now do we join in glad acknowledgment
that lies are false, and only truth is true.
We think of truth alone as we arise,
and spend five minutes practicing its ways,
encouraging our frightened minds with this:

*The power of decision is my own.*
*This day I will accept myself as what*
*my Father's Will created me to be.*

Then will we wait in silence, giving up
all self-deceptions, as we humbly ask
our Self that He reveal Himself to us.
And He Who never left will come again
to our awareness, grateful to restore
His home to God, as it was meant to be.

In patience wait for Him throughout the day,
and hourly invite Him with the words
with which the day began, concluding it
with this same invitation to your Self.
God's Voice will answer, for He speaks for you
and for your Father. He will substitute
the peace of God for all your frantic thoughts,
the truth of God for self-deceptions, and
God's Son for your illusions of yourself.

## LESSON 153

### In my defenselessness my safety lies.

You who feel threatened by this changing world,
its twists of fortune and its bitter jests,
its brief relationships and all the "gifts"
it merely lends to take away again;
attend this lesson well. The world provides
no safety. It is rooted in attack,
and all its "gifts" of seeming safety are
illusory deceptions. It attacks,
and then attacks again. No peace of mind
is possible where danger threatens thus.

The world gives rise but to defensiveness.
For threat brings anger, anger makes attack
seem reasonable, honestly provoked,
and righteous in the name of self-defense.
Yet is defensiveness a double threat.
For it attests to weakness, and sets up
a system of defense that cannot work.
Now are the weak still further undermined,
for there is treachery without and still
a greater treachery within. The mind
is now confused, and knows not where to turn
to find escape from its imaginings.

It is as if a circle held it fast,
wherein another circle bound it and
another one in that, until escape
no longer can be hoped for nor obtained.
Attack, defense; defense, attack, become
the circles of the hours and the days
that bind the mind in heavy bands of steel
with iron overlaid, returning but
to start again. There seems to be no break
nor ending in the ever-tightening grip
of the imprisonment upon the mind.

Defenses are the costliest of all
the prices which the ego would exact.
In them lies madness in a form so grim
that hope of sanity seems but to be
an idle dream, beyond the possible.
The sense of threat the world encourages
is so much deeper, and so far beyond
the frenzy and intensity of which
you can conceive, that you have no idea
of all the devastation it has wrought.

You are its slave. You know not what you do,
in fear of it. You do not understand
how much you have been made to sacrifice,
who feel its iron grip upon your heart.
You do not realize what you have done
to sabotage the holy peace of God
by your defensiveness. For you behold
the Son of God as but a victim to
attack by fantasies, by dreams, and by
illusions he has made; yet helpless in
their presence, needful only of defense
by still more fantasies, and dreams by which
illusions of his safety comfort him.

Defenselessness is strength. It testifies
to recognition of the Christ in you.
Perhaps you will recall the text maintains
that choice is always made between Christ's strength
and your own weakness, seen apart from Him.
Defenselessness can never be attacked,
because it recognizes strength so great
attack is folly, or a silly game
a tired child might play, when he becomes
too sleepy to remember what he wants.

Defensiveness is weakness. It proclaims
you have denied the Christ and come to fear
His Father's anger. What can save you now
from your delusion of an angry god,
whose fearful image you believe you see
at work in all the evils of the world?
What but illusions could defend you now,
when it is but illusions that you fight?

We will not play such childish games today.
For our true purpose is to save the world,
and we would not exchange for foolishness
the endless joy our function offers us.
We would not let our happiness slip by
because a fragment of a senseless dream
happened to cross our minds, and we mistook
the figures in it for the Son of God;
its tiny instant for eternity.

We look past dreams today, and recognize
that we need no defense because we are
created unassailable, without

all thought or wish or dream in which attack
has any meaning. Now we cannot fear,
for we have left all fearful thoughts behind.
And in defenselessness we stand secure,
serenely certain of our safety now,
sure of salvation; sure we will fulfill
our chosen purpose, as our ministry
extends its holy blessing through the world.

Be still a moment, and in silence think
how holy is your purpose, how secure
you rest, untouchable within its light.
God's ministers have chosen that the truth
be with them. Who is holier than they?
Who could be surer that his happiness
is fully guaranteed? And who could be
more mightily protected? What defense
could possibly be needed by the ones
who are among the chosen ones of God,
by His election and their own as well?

It is the function of God's ministers
to help their brothers choose as they have done.
God has elected all, but few have come
to realize His Will is but their own.
And while you fail to teach what you have learned,
salvation waits and darkness holds the world
in grim imprisonment. Nor will you learn
that light has come to you, and your escape
has been accomplished. For you will not see
the light, until you offer it to all
your brothers. As they take it from your hands,
so will you recognize it as your own.

Salvation can be thought of as a game
that happy children play. It was designed
by One Who loves His children, and Who would
replace their fearful toys with joyous games,
which teach them that the game of fear is gone.
His game instructs in happiness because
there is no loser. Everyone who plays
must win, and in his winning is the gain
to everyone ensured. The game of fear
is gladly laid aside, when children come
to see the benefits salvation brings.

You who have played that you are lost to hope,
abandoned by your Father, left alone
in terror in a fearful world made mad
by sin and guilt; be happy now. That game
is over. Now a quiet time has come,
in which we put away the toys of guilt,
and lock our quaint and childish thoughts of sin
forever from the pure and holy minds
of Heaven's children and the Son of God.

We pause but for a moment more, to play
our final, happy game upon this earth.
And then we go to take our rightful place
where truth abides and games are meaningless.
So is the story ended. Let this day
bring the last chapter closer to the world,
that everyone may learn the tale he reads
of terrifying destiny, defeat
of all his hopes, his pitiful defense
against a vengeance he can not escape,
is but his own deluded fantasy.
God's ministers have come to waken him
from the dark dreams this story has evoked
in his confused, bewildered memory
of this distorted tale. God's Son can smile
at last, on learning that it is not true.

Today we practice in a form we will
maintain for quite a while. We will begin
each day by giving our attention to
the daily thought as long as possible.
Five minutes now becomes the least we give
to preparation for a day in which
salvation is the only goal we have.
Ten would be better; fifteen better still.
And as distraction ceases to arise
to turn us from our purpose, we will find
that half an hour is too short a time
to spend with God. Nor will we willingly
give less at night, in gratitude and joy.

Each hour adds to our increasing peace,
as we remember to be faithful to
the Will we share with God. At times, perhaps,
a minute, even less, will be the most
that we can offer as the hour strikes.
Sometimes we will forget. At other times
the business of the world will close on us,
and we will be unable to withdraw
a little while, and turn our thoughts to God.

Yet when we can, we will observe our trust
as ministers of God, in hourly
remembrance of our mission and His Love.

And we will quietly sit by and wait
on Him and listen to His Voice, and learn
what He would have us do the hour that
is yet to come; while thanking Him for all
the gifts He gave us in the one gone by.

In time, with practice, you will never cease
to think of Him, and hear His loving Voice
guiding your footsteps into quiet ways,
where you will walk in true defenselessness.
For you will know that Heaven goes with you.
Nor would you keep your mind away from Him
a moment, even though your time is spent
in offering salvation to the world.
Think you He will not make this possible,
for you who chose to carry out His plan
for the salvation of the world and yours?

Today our theme is our defenselessness.
We clothe ourselves in it, as we prepare
to meet the day. We rise up strong in Christ,
and let our weakness disappear, as we
remember that His strength abides in us.
We will remind ourselves that He remains
beside us through the day, and never leaves
our weakness unsupported by His strength.
We call upon His strength each time we feel
the threat of our defenses undermine
our certainty of purpose. We will pause
a moment, as He tells us, "I am here."

Your practicing will now begin to take
the earnestness of love, to help you keep
your mind from wandering from its intent.
Be not afraid nor timid. There can be
no doubt that you will reach your final goal.
The ministers of God can never fail,
because the love and strength and peace that shine
from them to all their brothers come from Him.
These are His gifts to you. Defenselessness
is all you need to give Him in return.
You lay aside but what was never real,
to look on Christ and see His sinlessness.

# LESSON 154

**I am among the ministers of God.**

Let us today be neither arrogant nor falsely humble. We have gone beyond such foolishness. We cannot judge ourselves, nor need we do so. These are but attempts to hold decision off, and to delay commitment to our function. It is not our part to judge our worth, nor can we know what role is best for us; what we can do within a larger plan we cannot see in its entirety. Our part is cast in Heaven, not in hell. And what we think is weakness can be strength; what we believe to be our strength is often arrogance.

Whatever your appointed role may be, it was selected by the Voice for God, Whose function is to speak for you as well. Seeing your strengths exactly as they are, and equally aware of where they can be best applied, for what, to whom and when, He chooses and accepts your part for you. He does not work without your own consent. But He is not deceived in what you are, and listens only to His Voice in you.

It is through His ability to hear one Voice Which is His Own that you become aware at last there is one Voice in you. And that one Voice appoints your function, and relays it to you, giving you the strength to understand it, do what it entails, and to succeed in everything you do that is related to it. God has joined His Son in this, and thus His Son becomes His messenger of unity with Him.

It is this joining, through the Voice for God, of Father and of Son, that sets apart salvation from the world. It is this Voice Which speaks of laws the world does not obey; Which promises salvation from all sin, with guilt abolished in the mind that God created sinless. Now this mind becomes aware again of Who created it, and of His lasting union with itself. So is its Self the one reality in Which its will and that of God are joined.

A messenger is not the one who writes the message he delivers. Nor does he question the right of him who does, nor ask why he has chosen those who will receive the message that he brings. It is enough that he accept it, give it to the ones for whom it is intended, and fulfill his role in its delivery. If he determines what the messages should be, or what their purpose is, or where they should be carried, he is failing to perform his proper part as bringer of the Word.

There is one major difference in the role of Heaven's messengers, which sets them off from those the world appoints. The messages that they deliver are intended first for them. And it is only as they can accept them for themselves that they become able to bring them further, and to give them everywhere that they were meant to be. Like earthly messengers, they did not write the messages they bear, but they become their first receivers in the truest sense, receiving to prepare themselves to give.

An earthly messenger fulfills his role by giving all his messages away. The messengers of God perform their part by their acceptance of His messages as for themselves, and show they understand the messages by giving them away. They choose no roles that are not given them by His authority. And so they gain by every message that they give away.

Would you receive the messages of God? For thus do you become His messenger. You are appointed now. And yet you wait to give the messages you have received. And so you do not know that they are yours, and do not recognize them. No one can receive and understand he has received until he gives. For in the giving is his own acceptance of what he received.

You who are now the messengers of God, receive His messages. For that is part of your appointed role. God has not failed to offer what you need, nor has it been left unaccepted. Yet another part of your appointed task is yet to be accomplished. He Who has received for you the messages of God would have them be received by you as well. For thus do you identify with Him and claim your own.

It is this joining that we undertake to recognize today. We will not seek to keep our minds apart from Him Who speaks for us, for it is but our voice we hear as we attend Him. He alone can speak to us and for us, joining in one Voice the getting and the giving of God's Word; the giving and receiving of His Will.

We practice giving Him what He would have, that we may recognize His gifts to us. He needs our voice that He may speak through us. He needs our hands to hold His messages, and carry them to those whom He appoints. He needs our feet to bring us where He wills, that those who wait in misery may be at last delivered. And He needs our will united with His Own, that we may be the true receivers of the gifts He gives.

Let us but learn this lesson for today: We will not recognize what we receive until we give it. You have heard this said a hundred ways, a hundred times, and yet belief is lacking still. But this is sure; until belief is given it, you will receive a thousand miracles and then receive a thousand more, but will not know that God Himself has left no gift beyond what you already have; nor has denied the tiniest of blessings to His Son. What can this mean to you, until you have identified with Him and with His Own?

Our lesson for today is stated thus:

*I am among the ministers of God, and I am grateful that I have the means by which to recognize that I am free.*

The world recedes as we light up our minds, and realize these holy words are true. They are the message sent to us today from our Creator. Now we demonstrate how they have changed our minds about ourselves, and what our function is. For as we prove that we accept no will we do not share, our many gifts from our Creator will spring to our sight and leap into our hands, and we will recognize what we received.

## LESSON 155

**I will step back and let Him lead the way.**

There is a way of living in the world
that is not here, although it seems to be.
You do not change appearance, though you smile
more frequently. Your forehead is serene;
your eyes are quiet. And the ones who walk
the world as you do recognize their own.
Yet those who have not yet perceived the way
will recognize you also, and believe
that you are like them, as you were before.

The world is an illusion. Those who choose
to come to it are seeking for a place
where they can be illusions, and avoid
their own reality. Yet when they find
their own reality is even here,
then they step back and let it lead the way.
What other choice is really theirs to make?
To let illusions walk ahead of truth
is madness. But to let illusion sink
behind the truth and let the truth stand forth
as what it is, is merely sanity.

This is the simple choice we make today.
The mad illusion will remain awhile
in evidence, for those to look upon
who chose to come, and have not yet rejoiced
to find they were mistaken in their choice.
They cannot learn directly from the truth,
because they have denied that it is so.
And so they need a Teacher Who perceives
their madness, but Who still can look beyond
illusion to the simple truth in them.

If truth demanded they give up the world,
it would appear to them as if it asked
the sacrifice of something that is real.
Many have chosen to renounce the world
while still believing its reality.
And they have suffered from a sense of loss,
and have not been released accordingly.
Others have chosen nothing but the world,
and they have suffered from a sense of loss
still deeper, which they did not understand.

Between these paths there is another road
that leads away from loss of every kind,
for sacrifice and deprivation both
are quickly left behind. This is the way
appointed for you now. You walk this path
as others walk, nor do you seem to be
distinct from them, although you are indeed.
Thus can you serve them while you serve yourself,
and set their footsteps on the way that God
has opened up to you, and them through you.

Illusion still appears to cling to you,
that you may reach them. Yet it has stepped back.
And it is not illusion that they hear
you speak of, nor illusion that you bring
their eyes to look on and their minds to grasp.
Nor can the truth, which walks ahead of you,
speak to them through illusions, for the road
leads past illusion now, while on the way
you call to them, that they may follow you.

All roads will lead to this one in the end.
For sacrifice and deprivation are
paths that lead nowhere, choices for defeat,
and aims that will remain impossible.
All this steps back as truth comes forth in you,
to lead your brothers from the ways of death,
and set them on the way to happiness.
Their suffering is but illusion. Yet
they need a guide to lead them out of it,
for they mistake illusion for the truth.

Such is salvation's call, and nothing more.
It asks that you accept the truth, and let
it go before you, lighting up the path
of ransom from illusion. It is not
a ransom with a price. There is no cost,
but only gain. Illusion can but seem
to hold in chains the holy Son of God.
It is but from illusions he is saved.
As they step back, he finds himself again.

Walk safely now, yet carefully, because
this path is new to you. And you may find
that you are tempted still to walk ahead
of truth, and let illusions be your guide.
Your holy brothers have been given you,
to follow in your footsteps as you walk

with certainty of purpose to the truth.
It goes before you now, that they may see
something with which they can identify;
something they understand to lead the way.

Yet at the journey's ending there will be
no gap, no distance between truth and you.
And all illusions walking in the way
you travelled will be gone from you as well,
with nothing left to keep the truth apart
from God's completion, holy as Himself.
Step back in faith and let truth lead the way.
You know not where you go. But One Who knows
goes with you. Let Him lead you with the rest.

When dreams are over, time has closed the door
on all the things that pass and miracles
are purposeless, the holy Son of God
will make no journeys. There will be no wish
to be illusion rather than the truth.
And we step forth toward this, as we progress
along the way that truth points out to us.
This is our final journey, which we make
for everyone. We must not lose our way.
For as truth goes before us, so it goes
before our brothers who will follow us.

We walk to God. Pause and reflect on this.
Could any way be holier, or more
deserving of your effort, of your love
and of your full intent? What way could give
you more than everything, or offer less
and still content the holy Son of God?
We walk to God. The truth that walks before
us now is one with Him, and leads us to
where He has always been. What way but this
could be a path that you would choose instead?

Your feet are safely set upon the road
that leads the world to God. Look not to ways
that seem to lead you elsewhere. Dreams are not
a worthy guide for you who are God's Son.
Forget not He has placed His Hand in yours,
and given you your brothers in His Trust
that you are worthy of His Trust in you.
He cannot be deceived. His Trust has made
your pathway certain and your goal secure.
You will not fail your brothers nor your Self.

And now He asks but that you think of Him
a while each day, that He may speak to you
and tell you of His Love, reminding you
how great His Trust; how limitless His Love.
In your name and His Own, which are the same,
we practice gladly with this thought today:

*I will step back and let Him lead the way,*
*For I would walk along the road to Him.*

## LESSON 156

**I walk with God in perfect holiness.**

Today's idea but states the simple truth that makes the thought of sin impossible. It promises there is no cause for guilt, and being causeless it does not exist. It follows surely from the basic thought so often mentioned in the text; ideas leave not their source. If this be true, how can you be apart from God? How could you walk the world alone and separate from your Source?

We are not inconsistent in the thoughts that we present in our curriculum. Truth must be true throughout, if it be true. It cannot contradict itself, nor be in parts uncertain and in others sure. You cannot walk the world apart from God, because you could not be without Him. He is what your life is. Where you are He is. There is one life. That life you share with Him. Nothing can be apart from Him and live.

Yet where He is, there must be holiness as well as life. No attribute of His remains unshared by everything that lives. What lives is holy as Himself, because what shares His life is part of Holiness, and could no more be sinful than the sun could choose to be of ice; the sea elect to be apart from water, or the grass to grow with roots suspended in the air.

There is a light in you which cannot die; whose presence is so holy that the world is sanctified because of you. All things that live bring gifts to you, and offer them in gratitude and gladness at your feet. The scent of flowers is their gift to you. The waves bow down before you, and the trees extend their arms to shield you from the heat, and lay their leaves before you on the ground that you may walk in softness, while the wind sinks to a whisper round your holy head.

The light in you is what the universe longs to behold. All living things are still before you, for they recognize Who walks with you. The light you carry is their own. And thus they see in you their holiness, saluting you as savior and as God. Accept their reverence, for it is due to Holiness Itself, Which walks with you, transforming in Its gentle Light all things unto Its likeness and Its purity.

This is the way salvation works. As you step back, the light in you steps forward and encompasses the world. It heralds not the end of sin in punishment and death. In lightness and in laughter is sin gone, because its quaint absurdity is seen. It is a foolish thought, a silly dream, not frightening, ridiculous perhaps, but who would waste an instant in approach to God Himself for such a senseless whim?

Yet you have wasted many, many years on just this foolish thought. The past is gone, with all its fantasies. They keep you bound no longer. The approach to God is near. And in the little interval of doubt that still remains, you may perhaps lose sight of your Companion, and mistake Him for the senseless, ancient dream that now is past.

"Who walks with me?" This question should be asked a thousand times a day, till certainty has ended doubting and established peace. Today let doubting cease. God speaks for you in answering your question with these words:

*I walk with God in perfect holiness.*
*I light the world, I light my mind and all*
*the minds which God created one with me.*

## LESSON 157

**Into His Presence would I enter now.**

This is a day of silence and oftrust.
It is a special time of promise in
your calendar of days. It is a time
Heaven has set apart to shine upon,
and cast a timeless light upon this day,
when echoes of eternity are heard.
This day is holy, for it ushers in
a new experience; a different kind
of feeling and awareness. You have spent
long days and nights in celebrating death.
Today you learn to feel the joy of life.

This is another crucial turning point
in the curriculum. We add a new
dimension now; a fresh experience
that sheds a light on all that we have learned
already, and prepares us for what we
have yet to learn. It brings us to the door
where learning ceases, and we catch a glimpse
of what lies past the highest reaches it
can possibly attain. It leaves us here
an instant, and we go beyond it, sure
of our direction and our only goal.

Today it will be given you to feel
a touch of Heaven, though you will return
to paths of learning. Yet you have come far
enough along the way to alter time
sufficiently to rise above its laws,
and walk into eternity a while.
This you will learn to do increasingly,
as every lesson, faithfully rehearsed,
brings you more swiftly to this holy place
and leaves you, for a moment, to your Self.

He will direct your practicing today,
for what you ask for now is what He wills.
And having joined your will with His this day,
what you are asking must be given you.
Nothing is needed but today's idea
to light your mind, and let it rest in still
anticipation and in quiet joy,
wherein you quickly leave the world behind.

From this day forth, your ministry takes on
a genuine devotion, and a glow
that travels from your fingertips to those
you touch, and blesses those you look upon.
A vision reaches everyone you meet,
and everyone you think of, or who thinks
of you. For your experience today
will so transform your mind that it becomes
the touchstone for the holy Thoughts of God.

Your body will be sanctified today,
its only purpose being now to bring
the vision of what you experience
this day to light the world. We cannot give
experience like this directly. Yet
it leaves a vision in our eyes which we
can offer everyone, that he may come
the sooner to the same experience
in which the world is quietly forgot,
and Heaven is remembered for a while.

As this experience increases and
all goals but this become of little worth,
the world to which you will return becomes
a little closer to the end of time;
a little more like Heaven in its ways;
a little nearer its deliverance.
And you who bring it light will come to see
the light more sure; the vision more distinct.
The time will come when you will not return
in the same form in which you now appear,
for you will have no need of it. Yet now
it has a purpose, and will serve it well.

Today we will embark upon a course
you have not dreamed of. But the Holy One,
the Giver of the happy dreams of life,
Translator of perception into truth,
the holy Guide to Heaven given you,
has dreamed for you this journey which you make
and start today, with the experience
this day holds out to you to be your own.

Into Christ's Presence will we enter now,
serenely unaware of everything
except His shining face and perfect Love.
The vision of His face will stay with you,
but there will be an instant which transcends
all vision, even this, the holiest.
This you will never teach, for you attained
it not through learning. Yet the vision speaks
of your remembrance of what you knew
that instant, and will surely know again.

## LESSON 158

### Today I learn to give as I receive.

What has been given you? The knowledge that you are a mind, in Mind and purely mind, sinless forever, wholly unafraid, because you were created out of Love. Nor have you left your Source, remaining as you were created. This was given you as knowledge which you cannot lose. It was given as well to every living thing, for by that knowledge only does it live.

You have received all this. No one who walks the world but has received it. It is not this knowledge which you give, for that is what creation gave. All this cannot be learned. What, then, are you to learn to give today? Our lesson yesterday evoked a theme found early in the text. Experience cannot be shared directly, in the way that vision can. The revelation that the Father and the Son are one will come in time to every mind. Yet is that time determined by the mind itself, not taught.

The time is set already. It appears to be quite arbitrary. Yet there is no step along the road that anyone takes but by chance. It has already been taken by him, although he has not yet embarked on it. For time but seems to go in one direction. We but undertake a journey that is over. Yet it seems to have a future still unknown to us.

Time is a trick, a sleight of hand, a vast illusion in which figures come and go as if by magic. Yet there is a plan behind appearances that does not change. The script is written. When experience will come to end your doubting has been set. For we but see the journey from the point at which it ended, looking back on it, imagining we make it once again; reviewing mentally what has gone by.

A teacher does not give experience, because he did not learn it. It revealed itself to him at its appointed time.

But vision is his gift. This he can give directly, for Christ's knowledge is not lost, because He has a vision He can give to anyone who asks. The Father's Will and His are joined in knowledge. Yet there is a vision which the Holy Spirit sees because the mind of Christ beholds it too.

Here is the joining of the world of doubt and shadows made with the intangible. Here is a quiet place within the world made holy by forgiveness and by love. Here are all contradictions reconciled, for here the journey ends. Experience - unlearned, untaught, unseen - is merely there. This is beyond our goal, for it transcends what needs to be accomplished. Our concern is with Christ's vision. This we can attain.

Christ's vision has one law. It does not look upon a body, and mistake it for the Son whom God created. It beholds a light beyond the body; an idea beyond what can be touched, a purity undimmed by errors, pitiful mistakes, and fearful thoughts of guilt from dreams of sin. It sees no separation. And it looks on everyone, on every circumstance, all happenings and all events, without the slightest fading of the light it sees.

This can be taught; and must be taught by all who would achieve it. It requires but the recognition that the world can not give anything that faintly can compare with this in value; nor set up a goal that does not merely disappear when this has been perceived. And this you give today: See no one as a body. Greet him as the Son of God he is, acknowledging that he is one with you in holiness.

Thus are his sins forgiven him, for Christ has vision that has power to overlook them all. In His forgiveness are they gone. Unseen by One they merely disappear, because a vision of the holiness

that lies beyond them comes to take their place.
It matters not what form they took, nor how
enormous they appeared to be, nor who
seemed to be hurt by them. They are no more.
And all effects they seemed to have are gone
with them, undone and never to be done.

Thus do you learn to give as you receive.
And thus Christ's vision looks on you as well.
This lesson is not difficult to learn,
if you remember in your brother you
but see yourself. If he be lost in sin,
so must you be; if you see light in him,
your sins have been forgiven by yourself.
Each brother whom you meet today provides
another chance to let Christ's vision shine
on you, and offer you the peace of God.

It matters not when revelation comes,
for that is not of time. Yet time has still
one gift to give, in which true knowledge is
reflected in a way so accurate
its image shares its unseen holiness;
its likeness shines with its immortal love.
We practice seeing with the eyes of Christ
today. And by the holy gifts we give,
Christ's vision looks upon ourselves as well.

## LESSON 159

**I give the miracles I have received.**

No one can give what he has not received. To give a thing requires first you have it in your own possession. Here the laws of Heaven and the world agree. But here they also separate. The world believes that to possess a thing, it must be kept. Salvation teaches otherwise. To give is how to recognize you have received. It is the proof that what you have is yours.

You understand that you are healed when you give healing. You accept forgiveness as accomplished in yourself when you forgive. You recognize your brother as yourself, and thus do you perceive that you are whole. There is no miracle you cannot give, for all are given you. Receive them now by opening the storehouse of your mind where they are laid, and giving them away.

Christ's vision is a miracle. It comes from far beyond itself, for it reflects Eternal Love and the rebirth of love which never dies, but has been kept obscure. Christ's vision pictures Heaven, for it sees a world so like to Heaven that what God created perfect can be mirrored there. The darkened glass the world presents can show but twisted images in broken parts. The real world pictures Heaven's innocence.

Christ's vision is the miracle in which all miracles are born. It is their source, remaining with each miracle you give, and yet remaining yours. It is the bond by which the giver and receiver are united in extension here on earth, as they are one in Heaven. Christ beholds no sin in anyone. And in His sight the sinless are as one. Their holiness was given by His Father and Himself.

Christ's vision is the bridge between the worlds. And in its power can you safely trust to carry you from this world into one made holy by forgiveness. Things which seem quite solid here are merely shadows there; transparent, faintly seen, at times forgot, and never able to obscure the light that shines beyond them. Holiness has been restored to vision, and the blind can see.

This is the Holy Spirit's single gift; the treasure house to which you can appeal with perfect certainty for all the things that can contribute to your happiness. All are laid here already. All can be received but for the asking. Here the door is never locked, and no one is denied his least request or his most urgent need. There is no sickness not already healed, no lack unsatisfied, no need unmet within this golden treasury of Christ.

Here does the world remember what was lost when it was made. For here it is repaired, made new again, but in a different light. What was to be the home of sin becomes the center of redemption and the hearth of mercy, where the suffering are healed and welcome. No one will be turned away from this new home, where his salvation waits. No one is stranger to him. No one asks for anything of him except the gift of his acceptance of his welcoming.

Christ's vision is the holy ground in which the lilies of forgiveness set their roots. This is their home. They can be brought from here back to the world, but they can never grow in its unnourishing and shallow soil. They need the light and warmth and kindly care Christ's charity provides. They need the love with which He looks on them. And they become His messengers, who give as they received.

Take from His storehouse, that its treasures may increase. His lilies do not leave their home when they are carried back into the world. Their roots remain. They do not leave their source, but carry its beneficence with them, and turn the world into a garden like the one they came from, and to which they go again with added fragrance. Now are they

twice blessed. The messages they brought from Christ
have been delivered, and returned to them.
And they return them gladly unto Him.

Behold the store of miracles set out
for you to give. Are you not worth the gift,
when God appointed it be given you?
Judge not God's Son, but follow in the way
He has established. Christ has dreamed the dream
of a forgiven world. It is His gift,
whereby a sweet transition can be made
from death to life; from hopelessness to hope.
Let us an instant dream with Him. His dream
awakens us to truth. His vision gives
the means for a return to our unlost
and everlasting sanctity in God.

# LESSON 160

**I am at home. Fear is the stranger here.**

Fear is a stranger to the ways of love. Identify with fear, and you will be a stranger to yourself. And thus you are unknown to you. What is your Self remains an alien to the part of you which thinks that it is real, but different from yourself. Who could be sane in such a circumstance? Who but a madman could believe he is what he is not, and judge against himself?

There is a stranger in our midst, who comes from an idea so foreign to the truth he speaks a different language, looks upon a world truth does not know, and understands what truth regards as senseless. Stranger yet, he does not recognize to whom he comes, and yet maintains his home belongs to him, while he is alien now who is at home. And yet, how easy it would be to say, "This is my home. Here I belong, and will not leave because a madman says I must."

What reason is there for not saying this? What could the reason be except that you had asked this stranger in to take your place, and let you be a stranger to yourself? No one would let himself be dispossessed so needlessly, unless he thought there were another home more suited to his tastes.

Who is the stranger? Is it fear or you who are unsuited to the home which God provided for His Son? Is fear His Own, created in His likeness? Is it fear that love completes, and is completed by? There is no home can shelter love and fear. They cannot coexist. If you are real, then fear must be illusion. And if fear is real, then you do not exist at all.

How simply, then, the question is resolved. Who fears has but denied himself and said, "I am the stranger here. And so I leave my home to one more like me than myself, and give him all I thought belonged to me." Now is he exiled of necessity, not knowing who he is, uncertain of all things but this; that he is not himself, and that his home has been denied to him.

What does he search for now? What can he find? A stranger to himself can find no home wherever he may look, for he has made return impossible. His way is lost, except a miracle will search him out and show him that he is no stranger now. The miracle will come. For in his home his Self remains. It asked no stranger in, and took no alien thought to be Itself. And It will call Its Own unto Itself in recognition of what is Its Own.

Who is the stranger? Is he not the one your Self calls not? You are unable now to recognize this stranger in your midst, for you have given him your rightful place. Yet is your Self as certain of Its Own as God is of His Son. He cannot be confused about creation. He is sure of what belongs to Him. No stranger can be interposed between His knowledge and His Son's reality. He does not know of strangers. He is certain of His Son.

God's certainty suffices. Who He knows to be His Son belongs where He has set His Son forever. He has answered you who ask, "Who is the stranger?" Hear His Voice assure you, quietly and sure, that you are not a stranger to your Father, nor is your Creator stranger made to you. Whom God has joined remain forever one, at home in Him, no stranger to Himself.

Today we offer thanks that Christ has come to search the world for what belongs to Him. His vision sees no strangers, but beholds His Own and joyously unites with them. They see Him as a stranger, for they do not recognize themselves. Yet as they give Him welcome, they remember. And He leads them gently home again, where they belong.

Not one does Christ forget. Not one He fails
to give you to remember, that your home
may be complete and perfect as it was
established. He has not forgotten you.
But you will not remember Him until
you look on all as He does. Who denies
his brother is denying Him, and thus
refusing to accept the gift of sight
by which his Self is clearly recognized,
his home remembered and salvation come.

## LESSON 161

**Give me your blessing, holy Son of God.**

Today we practice differently, and take a stand against our anger, that our fears may disappear and offer room to love. Here is salvation in the simple words in which we practice with today's idea. Here is the answer to temptation which can never fail to welcome in the Christ where fear and anger had prevailed before. Here is Atonement made complete, the world passed safely by and Heaven now restored. Here is the answer of the Voice for God.

Complete abstraction is the natural condition of the mind. But part of it is now unnatural. It does not look on everything as one. It sees instead but fragments of the whole, for only thus could it invent the partial world you see. The purpose of all seeing is to show you what you wish to see. All hearing but brings to your mind the sounds it wants to hear.

Thus were specifics made. And now it is specifics we must use in practicing. We give them to the Holy Spirit, that He may employ them for a purpose which is different from the one we gave to them. Yet He can use but what we made, to teach us from a different point of view, so we can see a different use in everything.

One brother is all brothers. Every mind contains all minds, for every mind is one. Such is the truth. Yet do these thoughts make clear the meaning of creation? Do these words bring perfect clarity with them to you? What can they seem to be but empty sounds; pretty, perhaps, correct in sentiment, yet fundamentally not understood nor understandable. The mind that taught itself to think specifically can no longer grasp abstraction in the sense that it is all-encompassing. We need to see a little, that we learn a lot.

It seems to be the body that we feel limits our freedom, makes us suffer, and at last puts out our life. Yet bodies are but symbols for a concrete form of fear. Fear without symbols calls for no response, for symbols can stand for the meaningless. Love needs no symbols, being true. But fear attaches to specifics, being false.

Bodies attack, but minds do not. This thought is surely reminiscent of our text, where it is often emphasized. This is the reason bodies easily become fear's symbols. You have many times been urged to look beyond the body, for its sight presents the symbol of love's "enemy" Christ's vision does not see. The body is the target for attack, for no one thinks he hates a mind. Yet what but mind directs the body to attack? What else could be the seat of fear except what thinks of fear?

Hate is specific. There must be a thing to be attacked. An enemy must be perceived in such a form he can be touched and seen and heard, and ultimately killed. When hatred rests upon a thing, it calls for death as surely as God's Voice proclaims there is no death. Fear is insatiable, consuming everything its eyes behold, seeing itself in everything, compelled to turn upon itself and to destroy.

Who sees a brother as a body sees him as fear's symbol. And he will attack, because what he beholds is his own fear external to himself, poised to attack, and howling to unite with him again. Mistake not the intensity of rage projected fear must spawn. It shrieks in wrath, and claws the air in frantic hope it can reach to its maker and devour him.

This do the body's eyes behold in one whom Heaven cherishes, the angels love and God created perfect. This is his reality. And in Christ's vision is

his loveliness reflected in a form
so holy and so beautiful that you
could scarce refrain from kneeling at his feet.
Yet you will take his hand instead, for you
are like him in the sight that sees him thus.
Attack on him is enemy to you,
for you will not perceive that in his hands
is your salvation. Ask him but for this,
and he will give it to you. Ask him not
to symbolize your fear. Would you request
that love destroy itself? Or would you have
it be revealed to you and set you free?

Today we practice in a form we have
attempted earlier. Your readiness
is closer now, and you will come today
nearer Christ's vision. If you are intent
on reaching it, you will succeed today.
And once you have succeeded, you will not
be willing to accept the witnesses
your body's eyes call forth. What you will see
will sing to you of ancient melodies
you will remember. You are not forgot
in Heaven. Would you not remember it?

Select one brother, symbol of the rest,
and ask salvation of him. See him first
as clearly as you can, in that same form
to which you are accustomed. See his face,
his hands and feet, his clothing. Watch him smile,
and see familiar gestures which he makes
so frequently. Then think of this: What you
are seeing now conceals from you the sight
of one who can forgive you all your sins;
whose sacred hands can take away the nails
which pierce your own, and lift the crown of thorns
which you have placed upon your bleeding head.
Ask this of him, that he may set you free:

*Give me your blessing, holy Son of God.*
*I would behold you with the eyes of Christ,*
*and see my perfect sinlessness in you.*

And He will answer Whom you called upon.
For He will hear the Voice for God in you,
and answer in your own. Behold him now,
whom you have seen as merely flesh and bone,
and recognize that Christ has come to you.
Today's idea is your safe escape
from anger and from fear. Be sure you use
it instantly, should you be tempted to
attack a brother and perceive in him
the symbol of your fear. And you will see
him suddenly transformed from enemy
to savior; from the devil into Christ.

## LESSON 162

**I am as God created me.**

This single thought, held firmly in the mind, would save the world. From time to time we will repeat it, as we reach another stage in learning. It will mean far more to you as you advance. These words are sacred, for they are the words God gave in answer to the world you made. By them it disappears, and all things seen within its misty clouds and vaporous illusions vanish as these words are spoken. For they come from God.

Here is the Word by which the Son became His Father's happiness, His Love and His completion. Here creation is proclaimed, and honored as it is. There is no dream these words will not dispel; no thought of sin and no illusion which the dream contains that will not fade away before their might. They are the trumpet of awakening that sounds around the world. The dead awake in answer to its call. And those who live and hear this sound will never look on death.

Holy indeed is he who makes these words his own; arising with them in his mind, recalling them throughout the day, at night bringing them with him as he goes to sleep. His dreams are happy and his rest secure, his safety certain and his body healed, because he sleeps and wakens with the truth before him always. He will save the world, because he gives the world what he receives each time he practices the words of truth.

Today we practice simply. For the words we use are mighty, and they need no thoughts beyond themselves to change the mind of him who uses them. So wholly is it changed that it is now the treasury in which God places all His gifts and all His Love, to be distributed to all the world, increased in giving; kept complete because its sharing is unlimited. And thus you learn to think with God. Christ's vision has restored your sight by salvaging your mind.

We honor you today. Yours is the right to perfect holiness you now accept. With this acceptance is salvation brought to everyone, for who could cherish sin when holiness like this has blessed the world? Who could despair when perfect joy is yours, available to all as remedy for grief and misery, all sense of loss, and for complete escape from sin and guilt?

And who would not be brother to you now; you, his redeemer and his savior. Who could fail to welcome you into his heart with loving invitation, eager to unite with one like him in holiness? You are as God created you. These words dispel the night, and darkness is no more. The light is come today to bless the world. For you have recognized the Son of God, and in that recognition is the world's.

## LESSON 163

### There is no death. The Son of God is free.

Death is a thought that takes on many forms, often unrecognized. It may appear as sadness, fear, anxiety or doubt; as anger, faithlessness and lack of trust; concern for bodies, envy, and all forms in which the wish to be as you are not may come to tempt you. All such thoughts are but reflections of the worshipping of death as savior and as giver of release.

Embodiment of fear, the host of sin, god of the guilty and the lord of all illusions and deceptions, does the thought of death seem mighty. For it seems to hold all living things within its withered hand; all hopes and wishes in its blighting grasp; all goals perceived but in its sightless eyes. The frail, the helpless and the sick bow down before its image, thinking it alone is real, inevitable, worthy of their trust. For it alone will surely come.

All things but death are seen to be unsure, too quickly lost however hard to gain, uncertain in their outcome, apt to fail the hopes they once engendered, and to leave the taste of dust and ashes in their wake, in place of aspirations and of dreams. But death is counted on. For it will come with certain footsteps when the time has come for its arrival. It will never fail to take all life as hostage to itself.

Would you bow down to idols such as this? Here is the strength and might of God Himself perceived within an idol made of dust. Here is the opposite of God proclaimed as lord of all creation, stronger than God's Will for life, the endlessness of love and Heaven's perfect, changeless constancy. Here is the Will of Father and of Son defeated finally, and laid to rest beneath the headstone death has placed upon the body of the holy Son of God.

Unholy in defeat, he has become what death would have him be. His epitaph, which death itself has written, gives no name to him, for he has passed to dust. It says but this: "Here lies a witness God is dead." And this it writes again and still again, while all the while its worshippers agree, and kneeling down with foreheads to the ground, they whisper fearfully that it is so.

It is impossible to worship death in any form, and still select a few you would not cherish and would yet avoid, while still believing in the rest. For death is total. Either all things die, or else they live and cannot die. No compromise is possible. For here again we see an obvious position, which we must accept if we be sane; what contradicts one thought entirely can not be true, unless its opposite is proven false.

The idea of the death of God is so preposterous that even the insane have difficulty in believing it. For it implies that God was once alive and somehow perished; killed, apparently, by those who did not want Him to survive. Their stronger will could triumph over His, and so eternal life gave way to death. And with the Father died the Son as well.

Death's worshippers may be afraid. And yet, can thoughts like these be fearful? If they saw that it is only this which they believe, they would be instantly released. And you will show them this today. There is no death, and we renounce it now in every form, for their salvation and our own as well. God made not death. Whatever form it takes must therefore be illusion. This the stand we take today. And it is given us to look past death, and see the life beyond.

*Our Father, bless our eyes today. We are Your messengers, and we would look upon the glorious reflection of Your Love which shines in everything. We live and move in You alone. We are not separate from Your eternal life. There is no death, for death is not Your Will. And we abide where You have placed us, in the life we share with You and with all living things, to be like You and part of You forever. We accept Your Thoughts as ours, and our will is one with Yours eternally. Amen.*

# LESSON 164

**Now are we one with Him Who is our Source.**

What time but now can truth be recognized? The present is the only time there is. And so today, this instant, now, we come to look upon what is forever there; not in our sight, but in the eyes of Christ. He looks past time, and sees eternity as represented there. He hears the sounds the senseless, busy world engenders, yet He hears them faintly. For beyond them all He hears the song of Heaven, and the Voice for God more clear, more meaningful, more near.

The world fades easily away before His sight. Its sounds grow dim. A melody from far beyond the world increasingly is more and more distinct; an ancient Call to Which He gives an ancient answer. You will recognize them both, for they are but your answer to your Father's Call to you. Christ answers for you, echoing your Self, using your voice to give His glad consent; accepting your deliverance for you.

How holy is your practicing today, as Christ gives you His sight and hears for you, and answers in your name the Call He hears! How quiet is the time you give to spend with Him, beyond the world. How easily are all your seeming sins forgot, and all your sorrows unremembered. On this day is grief laid by, for sights and sounds that come from nearer than the world are clear to you who will today accept the gifts He gives.

There is a silence into which the world can not intrude. There is an ancient peace you carry in your heart and have not lost. There is a sense of holiness in you the thought of sin has never touched. All this today you will remember. Faithfulness in practicing today will bring rewards so great and so completely different from all things you sought before, that you will know that here your treasure is, and here your rest.

This is the day when vain imaginings part like a curtain, to reveal what lies beyond them. Now is what is really there made visible, while all the shadows which appeared to hide it merely sink away. Now is the balance righted, and the scale of judgment left to Him Who judges true. And in His judgment will a world unfold in perfect innocence before your eyes. Now will you see it with the eyes of Christ. Now is its transformation clear to you.

Brother, this day is sacred to the world. Your vision, given you from far beyond all things within the world, looks back on them in a new light. And what you see becomes the healing and salvation of the world. The valuable and valueless are both perceived and recognized for what they are. And what is worthy of your love receives your love, while nothing to be feared remains.

We will not judge today. We will receive but what is given us from judgment made beyond the world. Our practicing today becomes our gift of thankfulness for our release from blindness and from misery. All that we see will but increase our joy, because its holiness reflects our own. We stand forgiven in the sight of Christ, with all the world forgiven in our own. We bless the world, as we behold it in the light in which our Savior looks on us, and offer it the freedom given us through His forgiving vision, not our own.

Open the curtain in your practicing by merely letting go all things you think you want. Your trifling treasures put away, and leave a clean and open space within your mind where Christ can come, and offer you the treasure of salvation. He has need of your most holy mind to save the world. Is not this purpose worthy to be yours? Is not Christ's vision worthy to be sought above the world's unsatisfying goals?

Let not today slip by without the gifts it holds for you receiving your consent

and your acceptance. We can change the world,
if you acknowledge them. You may not see
the value your acceptance gives the world.
But this you surely want; you can exchange
all suffering for joy this very day.

Practice in earnest, and the gift is yours.
Would God deceive you? Can His promise fail?
Can you withhold so little, when His Hand
holds out complete salvation to His Son?

# LESSON 165

### Let not my mind deny the Thought of God.

What makes this world seem real except your own denial of the truth that lies beyond? What but your thoughts of misery and death obscure the perfect happiness and the eternal life your Father wills for you? And what could hide what cannot be concealed except illusion? What could keep from you what you already have except your choice to see it not, denying it is there?

The Thought of God created you. It left you not, nor have you ever been apart from it an instant. It belongs to you. By it you live. It is your Source of life, holding you one with it, and everything is one with you because it left you not. The Thought of God protects you, cares for you, makes soft your resting place and smooth your way, lighting your mind with happiness and love. Eternity and everlasting life shine in your mind, because the Thought of God has left you not, and still abides with you.

Who would deny his safety and his peace, his joy, his healing and his peace of mind, his quiet rest, his calm awakening, if he but recognized where they abide? Would he not instantly prepare to go where they are found, abandoning all else as worthless in comparison with them? And having found them, would he not make sure they stay with him, and he remain with them?

Deny not Heaven. It is yours today, but for the asking. Nor need you perceive how great the gift, how changed your mind will be before it comes to you. Ask to receive, and it is given you. Conviction lies within it. Till you welcome it as yours, uncertainty remains. Yet God is fair. Sureness is not required to receive what only your acceptance can bestow.

Ask with desire. You need not be sure that you request the only thing you want. But when you have received, you will be sure you have the treasure you have always sought. What would you then exchange for it? What would induce you now to let it fade away from your ecstatic vision? For this sight proves that you have exchanged your blindness for the seeing eyes of Christ; your mind has come to lay aside denial, and accept the Thought of God as your inheritance.

Now is all doubting past, the journey's end made certain, and salvation given you. Now is Christ's power in your mind, to heal as you were healed. For now you are among the saviors of the world. Your destiny lies there and nowhere else. Would God consent to let His Son remain forever starved by his denial of the nourishment he needs to live? Abundance dwells in him, and deprivation cannot cut him off from God's sustaining Love and from his home.

Practice today in hope. For hope indeed is justified. Your doubts are meaningless, for God is certain. And the Thought of Him is never absent. Sureness must abide within you who are host to Him. This course removes all doubts which you have interposed between Him and your certainty of Him.

We count on God, and not upon ourselves, to give us certainty. And in His Name we practice as His Word directs we do. His sureness lies beyond our every doubt. His Love remains beyond our every fear. The Thought of Him is still beyond all dreams and in our minds, according to His Will.

# LESSON 166

## I am entrusted with the gifts of God.

All things are given you. God's trust in you is limitless. He knows His Son. He gives without exception, holding nothing back that can contribute to your happiness. And yet, unless your will is one with His, His gifts are not received. But what would make you think there is another will than His?

Here is the paradox that underlies the making of the world. This world is not the Will of God, and so it is not real. Yet those who think it real must still believe there is another will, and one that leads to opposite effects from those He wills. Impossible indeed; but every mind that looks upon the world and judges it as certain, solid, trustworthy and true believes in two creators; or in one, himself alone. But never in one God.

The gifts of God are not acceptable to anyone who holds such strange beliefs. He must believe that to accept God's gifts, however evident they may become, however urgently he may be called to claim them as his own, is to be pressed to treachery against himself. He must deny their presence, contradict the truth, and suffer to preserve the world he made.

Here is the only home he thinks he knows. Here is the only safety he believes that he can find. Without the world he made is he an outcast; homeless and afraid. He does not realize that it is here he is afraid indeed, and homeless, too; an outcast wandering so far from home, so long away, he does not realize he has forgotten where he came from, where he goes, and even who he really is.

Yet in his lonely, senseless wanderings, God's gifts go with him, all unknown to him. He cannot lose them. But he will not look at what is given him. He wanders on, aware of the futility he sees about him everywhere, perceiving how his little lot but dwindles, as he goes ahead to nowhere. Still he wanders on in misery and poverty, alone though God is with him, and a treasure his so great that everything the world contains is valueless before its magnitude.

He seems a sorry figure; weary, worn, in threadbare clothing, and with feet that bleed a little from the rocky road he walks. No one but has identified with him, for everyone who comes here has pursued the path he follows, and has felt defeat and hopelessness as he is feeling them. Yet is he really tragic, when you see that he is following the way he chose, and need but realize Who walks with him and open up his treasures to be free?

This is your chosen self, the one you made as a replacement for reality. This is the self you savagely defend against all reason, every evidence, and all the witnesses with proof to show this is not you. You heed them not. You go on your appointed way, with eyes cast down lest you might catch a glimpse of truth, and be released from self-deception and set free.

You cower fearfully lest you should feel Christ's touch upon your shoulder, and perceive His gentle hand directing you to look upon your gifts. How could you then proclaim your poverty in exile? He would make you laugh at this perception of yourself. Where is self-pity then? And what becomes of all the tragedy you sought to make for him whom God intended only joy?

Your ancient fear has come upon you now, and justice has caught up with you at last. Christ's hand has touched your shoulder, and you feel that you are not alone. You even think the miserable self you thought was you may not be your Identity. Perhaps

God's Word is truer than your own. Perhaps
His gifts to you are real. Perhaps He has
not wholly been outwitted by your plan
to keep His Son in deep oblivion,
and go the way you chose without your Self.

God's Will does not oppose. It merely is.
It is not God you have imprisoned in
your plan to lose your Self. He does not know
about a plan so alien to His Will.
There was a need He did not understand,
to which He gave an Answer. That is all.
And you who have this Answer given you
have need no more of anything but This.

Now do we live, for now we cannot die.
The wish for death is answered, and the sight
that looked upon it now has been replaced
by vision which perceives that you are not
what you pretend to be. One walks with you
Who gently answers all your fears with this
one merciful reply, "It is not so."
He points to all the gifts you have each time
the thought of poverty oppresses you,
and speaks of His Companionship when you
perceive yourself as lonely and afraid.

Yet He reminds you still of one thing more
you had forgotten. For His touch on you
has made you like Himself. The gifts you have
are not for you alone. What He has come
to offer you, you now must learn to give.
This is the lesson that His giving holds,
for He has saved you from the solitude
you sought to make in which to hide from God.
He has reminded you of all the gifts
that God has given you. He speaks as well
of what becomes your will when you accept
these gifts, and recognize they are your own.

The gifts are, yours entrusted to your care,
to give to all who chose the lonely road
you have escaped. They do not understand
they but pursue their wishes. It is you
who teach them now. For you have learned of Christ
there is another way for them to walk.
Teach them by showing them the happiness
that comes to those who feel the touch of Christ,
and recognize God's gifts. Let sorrow not
tempt you to be unfaithful to your trust.

Your sighs will now betray the hopes of those
who look to you for their release. Your tears
are theirs. If you are sick, you but withhold
their healing. What you fear but teaches them
their fears are justified. Your hand becomes
the giver of Christ's touch; your change of mind
becomes the proof that who accepts God's gifts
can never suffer anything. You are entrusted
with the world's release from pain.

Betray it not. Become the living proof
of what Christ's touch can offer everyone.
God has entrusted all His gifts to you.
Be witness in your happiness to how
transformed the mind becomes which chooses to
accept His gifts, and feel the touch of Christ.
Such is your mission now. For God entrusts
the giving of His gifts to all who have
received them. He has shared His joy with you.
And now you go to share it with the world.

# LESSON 167

**There is one life, and that I share with God.**

There are not different kinds of life, for life is like the truth. It does not have degrees. It is the one condition in which all that God created share. Like all His Thoughts, it has no opposite. There is no death because what God created shares His Life. There is no death because an opposite to God does not exist. There is no death because the Father and the Son are one.

In this world, there appears to be a state that is life's opposite. You call it death. Yet we have learned that the idea of death takes many forms. It is the one idea which underlies all feelings that are not supremely happy. It is the alarm to which you give response of any kind that is not perfect joy. All sorrow, loss, anxiety and suffering and pain, even a little sigh of weariness, a slight discomfort or the merest frown, acknowledge death. And thus deny you live.

You think that death is of the body. Yet it is but an idea, irrelevant to what is seen as physical. A thought is in the mind. It can be then applied as mind directs it. But its origin is where it must be changed, if change occurs. Ideas leave not their source. The emphasis this course has placed on that idea is due to its centrality in our attempts to change your mind about yourself. It is the reason you can heal. It is the cause of healing. It is why you cannot die. Its truth established you as one with God.

Death is the thought that you are separate from your Creator. It is the belief conditions change, emotions alternate because of causes you cannot control, you did not make, and you can never change. It is the fixed belief ideas can leave their source, and take on qualities the source does not contain, becoming different from their own origin, apart from it in kind as well as distance, time and form.

Death cannot come from life. Ideas remain united to their source. They can extend all that their source contains. In that, they can go far beyond themselves. But they can not give birth to what was never given them. As they are made, so will their making be. As they were born, so will they then give birth. And where they come from, there will they return.

The mind can think it sleeps, but that is all. It cannot change what is its waking state. It cannot make a body, nor abide within a body. What is alien to the mind does not exist, because it has no source. For mind creates all things that are, and cannot give them attributes it lacks, nor change its own eternal, mindful state. It cannot make the physical. What seems to die is but the sign of mind asleep.

The opposite of life can only be another form of life. As such, it can be reconciled with what created it, because it is not opposite in truth. Its form may change; it may appear to be what it is not. Yet mind is mind, awake or sleeping. It is not its opposite in anything created, nor in what it seems to make when it believes it sleeps.

God creates only mind awake. He does not sleep, and His creations cannot share what He gives not, nor make conditions which He does not share with them. The thought of death is not the opposite to thoughts of life. Forever unopposed by opposites of any kind, the Thoughts of God remain forever changeless, with the power to extend forever changelessly, but yet within themselves, for they are everywhere.

What seems to be the opposite of life is merely sleeping. When the mind elects to be what it is not, and to assume an alien power which it does not have,

a foreign state it cannot enter, or
a false condition not within its Source,
it merely seems to go to sleep a while.
It dreams of time; an interval in which
what seems to happen never has occurred,
the changes wrought are substanceless, and all
events are nowhere. When the mind awakes,
it but continues as it always was.

Let us today be children of the truth,
and not deny our holy heritage.
Our life is not as we imagine it.
Who changes life because he shuts his eyes,
or makes himself what he is not because
he sleeps, and sees in dreams an opposite
to what he is? We will not ask for death
in any form today. Nor will we let
imagined opposites to life abide
even an instant where the Thought of life
eternal has been set by God Himself.

His holy home we strive to keep today
as He established it, and wills it be
forever and forever. He is Lord
of what we think today. And in His Thoughts,
which have no opposite, we understand
there is one life, and that we share with Him,
with all creation, with their thoughts as well,
whom He created in a unity
of life that cannot separate in death
and leave the Source of life from where it came.

We share one life because we have one Source,
a Source from Which perfection comes to us,
remaining always in the holy minds
which He created perfect. As we were,
so are we now and will forever be.
A sleeping mind must waken, as it sees
its own perfection mirroring the Lord
of Life so perfectly it fades into
what is reflected there. And now it is
no more a mere reflection. It becomes
the thing reflected, and the light which makes
reflection possible. No vision now
is needed. For the wakened mind is one
that knows its Source, its Self, its Holiness.

## LESSON 168

**Your grace is given me. I claim it now.**

God speaks to us. Shall we not speak to Him? He is not distant. He makes no attempt to hide from us. We try to hide from Him, and suffer from deception. He remains entirely accessible. He loves His Son. There is no certainty but this, yet this suffices. He will love His Son forever. When his mind remains asleep, He loves him still. And when his mind awakes, He loves him with a never-changing Love.

If you but knew the meaning of His Love, hope and despair would be impossible. For hope would be forever satisfied; despair of any kind unthinkable. His grace His answer is to all despair, for in it lies remembrance of His Love. Would He not gladly give the means by which His Will is recognized? His grace is yours by your acknowledgment. And memory of Him awakens in the mind that asks the means of Him whereby its sleep is done.

Today we ask of God the gift He has most carefully preserved within our hearts, waiting to be acknowledged. This the gift by which God leans to us and lifts us up, taking salvation's final step Himself. All steps but this we learn, instructed by His Voice. But finally He comes Himself, and takes us in His Arms and sweeps away the cobwebs of our sleep. His gift of grace is more than just an answer. It restores all memories the sleeping mind forgot; all certainty of what Love's meaning is.

God loves His Son. Request Him now to give the means by which this world will disappear, and vision first will come, with knowledge but an instant later. For in grace you see a light that covers all the world in love, and watch fear disappear from every face as hearts rise up and claim the light as theirs. What now remains that Heaven be delayed an instant longer? What is still undone when your forgiveness rests on everything?

It is a new and holy day today, for we receive what has been given us. Our faith lies in the Giver, not our own acceptance. We acknowledge our mistakes, but He to Whom all error is unknown is yet the One Who answers our mistakes by giving us the means to lay them down, and rise to Him in gratitude and love.

And He descends to meet us, as we come to Him. For what He has prepared for us He gives and we receive. Such is His Will, because He loves His Son. To Him we pray today, returning but the word He gave to us through His Own Voice, His Word, His Love:

*Your grace is given me. I claim it now.*
*Father, I come to You. And You will come*
*to me who ask. I am the Son You love.*

## LESSON 169

**By grace I live. By grace I am released.**

Grace is an aspect of the Love of God which is most like the state prevailing in the unity of truth. It is the world's most lofty aspiration, for it leads beyond the world entirely. It is past learning, yet the goal of learning, for grace cannot come until the mind prepares itself for true acceptance. Grace becomes inevitable instantly in those who have prepared a table where it can be gently laid and willingly received; an altar clean and holy for the gift.

Grace is acceptance of the Love of God within a world of seeming hate and fear. By grace alone the hate and fear are gone, for grace presents a state so opposite to everything the world contains, that those whose minds are lighted by the gift of grace can not believe the world of fear is real.

Grace is not learned. The final step must go beyond all learning. Grace is not the goal this course aspires to attain. Yet we prepare for grace in that an open mind can hear the Call to waken. It is not shut tight against God's Voice. It has become aware that there are things it does not know, and thus is ready to accept a state completely different from experience with which it is familiarly at home.

We have perhaps appeared to contradict our statement that the revelation of the Father and the Son as one has been already set. But we have also said the mind determines when that time will be, and has determined it. And yet we urge you to bear witness to the Word of God to hasten the experience of truth, and speed its advent into every mind that recognizes truth's effects on you.

Oneness is simply the idea God is. And in His Being, He encompasses all things. No mind holds anything but Him. We say "God is," and then we cease to speak, for in that knowledge words are meaningless. There are no lips to speak them, and no part of mind sufficiently distinct to feel that it is now aware of something not itself. It has united with its Source. And like its Source Itself, it merely is.

We cannot speak nor write nor even think of this at all. It comes to every mind when total recognition that its will is God's has been completely given and received completely. It returns the mind into the endless present, where the past and future cannot be conceived. It lies beyond salvation; past all thought of time, forgiveness and the holy face of Christ. The Son of God has merely disappeared into his Father, as his Father has in him. The world has never been at all. Eternity remains a constant state.

This is beyond experience we try to hasten. Yet forgiveness, taught and learned, brings with it the experiences which bear witness that the time the mind itself determined to abandon all but this is now at hand. We do not hasten it, in that what you will offer was concealed from Him Who teaches what forgiveness means.

All learning was already in His Mind, accomplished and complete. He recognized all that time holds, and gave it to all minds that each one might determine, from a point where time was ended, when it is released to revelation and eternity. We have repeated several times before that you but make a journey that is done.

For oneness must be here. Whatever time the mind has set for revelation is entirely irrelevant to what must be a constant state, forever as it always was; forever to remain as it is now. We merely take the part assigned long since, and fully recognized as perfectly fulfilled by Him Who wrote

salvation's script in His Creator's Name,
and in the Name of His Creator's Son.

There is no need to further clarify
what no one in the world can understand.
When revelation of your oneness comes,
it will be known and fully understood.
Now we have work to do, for those in time
can speak of things beyond, and listen to
words which explain what is to come is past
already. Yet what meaning can the words
convey to those who count the hours still,
and rise and work and go to sleep by them?

Suffice it, then, that you have work to do
to play your part. The ending must remain
obscure to you until your part is done.
It does not matter. For your part is still
what all the rest depends on. As you take
the role assigned to you, salvation comes
a little nearer each uncertain heart
that does not beat as yet in tune with God.

Forgiveness is the central theme that runs
throughout salvation, holding all its parts
in meaningful relationships, the course
it runs directed and its outcome sure.
And now we ask for grace, the final gift
salvation can bestow. Experience
that grace provides will end in time, for grace
foreshadows Heaven, yet does not replace
the thought of time but for a little while.

The interval suffices. It is here
that miracles are laid; to be returned
by you from holy instants you receive,
through grace in your experience, to all
who see the light that lingers in your face.
What is the face of Christ but his who went
a moment into timelessness, and brought
a clear reflection of the unity
he felt an instant back to bless the world?
How could you finally attain to it
forever, while a part of you remains
outside, unknowing, unawakened, and
in need of you as witness to the truth?

Be grateful to return, as you were glad
to go an instant, and accept the gifts
that grace provided you. You carry them
back to yourself. And revelation stands
not far behind. Its coming is ensured.
We ask for grace, and for experience
that comes from grace. We welcome the release
it offers everyone. We do not ask
for the unaskable. We do not look
beyond what grace can give. For this we can
give in the grace that has been given us.

Our learning goal today does not exceed
this prayer. Yet in the world, what could be more
than what we ask this day of Him Who gives
the grace we ask, as it was given Him?

*By grace I live. By grace I am released.*
*By grace I give. By grace I will release.*

# LESSON 170

## There is no cruelty in God and none in me.

No one attacks without intent to hurt. This can have no exception. When you think that you attack in self-defense, you mean that to be cruel is protection; you are safe because of cruelty. You mean that you believe to hurt another brings you freedom. And you mean that to attack is to exchange the state in which you are for something better, safer, more secure from dangerous invasion and from fear.

How thoroughly insane is the idea that to defend from fear is to attack! For here is fear begot and fed with blood, to make it grow and swell and rage. And thus is fear protected, not escaped. Today we learn a lesson which can save you more delay and needless misery than you can possibly imagine. It is this:

*You make what you defend against, and by your own defense against it is it real and inescapable. Lay down your arms, and only then do you perceive it false.*

It seems to be the enemy without that you attack. Yet your defense sets up an enemy within; an alien thought at war with you, depriving you of peace, splitting your mind into two camps which seem wholly irreconcilable. For love now has an "enemy," an opposite; and fear, the alien, now needs your defense against the threat of what you really are.

If you consider carefully the means by which your fancied self-defense proceeds on its imagined way, you will perceive the premises on which the idea stands. First, it is obvious ideas must leave their source, for it is you who make attack, and must have first conceived of it. Yet you attack outside yourself, and separate your mind from him who is to be attacked, with perfect faith the split you made is real.

Next, are the attributes of love bestowed upon its "enemy." For fear becomes your safety and protector of your peace, to which you turn for solace and escape from doubts about your strength, and hope of rest in dreamless quiet. And as love is shorn of what belongs to it and it alone, love is endowed with attributes of fear. For love would ask you lay down all defense as merely foolish. And your arms indeed would crumble into dust. For such they are.

With love as enemy, must cruelty become a god. And gods demand that those who worship them obey their dictates, and refuse to question them. Harsh punishment is meted out relentlessly to those who ask if the demands are sensible or even sane. It is their enemies who are unreasonable and insane, while they are always merciful and just.

Today we look upon this cruel god dispassionately. And we note that though his lips are smeared with blood, and fire seems to flame from him, he is but made of stone. He can do nothing. We need not defy his power. He has none. And those who see in him their safety have no guardian, no strength to call upon in danger, and no mighty warrior to fight for them.

This moment can be terrible. But it can also be the time of your release from abject slavery. You make a choice, standing before this idol, seeing him exactly as he is. Will you restore to love what you have sought to wrest from it and lay before this mindless piece of stone? Or will you make another idol to replace it? For the god of cruelty takes many forms. Another can be found.

Yet do not think that fear is the escape from fear. Let us remember what the text has stressed about the obstacles to peace. The final one, the hardest to believe

is nothing, and a seeming obstacle
with the appearance of a solid block,
impenetrable, fearful and beyond
surmounting, is the fear of God Himself.
Here is the basic premise which enthrones
the thought of fear as god. For fear is loved
by those who worship it, and love appears
to be invested now with cruelty.

Where does the totally insane belief
in gods of vengeance come from? Love has not
confused its attributes with those of fear.
Yet must the worshippers of fear perceive
their own confusion in fear's "enemy";
its cruelty as now a part of love.
And what becomes more fearful than the Heart
of Love Itself? The blood appears to be
upon His Lips; the fire comes from Him.
And He is terrible above all else,
cruel beyond conception, striking down
all who acknowledge Him to be their God.

The choice you make today is certain. For
you look for the last time upon this bit
of carven stone you made, and call it god
no longer. You have reached this place before,
but you have chosen that this cruel god
remain with you in still another form.
And so the fear of God returned with you.

This time you leave it there. And you return
to a new world, unburdened by its weight;
beheld not in its sightless eyes, but in
the vision that your choice restored to you.

Now do your eyes belong to Christ, and He
looks through them. Now your voice belongs to God
and echoes His. And now your heart remains
at peace forever. You have chosen Him
in place of idols, and your attributes,
given by your Creator, are restored
to you at last. The Call for God is heard
and answered. Now has fear made way for love,
as God Himself replaces cruelty.

*Father, we are like You. No cruelty*
*abides in us, for there is none in You.*
*Your peace is ours. And we bless the world*
*with what we have received from You alone.*
*We choose again, and make our choice for all*
*our brothers, knowing they are one with us.*
*We bring them Your salvation as we have*
*received it now. And we give thanks for them*
*who render us complete. In them we see*
*Your glory, and in them we find our peace.*
*Holy are we because Your holiness*
*has set us free. And we give thanks. Amen.*

# REVIEW V

**Introduction**

We now review again. This time we are ready to give more effort and more time to what we undertake. We recognize we are preparing for another phase of understanding. We would take this step completely, that we may go on again more certain, more sincere, with faith upheld more surely. Our footsteps have not been unwavering, and doubts have made us walk uncertainly and slowly on the road this course sets forth. But now we hasten on, for we approach a greater certainty, a firmer purpose and a surer goal.

*Steady our feet, our Father. Let our doubts be quiet and our holy minds be still, and speak to us. We have no words to give to You. We would but listen to Your Word, and make it ours. Lead our practicing as does a father lead a little child along a way he does not understand. Yet does he follow, sure that he is safe because his father leads the way for him.*

*So do we bring our practicing to You. And if we stumble, You will raise us up. If we forget the way, we count upon Your sure remembering. We wander off, but You will not forget to call us back. Quicken our footsteps now, that we may walk more certainly and quickly unto You. And we accept the Word You offer us to unify our practicing, as we review the thoughts that You have given us.*

This is the thought which should precede the thoughts that we review. Each one but clarifies some aspect of this thought, or helps it be more meaningful, more personal and true, and more descriptive of the holy Self we share and now prepare to know again:

*God is but Love, and therefore so am I.*

This Self alone knows love. This Self alone is perfectly consistent in Its thoughts; knows Its Creator, understands Itself, is perfect in Its knowledge and Its love, and never changes from Its constant state of union with Its Father and Itself.

And it is This That waits to meet us at the journey's ending. Every step we take brings us a little nearer. This review will shorten time immeasurably, if we keep in mind that This remains our goal, and as we practice it is This to Which we are approaching. Let us raise our hearts from dust to life, as we remember This is promised us, and that this course was sent to open up the path of light to us, and teach us, step by step, how to return to the eternal Self we thought we lost.

I take the journey with you. For I share your doubts and fears a little while, that you may come to me who recognize the road by which all fears and doubts are overcome. We walk together. I must understand uncertainty and pain, although I know they have no meaning. Yet a savior must remain with those he teaches, seeing what they see, but still retaining in his mind the way that led him out, and now will lead you out with him. God's Son is crucified until you walk along the road with me.

My resurrection comes again each time I lead a brother safely to the place at which the journey ends and is forgot. I am renewed each time a brother learns there is a way from misery and pain. I am reborn each time a brother's mind turns to the light in him and looks for me. I have forgotten no one. Help me now to lead you back to where the journey was begun, to make another choice with me.

Release me as you practice once again the thoughts I brought to you from Him Who sees your bitter need, and knows the answer God has given Him. Together we review these thoughts. Together we devote our time and effort to them. And together we

will teach them to our brothers. God would not
have Heaven incomplete. It waits for you,
as I do. I am incomplete without
your part in me. And as I am made whole
we go together to our ancient home,
prepared for us before time was and kept
unchanged by time, immaculate and safe,
as it will be at last when time is done.

Let this review be then your gift to me.
For this alone I need; that you will hear
the words I speak, and give them to the world.
You are my voice, my eyes, my feet, my hands
through which I save the world. The Self from Which
I call to you is but your own. To Him
we go together. Take your brother's hand,
for this is not a way we walk alone.
In him I walk with you, and you with me.
Our Father wills His Son be one with Him.
What lives but must not then be one with you?

Let this review become a time in which
we share a new experience for you,
yet one as old as time and older still.
Hallowed your name. Your glory undefiled
forever. And your wholeness now complete,
as God established it. You are His Son,
completing His extension in your own.
We practice but an ancient truth we knew
before illusion seemed to claim the world.
And we remind the world that it is free
of all illusions every time we say:

*God is but Love, and therefore so am I.*

With this we start each day of our review.
With this we start and end each period
of practice time. And with this thought we sleep,
to waken once again with these same words
upon our lips, to greet another day.
No thought that we review but we surround
with it, and use the thoughts to hold it up
before our minds, and keep it clear in our
rememberance throughout the day. And thus,
when we have finished this review, we will
have recognized the words we speak are true.

Yet are the words but aids, and to be used,
except at the beginning and the end
of practice periods, but to recall
the mind, as needed, to its purpose. We
place faith in the experience that comes
from practice, not the means we use. We wait
for the experience, and recognize
that it is only here conviction lies.
We use the words, and try and try again
to go beyond them to their meaning, which
is far beyond their sound. The sound grows dim
and disappears, as we approach the Source
of meaning. It is Here that we find rest.

## LESSON 171

**God is but Love, and therefore so am I.**
All things are echoes of the Voice for God.
**God is but Love, and therefore so am I.**
The power of decision is my own.
**God is but Love, and therefore so am I.**

## LESSON 172

**God is but Love, and therefore so am I.**
In my defenselessness my safety lies.
**God is but Love, and therefore so am I.**
I am among the ministers of God.
**God is but Love, and therefore so am I.**

## LESSON 173

**God is but Love, and therefore so am I.**
I will step back and let Him lead the way.
**God is but Love, and therefore so am I.**
I walk with God in perfect holiness.
**God is but Love, and therefore so am I.**

## LESSON 174

**God is but Love, and therefore so am I.**
Into His Presence would I enter now.
**God is but Love, and therefore so am I.**
Today I learn to give as I receive.
**God is but Love, and therefore so am I.**

## LESSON 175

**God is but Love, and therefore so am I.**
I give the miracles I have received.
**God is but Love, and therefore so am I.**
I am at home. Fear is the stranger here.
**God is but Love, and therefore so am I.**

## LESSON 176

**God is but Love, and therefore so am I.**
Give me your blessing, holy Son of God.
**God is but Love, and therefore so am I.**
I am as God created me.
**God is but Love, and therefore so am I.**

## LESSON 177

**God is but Love, and therefore so am I.**
There is no death. The Son of God is free.
**God is but Love, and therefore so am I.**
Now are we one with Him Who is our Source.
**God is but Love, and therefore so am I.**

## LESSON 178

**God is but Love, and therefore so am I.**
Let not my mind deny the Thought of God.
**God is but Love, and therefore so am I.**
I am entrusted with the gifts of God.
**God is but Love, and therefore so am I.**

## LESSON 179

**God is but Love, and therefore so am I.**
There is one life, and that I share with God.
**God is but Love, and therefore so am I.**
Your grace is given me. I claim it now.
**God is but Love, and therefore so am I.**

## LESSON 180

**God is but Love, and therefore so am I.**
By grace I live. By grace I am released.
**God is but Love, and therefore so am I.**
There is no cruelty in God and none in me.
**God is but Love, and therefore so am I.**

# INTRODUCTION TO LESSONS 181 TO 220

Our next few lessons make a special point of firming up your willingness to make your weak commitment strong; your scattered goals blend into one intent. You are not asked for total dedication all the time as yet. But you are asked to practice now in order to attain the sense of peace such unified commitment will bestow, if only intermittently. It is experiencing this that makes it sure that you will give your total willingness to following the way the course sets forth.

Our lessons now are geared specifically to widening horizons, and direct approaches to the special blocks that keep your vision narrow, and too limited to let you see the value of our goal. We are attempting now to lift these blocks, however briefly. Words alone can not convey the sense of liberation which their lifting brings. But the experience of freedom and of peace that comes as you give up your tight control of what you see speaks for itself. Your motivation will be so intensified that words become of little consequence. You will be sure of what you want, and what is valueless.

And so we start our journey beyond words by concentrating first on what impedes your progress still. Experience of what exists beyond defensiveness remains beyond achievement while it is denied. It may be there, but you cannot accept its presence. So we now attempt to go past all defenses for a little while each day. No more than this is asked, because no more than this is needed. It will be enough to guarantee the rest will come.

# LESSON 181

### I trust my brothers, who are one with me.

Trusting your brothers is essential to establishing and holding up your faith in your ability to transcend doubt and lack of sure conviction in yourself. When you attack a brother, you proclaim that he is limited by what you have perceived in him. You do not look beyond his errors. Rather, they are magnified, becoming blocks to your awareness of the Self That lies beyond your own mistakes, and past his seeming sins as well as yours.

Perception has a focus. It is this that gives consistency to what you see. Change but this focus, and what you behold will change accordingly. Your vision now will shift, to give support to the intent which has replaced the one you held before. Remove your focus on your brother's sins, and you experience the peace that comes from faith in sinlessness. This faith receives its only sure support from what you see in others past their sins. For their mistakes, if focused on, are witnesses to sins in you. And you will not transcend their sight and see the sinlessness that lies beyond.

Therefore, in practicing today, we first let all such little focuses give way to our great need to let our sinlessness become apparent. We instruct our minds that it is this we seek, and only this, for just a little while. We do not care about our future goals. And what we saw an instant previous has no concern for us within this interval of time wherein we practice changing our intent. We seek for innocence and nothing else. We seek for it with no concern but now.

A major hazard to success has been involvement with your past and future goals. You have been quite preoccupied with how extremely different the goals this course is advocating are from those you held before. And you have also been dismayed by the depressing and restricting thought that, even if you should succeed, you will inevitably lose your way again.

How could this matter? For the past is gone; the future but imagined. These concerns are but defenses against present change of focus in perception. Nothing more. We lay these pointless limitations by a little while. We do not look to past beliefs, and what we will believe will not intrude upon us now. We enter in the time of practicing with one intent; to look upon the sinlessness within.

We recognize that we have lost this goal if anger blocks our way in any form. And if a brother's sins occur to us, our narrowed focus will restrict our sight, and turn our eyes upon our own mistakes, which we will magnify and call our "sins." So, for a little while, without regard to past or future, should such blocks arise we will transcend them with instructions to our minds to change their focus, as we say:

*It is not this that I would look upon.*
*I trust my brothers, who are one with me.*

And we will also use this thought to keep us safe throughout the day. We do not seek for long-range goals. As each obstruction seems to block the vision of our sinlessness, we seek but for surcease an instant from the misery the focus upon sin will bring, and uncorrected will remain.

Nor do we ask for fantasies. For what we seek to look upon is really there. And as our focus goes beyond mistakes, we will behold a wholly sinless world. When seeing this is all we want to see, when this is all we seek for in the name of true perception, are the eyes of Christ inevitably ours. And the Love He feels for us becomes our own as well. This will become the only thing we see reflected in the world and in ourselves.

The world which once proclaimed our sins becomes
the proof that we are sinless. And our love
for everyone we look upon attests
to our remembrance of the holy Self
Which knows no sin, and never could conceive
of anything without Its sinlessness.

We seek for this remembrance as we turn
our minds to practicing today. We look
neither ahead nor backwards. We look straight
into the present. And we give our trust
to the experience we ask for now.
Our sinlessness is but the Will of God.
This instant is our willing one with His.

## LESSON 182

### I will be still an instant and go home.

This world you seem to live in is not home to you. And somewhere in your mind you know that this is true. A memory of home keeps haunting you, as if there were a place that called you to return, although you do not recognize the voice, nor what it is the voice reminds you of. Yet still you feel an alien here, from somewhere all unknown. Nothing so definite that you could say with certainty you are an exile here. Just a persistent feeling, sometimes not more than a tiny throb, at other times hardly remembered, actively dismissed, but surely to return to mind again.

No one but knows whereof we speak. Yet some try to put by their suffering in games they play to occupy their time, and keep their sadness from them. Others will deny that they are sad, and do not recognize their tears at all. Still others will maintain that what we speak of is illusion, not to be considered more than but a dream. Yet who, in simple honesty, without defensiveness and self-deception, would deny he understands the words we speak?

We speak today for everyone who walks this world, for he is not at home. He goes uncertainly about in endless search, seeking in darkness what he cannot find; not recognizing what it is he seeks. A thousand homes he makes, yet none contents his restless mind. He does not understand he builds in vain. The home he seeks can not be made by him. There is no substitute for Heaven. All he ever made was hell.

Perhaps you think it is your childhood home that you would find again. The childhood of your body, and its place of shelter, are a memory now so distorted that you merely hold a picture of a past that never happened. Yet there is a Child in you Who seeks His Father's house, and knows that He is alien here. This childhood is eternal, with an innocence that will endure forever. Where this Child shall go is holy ground. It is His holiness that lights up Heaven, and that brings to earth the pure reflection of the light above, wherein are earth and Heaven joined as one.

It is this Child in you your Father knows as His Own Son. It is this Child Who knows His Father. He desires to go home so deeply, so unceasingly, His voice cries unto you to let Him rest a while. He does not ask for more than just a few instants of respite; just an interval in which He can return to breathe again the holy air that fills His Father's house. You are His home as well. He will return. But give Him just a little time to be Himself, within the peace that is His home, resting in silence and in peace and love.

This Child needs your protection. He is far from home. He is so little that He seems so easily shut out, His tiny voice so readily obscured, His call for help almost unheard amid the grating sounds and harsh and rasping noises of the world. Yet does He know that in you still abides His sure protection. You will fail Him not. He will go home, and you along with Him.

This Child is your defenselessness; your strength. He trusts in you. He came because He knew you would not fail. He whispers of His home unceasingly to you. For He would bring you back with Him, that He Himself might stay, and not return again where He does not belong, and where He lives an outcast in a world of alien thoughts. His patience has no limits. He will wait until you hear His gentle Voice within you, calling you to let Him go in peace, along with you, to where He is at home and you with Him.

When you are still an instant, when the world recedes from you, when valueless ideas

cease to have value in your restless mind,
then will you hear His Voice. So poignantly
He calls to you that you will not resist
Him longer. In that instant He will take
you to His home, and you will stay with Him
in perfect stillness, silent and at peace,
beyond all words, untouched by fear and doubt,
sublimely certain that you are at home.

Rest with Him frequently today. For He
was willing to become a little Child
that you might learn of Him how strong is he
who comes without defenses, offering
only love's messages to those who think
he is their enemy. He holds the might
of Heaven in His hand and calls them friend,
and gives His strength to them, that they may see
He would be Friend to them. He asks that they
protect Him, for His home is far away,
and He will not return to it alone.

Christ is reborn as but a little Child
each time a wanderer would leave his home.
For he must learn that what he would protect
is but this Child, Who comes defenseless and
Who is protected by defenselessness.
Go home with Him from time to time today.

You are as much an alien here as He.

Take time today to lay aside your shield
which profits nothing, and lay down the spear
and sword you raised against an enemy
without existence. Christ has called you friend
and brother. He has even come to ask
your help in letting Him go home today,
completed and completely. He has come
as does a little child, who must beseech
his father for protection and for love.
He rules the universe, and yet He asks
unceasingly that you return with Him,
and take illusions as your gods no more.

You have not lost your innocence. It is
for this you yearn. This is your heart's desire.
This is the voice you hear, and this the call
which cannot be denied. The holy Child
remains with you. His home is yours. Today
He gives you His defenselessness, and you
accept it in exchange for all the toys
of battle you have made. And now the way
is open, and the journey has an end
in sight at last. Be still an instant and
go home with Him, and be at peace a while.

## LESSON 183

**I call upon God's Name and on my own.**

God's Name is holy, but no holier than yours. To call upon His Name is but to call upon your own. A father gives his son his name, and thus identifies the son with him. His brothers share his name, and thus are they united in a bond to which they turn for their identity. Your Father's Name reminds you who you are, even within a world that does not know; even though you have not remembered it.

God's Name can not be heard without response, nor said without an echo in the mind that calls you to remember. Say His Name, and you invite the angels to surround the ground on which you stand, and sing to you as they spread out their wings to keep you safe, and shelter you from every worldly thought that would intrude upon your holiness.

Repeat God's Name, and all the world responds by laying down illusions. Every dream the world holds dear has suddenly gone by, and where it seemed to stand you find a star; a miracle of grace. The sick arise, healed of their sickly thoughts. The blind can see; the deaf can hear. The sorrowful cast off their mourning, and the tears of pain are dried as happy laughter comes to bless the world.

Repeat the Name of God, and little names have lost their meaning. No temptation but becomes a nameless and unwanted thing before God's Name. Repeat His Name, and see how easily you will forget the names of all the gods you valued. They have lost the name of god you gave them. They become anonymous and valueless to you, although before you let the Name of God replace their little names, you stood before them worshipfully, naming them as gods.

Repeat the Name of God, and call upon your Self, Whose Name is His. Repeat His Name, and all the tiny, nameless things on earth slip into right perspective. Those who call upon the Name of God can not mistake the nameless for the Name, nor sin for grace, nor bodies for the holy Son of God. And should you join a brother as you sit with him in silence, and repeat God's Name along with him within your quiet mind, you have established there an altar which reaches to God Himself and to His Son.

Practice but this today; repeat God's Name slowly again and still again. Become oblivious to every name but His. Hear nothing else. Let all your thoughts become anchored on This. No other word we use except at the beginning, when we say today's idea but once. And then God's Name becomes our only thought, our only word, the only thing that occupies our minds, the only wish we have, the only sound with any meaning, and the only Name of everything that we desire to see; of everything that we would call our own.

Thus do we give an invitation which can never be refused. And God will come, and answer it Himself. Think not He hears the little prayers of those who call on Him with names of idols cherished by the world. They cannot reach Him thus. He cannot hear requests that He be not Himself, or that His Son receive another name than His.

Repeat God's Name, and you acknowledge Him as sole Creator of reality. And you acknowledge also that His Son is part of Him, creating in His Name. Sit silently, and let His Name become the all-encompassing idea that holds your mind completely. Let all thoughts be still except this one. And to all other thoughts respond with this, and see God's Name replace the thousand little names you gave your thoughts, not realizing that there is one Name for all there is, and all that there will be.

Today you can achieve a state in which you will experience the gift of grace. You can escape all bondage of the world,

and give the world the same release you found.
You can remember what the world forgot,
and offer it your own remembering.
You can accept today the part you play
in its salvation, and your own as well.
And both can be accomplished perfectly.

Turn to the Name of God for your release,
and it is given you. No prayer but this
is necessary, for it holds them all
within it. Words are insignificant,
and all requests unneeded when God's Son
calls on his Father's Name. His Father's Thoughts
become his own. He makes his claim to all
his Father gave, is giving still, and will
forever give. He calls on Him to let
all things he thought he made be nameless now,
and in their place the holy Name of God
becomes his judgment of their worthlessness.

All little things are silent. Little sounds
are soundless now. The little things of earth
have disappeared. The universe consists
of nothing but the Son of God, who calls
upon his Father. And his Father's Voice
gives answer in his Father's holy Name.
In this eternal, still relationship,
in which communication far transcends
all words, and yet exceeds in depth and height
whatever words could possibly convey,
is peace eternal. In our Father's Name,
we would experience this peace today.
And in His Name, it shall be given us.

# LESSON 184

## The Name of God is my inheritance.

You live by symbols. You have made up names for everything you see. Each one becomes a separate entity, identified by its own name. By this you carve it out of unity. By this you designate its special attributes, and set it off from other things by emphasizing space surrounding it. This space you lay between all things to which you give a different name; all happenings in terms of place and time; all bodies which are greeted by a name.

This space you see as setting off all things from one another is the means by which the world's perception is achieved. You see something where nothing is, and see as well nothing where there is unity; a space between all things, between all things and you. Thus do you think that you have given life in separation. By this split you think you are established as a unity which functions with an independent will.

What are these names by which the world becomes a series of discrete events, of things ununified, of bodies kept apart and holding bits of mind as separate awarenesses? You gave these names to them, establishing perception as you wished to have perception be. The nameless things were given names, and thus reality was given them as well. For what is named is given meaning and will then be seen as meaningful; a cause of true effect, with consequence inherent in itself.

This is the way reality is made by partial vision, purposefully set against the given truth. Its enemy is wholeness. It conceives of little things and looks upon them. And a lack of space, a sense of unity or vision that sees differently, become the threats which it must overcome, conflict with and deny.

Yet does this other vision still remain a natural direction for the mind to channel its perception. It is hard to teach the mind a thousand alien names, and thousands more. Yet you believe this is what learning means; its one essential goal by which communication is achieved, and concepts can be meaningfully shared.

This is the sum of the inheritance the world bestows. And everyone who learns to think that it is so accepts the signs and symbols that assert the world is real. It is for this they stand. They leave no doubt that what is named is there. It can be seen, as is anticipated. What denies that it is true is but illusion, for it is the ultimate reality. To question it is madness; to accept its presence is the proof of sanity.

Such is the teaching of the world. It is a phase of learning everyone who comes must go through. But the sooner he perceives on what it rests, how questionable are its premises, how doubtful its results, the sooner does he question its effects. Learning that stops with what the world would teach stops short of meaning. In its proper place, it serves but as a starting point from which another kind of learning can begin, a new perception can be gained, and all the arbitrary names the world bestows can be withdrawn as they are raised to doubt.

Think not you made the world. Illusions, yes! But what is true in earth and Heaven is beyond your naming. When you call upon a brother, it is to his body that you make appeal. His true Identity is hidden from you by what you believe he really is. His body makes response to what you call him, for his mind consents to take the name you give him as his own. And thus his unity is twice denied, for you perceive him separate from you, and he accepts this separate name as his.

It would indeed be strange if you were asked

to go beyond all symbols of the world,
forgetting them forever; yet were asked
to take a teaching function. You have need
to use the symbols of the world a while.
But be you not deceived by them as well.
They do not stand for anything at all,
and in your practicing it is this thought
that will release you from them. They become
but means by which you can communicate
in ways the world can understand, but which
you recognize is not the unity
where true communication can be found.

Thus what you need are intervals each day
in which the learning of the world becomes
a transitory phase; a prison house
from which you go into the sunlight and
forget the darkness. Here you understand
the Word, the Name Which God has given you;
the one Identity Which all things share;
the one acknowledgment of what is true.
And then step back to darkness, not because
you think it real, but only to proclaim
its unreality in terms which still
have meaning in the world that darkness rules.

Use all the little names and symbols which
delineate the world of darkness. Yet
accept them not as your reality.
The Holy Spirit uses all of them,
but He does not forget creation has
one Name, one Meaning, and a single Source
Which unifies all things within Itself.
Use all the names the world bestows on them
but for convenience, yet do not forget
they share the Name of God along with you.

God has no name. And yet His Name becomes
the final lesson that all things are one,
and at this lesson does all learning end.
All names are unified; all space is filled
with truth's reflection. Every gap is closed,
and separation healed. The Name of God
is the inheritance He gave to those
who chose the teaching of the world to take
the place of Heaven. In our practicing,
our purpose is to let our minds accept
what God has given as the answer to
the pitiful inheritance you made
as fitting tribute to the Son He loves.

No one can fail who seeks the meaning of
the Name of God. Experience must come
to supplement the Word. But first you must
accept the Name for all reality,
and realize the many names you gave
its aspects have distorted what you see,
but have not interfered with truth at all.
One Name we bring into our practicing.
One Name we use to unify our sight.

And though we use a different name for each
awareness of an aspect of God's Son,
we understand that they have but one Name,
Which He has given them. It is this Name
we use in practicing. And through Its use,
all foolish separations disappear
which kept us blind. And we are given strength
to see beyond them. Now our sight is blessed
with blessings we can give as we receive.

*Father, our Name is Yours. In It we are
united with all living things, and You
Who are their one Creator. What we made
and call by many different names is but
a shadow we have tried to cast across
Your Own Reality. And we are glad
and thankful we were wrong. All our mistakes
we give to You, that we may be absolved
from all effects our errors seemed to have.
And we accept the truth You give, in place
of every one of them. Your Name is our
salvation and escape from what we made.
Your Name unites us in the oneness which
is our inheritance and peace. Amen.*

# LESSON 185

## I want the peace of God.

To say these words is nothing. But to mean these words is everything. If you could but mean them for just an instant, there would be no further sorrow possible for you in any form; in any place or time. Heaven would be completely given back to full awareness, memory of God entirely restored, the resurrection of all creation fully recognized.

No one can mean these words and not be healed. He cannot play with dreams, nor think he is himself a dream. He cannot make a hell and think it real. He wants the peace of God, and it is given him. For that is all he wants, and that is all he will receive. Many have said these words. But few indeed have meant them. You have but to look upon the world you see around you to be sure how very few they are. The world would be completely changed, should any two agree these words express the only thing they want.

Two minds with one intent become so strong that what they will becomes the Will of God. For minds can only join in truth. In dreams, no two can share the same intent. To each, the hero of the dream is different; the outcome wanted not the same for both. Loser and gainer merely shift about in changing patterns, as the ratio of gain to loss and loss to gain takes on a different aspect or another form.

Yet compromise alone a dream can bring. Sometimes it takes the form of union, but only the form. The meaning must escape the dream, for compromising is the goal of dreaming. Minds cannot unite in dreams. They merely bargain. And what bargain can give them the peace of God? Illusions come to take His place. And what He means is lost to sleeping minds intent on compromise, each to his gain and to another's loss.

To mean you want the peace of God is to renounce all dreams. For no one means these words who wants illusions, and who therefore seeks the means which bring illusions. He has looked on them, and found them wanting. Now he seeks to go beyond them, recognizing that another dream would offer nothing more than all the others. Dreams are one to him. And he has learned their only difference is one of form, for one will bring the same despair and misery as do the rest.

The mind which means that all it wants is peace must join with other minds, for that is how peace is obtained. And when the wish for peace is genuine, the means for finding it is given, in a form each mind that seeks for it in honesty can understand. Whatever form the lesson takes is planned for him in such a way that he can not mistake it, if his asking is sincere. But if he asks without sincerity, there is no form in which the lesson will meet with acceptance and be truly learned.

Let us today devote our practicing to recognizing that we really mean the words we say. We want the peace of God. This is no idle wish. These words do not request another dream be given us. They do not ask for compromise, nor try to make another bargain in the hope that there may yet be one that can succeed where all the rest have failed. To mean these words acknowledges illusions are in vain, requesting the eternal in the place of shifting dreams which seem to change in what they offer, but are one in nothingness.

Today devote your practice periods to careful searching of your mind, to find the dreams you cherish still. What do you ask for in your heart? Forget the words you use in making your requests. Consider but what you believe will comfort you, and bring you happiness. But be you not dismayed by lingering illusions, for their form is not what matters now. Let not some dreams be more acceptable, reserving shame and secrecy for others. They are one. And being one, one question should be asked of all of them, "Is this what I would have, in place of Heaven and the peace of God?"

This is the choice you make. Be not deceived that it is otherwise. No compromise is possible in this. You choose God's peace, or you have asked for dreams. And dreams will come as you requested them. Yet will God's peace come just as certainly, and to remain with you forever. It will not be gone with every twist and turning of the road, to reappear, unrecognized, in forms which shift and change with every step you take.

You want the peace of God. And so do all who seem to seek for dreams. For them as well as for yourself, you ask but this when you make this request with deep sincerity. For thus you reach to what they really want, and join your own intent with what they seek above all things, perhaps unknown to them, but sure to you. You have been weak at times, uncertain in your purpose, and unsure of what you wanted, where to look for it, and where to turn for help in the attempt. Help has been given you. And would you not avail yourself of it by sharing it?

No one who truly seeks the peace of God can fail to find it. For he merely asks that he deceive himself no longer by denying to himself what is God's Will.

Who can remain unsatisfied who asks for what he has already? Who could be unanswered who requests an answer which is his to give? The peace of God is yours.

For you was peace created, given you by its Creator, and established as His Own eternal gift. How can you fail, when you but ask for what He wills for you? And how could your request be limited to you alone? No gift of God can be unshared. It is this attribute that sets the gifts of God apart from every dream that ever seemed to take the place of truth.

No one can lose and everyone must gain whenever any gift of God has been requested and received by anyone. God gives but to unite. To take away is meaningless to Him. And when it is as meaningless to you, you can be sure you share one Will with Him, and He with you. And you will also know you share one Will with all your brothers, whose intent is yours.

It is this one intent we seek today, uniting our desires with the need of every heart, the call of every mind, the hope that lies beyond despair, the love attack would hide, the brotherhood that hate has sought to sever, but which still remains as God created it. With Help like this beside us, can we fail today as we request the peace of God be given us?

## LESSON 186

### Salvation of the world depends on me.

Here is the statement that will one day take all arrogance away from every mind. Here is the thought of true humility, which holds no function as your own but that which has been given you. It offers your acceptance of a part assigned to you, without insisting on another role. It does not judge your proper role. It but acknowledges the Will of God is done on earth as well as Heaven. It unites all wills on earth in Heaven's plan to save the world, restoring it to Heaven's peace.

Let us not fight our function. We did not establish it. It is not our idea. The means are given us by which it will be perfectly accomplished. All that we are asked to do is to accept our part in genuine humility, and not deny with self-deceiving arrogance that we are worthy. What is given us to do, we have the strength to do. Our minds are suited perfectly to take the part assigned to us by One Who knows us well.

Today's idea may seem quite sobering, until you see its meaning. All it says is that your Father still remembers you, and offers you the perfect trust He holds in you who are His Son. It does not ask that you be different in any way from what you are. What could humility request but this? And what could arrogance deny but this? Today we will not shrink from our assignment on the specious grounds that modesty is outraged. It is pride that would deny the Call for God Himself.

All false humility we lay aside today, that we may listen to God's Voice reveal to us what He would have us do. We do not doubt our adequacy for the function He will offer us. We will be certain only that He knows our strengths, our wisdom and our holiness. And if He deems us worthy, so we are. It is but arrogance that judges otherwise.

There is one way, and only one, to be released from the imprisonment your plan to prove the false is true has brought to you. Accept the plan you did not make instead. Judge not your value to it. If God's Voice assures you that salvation needs your part, and that the whole depends on you, be sure that it is so. The arrogant must cling to words, afraid to go beyond them to experience which might affront their stance. Yet are the humble free to hear the Voice Which tells them what they are, and what to do.

Arrogance makes an image of yourself that is not real. It is this image which quails and retreats in terror, as the Voice for God assures you that you have the strength, the wisdom and the holiness to go beyond all images. You are not weak, as is the image of yourself. You are not ignorant and helpless. Sin can not tarnish the truth in you, and misery can come not near the holy home of God.

All this the Voice for God relates to you. And as He speaks, the image trembles and seeks to attack the threat it does not know, sensing its basis crumble. Let it go. Salvation of the world depends on you, and not upon this little pile of dust. What can it tell the holy Son of God? Why need he be concerned with it at all?

And so we find our peace. We will accept the function God has given us, for all illusions rest upon the weird belief that we can make another for ourselves. Our self-made roles are shifting, and they seem to change from mourner to ecstatic bliss of love and loving. We can laugh or weep, and greet the day with welcome or with tears. Our very being seems to change as we experience a thousand shifts in mood, and our emotions raise us high indeed, or dash us to the ground in hopelessness.

Is this the Son of God? Could He create
such instability and call it Son?
He Who is changeless shares His attributes
with His creation. All the images
His Son appears to make have no effect
on what he is. They blow across his mind
like wind-swept leaves that form a patterning
an instant, break apart to group again,
and scamper off. Or like mirages seen
above a desert, rising from the dust.

These unsubstantial images will go,
and leave your mind unclouded and serene,
when you accept the function given you.
The images you make give rise to but
conflicting goals, impermanent and vague,
uncertain and ambiguous. Who could
be constant in his efforts, or direct
his energies and concentrated drive
toward goals like these?
The functions which the world
esteems are so uncertain that they change
ten times an hour at their most secure.
What hope of gain can rest on goals like this?

In lovely contrast, certain as the sun's
return each morning to dispel the night,
your truly given function stands out clear
and wholly unambiguous. There is
no doubt of its validity. It comes
from One Who knows no error, and His Voice
is certain of Its messages. They will
not change, nor be in conflict. All of them
point to one goal, and one you can attain.
Your plan may be impossible, but God's
can never fail because He is its Source.

Do as God's Voice directs. And if It asks
a thing of you which seems impossible,
remember Who it is That asks, and who
would make denial. Then consider this;
which is more likely to be right? The Voice
That speaks for the Creator of all things,
Who knows all things exactly as they are,
or a distorted image of yourself,
confused, bewildered, inconsistent and
unsure of everything? Let not its voice
direct you. Hear instead a certain Voice,
Which tells you of a function given you
by your Creator Who remembers you,
and urges that you now remember Him.

His gentle Voice is calling from the known
to the unknowing. He would comfort you,
although He knows no sorrow. He would make
a restitution, though He is complete;
a gift to you, although He knows that you
have everything already. He has Thoughts
which answer every need His Son perceives,
although He sees them not. For Love must give,
and what is given in His Name takes on
the form most useful in a world of form.

These are the forms which never can deceive,
because they come from Formlessness Itself.
Forgiveness is an earthly form of love,
which as it is in Heaven has no form.
Yet what is needed here is given here
as it is needed. In this form you can
fulfill your function even here, although
what love will mean to you when formlessness
has been restored to you is greater still.
Salvation of the world depends on you
who can forgive. Such is your function here.

## LESSON 187

**I bless the world because I bless myself.**

No one can give unless he has. In fact, giving is proof of having. We have made this point before. What seems to make it hard to credit is not this. No one can doubt that you must first possess what you would give. It is the second phase on which the world and true perception differ. Having had and given, then the world asserts that you have lost what you possessed. The truth maintains that giving will increase what you possess.

How is this possible? For it is sure that if you give a finite thing away, your body's eyes will not perceive it yours. Yet we have learned that things but represent the thoughts that make them. And you do not lack for proof that when you give ideas away, you strengthen them in your own mind. Perhaps the form in which the thought seems to appear is changed in giving. Yet it must return to him who gives. Nor can the form it takes be less acceptable. It must be more.

Ideas must first belong to you, before you give them. If you are to save the world, you first accept salvation for yourself. But you will not believe that this is done until you see the miracles it brings to everyone you look upon. Herein is the idea of giving clarified and given meaning. Now you can perceive that by your giving is your store increased.

Protect all things you value by the act of giving them away, and you are sure that you will never lose them. What you thought you did not have is thereby proven yours. Yet value not its form. For this will change and grow unrecognizable in time, however much you try to keep it safe. No form endures. It is the thought behind the form of things that lives unchangeable.

Give gladly. You can only gain thereby. The thought remains, and grows in strength as it is reinforced by giving. Thoughts extend as they are shared, for they can not be lost.

There is no giver and receiver in the sense the world conceives of them. There is a giver who retains; another who will give as well. And both must gain in this exchange, for each will have the thought in form most helpful to him. What he seems to lose is always something he will value less than what will surely be returned to him.

Never forget you give but to yourself. Who understands what giving means must laugh at the idea of sacrifice. Nor can he fail to recognize the many forms which sacrifice may take. He laughs as well at pain and loss, at sickness and at grief, at poverty, starvation and at death. He recognizes sacrifice remains the one idea that stands behind them all, and in his gentle laughter are they healed.

Illusion recognized must disappear. Accept not suffering, and you remove the thought of suffering. Your blessing lies on everyone who suffers, when you choose to see all suffering as what it is. The thought of sacrifice gives rise to all the forms that suffering appears to take. And sacrifice is an idea so mad that sanity dismisses it at once.

Never believe that you can sacrifice. There is no place for sacrifice in what has any value. If the thought occurs, its very presence proves that error has arisen and correction must be made. Your blessing will correct it. Given first to you, it now is yours to give as well. No form of sacrifice and suffering can long endure before the face of one who has forgiven and has blessed himself.

The lilies that your brother offers you are laid upon your altar, with the ones you offer him beside them. Who could fear to look upon such lovely holiness? The great illusion of the fear of God diminishes to nothingness before

the purity that you will look on here.
Be not afraid to look. The blessedness
you will behold will take away all thought
of form, and leave instead the perfect gift
forever there, forever to increase,
forever yours, forever given away.

Now are we one in thought, for fear has gone.
And here, before the altar to one God,
one Father, one Creator and one Thought,
we stand together as one Son of God.
Not separate from Him Who is our Source;
not distant from one brother who is part
of our one Self Whose innocence has joined
us all as one, we stand in blessedness,
and give as we receive. The Name of God
is on our lips. And as we look within,
we see the purity of Heaven shine
in our reflection of our Father's Love.

Now are we blessed, and now we bless the world.
What we have looked upon we would extend,
for we would see it everywhere. We would
behold it shining with the grace of God
in everyone. We would not have it be
withheld from anything we look upon.
And to ensure this holy sight is ours,
we offer it to everything we see.
For where we see it, it will be returned
to us in form of lilies we can lay
upon our altar, making it a home
for Innocence Itself, Who dwells in us
and offers us His Holiness as ours.

## LESSON 188

### The peace of God is shining in me now.

Why wait for Heaven? Those who seek the light are merely covering their eyes. The light is in them now. Enlightenment is but a recognition, not a change at all. Light is not of the world, yet you who bear the light in you are alien here as well. The light came with you from your native home, and stayed with you because it is your own. It is the only thing you bring with you from Him Who is your Source. It shines in you because it lights your home, and leads you back to where it came from and you are at home.

This light can not be lost. Why wait to find it in the future, or believe it has been lost already, or was never there? It can so easily be looked upon that arguments which prove it is not there become ridiculous. Who can deny the presence of what he beholds in him? It is not difficult to look within, for there all vision starts. There is no sight, be it of dreams or from a truer Source, that is not but the shadow of the seen through inward vision. There perception starts, and there it ends. It has no source but this.

The peace of God is shining in you now, and from your heart extends around the world. It pauses to caress each living thing, and leaves a blessing with it that remains forever and forever. What it gives must be eternal. It removes all thoughts of the ephemeral and valueless. It brings renewal to all tired hearts, and lights all vision as it passes by. All of its gifts are given everyone, and everyone unites in giving thanks to you who give, and you who have received.

The shining in your mind reminds the world of what it has forgotten, and the world restores the memory to you as well. From you salvation radiates with gifts beyond all measure, given and returned. To you, the giver of the gift, does God Himself give thanks. And in His blessing does the light in you shine brighter, adding to the gifts you have to offer to the world.

The peace of God can never be contained. Who recognizes it within himself must give it. And the means for giving it are in his understanding. He forgives because he recognized the truth in him. The peace of God is shining in you now, and in all living things. In quietness is it acknowledged universally. For what your inward vision looks upon is your perception of the universe.

Sit quietly and close your eyes. The light within you is sufficient. It alone has power to give the gift of sight to you. Exclude the outer world, and let your thoughts fly to the peace within. They know the way. For honest thoughts, untainted by the dream of worldly things outside yourself, become the holy messengers of God Himself.

These thoughts you think with Him. They recognize their home. And they point surely to their Source, Where God the Father and the Son are one. God's peace is shining on them, but they must remain with you as well, for they were born within your mind, as yours was born in God's. They lead you back to peace, from where they came but to remind you how you must return.

They heed your Father's Voice when you refuse to listen. And they urge you gently to accept His Word for what you are, instead of fantasies and shadows. They remind you that you are the co-creator of all things that live. For as the peace of God is shining in you, it must shine on them.

We practice coming nearer to the light in us today. We take our wandering thoughts, and gently bring them back to where they fall in line with all the thoughts we share with God. We will not let them stray. We let the light

within our minds direct them to come home.
We have betrayed them, ordering that they
depart from us. But now we call them back,
and wash them clean of strange desires and
disordered wishes. We restore to them
the holiness of their inheritance.

Thus are our minds restored with them, and we
acknowledge that the peace of God still shines
in us, and from us to all living things
that share our life. We will forgive them all,
absolving all the world from what we thought
it did to us. For it is we who make
the world as we would have it. Now we choose
that it be innocent, devoid of sin
and open to salvation. And we lay
our saving blessing on it, as we say:

*The peace of God is shining in me now.*
*Let all things shine upon me in that peace,*
*And let me bless them with the light in me.*

# LESSON 189

### I feel the Love of God within me now.

There is a light in you the world can not
perceive. And with its eyes you will not see
this light, for you are blinded by the world.
Yet you have eyes to see it. It is there
for you to look upon. It was not placed
in you to be kept hidden from your sight.
This light is a reflection of the thought
we practice now. To feel the Love of God
within you is to see the world anew,
shining in innocence, alive with hope,
and blessed with perfect charity and love.

Who could feel fear in such a world as this?
It welcomes you, rejoices that you came,
and sings your praises as it keeps you safe
from every form of danger and of pain.
It offers you a warm and gentle home
in which to stay a while. It blesses you
throughout the day, and watches through the night
as silent guardian of your holy sleep.
It sees salvation in you, and protects
the light in you, in which it sees its own.
It offers you its flowers and its snow,
in thankfulness for your benevolence.

This is the world the Love of God reveals.
It is so different from the world you see
through darkened eyes of malice and of fear,
that one belies the other. Only one
can be perceived at all. The other one
is wholly meaningless. A world in which
forgiveness shines on everything, and peace
offers its gentle light to everyone,
is inconceivable to those who see
a world of hatred rising from attack,
poised to avenge, to murder and destroy.

Yet is the world of hatred equally
unseen and inconceivable to those
who feel God's Love in them. Their world reflects
the quietness and peace that shines in them;
the gentleness and innocence they see
surrounding them; the joy with which they look
out from the endless wells of joy within.
What they have felt in them they look upon,
and see its sure reflection everywhere.

What would you see? The choice is given you.
But learn and do not let your mind forget
this law of seeing: You will look upon
that which you feel within. If hatred finds
a place within your heart, you will perceive
a fearful world, held cruelly in death's
sharp-pointed, bony fingers. If you feel
the Love of God within you, you will look
out on a world of mercy and of love.

Today we pass illusions, as we seek
to reach to what is true in us, and feel
its all-embracing tenderness, its Love
which knows us perfect as itself, its sight
which is the gift its Love bestows on us.
We learn the way today. It is as sure
as Love itself, to which it carries us.
For its simplicity avoids the snares
the foolish convolutions of the world's
apparent reasoning but serve to hide.

Simply do this: Be still, and lay aside
all thoughts of what you are and what God is;
all concepts you have learned about the world;
all images you hold about yourself.
Empty your mind of everything it thinks
is either true or false, or good or bad,
of every thought it judges worthy, and
all the ideas of which it is ashamed.
Hold onto nothing. Do not bring with you
one thought the past has taught, nor one belief
you ever learned before from anything.
Forget this world, forget this course, and come
with wholly empty hands unto your God.

Is it not He Who knows the way to you?
You need not know the way to Him. Your part
is simply to allow all obstacles
that you have interposed between the Son
and God the Father to be quietly
removed forever. God will do His part
in joyful and immediate response.
Ask and receive. But do not make demands,
nor point the road to God by which He should
appear to you. The way to reach Him is
merely to let Him be. For in that way

is your reality proclaimed as well.

And so today we do not choose the way
in which we go to Him. But we do choose
to let Him come. And with this choice we rest.
And in our quiet hearts and open minds,
His Love will blaze its pathway of itself.
What has not been denied is surely there,
if it be true and can be surely reached.
God knows His Son, and knows the way to him.
He does not need His Son to show Him how
to find His way. Through every opened door
His Love shines outward from its home within,
and lightens up the world in innocence.

*Father, we do not know the way to You.*
*But we have called, and You have answered us.*
*We will not interfere. Salvation's ways*
*are not our own, for they belong to You.*
*And it is unto You we look for them.*
*Our hands are open to receive Your gifts.*
*We have no thoughts we think apart from You,*
*and cherish no beliefs of what we are,*
*or Who created us. Yours is the way*
*that we would find and follow. And we ask*
*but that Your Will, which is our own as well,*
*be done in us and in the world, that it*
*become a part of Heaven now. Amen.*

# LESSON 190

### I choose the joy of God instead of pain.

Pain is a wrong perspective. When it is experienced in any form, it is a proof of self-deception. It is not a fact at all. There is no form it takes that will not disappear if seen aright. For pain proclaims God cruel. How could it be real in any form? It witnesses to God the Father's hatred of His Son, the sinfulness He sees in him, and His insane desire for revenge and death.

Can such projections be attested to? Can they be anything but wholly false? Pain is but witness to the Son's mistakes in what he thinks he is. It is a dream of fierce retaliation for a crime that could not be committed; for attack on what is wholly unassailable. It is a nightmare of abandonment by an Eternal Love, Which could not leave the Son whom It created out of love.

Pain is a sign illusions reign in place of truth. It demonstrates God is denied, confused with fear, perceived as mad, and seen as traitor to Himself. If God is real, there is no pain. If pain is real, there is no God. For vengeance is not part of love. And fear, denying love and using pain to prove that God is dead, has shown that death is victor over life. The body is the Son of God, corruptible in death, as mortal as the Father he has slain.

Peace to such foolishness! The time has come to laugh at such insane ideas. There is no need to think of them as savage crimes, or secret sins with weighty consequence. Who but a madman could conceive of them as cause of anything? Their witness, pain, is mad as they, and no more to be feared than the insane illusions which it shields, and tries to demonstrate must still be true.

It is your thoughts alone that cause you pain. Nothing external to your mind can hurt or injure you in any way. There is no cause beyond yourself that can reach down and bring oppression. No one but yourself affects you. There is nothing in the world that has the power to make you ill or sad, or weak or frail. But it is you who have the power to dominate all things you see by merely recognizing what you are. As you perceive the harmlessness in them, they will accept your holy will as theirs. And what was seen as fearful now becomes a source of innocence and holiness.

My holy brother, think of this awhile: The world you see does nothing. It has no effects at all. It merely represents your thoughts. And it will change entirely as you elect to change your mind, and choose the joy of God as what you really want. Your Self is radiant in this holy joy, unchanged, unchanging and unchangeable, forever and forever. And would you deny a little corner of your mind its own inheritance, and keep it as a hospital for pain; a sickly place where living things must come at last to die?

The world may seem to cause you pain. And yet the world, as causeless, has no power to cause. As an effect, it cannot make effects. As an illusion, it is what you wish. Your idle wishes represent its pains. Your strange desires bring it evil dreams. Your thoughts of death envelop it in fear, while in your kind forgiveness does it live.

Pain is the thought of evil taking form, and working havoc in your holy mind. Pain is the ransom you have gladly paid not to be free. In pain is God denied the Son He loves. In pain does fear appear to triumph over love, and time replace eternity and Heaven. And the world becomes a cruel and a bitter place, where sorrow rules and little joys give way before the onslaught of the savage pain that waits to end all joy in misery.

Lay down your arms, and come without defense
into the quiet place where Heaven's peace
holds all things still at last. Lay down all thoughts
of danger and of fear. Let no attack
enter with you. Lay down the cruel sword
of judgment that you hold against your throat,
and put aside the withering assaults
with which you seek to hide your holiness.

Here will you understand there is no pain.
Here does the joy of God belong to you.
This is the day when it is given you
to realize the lesson that contains
all of salvation's power. It is this:

Pain is illusion; joy, reality.
Pain is but sleep; joy is awakening.
Pain is deception; joy alone is truth.

And so again we make the only choice
that ever can be made; we choose between
illusions and the truth, or pain and joy,
or hell and Heaven. Let our gratitude
unto our Teacher fill our hearts, as we
are free to choose our joy instead of pain,
our holiness in place of sin, the peace
of God instead of conflict, and the light
of Heaven for the darkness of the world.

# LESSON 191

## I am the holy Son of God Himself.

Here is your declaration of release
from bondage of the world. And here as well
is all the world released. You do not see
what you have done by giving to the world
the role of jailer to the Son of God.
What could it be but vicious and afraid,
fearful of shadows, punitive and wild,
lacking all reason, blind, insane with hate?

What have you done that this should be your world?
What have you done that this is what you see?
Deny your own Identity, and this
is what remains. You look on chaos and
proclaim it is yourself. There is no sight
that fails to witness this to you. There is
no sound that does not speak of frailty
within you and without; no breath you draw
that does not seem to bring you nearer death;
no hope you hold but will dissolve in tears.

Deny your own Identity, and you
will not escape the madness which induced
this weird, unnatural and ghostly thought
that mocks creation and that laughs at God.
Deny your own Identity, and you
assail the universe alone, without
a friend, a tiny particle of dust
against the legions of your enemies.
Deny your own Identity, and look
on evil, sin and death, and watch despair
snatch from your fingers every scrap of hope,
leaving you nothing but the wish to die.

Yet what is it except a game you play
in which identity can be denied?
You are as God created you. All else
but this one thing is folly to believe.
In this one thought is everyone set free.
In this one truth are all illusions gone.
In this one fact is sinlessness proclaimed
to be forever part of everything,
the central core of its existence and
its guarantee of immortality.

But let today's idea find a place
among your thoughts and you have risen far
above the world, and all the worldly thoughts
that hold it prisoner. And from this place
of safety and escape you will return
and set it free. For he who can accept
his true Identity is truly saved.
And his salvation is the gift he gives
to everyone, in gratitude to Him
Who pointed out the way to happiness
that changed his whole perspective of the world.

One holy thought like this and you are free:
You are the holy Son of God Himself.
And with this holy thought you learn as well
that you have freed the world. You have no need
to use it cruelly, and then perceive
this savage need in it. You set it free
of your imprisonment. You will not see
a devastating image of yourself
walking the world in terror, with the world
twisting in agony because your fears
have laid the mark of death upon its heart.

Be glad today how very easily
is hell undone. You need but tell yourself:

*I am the holy Son of God Himself.*
*I cannot suffer, cannot be in pain;*
*I cannot suffer loss, nor fail to do*
*all that salvation asks.*

And in that thought
is everything you look on wholly changed.

A miracle has lighted up all dark
and ancient caverns, where the rites of death
echoed since time began. For time has lost
its hold upon the world. The Son of God
has come in glory to redeem the lost,
to save the helpless, and to give the world
the gift of his forgiveness. Who could see
the world as dark and sinful, when God's Son
has come again at last to set it free?

You who perceive yourself as weak and frail,
with futile hopes and devastated dreams,
born but to die, to weep and suffer pain,
hear this: All power is given unto you

in earth and Heaven. There is nothing that
you cannot do. You play the game of death,
of being helpless, pitifully tied
to dissolution in a world which shows
no mercy to you. Yet when you accord
it mercy, will its mercy shine on you.

Then let the Son of God awaken from
his sleep, and opening his holy eyes,
return again to bless the world he made.
In error it began, but it will end
in the reflection of his holiness.
And he will sleep no more and dream of death.
Then join with me today. Your glory is
the light that saves the world. Do not withhold
salvation longer. Look about the world,
and see the suffering there. Is not your heart
willing to bring your weary brothers rest?

They must await your own release. They stay
in chains till you are free. They cannot see
the mercy of the world until you find
it in yourself. They suffer pain until
you have denied its hold on you. They die
till you accept your own eternal life.
You are the holy Son of God Himself.
Remember this, and all the world is free.
Remember this, and earth and Heaven are one.

# LESSON 192

**I have a function God would have me fill.**

It is your Father's holy Will that you complete Himself, and that your Self shall be His sacred Son, forever pure as He, of Love created and in love preserved, extending love, creating in its Name, forever one with God and with your Self. Yet what can such a function mean within a world of envy, hatred and attack?

Therefore, you have a function in the world in its own terms. For who can understand a language far beyond his simple grasp? Forgiveness represents your function here. It is not God's creation, for it is the means by which untruth can be undone. And who would pardon Heaven? Yet on earth, you need the means to let illusions go. Creation merely waits for your return to be acknowledged, not to be complete.

Creation cannot even be conceived of in the world. It has no meaning here. Forgiveness is the closest it can come to earth. For being Heaven-born, it has no form at all. Yet God created One Who has the power to translate in form the wholly formless. What He makes are dreams, but of a kind so close to waking that the light of day already shines in them, and eyes already opening behold the joyful sights their offerings contain.

Forgiveness gently looks upon all things unknown in Heaven, sees them disappear, and leaves the world a clean and unmarked slate on which the Word of God can now replace the senseless symbols written there before. Forgiveness is the means by which the fear of death is overcome, because it holds no fierce attraction now and guilt is gone. Forgiveness lets the body be perceived as what it is; a simple teaching aid, to be laid by when learning is complete, but hardly changing him who learns at all.

The mind without the body cannot make mistakes. It cannot think that it will die, nor be the prey of merciless attack. Anger becomes impossible, and where is terror then? What fears could still assail those who have lost the source of all attack, the core of anguish and the seat of fear? Only forgiveness can relieve the mind of thinking that the body is its home. Only forgiveness can restore the peace that God intended for His holy Son. Only forgiveness can persuade the Son to look again upon his holiness.

With anger gone, you will indeed perceive that, for Christ's vision and the gift of sight, no sacrifice was asked, and only pain was lifted from a sick and tortured mind. Is this unwelcome? Is it to be feared? Or is it to be hoped for, met with thanks and joyously accepted? We are one, and therefore give up nothing. But we have indeed been given everything by God.

Yet do we need forgiveness to perceive that this is so. Without its kindly light we grope in darkness, using reason but to justify our rage and our attack. Our understanding is so limited that what we think we understand is but confusion born of error. We are lost in mists of shifting dreams and fearful thoughts, our eyes shut tight against the light; our minds engaged in worshipping what is not there.

Who can be born again in Christ but him who has forgiven everyone he sees or thinks of or imagines? Who could be set free while he imprisons anyone? A jailer is not free, for he is bound together with his prisoner. He must be sure that he does not escape, and so he spends his time in keeping watch on him. The bars that limit him become the world in which his jailer lives, along with him. And it is on his freedom that the way to liberty depends for both of them.

Therefore, hold no one prisoner. Release instead of bind, for thus are you made free. The way is simple. Every time you feel a stab of anger, realize you hold a sword above your head. And it will fall or be averted as you choose to be condemned or free. Thus does each one who seems to tempt you to be angry represent your savior from the prison house of death. And so you owe him thanks instead of pain.

Be merciful today. The Son of God deserves your mercy. It is he who asks that you accept the way to freedom now. Deny him not. His Father's Love for him belongs to you. Your function here on earth is only to forgive him, that you may accept him back as your Identity. He is as God created him. And you are what he is. Forgive him now his sins, and you will see that you are one with him.

# LESSON 193

### All things are lessons God would have me learn.

God does not know of learning. Yet His Will extends to what He does not understand, in that He wills the happiness His Son inherited of Him be undisturbed; eternal and forever gaining scope, eternally expanding in the joy of full creation, and eternally open and wholly limitless in Him. That is His Will. And thus His Will provides the means to guarantee that it is done.

God sees no contradictions. Yet His Son believes he sees them. Thus he has a need for One Who can correct his erring sight, and give him vision that will lead him back to where perception ceases. God does not perceive at all. Yet it is He Who gives the means by which perception is made true and beautiful enough to let the light of Heaven shine upon it. It is He Who answers what His Son would contradict, and keeps his sinlessness forever safe.

These are the lessons God would have you learn. His Will reflects them all, and they reflect His loving kindness to the Son He loves. Each lesson has a central thought, the same in all of them. The form alone is changed, with different circumstances and events; with different characters and different themes, apparent but not real. They are the same in fundamental content. It is this:

*Forgive, and you will see this differently.*

Certain it is that all distress does not appear to be but unforgiveness. Yet that is the content underneath the form. It is this sameness which makes learning sure, because the lesson is so simple that it cannot be rejected in the end. No one can hide forever from a truth so very obvious that it appears in countless forms, and yet is recognized as easily in all of them, if one but wants to see the simple lesson there.

*Forgive, and you will see this differently.*

These are the words the Holy Spirit speaks in all your tribulations, all your pain, all suffering regardless of its form. These are the words with which temptation ends, and guilt, abandoned, is revered no more. These are the words which end the dream of sin, and rid the mind of fear. These are the words by which salvation comes to all the world.

Shall we not learn to say these words when we are tempted to believe that pain is real, and death becomes our choice instead of life? Shall we not learn to say these words when we have understood their power to release all minds from bondage? These are words which give you power over all events that seem to have been given power over you. You see them rightly when you hold these words in full awareness, and do not forget these words apply to everything you see or any brother looks upon amiss.

How can you tell when you are seeing wrong, or someone else is failing to perceive the lesson he should learn? Does pain seem real in the perception? If it does, be sure the lesson is not learned. And there remains an unforgiveness hiding in the mind that sees the pain through eyes the mind directs.

God would not have you suffer thus. He would help you forgive yourself. His Son does not remember who he is. And God would have him not forget His Love, and all the gifts His Love brings with it. Would you now renounce your own salvation? Would you fail to learn the simple lessons Heaven's Teacher sets before you, that all pain may disappear and God may be remembered by His Son?

All things are lessons God would have you learn. He would not leave an unforgiving thought without correction, nor one thorn or nail to hurt His holy Son in any way. He would ensure his holy rest remain

untroubled and serene, without a care,
in an eternal home which cares for him.
And He would have all tears be wiped away,
with none remaining yet unshed, and none
but waiting their appointed time to fall.
For God has willed that laughter should replace
each one, and that His Son be free again.

We will attempt today to overcome
a thousand seeming obstacles to peace
in just one day. Let mercy come to you
more quickly. Do not try to hold it off
another day, another minute or
another instant. Time was made for this.
Use it today for what its purpose is.
Morning and night, devote what time you can
to serve its proper aim, and do not let
the time be less than meets your deepest need.

Give all you can, and give a little more.
For now we would arise in haste and go
unto our Father's house. We have been gone
too long, and we would linger here no more.
And as we practice, let us think about
all things we saved to settle by ourselves,
and kept apart from healing. Let us give
them all to Him Who knows the way to look
upon them so that they will disappear.
Truth is His message; truth His teaching is.
His are the lessons God would have us learn.

Each hour, spend a little time today,
and in the days to come, in practicing
the lesson in forgiveness in the form
established for the day. And try to give
it application to the happenings
the hour brought, so that the next one is
free of the one before. The chains of time
are easily unloosened in this way.
Let no one hour cast its shadow on
the one that follows, and when that one goes,
let everything that happened in its course
go with it. Thus will you remain unbound,
in peace eternal in the world of time.

This is the lesson God would have you learn:
There is a way to look on everything
that lets it be to you another step
to Him, and to salvation of the world.
To all that speaks of terror, answer thus:

*I will forgive, and this will disappear.*

To every apprehension, every care
and every form of suffering, repeat
these selfsame words. And then you hold the key
that opens Heaven's gate, and brings the Love
of God the Father down to earth at last,
to raise it up to Heaven. God will take
this final step Himself. Do not deny
the little steps He asks you take to Him.

## LESSON 194

### I place the future in the Hands of God.

Today's idea takes another step
toward quick salvation, and a giant stride
it is indeed! So great the distance is
that it encompasses, it sets you down
just short of Heaven, with the goal in sight
and obstacles behind. Your foot has reached
the lawns that welcome you to Heaven's gate;
the quiet place of peace, where you await
with certainty the final step of God.
How far are we progressing now from earth!
How close are we approaching to our goal!
How short the journey still to be pursued!

Accept today's idea, and you have
passed all anxiety, all pits of hell,
all blackness of depression, thoughts of sin,
and devastation brought about by guilt.
Accept today's idea, and you have
released the world from all imprisonment
by loosening the heavy chains that locked
the door to freedom on it. You are saved,
and your salvation thus becomes the gift
you give the world, because you have received.

In no one instant is depression felt,
or pain experienced or loss perceived.
In no one instant sorrow can be set
upon a throne, and worshipped faithfully.
In no one instant can one even die.
And so each instant given unto God
in passing, with the next one given Him
already, is a time of your release
from sadness, pain and even death itself.

God holds your future as He holds your past
and present. They are one to Him, and so
they should be one to you. Yet in this world,
the temporal progression still seems real.
And so you are not asked to understand
the lack of sequence really found in time.
You are but asked to let the future go,
and place it in God's Hands. And you will see
by your experience that you have laid
the past and present in His Hands as well,
because the past will punish you no more,
and future dread will now be meaningless.

Release the future. For the past is gone,
and what is present, freed from its bequest
of grief and misery, of pain and loss,
becomes the instant in which time escapes
the bondage of illusions where it runs
its pitiless, inevitable course.
Then is each instant which was slave to time
transformed into a holy instant, when
the light that was kept hidden in God's Son
is freed to bless the world. Now is he free,
and all his glory shines upon a world
made free with him, to share his holiness.

If you can see the lesson for today
as the deliverance it really is,
you will not hesitate to give as much
consistent effort as you can, to make
it be a part of you. As it becomes
a thought that rules your mind, a habit in
your problem-solving repertoire, a way
of quick reaction to temptation, you
extend your learning to the world. And as
you learn to see salvation in all things,
so will the world perceive that it is saved.

What worry can beset the one who gives
his future to the loving Hands of God?
What can he suffer? What can cause him pain,
or bring experience of loss to him?
What can he fear? And what can he regard
except with love? For he who has escaped
all fear of future pain has found his way
to present peace, and certainty of care
the world can never threaten. He is sure
that his perception may be faulty, but
will never lack correction. He is free
to choose again when he has been deceived;
to change his mind when he has made mistakes.

Place, then, your future in the Hands of God.
For thus you call the memory of Him
to come again, replacing all your thoughts
of sin and evil with the truth of love.
Think you the world could fail to gain thereby,
and every living creature not respond
with healed perception? Who entrusts himself

to God has also placed the world within
the Hands to which he has himself appealed
for comfort and security. He lays
aside the sick illusions of the world
along with his, and offers peace to both.

Now are we saved indeed. For in God's Hands
we rest untroubled, sure that only good
can come to us. If we forget, we will
be gently reassured. If we accept
an unforgiving thought, it will be soon
replaced by love's reflection. And if we
are tempted to attack, we will appeal
to Him Who guards our rest to make the choice
for us that leaves temptation far behind.
No longer is the world our enemy,
for we have chosen that we be its Friend.

# LESSON 195

## Love is the way I walk in gratitude.

Gratitude is a lesson hard to learn
for those who look upon the world amiss.
The most that they can do is see themselves
as better off than others. And they try
to be content because another seems
to suffer more than they. How pitiful
and deprecating are such thoughts! For who
has cause for thanks while others have less cause?
And who could suffer less because he sees
another suffer more? Your gratitude
is due to Him alone Who made all cause
of sorrow disappear throughout the world.

It is insane to offer thanks because
of suffering. But it is equally
insane to fail in gratitude to One
Who offers you the certain means whereby
all pain is healed, and suffering replaced
with laughter and with happiness. Nor could
the even partly sane refuse to take
the steps which He directs, and follow in
the way He sets before them, to escape
a prison that they thought contained no door
to the deliverance they now perceive.

Your brother is your "enemy" because
you see in him the rival for your peace;
a plunderer who takes his joy from you,
and leaves you nothing but a black despair
so bitter and relentless that there is
no hope remaining. Now is vengeance all
there is to wish for. Now can you but try
to bring him down to lie in death with you,
as useless as yourself; as little left
within his grasping fingers as in yours.

You do not offer God your gratitude
because your brother is more slave than you,
nor could you sanely be enraged if he
seems freer. Love makes no comparisons.
And gratitude can only be sincere
if it be joined to love. We offer thanks
to God our Father that in us all things
will find their freedom. It will never be
that some are loosed while others still are bound.
For who can bargain in the name of love?

Therefore give thanks, but in sincerity.
And let your gratitude make room for all
who will escape with you; the sick, the weak,
the needy and afraid, and those who mourn
a seeming loss or feel apparent pain,
who suffer cold or hunger, or who walk
the way of hatred and the path of death.
All these go with you. Let us not compare
ourselves with them, for thus we split them off
from our awareness of the unity
we share with them, as they must share with us.

We thank our Father for one thing alone;
that we are separate from no living thing,
and therefore one with Him. And we rejoice
that no exceptions ever can be made
which would reduce our wholeness, nor impair
or change our function to complete the One
Who is Himself completion. We give thanks
for every living thing, for otherwise
we offer thanks for nothing, and we fail
to recognize the gifts of God to us.

Then let our brothers lean their tired heads
against our shoulders as they rest a while.
We offer thanks for them. For if we can
direct them to the peace that we would find,
the way is opening at last to us.
An ancient door is swinging free again;
a long forgotten Word re-echoes in
our memory, and gathers clarity
as we are willing once again to hear.

Walk, then, in gratitude the way of love.
For hatred is forgotten when we lay
comparisons aside. What more remains
as obstacles to peace? The fear of God
is now undone at last, and we forgive
without comparing. Thus we cannot choose
to overlook some things, and yet retain
some other things still locked away as "sins."
When your forgiveness is complete you will
have total gratitude, for you will see
that everything has earned the right to love
by being loving, even as your Self.

Today we learn to think of gratitude

in place of anger, malice and revenge.
We have been given everything. If we
refuse to recognize it, are we not
entitled therefore to our bitterness,
and to a self-perception which regards
us in a place of merciless pursuit,
where we are badgered ceaselessly, and pushed
about without a thought or care for us
or for our future? Gratitude becomes
the single thought we substitute for these
insane perceptions. God has cared for us,
and calls us Son. Can there be more than this?

Our gratitude will pave the way to Him,
and shorten our learning time by more
than you could ever dream of. Gratitude
goes hand in hand with love, and where one is
the other must be found. For gratitude
is but an aspect of the Love which is
the Source of all creation. God gives thanks
to you, His Son, for being what you are;
His Own completion and the Source of love,
along with Him. Your gratitude to Him
is one with His to you. For love can walk
no road except the way of gratitude,
and thus we go who walk the way to God.

## LESSON 196

### It can be but myself I crucify.

When this is firmly understood and kept in full awareness, you will not attempt to harm yourself, nor make your body slave to vengeance. You will not attack yourself, and you will realize that to attack another is but to attack yourself. You will be free of the insane belief that to attack a brother saves yourself. And you will understand his safety is your own, and in his healing you are healed.

Perhaps at first you will not understand how mercy, limitless and with all things held in its sure protection, can be found in the idea we practice for today. It may, in fact, appear to be a sign that punishment can never be escaped because the ego, under what it sees as threat, is quick to cite the truth to save its lies. Yet must it fail to understand the truth it uses thus. But you can learn to see these foolish applications, and deny the meaning they appear to have.

Thus do you also teach your mind that you are not an ego. For the ways in which the ego would distort the truth will not deceive you longer. You will not believe you are a body to be crucified. And you will see within today's idea the light of resurrection, looking past all thoughts of crucifixion and of death, to thoughts of liberation and of life.

Today's idea is one step we take in leading us from bondage to the state of perfect freedom. Let us take this step today, that we may quickly go the way salvation shows us, taking every step in its appointed sequence, as the mind relinquishes its burdens one by one. It is not time we need for this. It is but willingness. For what would seem to need a thousand years can easily be done in just one instant by the grace of God.

The dreary, hopeless thought that you can make attacks on others and escape yourself has nailed you to the cross. Perhaps it seemed to be salvation. Yet it merely stood for the belief the fear of God is real. And what is that but hell? Who could believe his Father is his deadly enemy, separate from him, and waiting to destroy his life and blot him from the universe, without the fear of hell upon his heart?

Such is the form of madness you believe, if you accept the fearful thought you can attack another and be free yourself. Until this form is changed, there is no hope. Until you see that this, at least, must be entirely impossible, how could there be escape? The fear of God is real to anyone who thinks this thought is true. And he will not perceive its foolishness, or even see that it is there, so that it would be possible to question it.

To question it at all, its form must first be changed at least as much as will permit fear of retaliation to abate, and the responsibility returned to some extent to you. From there you can at least consider if you want to go along this painful path. Until this shift has been accomplished, you can not perceive that it is but your thoughts that bring you fear, and your deliverance depends on you.

Our next steps will be easy, if you take this one today. From there we go ahead quite rapidly. For once you understand it is impossible that you be hurt except by your own thoughts, the fear of God must disappear. You cannot then believe that fear is caused without. And God, Whom you had thought to banish, can be welcomed back within the holy mind He never left.

Salvation's song can certainly be heard in the idea we practice for today. If it can but be you you crucify, you did not hurt the world, and need not fear

its vengeance and pursuit. Nor need you hide in terror from the deadly fear of God projection hides behind. The thing you dread the most is your salvation. You are strong, and it is strength you want. And you are free, and glad of freedom. You have sought to be both weak and bound, because you feared your strength
and freedom. Yet salvation lies in them.

There is an instant in which terror seems to grip your mind so wholly that escape appears quite hopeless. When you realize, once and for all, that it is you you fear, the mind perceives itself as split. And this had been concealed while you believed attack could be directed outward, and returned from outside to within. It seemed to be an enemy outside you had to fear. And thus a god outside yourself became your mortal enemy; the source of fear.

Now, for an instant, is a murderer perceived within you, eager for your death, intent on plotting punishment for you until the time when it can kill at last. Yet in this instant is the time as well in which salvation comes. For fear of God has disappeared. And you can call on Him to save you from illusions by His Love, calling Him Father and yourself His Son. Pray that the instant may be soon, – today. Step back from fear, and make advance to love.

There is no Thought of God that does not go with you to help you reach that instant, and to go beyond it quickly, surely and forever. When the fear of God is gone, there are no obstacles that still remain between you and the holy peace of God. How kind and merciful is the idea we practice! Give it welcome, as you should, for it is your release. It is indeed but you your mind can try to crucify. Yet your redemption, too, will come from you.

# LESSON 197

### It can be but my gratitude I earn.

Here is the second step we take to free your mind from the belief in outside force pitted against your own. You make attempts at kindness and forgiveness. Yet you turn them to attack again, unless you find external gratitude and lavish thanks. Your gifts must be received with honor, lest they be withdrawn. And so you think God's gifts are loans at best; at worst, deceptions which would cheat you of defenses, to ensure that when He strikes He will not fail to kill.

How easily are God and guilt confused by those who know not what their thoughts can do. Deny your strength, and weakness must become salvation to you. See yourself as bound, and bars become your home. Nor will you leave the prison house, or claim your strength, until guilt and salvation are not seen as one, and freedom and salvation are perceived as joined, with strength beside them, to be sought and claimed, and found and fully recognized.

The world must thank you when you offer it release from your illusions. Yet your thanks belong to you as well, for its release can only mirror yours. Your gratitude is all your gifts require, that they be a lasting offering of a thankful heart, released from hell forever. Is it this you would undo by taking back your gifts, because they were not honored? It is you who honor them and give them fitting thanks, for it is you who have received the gifts.

It does not matter if another thinks your gifts unworthy. In his mind there is a part that joins with yours in thanking you. It does not matter if your gifts seem lost and ineffectual. They are received where they are given. In your gratitude are they accepted universally, and thankfully acknowledged by the Heart of God Himself. And would you take them back, when He has gratefully accepted them?

God blesses every gift you give to Him, and every gift is given Him, because it can be given only to yourself.

And what belongs to God must be His Own. Yet you will never realize His gifts are sure, eternal, changeless, limitless, forever giving out, extending love and adding to your never-ending joy while you forgive but to attack again.

Withdraw the gifts you give, and you will think that what is given you has been withdrawn. But learn to let forgiveness take away the sins you think you see outside yourself, and you can never think the gifts of God are lent but for a little while, before He snatches them away again in death. For death will have no meaning for you then.

And with the end of this belief is fear forever over. Thank your Self for this, for He is grateful only unto God, and He gives thanks for you unto Himself. To everyone who lives will Christ yet come, for everyone must live and move in Him. His Being in His Father is secure, because Their Will is one. Their gratitude to all They have created has no end, for gratitude remains a part of love.

Thanks be to you, the holy Son of God. For as you were created, you contain all things within your Self. And you are still as God created you. Nor can you dim the light of your perfection. In your heart the Heart of God is laid. He holds you dear, because you are Himself. All gratitude belongs to you, because of what you are.

Give thanks as you receive it. Be you free of all ingratitude to anyone who makes your Self complete. And from this Self is no one left outside. Give thanks for all the countless channels which extend this Self. All that you do is given unto Him. All that you think can only be His Thoughts, sharing with Him the holy Thoughts of God. Earn now the gratitude you have denied yourself when you forgot the function God has given you. But never think that He has ever ceased to offer thanks to you.

## LESSON 198

**Only my condemnation injures me.**

Injury is impossible. And yet illusion makes illusion. If you can condemn, you can be injured. For you have believed that you can injure, and the right you have established for yourself can be now used against you, till you lay it down as valueless, unwanted and unreal. Then does illusion cease to have effects, and those it seemed to have will be undone. Then are you free, for freedom is your gift, and you can now receive the gift you gave.

Condemn and you are made a prisoner. Forgive and you are freed. Such is the law that rules perception. It is not a law that knowledge understands, for freedom is a part of knowledge. To condemn is thus impossible in truth. What seems to be its influence and its effects have not occurred at all. Yet must we deal with them a while as if they had. Illusion makes illusion. Except one. Forgiveness is illusion that is answer to the rest.

Forgiveness sweeps all other dreams away, and though it is itself a dream, it breeds no others. All illusions save this one must multiply a thousandfold. But this is where illusions end. Forgiveness is the end of dreams, because it is a dream of waking. It is not itself the truth. Yet does it point to where the truth must be, and gives direction with the certainty of God Himself. It is a dream in which the Son of God awakens to his Self and to his Father, knowing They are one.

Forgiveness is the only road that leads out of disaster, past all suffering, and finally away from death. How could there be another way, when this one is the plan of God Himself? And why would you oppose it, quarrel with it, seek to find a thousand ways in which it must be wrong; a thousand other possibilities?

Is it not wiser to be glad you hold the answer to your problems in your hand? Is it not more intelligent to thank the One Who gives salvation, and accept His gift with gratitude? And is it not a kindness to yourself to hear His Voice and learn the simple lessons He would teach, instead of trying to dismiss His words, and substitute your own in place of His?

His words will work. His words will save. His words contain all hope, all blessing and all joy that ever can be found upon this earth. His words are born in God, and come to you with Heaven's love upon them. Those who hear His words have heard the song of Heaven. For these are the words in which all merge as one at last. And as this one will fade away, the Word of God will come to take its place, for it will be remembered then and loved.

This world has many seeming separate haunts where mercy has no meaning, and attack appears as justified. Yet all are one; a place where death is offered to God's Son and to his Father. You may think They have accepted. But if you will look again upon the place where you beheld Their blood, you will perceive a miracle instead. How foolish to believe that They could die! How foolish to believe you can attack! How mad to think that you could be condemned, and that the holy Son of God can die!

The stillness of your Self remains unmoved, untouched by thoughts like these, and unaware of any condemnation which could need forgiveness. Dreams of any kind are strange and alien to the truth. And what but truth could have a Thought which builds a bridge to it that brings illusions to the other side?

Today we practice letting freedom come to make its home with you. The truth bestows these words upon your mind, that you may find the key to light and let the darkness end:

*Only my condemnation injures me.*

*Only my own forgiveness sets me free.*

Do not forget today that there can be no form of suffering that fails to hide an unforgiving thought. Nor can there be a form of pain forgiveness cannot heal.

Accept the one illusion which proclaims there is no condemnation in God's Son, and Heaven is remembered instantly; the world forgotten, all its weird beliefs forgotten with it, as the face of Christ appears unveiled at last in this one dream. This is the gift the Holy Spirit holds for you from God your Father. Let today be celebrated both on earth and in your holy home as well. Be kind to both, as you forgive the trespasses you thought them guilty of, and see your innocence shining upon you from the face of Christ.

Now is there silence all around the world. Now is there stillness where before there was a frantic rush of thoughts that made no sense. Now is there tranquil light across the face of earth, made quiet in a dreamless sleep. And now the Word of God alone remains upon it. Only that can be perceived an instant longer. Then are symbols done, and everything you ever thought you made completely vanished from the mind that God forever knows to be His only Son.

There is no condemnation in him. He is perfect in his holiness. He needs no thoughts of mercy. Who could give him gifts when everything is his? And who could dream of offering forgiveness to the Son of Sinlessness Itself, so like to Him Whose Son he is, that to behold the Son is to perceive no more, and only know the Father? In this vision of the Son, so brief that not an instant stands between this single sight and timelessness itself, you see the vision of yourself, and then you disappear forever into God.

Today we come still nearer to the end of everything that yet would stand between this vision and our sight. And we are glad that we have come this far, and recognize that He Who brought us here will not forsake us now. For He would give to us the gift that God has given us through Him today. Now is the time for your deliverance. The time has come. The time has come today.

## LESSON 199

**I am not a body. I am free.**

Freedom must be impossible as long as you perceive a body as yourself. The body is a limit. Who would seek for freedom in a body looks for it where it can not be found. The mind can be made free when it no longer sees itself as in a body, firmly tied to it and sheltered by its presence. If this were the truth, the mind were vulnerable indeed!

The mind that serves the Holy Spirit is unlimited forever, in all ways, beyond the laws of time and space, unbound by any preconceptions, and with strength and power to do whatever it is asked. Attack thoughts cannot enter such a mind, because it has been given to the Source of love, and fear can never enter in a mind that has attached itself to love. It rests in God. And who can be afraid who lives in Innocence, and only loves?

It is essential for your progress in this course that you accept today's idea, and hold it very dear. Be not concerned that to the ego it is quite insane. The ego holds the body dear because it dwells in it, and lives united with the home that it has made. It is a part of the illusion that has sheltered it from being found illusory itself.

Here does it hide, and here it can be seen as what it is. Declare your innocence and you are free. The body disappears, because you have no need of it except the need the Holy Spirit sees. For this, the body will appear as useful form for what the mind must do. It thus becomes a vehicle which helps forgiveness be extended to the all-inclusive goal that it must reach, according to God's plan.

Cherish today's idea, and practice it today and every day. Make it a part of every practice period you take. There is no thought that will not gain thereby in power to help the world, and none which will not gain in added gifts to you as well. We sound the call of freedom round the world with this idea. And would you be exempt from the acceptance of the gifts you give?

The Holy Spirit is the home of minds that seek for freedom. In Him they have found what they have sought. The body's purpose now is unambiguous. And it becomes perfect in the ability to serve an undivided goal. In conflict-free and unequivocal response to mind with but the thought of freedom as its goal, the body serves, and serves its purpose well. Without the power to enslave, it is a worthy servant of the freedom which the mind within the Holy Spirit seeks.

Be free today. And carry freedom as your gift to those who still believe they are enslaved within a body. Be you free, so that the Holy Spirit can make use of your escape from bondage, to set free the many who perceive themselves as bound and helpless and afraid. Let love replace their fears through you. Accept salvation now, and give your mind to Him Who calls to you to make this gift to Him. For He would give you perfect freedom, perfect joy, and hope that finds its full accomplishment in God.

You are God's Son. In immortality you live forever. Would you not return your mind to this? Then practice well the thought the Holy Spirit gives you for today. Your brothers stand released with you in it; the world is blessed along with you, God's Son will weep no more, and Heaven offers thanks for the increase of joy your practice brings even to it. And God Himself extends His Love and happiness each time you say:

*I am not a body. I am free.*
*I hear the Voice That God has given me,*
*and it is only This my mind obeys.*

# LESSON 200

## There is no peace except the peace of God.

Seek you no further. You will not find peace except the peace of God. Accept this fact, and save yourself the agony of yet more bitter disappointments, bleak despair, and sense of icy hopelessness and doubt. Seek you no further. There is nothing else for you to find except the peace of God, unless you seek for misery and pain.

This is the final point to which each one must come at last, to lay aside all hope of finding happiness where there is none; of being saved by what can only hurt; of making peace of chaos, joy of pain, and Heaven out of hell. Attempt no more to win through losing, nor to die to live. You cannot but be asking for defeat.

Yet you can ask as easily for love, for happiness, and for eternal life in peace that has no ending. Ask for this, and you can only win. To ask for what you have already must succeed. To ask that what is false be true can only fail. Forgive yourself for vain imaginings, and seek no longer what you cannot find. For what could be more foolish than to seek and seek and seek again for hell, when you have but to look with open eyes to find that Heaven lies before you, through a door that opens easily to welcome you?

Come home. You have not found your happiness in foreign places and in alien forms that have no meaning to you, though you sought to make them meaningful. This world is not where you belong. You are a stranger here. But it is given you to find the means whereby the world no longer seems to be a prison house or jail for anyone.

Freedom is given you where you beheld but chains and iron doors. But you must change your mind about the purpose of the world, if you would find escape. You will be bound till all the world is seen by you as blessed, and everyone made free of your mistakes and honored as he is. You made him not; no more yourself. And as you free the one, the other is accepted as he is.

What does forgiveness do? In truth it has no function, and does nothing. For it is unknown in Heaven. It is only hell where it is needed, and where it must serve a mighty function. Is not the escape of God's beloved Son from evil dreams that he imagines, yet believes are true, a worthy purpose? Who could hope for more, while there appears to be a choice to make between success and failure; love and fear?

There is no peace except the peace of God, because He has one Son who cannot make a world in opposition to God's Will and to his own, which is the same as His. What could he hope to find in such a world? It cannot have reality, because it never was created. Is it here that he would seek for peace? Or must he see that, as he looks on it, the world can but deceive? Yet can he learn to look on it another way, and find the peace of God.

Peace is the bridge that everyone will cross, to leave this world behind. But peace begins within the world perceived as different, and leading from this fresh perception to the gate of Heaven and the way beyond. Peace is the answer to conflicting goals, to senseless journeys, frantic, vain pursuits, and meaningless endeavors. Now the way is easy, sloping gently toward the bridge where freedom lies within the peace of God.

Let us not lose our way again today. We go to Heaven, and the path is straight. Only if we attempt to wander can there be delay, and needless wasted time on thorny byways. God alone is sure, and He will guide our footsteps. He will not desert His Son in need, nor let him stray forever from his home. The Father calls; the Son will hear. And that is all there is

to what appears to be a world apart
from God, where bodies have reality.

Now is there silence. Seek no further. You
have come to where the road is carpeted
with leaves of false desires, fallen from
the trees of hopelessness you sought before.
Now are they underfoot. And you look up
and on toward Heaven, with the body's eyes
but serving for an instant longer now.
Peace is already recognized at last,
and you can feel its soft embrace surround
your heart and mind with comfort and with love.

Today we seek no idols. Peace can not
be found in them. The peace of God is ours,
and only this will we accept and want.
Peace be to us today. For we have found
a simple, happy way to leave the world
of ambiguity, and to replace
our shifting goals and solitary dreams
with single purpose and companionship.
For peace is union, if it be of God.
We seek no further. We are close to home,
and draw still nearer every time we say:

*There is no peace except the peace of God,
And I am glad and thankful it is so.*

# REVIEW VI

## Introduction

For this review we take but one idea
each day, and practice it as often as
is possible. Besides the time you give
morning and evening, which should not be less
than fifteen minutes, and the hourly
remembrances you make throughout the day,
use the idea as often as you can
between them. Each of these ideas alone
would be sufficient for salvation, if
it were learned truly. Each would be enough
to give release to you and to the world
from every form of bondage, and invite
the memory of God to come again.

With this in mind we start our practicing,
in which we carefully review the thoughts
the Holy Spirit has bestowed on us
in our last twenty lessons. Each contains
the whole curriculum if understood,
practiced, accepted, and applied to all
the seeming happenings throughout the day.
One is enough. But from that one, there must
be no exceptions made. And so we need
to use them all and let them blend as one,
as each contributes to the whole we learn.

These practice sessions, like our last review,
are centered round a central theme with which
we start and end each lesson. It is this:

*I am not a body. I am free.*
*For I am still as God created me.*

The day begins and ends with this. And we
repeat it every time the hour strikes,
or we remember, in between, we have
a function that transcends the world we see.
Beyond this, and a repetition of
the special thought we practice for the day,
no form of exercise is urged, except
a deep relinquishment of everything
that clutters up the mind, and makes it deaf
to reason, sanity and simple truth.

We will attempt to get beyond all words
and special forms of practicing for this
review. For we attempt, this time, to reach
a quickened pace along a shorter path
to the serenity and peace of God.
We merely close our eyes, and then forget
all that we thought we knew and understood.
For thus is freedom given us from all
we did not know and failed to understand.

There is but one exception to this lack
of structuring. Permit no idle thought
to go unchallenged. If you notice one,
deny its hold and hasten to assure
your mind that this is not what it would have.
Then gently let the thought which you denied
be given up, in sure and quick exchange
for the idea we practice for the day.

When you are tempted, hasten to proclaim
your freedom from temptation, as you say:

*This thought I do not want. I choose instead ----*

And then repeat the idea for the day,
and let it take the place of what you thought.
Beyond such special applications of
each day's idea, we will add but a few
formal expressions or specific thoughts
to aid in practicing. Instead, we give
these times of quiet to the Teacher Who
instructs in quiet, speaks of peace, and gives
our thoughts whatever meaning they may have.

To Him I offer this review for you.
I place you in His charge, and let Him teach
you what to do and say and think, each time
you turn to Him. He will not fail to be
available to you, each time you call
to Him to help you. Let us offer Him
the whole review we now begin, and let
us also not forget to Whom it has
been given, as we practice day by day,
advancing toward the goal He set for us;
allowing Him to teach us how to go,
and trusting Him completely for the way
each practice period can best become
a loving gift of freedom to the world.

## LESSON 201

**I am not a body. I am free.**
**For I am still as God created me.**

I trust my brothers, who are one with me.

*No one but is my brother. I am blessed with oneness with the universe and God, my Father, one Creator of the whole that is my Self, forever one with me.*

**I am not a body. I am free.**
**For I am still as God created me.**

## LESSON 202

**I am not a body. I am free.**
**For I am still as God created me.**

I will be still an instant and go home.

*Why would I choose to stay an instant more where I do not belong, when God Himself has given me His Voice to call me home?*

**I am not a body. I am free.**
**For I am still as God created me.**

## LESSON 203

**I am not a body. I am free.**
**For I am still as God created me.**

I call upon God's Name and on my own.

*The Name of God is my deliverance from every thought of evil and of sin, because it is my own as well as His.*

**I am not a body. I am free.**
**For I am still as God created me.**

## LESSON 204

**I am not a body. I am free.**
**For I am still as God created me.**

The Name of God is my inheritance.

*God's Name reminds me that I am His Son, not slave to time, unbound by laws which rule the world of sick illusions, free in God, forever and forever one with Him.*

**I am not a body. I am free.**
**For I am still as God created me.**

## LESSON 205

**I am not a body. I am free.**
**For I am still as God created me.**

I want the peace of God.

*The peace of God is everything I want. The peace of God is my one goal; the aim of all my living here, the end I seek, my purpose and my function and my life, while I abide where I am not at home.*

**I am not a body. I am free.**
**For I am still as God created me.**

## LESSON 206

**I am not a body. I am free.**
**For I am still as God created me.**

Salvation of the world depends on me.

*I am entrusted with the gifts of God, because I am His Son. And I would give His gifts where He intended them to be.*

**I am not a body. I am free.**
**For I am still as God created me.**

## LESSON 207

**I am not a body. I am free.**
**For I am still as God created me.**

I bless the world because I bless myself.

*God's blessing shines upon me from within*
*my heart, where He abides. I need but turn*
*to Him, and every sorrow melts away,*
*as I accept His boundless Love for me.*

**I am not a body. I am free.**
**For I am still as God created me.**

## LESSON 208

**I am not a body. I am free.**
**For I am still as God created me.**

The peace of God is shining in me now.

*I will be still, and let the earth be still*
*along with me. And in that stillness we*
*will find the peace of God. It is within*
*my heart, which witnesses to God Himself.*

**I am not a body. I am free.**
**For I am still as God created me.**

## LESSON 209

**I am not a body. I am free.**
**For I am still as God created me.**

I feel the Love of God within me now.

*The Love of God is what created me.*
*The Love of God is everything I am.*
*The Love of God proclaimed me as His Son.*
*The Love of God within me sets me free.*

**I am not a body. I am free.**
**For I am still as God created me.**

## LESSON 210

**I am not a body. I am free.**
**For I am still as God created me.**

I choose the joy of God instead of pain.

*Pain is my own idea. It is not*
*a Thought of God, but one I thought apart*
*from Him and from His Will. His Will is joy,*
*and only joy for His beloved Son.*
*And that I choose, instead of what I made.*

**I am not a body. I am free.**
**For I am still as God created me.**

## LESSON 211

**I am not a body. I am free.**
**For I am still as God created me.**

I am the holy Son of God Himself.

*In silence and in true humility*
*I seek God's glory, to behold it in*
*the Son whom He created as my Self.*

**I am not a body. I am free.**
**For I am still as God created me.**

## LESSON 212

**I am not a body. I am free.**
**For I am still as God created me.**

I have a function God would have me fill.

*I seek the function that would set me free*
*from all the vain illusions of the world.*
*Only the function God has given me*
*can offer freedom. Only this I seek,*
*and only this will I accept as mine.*

**I am not a body. I am free.**
**For I am still as God created me.**

## LESSON 213

**I am not a body. I am free.**
**For I am still as God created me.**

All things are lessons God would have me learn.

*A lesson is a miracle which God*
*offers to me, in place of thoughts I made*
*that hurt me. What I learn of Him becomes*
*the way I am set free. And so I choose*
*to learn His lessons and forget my own.*

**I am not a body. I am free.**
**For I am still as God created me.**

## LESSON 214

**I am not a body. I am free.**
**For I am still as God created me.**

I place the future in the Hands of God.

*The past is gone; the future is not yet.*
*Now am I freed from both. For what God gives*
*can only be for good. And I accept*
*but what He gives as what belongs to me.*

**I am not a body. I am free.**
**For I am still as God created me.**

## LESSON 215

**I am not a body. I am free.**
**For I am still as God created me.**

Love is the way I walk in gratitude.

*The Holy Spirit is my only Guide.*
*He walks with me in love. And I give thanks*
*to Him for showing me the way to go.*

**I am not a body. I am free.**
**For I am still as God created me.**

## LESSON 216

**I am not a body. I am free.**
**For I am still as God created me.**

It can be but myself I crucify.

*All that I do I do unto myself.*
*If I attack, I suffer. But if I*
*forgive, salvation will be given me.*

**I am not a body. I am free.**
**For I am still as God created me.**

## LESSON 217

**I am not a body. I am free.**
**For I am still as God created me.**

It can be but my gratitude I earn.

*Who should give thanks for my salvation but*
*myself? And how but through salvation can*
*I find the Self to Whom my thanks are due?*

**I am not a body. I am free.**
**For I am still as God created me.**

## LESSON 218

**I am not a body. I am free.**
**For I am still as God created me.**

Only my condemnation injures me.

*My condemnation keeps my vision dark,*
*and through my sightless eyes I cannot see*
*the vision of my glory. Yet today*
*I can behold this glory and be glad.*

**I am not a body. I am free.**
**For I am still as God created me.**

## LESSON 219

**I am not a body. I am free.**
**For I am still as God created me.**

I am not a body. I am free.

*I am God's Son. Be still, my mind, and think a moment upon this. And then return to earth, without confusion as to what my Father loves forever as His Son*

**I am not a body. I am free.**
**For I am still as God created me.**

## LESSON 220

**I am not a body. I am free.**
**For I am still as God created me.**

There is no peace except the peace of God.

*Let me not wander from the way of peace, for I am lost on other roads than this. But let me follow Him Who leads me home, and peace is certain as the Love of God.*

**I am not a body. I am free.**
**For I am still as God created me.**

## PART II

### Introduction

Words will mean little now. We use them but as guides on which we do not now depend. For now we seek direct experience of truth alone. The lessons that remain are merely introductions to the times in which we leave the world of pain, and go to enter peace. Now we begin to reach the goal this course has set, and find the end toward which our practicing was always geared.

Now we attempt to let the exercise be merely a beginning. For we wait in quiet expectation for our God and Father. He has promised He will take the final step Himself. And we are sure His promises are kept. We have come far along the road, and now we wait for Him. We will continue spending time with Him each morning and at night, as long as makes us happy. We will not consider time a matter of duration now. We use as much as we will need for the result that we desire. Nor will we forget our hourly remembrance in between, calling to God when we have need of Him as we are tempted to forget our goal.

We will continue with a central thought for all the days to come, and we will use that thought to introduce our times of rest, and calm our minds at need. Yet we will not content ourselves with simple practicing in the remaining holy instants which conclude the year that we have given God. We say some simple words of welcome, and expect our Father to reveal Himself, as He has promised. We have called on Him, and He has promised that His Son will not remain unanswered when he calls His Name.

Now do we come to Him with but His Word upon our minds and hearts, and wait for Him to take the step to us that He has told us, through His Voice, He would not fail to take when we invited him. He has not left His Son in all his madness, nor betrayed His trust in Him. Has not His faithfulness earned Him the invitation that He seeks to make us happy? We will offer it, and it will be accepted. So our times with Him will now be spent. We say the words of invitation that His Voice suggests, and then we wait for Him to come to us.

Now is the time of prophecy fulfilled. Now are all ancient promises upheld and fully kept. No step remains for time to separate from its accomplishment. For now we cannot fail. Sit silently and wait upon your Father. He has willed to come to you when you have recognized it is your will He do so. And you could have never come this far unless you saw, however dimly, that it is your will.

I am so close to you we cannot fail. Father, we give these holy times to You, in gratitude to Him Who taught us how to leave the world of sorrow in exchange for its replacement, given us by You. We look not backward now. We look ahead, and fix our eyes upon the journey's end. Accept these little gifts of thanks from us, as through Christ's vision we behold a world beyond the one we made, and take that world to be the full replacement of our own.

And now we wait in silence, unafraid and certain of Your coming. We have sought to find our way by following the Guide You sent to us. We did not know the way, but You did not forget us. And we know that You will not forget us now. We ask but that Your ancient promises be kept which are Your Will to keep. We will with You in asking this. The Father and the Son, Whose holy Will created all that is, can fail in nothing. In this certainty, we undertake these last few steps to You, and rest in confidence upon Your Love, which will not fail the Son who calls to You.

And so we start upon the final part

of this one holy year, which we have spent
together in the search for truth and God,
Who is its one Creator. We have found
the way He chose for us, and made the choice
to follow it as He would have us go.
His Hand has held us up. His Thoughts have lit
the darkness of our minds. His Love has called
to us unceasingly since time began.

We had a wish that God would fail to have
the Son whom He created for Himself.
We wanted God to change Himself, and be
what we would make of Him. And we believed
that our insane desires were the truth.
Now we are glad that this is all undone,
and we no longer think illusions true.
The memory of God is shimmering
across the wide horizons of our minds.
A moment more, and it will rise again.
A moment more, and we who are God's Sons
are safely home, where He would have us be.

Now is the need for practice almost done.
For in this final section, we will come
to understand that we need only call
to God, and all temptations disappear.
Instead of words, we need but feel His Love.
Instead of prayers, we need but call His Name.
Instead of judging, we need but be still
and let all things be healed. We will accept
the way God's plan will end, as we received
the way it started. Now it is complete.
This year has brought us to eternity.

One further use for words we still retain.
From time to time, instructions on a theme
of special relevance will intersperse
our daily lessons and the periods
of wordless, deep experience which should
come afterwards. These special thoughts should be
reviewed each day, each one of them to be
continued till the next is given you.
They should be slowly read and thought about
a little while, preceding one of the
holy and blessed instants in the day.
We give the first of these instructions now.

## WHAT IS FORGIVENESS?

Forgiveness recognizes what you thought
your brother did to you has not occurred.
It does not pardon sins and make them real.
It sees there was no sin. And in that view
are all your sins forgiven. What is sin,
except a false idea about God's Son?
Forgiveness merely sees its falsity,
and therefore lets it go. What then is free
to take its place is now the Will of God.

An unforgiving thought is one which makes
a judgment that it will not raise to doubt,
although it is not true. The mind is closed,
and will not be released. The thought protects
projection, tightening its chains, so that
distortions are more veiled and more obscure;
less easily accessible to doubt,
and further kept from reason. What can come
between a fixed projection and the aim
that it has chosen as its wanted goal?

An unforgiving thought does many things.
In frantic action it pursues its goal,
twisting and overturning what it sees
as interfering with its chosen path.
Distortion is its purpose, and the means
by which it would accomplish it as well.
It sets about its furious attempts
to smash reality, without concern
for anything that would appear to pose
a contradiction to its point of view.

Forgiveness, on the other hand, is still,
and quietly does nothing. It offends
no aspect of reality, nor seeks
to twist it to appearances it likes.
It merely looks, and waits, and judges not.
He who would not forgive must judge, for he
must justify his failure to forgive.
But he who would forgive himself must learn
to welcome truth exactly as it is.

Do nothing, then, and let forgiveness show
you what to do, through Him Who is your Guide,
your Savior and Protector, strong in hope,
and certain of your ultimate success.
He has forgiven you already, for
such is His function, given Him by God.
Now must you share His function, and forgive
whom He has saved, whose sinlessness He sees,
and whom He honors as the Son of God.

## LESSON 221

**Peace to my mind. Let all my thoughts be still.**

*Father, I come to You today to seek*
*the peace that You alone can give. I come*
*in silence. In the quiet of my heart,*
*the deep recesses of my mind, I wait*
*and listen for Your Voice. My Father, speak*
*to me today. I come to hear Your Voice*
*in silence and in certainty and love,*
*sure You will hear my call and answer me.*

Now do we wait in quiet. God is here,
because we wait together. I am sure
that He will speak to you, and you will hear.
Accept my confidence, for it is yours.
Our minds are joined. We wait with one intent;
to hear our Father's answer to our call,
to let our thoughts be still and find His peace,
to hear Him speak to us of what we are,
and to reveal Himself unto His Son.

## LESSON 222

**God is with me. I live and move in Him.**

God is with me. He is my Source of life,
the life within, the air I breathe, the food
by which I am sustained, the water which
renews and cleanses me. He is my home,
wherein I live and move; the Spirit Which
directs my actions, offers me Its Thoughts,
and guarantees my safety from all pain.
He covers me with kindness and with care,
and holds in love the Son He shines upon,
who also shines on Him. How still is he
who knows the truth of what He speaks today!

*Father, we have no words except Your Name*
*upon our lips and in our minds, as we*
*come quietly into Your Presence now,*
*and ask to rest with You in peace a while.*

## LESSON 223

**God is my life. I have no life but His.**

I was mistaken when I thought I lived
apart from God, a separate entity
that moved in isolation, unattached,
and housed within a body. Now I know
my life is God's, I have no other home,
and I do not exist apart from Him.
He has no Thoughts that are not part of me,
and I have none but those which are of Him.

*Our Father, let us see the face of Christ*
*instead of our mistakes. For we who are*
*Your holy Son are sinless. We would look*
*upon our sinlessness, for guilt proclaims*
*that we are not Your Son. And we would not*
*forget You longer. We are lonely here,*
*and long for Heaven, where we are at home.*
*Today we would return. Our Name is Yours,*
*and we acknowledge that we are Your Son.*

## LESSON 224

**God is my Father, and He loves His Son.**

My true Identity is so secure,
so lofty, sinless, glorious and great,
wholly beneficent and free from guilt,
that Heaven looks to It to give it light.
It lights the world as well. It is the gift
my Father gave to me; the one as well
I give the world. There is no gift but This
that can be either given or received.
This is reality, and only This.
This is illusion's end. It is the truth.

*My Name, O Father, still is known to You.*
*I have forgotten it, and do not know*
*where I am going, who I am, or what*
*it is I do. Remind me, Father, now,*
*for I am weary of the world I see.*
*Reveal what You would have me see instead.*

## LESSON 225

**God is my Father, and His Son loves Him.**

*Father, I must return Your Love for me,*
*for giving and receiving are the same,*
*and You have given all Your Love to me.*
*I must return it, for I want it mine*
*in full awareness, blazing in my mind*
*and keeping it within its kindly light,*
*inviolate, beloved, with fear behind*
*and only peace ahead. How still the way*
*Your loving Son is led along to You!*

Brother, we find that stillness now. The way is open. Now we follow it in peace together. You have reached your hand to me, and I will never leave you. We are one, and it is but this oneness that we seek, as we accomplish these few final steps which end a journey that was not begun.

## LESSON 226

**My home awaits me. I will hasten there.**

If I so choose, I can depart this world entirely. It is not death which makes this possible, but it is change of mind about the purpose of the world. If I believe it has a value as I see it now, so will it still remain for me. But if I see no value in the world as I behold it, nothing that I want to keep as mine or search for as a goal, it will depart from me. For I have not sought for illusions to replace the truth.

*Father, my home awaits my glad return.*
*Your Arms are open and I hear Your Voice.*
*What need have I to linger in a place*
*of vain desires and of shattered dreams,*
*when Heaven can so easily be mine?*

## LESSON 227

**This is my holy instant of release.**

*Father, it is today that I am free,*
*because my will is Yours. I thought to make*
*another will. Yet nothing that I thought*
*apart from You exists. And I am free*
*because I was mistaken, and did not*
*affect my own reality at all*
*by my illusions. Now I give them up,*
*and lay them down before the feet of truth,*
*to be removed forever from my mind.*
*This is my holy instant of release.*
*Father, I know my will is one with Yours.*

And so today we find our glad return to Heaven, which we never really left. The Son of God this day lays down his dreams. The Son of God this day comes home again, released from sin and clad in holiness, with his right mind restored to him at last.

## LESSON 228

**God has condemned me not. No more do I.**

My Father knows my holiness. Shall I deny His knowledge, and believe in what His knowledge makes impossible? Shall I accept as true what He proclaims as false? Or shall I take His Word for what I am, since He is my Creator, and the One Who knows the true condition of His Son?

*Father, I was mistaken in myself,*
*because I failed to realize the Source*
*from Which I came. I have not left that Source*
*to enter in a body and to die.*
*My holiness remains a part of me,*
*as I am part of You. And my mistakes*
*about myself are dreams. I let them go*
*today. And I stand ready to receive*
*Your Word alone for what I really am.*

## LESSON 229

**Love, Which created me, is what I am.**

I seek my own Identity, and find
It in these words: "Love, Which created me,
is what I am." Now need I seek no more.
Love has prevailed. So still It waited for
my coming home, that I will turn away
no longer from the holy face of Christ.
And what I look upon attests the truth
of the Identity I sought to lose,
but Which my Father has kept safe for me.

*Father, my thanks to You for what I am;*
*for keeping my Identity untouched*
*and sinless, in the midst of all the thoughts*
*of sin my foolish mind made up. And thanks*
*to You for saving me from them. Amen.*

## LESSON 230

**Now will I seek and find the peace of God.**

In peace I was created. And in peace
do I remain. It is not given me
to change my Self. How merciful is God
my Father, that when He created me
He gave me peace forever. Now I ask
but to be what I am. And can this be
denied me, when it is forever true?

*Father, I seek the peace You gave as mine*
*in my creation. What was given then*
*must be here now, for my creation was*
*apart from time, and still remains beyond*
*all change. The peace in which Your Son was born*
*into Your Mind is shining there unchanged.*
*I am as You created me. I need*
*but call on You to find the peace You gave.*
*It is Your Will that gave it to Your Son.*

## WHAT IS SALVATION?

Salvation is a promise, made by God,
that you would find your way to Him at last.
It cannot but be kept. It guarantees
that time will have an end, and all the thoughts
that have been born in time will end as well.
God's Word is given every mind which thinks
that it has separate thoughts, and will replace
these thoughts of conflict with the Thought of peace.

The Thought of peace was given to God's Son
the instant that his mind had thought of war.
There was no need for such a Thought before,
for peace was given without opposite,
and merely was. But when the mind is split
there is a need of healing. So the Thought
that has the power to heal the split became
a part of every fragment of the mind
that still was one, but failed to recognize
its oneness. Now it did not know itself,
and thought its own Identity was lost.

Salvation is undoing in the sense
that it does nothing, failing to support
the world of dreams and malice. Thus it lets
illusions go. By not supporting them,
it merely lets them quietly go down
to dust. And what they hid is now revealed;
an altar to the holy Name of God
whereon His Word is written, with the gifts
of your forgiveness laid before it, and
the memory of God not far behind.

Let us come daily to this holy place,
and spend a while together. Here we share
our final dream. It is a dream in which
there is no sorrow, for it holds a hint
of all the glory given us by God.
The grass is pushing through the soil, the trees
are budding now, and birds have come to live
within their branches. Earth is being born
again in new perspective. Night has gone,
and we have come together in the light.

From here we give salvation to the world,
for it is here salvation was received.
The song of our rejoicing is the call
to all the world that freedom is returned,
that time is almost over, and God's Son
has but an instant more to wait until
his Father is remembered, dreams are done,
eternity has shined away the world,
and only Heaven now exists at all.

## LESSON 231

**Father, I will but to remember You.**

*What can I seek for, Father, but Your Love?
Perhaps I think I seek for something else;
a something I have called by many names.
Yet is Your Love the only thing I seek,
or ever sought. For there is nothing else
that I could ever really want to find.
Let me remember You. What else could I
desire but the truth about myself?*

This is your will, my brother. And you share this will with me, and with the One as well Who is our Father. To remember Him is Heaven. This we seek. And only this is what it will be given us to find.

## LESSON 232

**Be in my mind, my Father, through the day.**

*Be in my mind, my Father, when I wake,
and shine on me throughout the day today.
Let every minute be a time in which
I dwell with You. And let me not forget
my hourly thanksgiving that You have
remained with me, and always will be there
to hear my call to You and answer me.
As evening comes, let all my thoughts be still
of You and of Your Love. And let me sleep
sure of my safety, certain of Your care,
and happily aware I am Your Son.*

This is as every day should be. Today, practice the end of fear. Have faith in Him Who is your Father. Trust all things to Him. Let Him reveal all things to you, and be you undismayed because you are His Son.

## LESSON 233

**I give my life to God to guide today.**

*Father, I give You all my thoughts today.
I would have none of mine. In place of them,
give me Your Own. I give You all my acts
as well, that I may do Your Will instead
of seeking goals which cannot be obtained,
and wasting time in vain imaginings.
Today I come to You. I will step back
and merely follow You. Be You the Guide,
and I the follower who questions not
the wisdom of the Infinite, nor Love
whose tenderness I cannot comprehend,
but which is yet Your perfect gift to me.*

Today we have one Guide to lead us on. And as we walk together, we will give this day to Him with no reserve at all. This is His day. And so it is a day of countless gifts and mercies unto us.

## LESSON 234

**Father, today I am Your Son again.**

Today we will anticipate the time when dreams of sin and guilt are gone, and we have reached the holy peace we never left. Merely a tiny instant has elapsed between eternity and timelessness. So brief the interval there was no lapse in continuity, nor break in thoughts which are forever unified as one. Nothing has ever happened to disturb the peace of God the Father and the Son. This we accept as wholly true today.

*We thank You, Father, that we cannot lose
the memory of You and of Your Love.
We recognize our safety, and give thanks
for all the gifts You have bestowed on us,
for all the loving help we have received,
for Your eternal patience, and the Word
which You have given us that we are saved.*

## LESSON 235

**God in His mercy wills that I be saved.**

I need but look upon all things that seem to hurt me, and with perfect certainty assure myself, "God wills that I be saved from this," and merely watch them disappear. I need but keep in mind my Father's Will for me is only happiness, to find that only happiness has come to me. And I need but remember that God's Love surrounds His Son and keeps his sinlessness forever perfect, to be sure that I am saved and safe forever in His Arms. I am the Son He loves. And I am saved because God in His mercy wills it so.

*Father, Your holiness is mine. Your Love created me, and made my sinlessness forever part of You. I have no guilt nor sin in me, for there is none in You.*

## LESSON 236

**I rule my mind, which I alone must rule.**

I have a kingdom I must rule. At times, it does not seem I am its king at all. It seems to triumph over me, and tell me what to think, and what to do and feel. And yet it has been given me to serve whatever purpose I perceive in it. My mind can only serve. Today I give its service to the Holy Spirit to employ as He sees fit. I thus direct my mind, which I alone can rule. And thus I set it free to do the Will of God.

*Father, my mind is open to Your Thoughts, and closed today to every thought but Yours. I rule my mind, and offer it to You. Accept my gift, for it is Yours to me.*

## LESSON 237

**Now would I be as God created me.**

Today I will accept the truth about myself. I will arise in glory, and allow the light in me to shine upon the world throughout the day. I bring the world the tidings of salvation which I hear as God my Father speaks to me. And I behold the world that Christ would have me see, aware it ends the bitter dream of death; aware it is my Father's call to me.

*Christ is my eyes today, and He the ears that listen to the Voice for God today. Father, I come to You through Him Who is Your Son, and my true Self as well. Amen.*

## LESSON 238

**On my decision all salvation rests.**

*Father, Your trust in me has been so great, I must be worthy. You created me, and know me as I am. And yet You placed Your Son's salvation in my hands, and let it rest on my decision. I must be beloved of You indeed. And I must be steadfast in holiness as well, that You would give Your Son to me in certainty that he is safe Who still is part of You, and yet is mine, because He is my Self.*

And so, again today, we pause to think how much our Father loves us. And how dear His Son, created by His Love, remains to Him Whose Love is made complete in him.

## LESSON 239

**The glory of my Father is my own.**

Let not the truth about ourselves today
be hidden by a false humility.
Let us instead be thankful for the gifts
our Father gave us. Can we see in those
with whom He shares His glory any trace
of sin and guilt? And can it be that we
are not among them, when He loves His Son
forever and with perfect constancy,
knowing he is as He created him?

*We thank You, Father, for the light that shines
forever in us. And we honor it,
because You share it with us. We are one,
united in this light and one with You,
at peace with all creation and ourselves.*

## LESSON 240

**Fear is not justified in any form.**

Fear is deception. It attests that you
have seen yourself as you could never be,
and therefore look upon a world which is
impossible. Not one thing in this world
is true. It does not matter what the form
in which it may appear. It witnesses
but to your own illusions of yourself.
Let us not be deceived today. We are
the Sons of God. There is no fear in us,
for we are each a part of Love Itself.

*How foolish are our fears! Would You allow
Your Son to suffer? Give us faith today
to recognize Your Son, and set him free.
Let us forgive him in Your Name, that we
may understand his holiness, and feel
the love for him which is Your Own as well.*

# WHAT IS THE WORLD?

The world is false perception. It is born of error, and it has not left its source. It will remain no longer than the thought that gave it birth is cherished. When the thought of separation has been changed to one of true forgiveness, will the world be seen in quite another light; and one which leads to truth, where all the world must disappear and all its errors vanish. Now its source has gone, and its effects are gone as well.

The world was made as an attack on God. It symbolizes fear. And what is fear except love's absence? Thus the world was meant to be a place where God could enter not, and where His Son could be apart from Him. Here was perception born, for knowledge could not cause such insane thoughts. But eyes deceive, and ears hear falsely. Now mistakes become quite possible, for certainty has gone.

The mechanisms of illusion have been born instead. And now they go to find what has been given them to seek. Their aim is to fulfill the purpose which the world was made to witness and make real. They see in its illusions but a solid base where truth exists, upheld apart from lies. Yet everything that they report is but illusion which is kept apart from truth.

As sight was made to lead away from truth, it can be redirected. Sounds become the call of God, and all perception can be given a new purpose by the One Whom God appointed Savior to the world. Follow His Light, and see the world as He beholds it. Hear His Voice alone in all that speaks to you. And let Him give you peace and certainty, which you have thrown away, but Heaven has preserved for you in Him.

Let us not rest content until the world has joined our changed perception. Let us not be satisfied until forgiveness has been made complete. And let us not attempt to change our function. We must save the world. For we who made it must behold it through the eyes of Christ, that what was made to die can be restored to everlasting life.

## LESSON 241

**This holy instant is salvation come.**

What joy there is today! It is a time of special celebration. For today holds out the instant to the darkened world where its release is set. The day has come when sorrows pass away and pain is gone. The glory of salvation dawns today upon a world set free. This is the time of hope for countless millions. They will be united now, as you forgive them all. For I will be forgiven by you today.

*We have forgiven one another now, and so we come at last to You again. Father, Your Son, who never left, returns to Heaven and his home. How glad are we to have our sanity restored to us, and to remember that we all are one.*

## LESSON 242

**This day is God's. It is my gift to Him.**

I will not lead my life alone today. I do not understand the world, and so to try to lead my life alone must be but foolishness. But there is One Who knows all that is best for me. And He is glad to make no choices for me but the ones that lead to God. I give this day to Him, for I would not delay my coming home, and it is He Who knows the way to God.

*And so we give today to You. We come with wholly open minds. We do not ask for anything that we may think we want. Give us what You would have received by us. You know all our desires and our wants. And You will give us everything we need in helping us to find the way to You.*

## LESSON 243

**Today I will judge nothing that occurs.**

I will be honest with myself today. I will not think that I already know what must remain beyond my present grasp. I will not think I understand the whole from bits of my perception, which are all that I can see. Today I recognize that this is so. And so I am relieved of judgments that I cannot make. Thus do I free myself and what I look upon, to be in peace as God created us.

*Father, today I leave creation free to be itself. I honor all its parts, in which I am included. We are one because each part contains Your memory, and truth must shine in all of us as one.*

## LESSON 244

**I am in danger nowhere in the world.**

*Your Son is safe wherever he may be, for You are there with him. He need but call upon Your Name, and he will recollect his safety and Your Love, for they are one. How can he fear or doubt or fail to know he cannot suffer, be endangered, or experience unhappiness, when he belongs to You, beloved and loving, in the safety of Your Fatherly embrace?*

And there we are in truth. No storms can come into the hallowed haven of our home. In God we are secure. For what can come to threaten God Himself, or make afraid what will forever be a part of Him?

## LESSON 245

**Your peace is with me, Father. I am safe.**

*Your peace surrounds me, Father. Where I go,*
*Your peace goes there with me. It sheds its light*
*on everyone I meet. I bring it to*
*the desolate and lonely and afraid.*
*I give Your peace to those who suffer pain,*
*or grieve for loss, or think they are bereft*
*of hope and happiness. Send them to me,*
*my Father. Let me bring Your peace with me.*
*For I would save Your Son, as is Your Will,*
*that I may come to recognize my Self.*

And so we go in peace. To all the world
we give the message that we have received.
And thus we come to hear the Voice for God,
Who speaks to us as we relate His Word;
Whose Love we recognize because we share
the Word that He has given unto us.

## LESSON 246

**To love my Father is to love His Son.**

Let me not think that I can find the way
to God, if I have hatred in my heart.
Let me not try to hurt God's Son, and think
that I can know his Father or my Self.
Let me not fail to recognize myself,
and still believe that my awareness can
contain my Father, or my mind conceive
of all the love my Father has for me,
and all the love which I return to Him.

*I will accept the way You choose for me*
*to come to You, my Father. For in that*
*will I succeed, because it is Your Will.*
*And I would recognize that what You will*
*is what I will as well, and only that.*
*And so I choose to love Your Son. Amen.*

## LESSON 247

**Without forgiveness I will still be blind.**

Sin is the symbol of attack. Behold
it anywhere, and I will suffer. For
forgiveness is the only means whereby
Christ's vision comes to me. Let me accept
what His sight shows me as the simple truth,
and I am healed completely. Brother, come
and let me look on you. Your loveliness
reflects my own. Your sinlessness is mine.
You stand forgiven, and I stand with you.

*So would I look on everyone today.*
*My brothers are Your Sons. Your Fatherhood*
*created them, and gave them all to me*
*as part of You, and my own Self as well.*
*Today I honor You through them, and thus*
*I hope this day to recognize my Self.*

## LESSON 248

**Whatever suffers is not part of me.**

I have disowned the truth. Now let me be
as faithful in disowning falsity.
Whatever suffers is not part of me.
What grieves is not myself. What is in pain
is but illusion in my mind. What dies
was never living in reality,
and did but mock the truth about myself.
Now I disown self-concepts and deceits
and lies about the holy Son of God.
Now am I ready to accept him back
as God created him, and as he is.

*Father, my ancient love for You returns,*
*and lets me love Your Son again as well.*
*Father, I am as You created me.*
*Now is Your Love remembered, and my own.*
*Now do I understand that they are one.*

## LESSON 249

**Forgiveness ends all suffering and loss.**

Forgiveness paints a picture of a world where suffering is over, loss becomes impossible and anger makes no sense. Attack is gone, and madness has an end. What suffering is now conceivable? What loss can be sustained? The world becomes a place of joy, abundance, charity and endless giving. It is now so like to Heaven that it quickly is transformed into the light that it reflects. And so the journey which the Son of God began has ended in the light from which he came.

*Father, we would return our minds to You. We have betrayed them, held them in a vise of bitterness, and frightened them with thoughts of violence and death. Now would we rest again in You, as You created us.*

## LESSON 250

**Let me not see myself as limited.**

Let me behold the Son of God today, and witness to his glory. Let me not try to obscure the holy light in him, and see his strength diminished and reduced to frailty; nor perceive the lacks in him with which I would attack his sovereignty.

*He is Your Son, my Father. And today I would behold his gentleness instead of my illusions. He is what I am, and as I see him so I see myself. Today I would see truly, that this day I may at last identify with him.*

## WHAT IS SIN?

Sin is insanity. It is the means
by which the mind is driven mad, and seeks
to let illusions take the place of truth.
And being mad, it sees illusions where
the truth should be, and where it really is.
Sin gave the body eyes, for what is there
the sinless would behold? What need have they
of sights or sounds or touch? What would they hear
or reach to grasp? What would they sense at all?
To sense is not to know. And truth can be
but filled with knowledge, and with nothing else.

The body is the instrument the mind
made in its efforts to deceive itself.
Its purpose is to strive. Yet can the goal
of striving change. And now the body serves
a different aim for striving. What it seeks
for now is chosen by the aim the mind
has taken as replacement for the goal
of self-deception. Truth can be its aim
as well as lies. The senses then will seek
instead for witnesses to what is true.

Sin is the home of all illusions, which
but stand for things imagined, issuing
from thoughts that are untrue. They are the "proof"
that what has no reality is real.

Sin "proves" God's Son is evil; timelessness
must have an end; eternal life must die.
And God Himself has lost the Son He loves,
with but corruption to complete Himself,
His Will forever overcome by death,
love slain by hate, and peace to be no more.

A madman's dreams are frightening, and sin
appears indeed to terrify. And yet
what sin perceives is but a childish game.
The Son of God may play he has become
a body, prey to evil and to guilt,
with but a little life that ends in death.
But all the while his Father shines on him,
and loves him with an everlasting Love
which his pretenses cannot change at all.

How long, O Son of God, will you maintain
the game of sin? Shall we not put away
these sharp-edged children's toys? How soon will you
be ready to come home? Perhaps today?
There is no sin. Creation is unchanged.
Would you still hold return to Heaven back?
How long, O holy Son of God, how long?

## LESSON 251

**I am in need of nothing but the truth.**

I sought for many things, and found despair.
Now do I seek but one, for in that one
is all I need, and only what I need.
All that I sought before I needed not,
and did not even want. My only need
I did not recognize. But now I see
that I need only truth. In that all needs
are satisfied, all cravings end, all hopes
are finally fulfilled and dreams are gone.
Now have I everything that I could need.
Now have I everything that I could want.
And now at last I find myself at peace.

*And for that peace, our Father, we give thanks.
What we denied ourselves You have restored,
and only that is what we really want.*

## LESSON 252

**The Son of God is my Identity.**

My Self is holy beyond all the thoughts
of holiness of which I now conceive.
Its shimmering and perfect purity
is far more brilliant than is any light
that I have ever looked upon. Its love
is limitless, with an intensity
that holds all things within it, in the calm
of quiet certainty. Its strength comes not
from burning impulses which move the world,
but from the boundless Love of God Himself.
How far beyond this world my Self must be,
and yet how near to me and close to God!

*Father, You know my true Identity.
Reveal It now to me who am Your Son,
that I may waken to the truth in You,
and know that Heaven is restored to me.*

## LESSON 253

**My Self is ruler of the universe.**

It is impossible that anything
should come to me unbidden by myself.
Even in this world, it is I who rule
my destiny. What happens is what I
desire. What does not occur is what
I do not want to happen. This must I
accept. For thus am I led past this world
to my creations, children of my will,
in Heaven where my holy Self abides
with them and Him Who has created me.

*You are the Self Whom You created Son,
creating like Yourself and one with You.
My Self, Which rules the universe, is but
Your Will in perfect union with my own,
which can but offer glad assent to Yours,
that it may be extended to Itself.*

## LESSON 254

**Let every voice but God's be still in me.**

*Father, today I would but hear Your Voice.
In deepest silence I would come to You,
to hear Your Voice and to receive Your Word.
I have no prayer but this: I come to You
to ask You for the truth. And truth is but
Your Will, which I would share with You today.*

Today we let no ego thoughts direct
our words or actions. When such thoughts occur,
we quietly step back and look at them,
and then we let them go. We do not want
what they would bring with them. And so we do
not choose to keep them. They are silent now.
And in the stillness, hallowed by His Love,
God speaks to us and tells us of our will,
as we have chosen to remember Him.

## LESSON 255

**This day I choose to spend in perfect peace.**

It does not seem to me that I can choose to have but peace today. And yet, my God assures me that His Son is like Himself. Let me this day have faith in Him Who says I am God's Son. And let the peace I choose be mine today bear witness to the truth of what He says. God's Son can have no cares, and must remain forever in the peace of Heaven. In His Name, I give today to finding what my Father wills for me, accepting it as mine, and giving it to all my Father's Sons, along with me.

*And so, my Father, would I pass this day with You. Your Son has not forgotten You. The peace You gave him still is in his mind, and it is there I choose to spend today.*

## LESSON 256

**God is the only goal I have today.**

The way to God is through forgiveness here. There is no other way. If sin had not been cherished by the mind, what need would there have been to find the way to where you are? Who would still be uncertain? Who could be unsure of who he is? And who would yet remain asleep, in heavy clouds of doubt about the holiness of him whom God created sinless? Here we can but dream. But we can dream we have forgiven him in whom all sin remains impossible, and it is this we choose to dream today. God is our goal; forgiveness is the means by which our minds return to Him at last.

*And so, our Father, would we come to You in Your appointed way. We have no goal except to hear Your Voice, and find the way Your sacred Word has pointed out to us.*

## LESSON 257

**Let me remember what my purpose is.**

If I forget my goal I can be but confused, unsure of what I am, and thus conflicted in my actions. No one can serve contradicting goals and serve them well. Nor can he function without deep distress and great depression. Let us therefore be determined to remember what we want today, that we may unify our thoughts and actions meaningfully, and achieve only what God would have us do this day.

*Father, forgiveness is Your chosen means for our salvation. Let us not forget today that we can have no will but Yours. And thus our purpose must be Yours as well, if we would reach the peace You will for us.*

## LESSON 258

**Let me remember that my goal is God.**

All that is needful is to train our minds to overlook all little senseless aims, and to remember that our goal is God. His memory is hidden in our minds, obscured but by our pointless little goals which offer nothing, and do not exist. Shall we continue to allow God's grace to shine in unawareness, while the toys and trinkets of the world are sought instead? God is our only goal, our only Love. We have no aim but to remember Him.

*Our goal is but to follow in the way that leads to You. We have no goal but this. What could we want but to remember You? What could we seek but our Identity?*

## LESSON 259

**Let me remember that there is no sin.**

Sin is the only thought that makes the goal of God seem unattainable. What else could blind us to the obvious, and make the strange and the distorted seem more clear? What else but sin engenders our attacks? What else but sin could be the source of guilt, demanding punishment and suffering? And what but sin could be the source of fear, obscuring God's creation; giving love the attributes of fear and of attack?

*Father, I would not be insane today. I would not be afraid of love, nor seek for refuge in its opposite. For love can have no opposite. You are the Source of everything there is. And everything that is remains with You, and You with it.*

## LESSON 260

**Let me remember God created me.**

*Father, I did not make myself, although in my insanity I thought I did. Yet, as Your Thought, I have not left my Source, remaining part of Who created me. Your Son, my Father, calls on You today. Let me remember You created me. Let me remember my Identity. And let my sinlessness arise again before Christ's vision, through which I would look upon my brothers and myself today.*

Now is our Source remembered, and Therein we find our true Identity at last. Holy indeed are we, because our Source can know no sin. And we who are His Sons are like each other, and alike to Him.

## WHAT IS THE BODY?

The body is a fence the Son of God
imagines he has built, to separate
parts of his Self from other parts. It is
within this fence he thinks he lives, to die
as it decays and crumbles. For within
this fence he thinks that he is safe from love.
Identifying with his safety, he
regards himself as what his safety is.
How else could he be certain he remains
within the body, keeping love outside?

The body will not stay. Yet this he sees
as double safety. For the Son of God's
impermanence is "proof" his fences work,
and do the task his mind assigns to them.
For if his oneness still remained untouched,
who could attack and who could be attacked?
Who could be victor? Who could be his prey?
Who could be victim? Who the murderer?
And if he did not die, what "proof" is there
that God's eternal Son can be destroyed?

The body is a dream. Like other dreams
it sometimes seems to picture happiness,
but can quite suddenly revert to fear,
where every dream is born. For only love
creates in truth, and truth can never fear.
Made to be fearful, must the body serve
the purpose given it. But we can change
the purpose that the body will obey
by changing what we think that it is for.

The body is the means by which God's Son
returns to sanity. Though it was made
to fence him into hell without escape,
yet has the goal of Heaven been exchanged
for the pursuit of hell. The Son of God
extends his hand to reach his brother, and
to help him walk along the road with him.
Now is the body holy. Now it serves
to heal the mind that it was made to kill.

You will identify with what you think
will make you safe. Whatever it may be,
you will believe that it is one with you.
Your safety lies in truth, and not in lies.
Love is your safety. Fear does not exist.
Identify with love, and you are safe.
Identify with love, and you are home.
Identify with love, and find your Self.

## LESSON 261

**God is my refuge and security.**

I will identify with what I think
is refuge and security. I will
behold myself where I perceive my strength,
and think I live within the citadel
where I am safe and cannot be attacked.
Let me today seek not security
in danger, nor attempt to find my peace
in murderous attack. I live in God.
In Him I find my refuge and my strength.
In Him is my Identity. In Him
is everlasting peace. And only there
will I remember Who I really am.

*Let me not seek for idols. I would come,
my Father, home to You today. I choose
to be as You created me, and find
the Son whom You created as my Self.*

## LESSON 262

**Let me perceive no differences today.**

*Father, You have one Son. And it is he
that I would look upon today. He is
Your one creation. Why should I perceive
a thousand forms in what remains as one?
Why should I give this one a thousand names,
when only one suffices? For Your Son
must bear Your Name, for You created him.
Let me not see him as a stranger to
his Father, nor as stranger to myself.
For he is part of me and I of him,
and we are part of You Who are our Source,
eternally united in Your Love;
eternally the holy Son of God.*

We who are one would recognize this day
the truth about ourselves. We would come home,
and rest in unity. For there is peace,
and nowhere else can peace be sought and found.

## LESSON 263

**My holy vision sees all things as pure.**

*Father, Your Mind created all that is,
Your Spirit entered into it, Your Love
gave life to it. And would I look upon
what You created as if it could be
made sinful? I would not perceive such dark
and fearful images. A madman's dream
is hardly fit to be my choice, instead
of all the loveliness with which You blessed
creation; all its purity, its joy,
and its eternal, quiet home in You.*

And while we still remain outside the gate
of Heaven, let us look on all we see
through holy vision and the eyes of Christ.
Let all appearances seem pure to us,
that we may pass them by in innocence,
and walk together to our Father's house
as brothers and the holy Sons of God.

## LESSON 264

**I am surrounded by the Love of God.**

*Father, You stand before me and behind,
beside me, in the place I see myself,
and everywhere I go. You are in all
the things I look upon, the sounds I hear,
and every hand that reaches for my own.
In You time disappears, and place becomes
a meaningless belief. For what surrounds
Your Son and keeps him safe is Love Itself.
There is no Source but This, and nothing is
that does not share Its holiness; that stands
beyond Your one creation, or without
the Love Which holds all things within Itself.
Father, Your Son is like Yourself. We come
to You in Your Own Name today, to be
at peace within Your everlasting Love.*

My brothers, join with me in this today.
This is salvation's prayer. Must we not join
in what will save the world, along with us?

## LESSON 265

**Creation's gentleness is all I see.**

I have indeed misunderstood the world,
because I laid my sins on it and saw
them looking back at me. How fierce they seemed!
And how deceived was I to think that what
I feared was in the world, instead of in
my mind alone. Today I see the world
in the celestial gentleness with which
creation shines. There is no fear in it.
Let no appearance of my sins obscure
the light of Heaven shining on the world.
What is reflected there is in God's Mind.
The images I see reflect my thoughts.
Yet is my mind at one with God's. And so
I can perceive creation's gentleness.

*In quiet would I look upon the world,
which but reflects Your Thoughts, and mine as well.
Let me remember that they are the same,
and I will see creation's gentleness.*

## LESSON 266

**My holy Self abides in you, God's Son.**

*Father, You gave me all Your Sons, to be
my saviors and my counselors in sight;
the bearers of Your holy Voice to me.
In them are You reflected, and in them
does Christ look back upon me from my Self.
Let not Your Son forget Your holy Name.
Let not Your Son forget his holy Source.
Let not Your Son forget his name is Yours.*

This day we enter into paradise,
calling upon God's Name and on our own,
acknowledging our Self in each of us;
united in the holy Love of God.
How many saviors God has given us!
How can we lose the way to Him, when He
has filled the world with those who point to Him,
and given us the sight to look on them?

## LESSON 267

**My heart is beating in the peace of God.**

Surrounding me is all the life that God
created in His Love. It calls to me
in every heartbeat and in every breath;
in every action and in every thought.
Peace fills my heart, and floods my body with
the purpose of forgiveness. Now my mind
is healed, and all I need to save the world
is given me. Each heartbeat brings me peace;
each breath infuses me with strength. I am
a messenger of God, directed by
His Voice, sustained by Him in love, and held
forever quiet and at peace within
His loving Arms. Each heartbeat calls His Name,
and every one is answered by His Voice,
assuring me I am at home in Him.

*Let me attend Your Answer, not my own.
Father, my heart is beating in the peace
the Heart of Love created. It is there
and only there that I can be at home.*

## LESSON 268

**Let all things be exactly as they are.**

*Let me not be Your critic, Lord, today,
and judge against You. Let me not attempt
to interfere with Your creation, and
distort it into sickly forms. Let me
be willing to withdraw my wishes from
its unity, and thus to let it be
as You created it. For thus will I
be able, too, to recognize my Self
as You created me. In Love was I
created, and in Love will I remain
forever. What can frighten me, when I
let all things be exactly as they are?*

Let not our sight be blasphemous today,
nor let our ears attend to lying tongues.
Only reality is free of pain.
Only reality is free of loss.
Only reality is wholly safe.
And it is only this we seek today.

## LESSON 269

**My sight goes forth to look upon Christ's face.**

*I ask Your blessing on my sight today.*
*It is the means which You have chosen to*
*become the way to show me my mistakes,*
*and look beyond them. It is given me*
*to find a new perception through the Guide*
*You gave to me, and through His lessons to*
*surpass perception and return to truth.*
*I ask for the illusion which transcends*
*all those I made. Today I choose to see*
*a world forgiven, in which everyone*
*shows me the face of Christ, and teaches me*
*that what I look upon belongs to me;*
*that nothing is, except Your holy Son.*

Today our sight is blessed indeed. We share one vision, as we look upon the face of Him Whose Self is ours. We are one because of Him Who is the Son of God; of Him Who is our own Identity.

## LESSON 270

**I will not use the body's eyes today.**

*Father, Christ's vision is Your gift to me,*
*and it has power to translate all that*
*the body's eyes behold into the sight*
*of a forgiven world. How glorious*
*and gracious is this world! Yet how much more*
*will I perceive in it than sight can give.*
*The world forgiven signifies Your Son*
*acknowledges his Father, lets his dreams*
*be brought to truth, and waits expectantly*
*the one remaining instant more of time*
*which ends forever, as Your memory*
*returns to him. And now his will is one*
*with Yours. His function now is but Your Own,*
*and every thought except Your Own is gone.*

The quiet of today will bless our hearts, and through them peace will come to everyone. Christ is our eyes today. And through His sight we offer healing to the world through Him, the holy Son whom God created whole; the holy Son whom God created one.

## WHAT IS THE CHRIST?

Christ is God's Son as He created Him. He is the Self we share, uniting us with one another, and with God as well. He is the Thought Which still abides within the Mind that is His Source. He has not left His holy home, nor lost the innocence in which He was created. He abides unchanged forever in the Mind of God.

Christ is the link that keeps you one with God, and guarantees that separation is no more than an illusion of despair, for hope forever will abide in Him. Your mind is part of His, and His of yours. He is the part in which God's Answer lies; where all decisions are already made, and dreams are over. He remains untouched by anything the body's eyes perceive. For though in Him His Father placed the means for your salvation, yet does He remain the Self Who, like His Father, knows no sin.

Home of the Holy Spirit, and at home in God alone, does Christ remain at peace within the Heaven of your holy mind. This is the only part of you that has reality in truth. The rest is dreams.

Yet will these dreams be given unto Christ, to fade before His glory and reveal your holy Self, the Christ, to you at last.

The Holy Spirit reaches from the Christ in you to all your dreams, and bids them come to Him, to be translated into truth. He will exchange them for the final dream which God appointed as the end of dreams. For when forgiveness rests upon the world and peace has come to every Son of God, what could there be to keep things separate, for what remains to see except Christ's face?

And how long will this holy face be seen, when it is but the symbol that the time for learning now is over, and the goal of the Atonement has been reached at last? So therefore let us seek to find Christ's face and look on nothing else. As we behold His glory, will we know we have no need of learning or perception or of time, or anything except the holy Self, the Christ Whom God created as His Son.

## LESSON 271

**Christ's is the vision I will use today.**

Each day, each hour, every instant, I
am choosing what I want to look upon,
the sounds I want to hear, the witnesses
to what I want to be the truth for me.
Today I choose to look upon what Christ
would have me see, to listen to God's Voice,
and seek the witnesses to what is true
in God's creation. In Christ's sight, the world
and God's creation meet, and as they come
together all perception disappears.
His kindly sight redeems the world from death,
for nothing that He looks on but must live,
remembering the Father and the Son;
Creator and creation unified.

*Father, Christ's vision is the way to You.
What He beholds invites Your memory
to be restored to me. And this I choose
to be what I would look upon today.*

## LESSON 272

**How can illusions satisfy God's Son?**

*Father, the truth belongs to me. My home
is set in Heaven by Your Will and mine.
Can dreams content me? Can illusions bring
me happiness? What but Your memory
can satisfy Your Son? I will accept
no less than You have given me. I am
surrounded by Your Love, forever still,
forever gentle and forever safe.
God's Son must be as You created him.*

Today we pass illusions by. And if
we hear temptation call to us to stay
and linger in a dream, we turn aside
and ask ourselves if we, the Sons of God,
could be content with dreams, when Heaven can
be chosen just as easily as hell,
and love will happily replace all fear.

## LESSON 273

**The stillness of the peace of God is mine.**

Perhaps we are now ready for a day
of undisturbed tranquility. If this
is not yet feasible, we are content
and even more than satisfied to learn
how such a day can be achieved. If we
give way to a disturbance, let us learn
how to dismiss it and return to peace.
We need but tell our minds, with certainty,
"The stillness of the peace of God is mine,"
and nothing can intrude upon the peace
that God Himself has given to His Son.

*Father, Your peace is mine. What need have I
to fear that anything can rob me of
what You would have me keep? I cannot lose
Your gifts to me. And so the peace You gave
Your Son is with me still, in quietness
and in my own eternal love for You.*

## LESSON 274

**Today belongs to Love. Let me not fear.**

*Father, today I would let all things be
as You created them, and give Your Son
the honor due his sinlessness; the love
of brother to his brother and his Friend.
Through this I am redeemed. Through this as well
the truth will enter where illusions were,
light will replace all darkness, and Your Son
will know he is as You created him.*

A special blessing comes to us today,
from Him Who is our Father. Give this day
to Him, and there will be no fear today,
because the day is given unto Love.

## LESSON 275

**God's healing Voice protects all things today.**

Let us today attend the Voice for God, Which speaks an ancient lesson, no more true today than any other day. Yet has this day been chosen as the time when we will seek and hear and learn and understand. Join me in hearing. For the Voice for God tells us of things we cannot understand alone, nor learn apart. It is in this that all things are protected. And in this the healing of the Voice for God is found.

*Your healing Voice protects all things today, and so I leave all things to You. I need be anxious over nothing. For Your Voice will tell me what to do and where to go; to whom to speak and what to say to him, what thoughts to think, what words to give the world. The safety that I bring is given me. Father, Your Voice protects all things through me.*

## LESSON 276

**The Word of God is given me to speak.**

What is the Word of God? "My Son is pure and holy as Myself." And thus did God become the Father of the Son He loves, for thus was he created. This the Word His Son did not create with Him, because in this His Son was born. Let us accept His Fatherhood, and all is given us. Deny we were created in His Love and we deny our Self, to be unsure of who we are, of Who our Father is, and for what purpose we have come. And yet, we need but to acknowledge Him Who gave His Word to us in our creation, to remember Him and so recall our Self.

*Father, Your Word is mine. And it is this that I would speak to all my brothers, who are given me to cherish as my own, as I am loved and blessed and saved by You.*

## LESSON 277

**Let me not bind Your Son with laws I made.**

*Your Son is free, my Father. Let me not imagine I have bound him with the laws I made to rule the body. He is not subject to any laws I made by which I try to make the body more secure. He is not changed by what is changeable. He is not slave to any laws of time. He is as You created him, because he knows no law except the law of love.*

Let us not worship idols, nor believe in any law idolatry would make to hide the freedom of the Son of God. He is not bound except by his beliefs. Yet what he is, is far beyond his faith in slavery or freedom. He is free because he is his Father's Son. And he cannot be bound unless God's truth can lie, and God can will that He deceive Himself.

## LESSON 278

**If I am bound, my Father is not free.**

If I accept that I am prisoner within a body, in a world in which all things that seem to live appear to die, then is my Father prisoner with me. And this do I believe, when I maintain the laws the world obeys must I obey; the frailties and the sins which I perceive are real, and cannot be escaped. If I am bound in any way, I do not know my Father nor my Self. And I am lost to all reality. For truth is free, and what is bound is not a part of truth.

*Father, I ask for nothing but the truth. I have had many foolish thoughts about myself and my creation, and have brought a dream of fear into my mind. Today, I would not dream. I choose the way to You instead of madness and instead of fear. For truth is safe, and only love is sure.*

## LESSON 279

**Creation's freedom promises my own.**

The end of dreams is promised me, because
God's Son is not abandoned by His Love.
Only in dreams is there a time when he
appears to be in prison, and awaits
a future freedom, if it be at all.
Yet in reality his dreams are gone,
with truth established in their place. And now
is freedom his already. Should I wait
in chains which have been severed for release,
when God is offering me freedom now?

*I will accept Your promises today,*
*and give my faith to them. My Father loves*
*the Son Whom He created as His Own.*
*Would You withhold the gifts You gave to me?*

## LESSON 280

**What limits can I lay upon God's Son?**

Whom God created limitless is free.
I can invent imprisonment for him,
but only in illusions, not in truth.
No Thought of God has left its Father's Mind.
No Thought of God is limited at all.
No Thought of God but is forever pure.
Can I lay limits on the Son of God,
whose Father willed that he be limitless,
and like Himself in freedom and in love?

*Today let me give honor to Your Son,*
*for thus alone I find the way to You.*
*Father, I lay no limits on the Son*
*You love and You created limitless.*
*The honor that I give to him is Yours,*
*and what is Yours belongs to me as well.*

## WHAT IS THE HOLY SPIRIT?

The Holy Spirit mediates between illusions and the truth. Since He must bridge the gap between reality and dreams, perception leads to knowledge through the grace that God has given Him, to be His gift to everyone who turns to Him for truth. Across the bridge that He provides are dreams all carried to the truth, to be dispelled before the light of knowledge. There are sights and sounds forever laid aside. And where they were perceived before, forgiveness has made possible perception's tranquil end.

The goal the Holy Spirit's teaching sets is just this end of dreams. For sights and sounds must be translated from the witnesses of fear to those of love. And when this is entirely accomplished, learning has achieved the only goal it has in truth. For learning, as the Holy Spirit guides it to the outcome He perceives for it, becomes the means to go beyond itself, to be replaced by the Eternal Truth.

If you but knew how much your Father yearns to have you recognize your sinlessness, you would not let His Voice appeal in vain, nor turn away from His replacement for the fearful images and dreams you made. The Holy Spirit understands the means you made, by which you would attain what is forever unattainable. And if you offer them to Him, He will employ the means you made for exile to restore your mind to where it truly is at home.

From knowledge, where He has been placed by God, the Holy Spirit calls to you, to let forgiveness rest upon your dreams, and be restored to sanity and peace of mind. Without forgiveness will your dreams remain to terrify you. And the memory of all your Father's Love will not return to signify the end of dreams has come.

Accept your Father's gift. It is a call from Love to Love, that It be but Itself. The Holy Spirit is His gift, by which the quietness of Heaven is restored to God's beloved Son. Would you refuse to take the function of completing God, when all He wills is that you be complete?

## LESSON 281

**I can be hurt by nothing but my thoughts.**

*Father, Your Son is perfect. When I think
that I am hurt in any way, it is
because I have forgotten who I am,
and that I am as You created me.
Your Thoughts can only bring me happiness.
If ever I am sad or hurt or ill,
I have forgotten what You think, and put
my little meaningless ideas in place
of where Your Thoughts belong, and where they are.
I can be hurt by nothing but my thoughts.
The Thoughts I think with You can only bless.
The Thoughts I think with You alone are true.*

I will not hurt myself today. For I
am far beyond all pain. My Father placed
me safe in Heaven, watching over me.
And I would not attack the Son He loves,
for what He loves is also mine to love.


## LESSON 282

**I will not be afraid of love today.**

If I could realize but this today,
salvation would be reached for all the world.
This the decision not to be insane,
and to accept myself as God Himself,
my Father and my Source, created me.
This the determination not to be
asleep in dreams of death, while truth remains
forever living in the joy of love.
And this the choice to recognize the Self
Whom God created as the Son He loves,
and Who remains my one Identity.

*Father, Your Name is Love and so is mine.
Such is the truth. And can the truth be changed
by merely giving it another name?
The name of fear is simply a mistake.
Let me not be afraid of truth today.*


## LESSON 283

**My true Identity abides in You.**

*Father, I made an image of myself,
and it is this I call the Son of God.
Yet is creation as it always was,
for Your creation is unchangeable.
Let me not worship idols. I am he
my Father loves. My holiness remains
the light of Heaven and the Love of God.
Is not what is beloved of You secure?
Is not the light of Heaven infinite?
Is not Your Son my true Identity,
when You created everything that is?*

Now are we one in shared Identity,
with God our Father as our only Source,
and everything created part of us.
And so we offer blessing to all things,
uniting lovingly with all the world,
which our forgiveness has made one with us.


## LESSON 284

**I can elect to change all thoughts that hurt.**

Loss is not loss when properly perceived.
Pain is impossible. There is no grief
with any cause at all. And suffering
of any kind is nothing but a dream.
This is the truth, at first to be but said
and then repeated many times; and next
to be accepted as but partly true,
with many reservations. Then to be
considered seriously more and more,
and finally accepted as the truth.
I can elect to change all thoughts that hurt.
And I would go beyond these words today,
and past all reservations, and arrive
at full acceptance of the truth in them.

*Father, what You have given cannot hurt,
so grief and pain must be impossible.
Let me not fail to trust in You today,
accepting but the joyous as Your gifts;
accepting but the joyous as the truth.*

## LESSON 285

**My holiness shines bright and clear today.**

Today I wake with joy, expecting but
the happy things of God to come to me.
I ask but them to come, and realize
my invitation will be answered by
the thoughts to which it has been sent by me.
And I will ask for only joyous things
the instant I accept my holiness.
For what would be the use of pain to me,
what purpose would my suffering fulfill,
and how would grief and loss avail me if
insanity departs from me today,
and I accept my holiness instead?

*Father, my holiness is Yours. Let me
rejoice in it, and through forgiveness be
restored to sanity. Your Son is still
as You created him. My holiness
is part of me, and also part of You.
And what can alter Holiness Itself?*

## LESSON 286

**The hush of Heaven holds my heart today.**

*Father, how still today! How quietly
do all things fall in place! This is the day
that has been chosen as the time in which
I come to understand the lesson that
there is no need that I do anything.
In You is every choice already made.
In You has every conflict been resolved.
In You is everything I hope to find
already given me. Your peace is mine.
My heart is quiet, and my mind at rest.
Your Love is Heaven, and Your Love is mine.*

The stillness of today will give us hope
that we have found the way, and travelled far
along it to a wholly certain goal.
Today we will not doubt the end which God
Himself has promised us. We trust in Him,
and in our Self, Who still is one with Him.

## LESSON 287

**You are my goal, my Father. Only You.**

Where would I go but Heaven? What could be
a substitute for happiness? What gift
could I prefer before the peace of God?
What treasure would I seek and find and keep
that can compare with my Identity?
And would I rather live with fear than love?

*You are my goal, my Father. What but You
could I desire to have? What way but that
which leads to You could I desire to walk?
And what except the memory of You
could signify to me the end of dreams
and futile substitutions for the truth?
You are my only goal. Your Son would be
as You created him. What way but this
could I expect to recognize my Self,
and be at one with my Identity?*

## LESSON 288

**Let me forget my brother's past today.**

*This is the thought that leads the way to You,
and brings me to my goal. I cannot come
to You without my brother. And to know
my Source, I first must recognize what You
created one with me. My brother's is
the hand that leads me on the way to You.
His sins are in the past along with mine,
and I am saved because the past is gone.
Let me not cherish it within my heart,
or I will lose the way to walk to You.
My brother is my savior. Let me not
attack the savior You have given me.
But let me honor him who bears Your Name,
and so remember that It is my own.*

Forgive me, then, today. And you will know
you have forgiven me if you behold
your brother in the light of holiness.
He cannot be less holy than can I,
and you can not be holier than he.

## LESSON 289

**The past is over. It can touch me not.**

Unless the past is over in my mind, the real world must escape my sight. For I am really looking nowhere; seeing but what is not there. How can I then perceive the world forgiveness offers? This the past was made to hide, for this the world that can be looked on only now. It has no past. For what can be forgiven but the past, and if it is forgiven it is gone.

*Father, let me not look upon a past that is not there. For You have offered me Your Own replacement, in a present world the past has left untouched and free of sin. Here is the end of guilt. And here am I made ready for Your final step. Shall I demand that You wait longer for Your Son to find the loveliness You planned to be the end of all his dreams and all his pain?*

## LESSON 290

**My present happiness is all I see.**

Unless I look upon what is not there, my present happiness is all I see. Eyes that begin to open see at last. And I would have Christ's vision come to me this very day. What I perceive without God's Own Correction for the sight I made is frightening and painful to behold. Yet I would not allow my mind to be deceived by the belief the dream I made is real an instant longer. This the day I seek my present happiness, and look on nothing else except the thing I seek.

*With this resolve I come to You, and ask Your strength to hold me up today, while I but seek to do Your Will. You cannot fail to hear me, Father. What I ask have You already given me. And I am sure that I will see my happiness today.*

## WHAT IS THE REAL WORLD?

The real world is a symbol, like the rest
of what perception offers. Yet it stands
for what is opposite to what you made.
Your world is seen through eyes of fear, and brings
the witnesses of terror to your mind.
The real world cannot be perceived except
through eyes forgiveness blesses, so they see
a world where terror is impossible,
and witnesses to fear can not be found.

The real world holds a counterpart for each
unhappy thought reflected in your world;
a sure correction for the sights of fear
and sounds of battle which your world contains.
The real world shows a world seen differently,
through quiet eyes and with a mind at peace.
Nothing but rest is there. There are no cries
of pain and sorrow heard, for nothing there
remains outside forgiveness. And the sights
are gentle. Only happy sights and sounds
can reach the mind that has forgiven itself.

What need has such a mind for thoughts of death,
attack and murder? What can it perceive
surrounding it but safety, love and joy?
What is there it would choose to be condemned,
and what is there that it would judge against?

The world it sees arises from a mind
at peace within itself. No danger lurks
in anything it sees, for it is kind,
and only kindness does it look upon.

The real world is the symbol that the dream
of sin and guilt is over, and God's Son
no longer sleeps. His waking eyes perceive
the sure reflection of his Father's Love;
the certain promise that he is redeemed.
The real world signifies the end of time,
for its perception makes time purposeless.

The Holy Spirit has no need of time
when it has served His purpose. Now He waits
but that one instant more for God to take
His final step, and time has disappeared,
taking perception with it as it goes,
and leaving but the truth to be itself.
That instant is our goal, for it contains
the memory of God. And as we look
upon a world forgiven, it is He
Who calls to us and comes to take us home,
reminding us of our Identity
Which our forgiveness has restored to us.

### LESSON 291

**This is a day of stillness and of peace.**

Christ's vision looks through me today. His sight
shows me all things forgiven and at peace,
and offers this same vision to the world.
And I accept this vision in its name,
both for myself and for the world as well.
What loveliness we look upon today!
What holiness we see surrounding us!
And it is given us to recognize
it is a holiness in which we share;
it is the Holiness of God Himself.

*This day my mind is quiet, to receive
the Thoughts You offer me. And I accept
what comes from You, instead of from myself.
I do not know the way to You. But You
are wholly certain. Father, guide Your Son
along the quiet path that leads to You.
Let my forgiveness be complete, and let
the memory of You return to me.*

### LESSON 292

**A happy outcome to all things is sure.**

God's promises make no exceptions. And
He guarantees that only joy can be
the final outcome found for everything.
Yet it is up to us when this is reached;
how long we let an alien will appear
to be opposing His. And while we think
this will is real, we will not find the end
He has appointed as the outcome of
all problems we perceive, all trials we see,
and every situation that we meet.
Yet is the ending certain. For God's Will
is done in earth and Heaven. We will seek
and we will find according to His Will,
which guarantees that our will is done.

*We thank You, Father, for Your guarantee
of only happy outcomes in the end.
Help us not interfere, and so delay
the happy endings You have promised us
for every problem that we can perceive;
for every trial we think we still must meet.*

### LESSON 293

**All fear is past and only love is here.**

All fear is past, because its source is gone,
and all its thoughts gone with it. Love remains
the only present state, whose Source is here
forever and forever. Can the world
seem bright and clear and safe and welcoming,
with all my past mistakes oppressing it,
and showing me distorted forms of fear?
Yet in the present love is obvious,
and its effects apparent. All the world
shines in reflection of its holy light,
and I perceive a world forgiven at last.

*Father, let not Your holy world escape
my sight today. Nor let my ears be deaf
to all the hymns of gratitude the world
is singing underneath the sounds of fear.
There is a real world which the present holds
safe from all past mistakes. And I would see
only this world before my eyes today.*

### LESSON 294

**My body is a wholly neutral thing.**

I am a Son of God. And can I be
another thing as well? Did God create
the mortal and corruptible? What use
has God's beloved Son for what must die?
And yet a neutral thing does not see death,
for thoughts of fear are not invested there,
nor is a mockery of love bestowed
upon it. Its neutrality protects
it while it has a use. And afterwards,
without a purpose, it is laid aside.
It is not sick nor old nor hurt. It is
but functionless, unneeded and cast off.
Let me not see it more than this today;
of service for a while and fit to serve,
to keep its usefulness while it can serve,
and then to be replaced for greater good.

*My body, Father, cannot be Your Son.
And what is not created cannot be
sinful nor sinless; neither good nor bad.
Let me, then, use this dream to help Your plan
that we awaken from all dreams we made.*

## LESSON 295

**The Holy Spirit looks through me today.**

Christ asks that He may use my eyes today, and thus redeem the world. He asks this gift that He may offer peace of mind to me, and take away all terror and all pain. And as they are removed from me, the dreams that seemed to settle on the world are gone. Redemption must be one. As I am saved, the world is saved with me. For all of us must be redeemed together. Fear appears in many different forms, but love is one.

*My Father, Christ has asked a gift of me, and one I give that it be given me. Help me to use the eyes of Christ today, and thus allow the Holy Spirit's Love to bless all things which I may look upon, that His forgiving Love may rest on me.*

## LESSON 296

**The Holy Spirit speaks through me today.**

*The Holy Spirit needs my voice today, that all the world may listen to Your Voice, and hear Your Word through me. I am resolved to let You speak through me, for I would use no words but Yours, and have no thoughts which are apart from Yours, for only Yours are true. I would be savior to the world I made. For having damned it I would set it free, that I may find escape, and hear the Word Your holy Voice will speak to me today.*

We teach today what we would learn, and that alone. And so our learning goal becomes an unconflicted one, and possible of easy reach and quick accomplishment. How gladly does the Holy Spirit come to rescue us from hell, when we allow His teaching to persuade the world, through us, to seek and find the easy path to God.

## LESSON 297

**Forgiveness is the only gift I give.**

Forgiveness is the only gift I give, because it is the only gift I want. And everything I give I give myself. This is salvation's simple formula. And I, who would be saved, would make it mine, to be the way I live within a world that needs salvation, and that will be saved as I accept Atonement for myself.

*Father, how certain are Your ways; how sure their final outcome, and how faithfully is every step in my salvation set already, and accomplished by Your grace. Thanks be to You for Your eternal gifts, and thanks to You for my Identity.*

## LESSON 298

**I love You, Father, and I love Your Son.**

My gratitude permits my love to be accepted without fear. And thus am I restored to my Reality at last. All that intruded on my holy sight forgiveness takes away. And I draw near the end of senseless journeys, mad careers and artificial values. I accept instead what God establishes as mine, sure that in that alone I will be saved; sure that I go through fear to meet my Love.

*Father, I come to You today, because I would not follow any way but Yours. You are beside me. Certain is Your way. And I am grateful for Your holy gifts of certain sanctuary, and escape from everything that would obscure my love for God my Father and His holy Son.*

## LESSON 299

### Eternal holiness abides in me.

My holiness is far beyond my own
ability to understand or know.
Yet God, my Father, Who created it,
acknowledges my holiness as His.
Our Will, together, understands it. And
our Will, together, knows that it is so.

*Father, my holiness is not of me.*
*It is not mine to be destroyed by sin.*
*It is not mine to suffer from attack.*
*Illusions can obscure it, but can not*
*put out its radiance, nor dim its light.*
*It stands forever perfect and untouched.*
*In it are all things healed, for they remain*
*as You created them. And I can know*
*my holiness. For Holiness Itself*
*created me, and I can know my Source*
*because it is Your Will that You be known.*

## LESSON 300

### Only an instant does this world endure.

This is a thought which can be used to say
that death and sorrow are the certain lot
of all who come here, for their joys are gone
before they are possessed, or even grasped.
Yet this is also the idea that lets
no false perception keep us in its hold,
nor represent more than a passing cloud
upon a sky eternally serene.
And it is this serenity we seek,
unclouded, obvious and sure, today.

*We seek Your holy world today. For we,*
*Your loving Sons, have lost our way a while.*
*But we have listened to Your Voice, and learned*
*exactly what to do to be restored*
*to Heaven and our true Identity.*
*And we give thanks today the world endures*
*but for an instant. We would go beyond*
*that tiny instant to eternity.*

## WHAT IS THE SECOND COMING?

Christ's Second Coming, which is sure as God, is merely the correction of mistakes, and the return of sanity. It is a part of the condition that restores the never lost, and re-establishes what is forever and forever true. It is the invitation to God's Word to take illusion's place; the willingness to let forgiveness rest upon all things without exception and without reserve.

It is the all-inclusive nature of Christ's Second Coming that permits it to embrace the world and hold you safe within its gentle advent, which encompasses all living things with you. There is no end to the release the Second Coming brings, as God's creation must be limitless. Forgiveness lights the Second Coming's way, because it shines on everything as one. And thus is oneness recognized at last.

The Second Coming ends the lessons that the Holy Spirit teaches, making way for the Last Judgment, in which learning ends in one last summary that will extend beyond itself, and reaches up to God. The Second Coming is the time in which all minds are given to the hands of Christ, to be returned to spirit in the name of true creation and the Will of God.

The Second Coming is the one event in time which time itself can not affect. For every one who ever came to die, or yet will come or who is present now, is equally released from what he made. In this equality is Christ restored as one Identity, in Which the Sons of God acknowledge that they all are one. And God the Father smiles upon His Son, His one creation and His only joy.

Pray that the Second Coming will be soon, but do not rest with that. It needs your eyes and ears and hands and feet. It needs your voice. And most of all it needs your willingness. Let us rejoice that we can do God's Will, and join together in its holy light. Behold, the Son of God is one in us, and we can reach our Father's Love through Him.

## LESSON 301

**And God Himself shall wipe away all tears.**

*Father, unless I judge I cannot weep.*
*Nor can I suffer pain, or feel I am*
*abandoned or unneeded in the world.*
*This is my home because I judge it not,*
*and therefore is it only what You will.*
*Let me today behold it uncondemned,*
*through happy eyes forgiveness has released*
*from all distortion. Let me see Your world*
*instead of mine. And all the tears I shed*
*will be forgotten, for their source is gone.*
*Father, I will not judge Your world today.*

God's world is happy. Those who look on it
can only add their joy to it, and bless
it as a cause of further joy in them.
We wept because we did not understand.
But we have learned the world we saw was false,
and we will look upon God's world today.

## LESSON 302

**Where darkness was I look upon the light.**

*Father, our eyes are opening at last.*
*Your holy world awaits us, as our sight*
*is finally restored and we can see.*
*We thought we suffered. But we had forgot*
*the Son whom You created. Now we see*
*that darkness is our own imagining,*
*and light is there for us to look upon.*
*Christ's vision changes darkness into light,*
*for fear must disappear when love has come.*
*Let me forgive Your holy world today,*
*that I may look upon its holiness*
*and understand it but reflects my own.*

Our Love awaits us as we go to Him,
and walks beside us showing us the way.
He fails in nothing. He the end we seek,
and He the means by which we go to Him.

## LESSON 303

**The holy Christ is born in me today.**

Watch with me, angels, watch with me today.
Let all God's holy Thoughts surround me, and
be still with me while Heaven's Son is born.
Let earthly sounds be quiet, and the sights
to which I am accustomed disappear.
Let Christ be welcomed where He is at home.
And let Him hear the sounds He understands,
and see but sights that show His Father's Love.
Let Him no longer be a stranger here,
for He is born again in me today.

*Your Son is welcome, Father. He has come*
*to save me from the evil self I made.*
*He is the Self That You have given me.*
*He is but what I really am in truth.*
*He is the Son You love above all things.*
*He is my Self as You created me.*
*It is not Christ That can be crucified.*
*Safe in Your Arms let me receive Your Son.*

## LESSON 304

**Let not my world obscure the sight of Christ.**

I can obscure my holy sight, if I
intrude my world upon it. Nor can I
behold the holy sights Christ looks upon,
unless it is His vision that I use.
Perception is a mirror, not a fact.
And what I look on is my state of mind,
reflected outward. I would bless the world
by looking on it through the eyes of Christ.
And I will look upon the certain signs
that all my sins have been forgiven me.

*You lead me from the darkness to the light;*
*from sin to holiness. Let me forgive,*
*and thus receive salvation for the world.*
*It is Your gift, my Father, given me*
*to offer to Your holy Son, that he*
*may find again the memory of You,*
*and of Your Son as You created him.*

## LESSON 305

**There is a peace that Christ bestows on us.**

Who uses but Christ's vision finds a peace
so deep and quiet, undisturbable
and wholly changeless, that the world contains
no counterpart. Comparisons are still
before this peace. And all the world departs
in silence as this peace envelops it,
and gently carries it to truth, no more
to be the home of fear. For love has come,
and healed the world by giving it Christ's peace.

*Father, the peace of Christ is given us,
because it is Your Will that we be saved.
Help us today but to accept Your gift,
and judge it not. For it has come to us
to save us from our judgment on ourselves.*

## LESSON 306

**The gift of Christ is all I seek today.**

What but Christ's vision would I use today,
when it can offer me a day in which
I see a world so like to Heaven that
an ancient memory returns to me?
Today I can forget the world I made.
Today I can go past all fear, and be
restored to love and holiness and peace.
Today I am redeemed, and born anew
into a world of mercy and of care;
of loving kindness and the peace of God.

*And so, our Father, we return to You,
remembering we never went away;
remembering Your holy gifts to us.
In gratitude and thankfulness we come,
with empty hands and open hearts and minds,
asking but what You give. We cannot make
an offering sufficient for Your Son.
But in Your Love the gift of Christ is his.*

## LESSON 307

**Conflicting wishes cannot be my will.**

*Father, Your Will is mine, and only that.
There is no other will for me to have.
Let me not try to make another will,
for it is senseless and will cause me pain.
Your Will alone can bring me happiness,
and only Yours exists. If I would have
what only You can give, I must accept
Your Will for me, and enter into peace
where conflict is impossible, Your Son
is one with You in being and in will,
and nothing contradicts the holy truth
that I remain as You created me.*

And with this prayer we enter silently
into a state where conflict cannot come,
because we join our holy will with God's,
in recognition that they are the same.

## LESSON 308

**This instant is the only time there is.**

I have conceived of time in such a way
that I defeat my aim. If I elect
to reach past time to timelessness, I must
change my perception of what time is for.
Time's purpose cannot be to keep the past
and future one. The only interval
in which I can be saved from time is now.
For in this instant has forgiveness come
to set me free. The birth of Christ is now,
without a past or future. He has come
to give His present blessing to the world,
restoring it to timelessness and love.
And love is ever-present, here and now.

*Thanks for this instant, Father. It is now
I am redeemed. This instant is the time
You have appointed for Your Son's release,
and for salvation of the world in him.*

## LESSON 309

**I will not fear to look within today.**

Within me is Eternal Innocence,
because it is God's Will that It be there
forever and forever. I, His Son,
whose will is limitless as is His Own,
can will no change in this. For to deny
my Father's Will is to deny my own.
To look within is but to find my will
as God created it, and as it is.
I fear to look within because I think
I made another will that is not true,
and made it real. Yet it has no effects.
Within me is the holiness of God.
Within me is the memory of Him.

*The step I take today, my Father, is
my sure release from idle dreams of sin.
Your altar stands serene and undefiled.
It is the holy altar to my Self,
and there I find my true Identity.*

## LESSON 310

**In fearlessness and love I spend today.**

*This day, my Father, would I spend with You,
as You have chosen all my days should be.
And what I will experience is not
of time at all. The joy that comes to me
is not of days nor hours, for it comes
from Heaven to Your Son. This day will be
Your sweet reminder to remember You,
Your gracious calling to Your holy Son,
the sign Your grace has come to me, and that
it is Your Will I be set free today.*

We spend this day together, you and I.
And all the world joins with us in our song
of thankfulness and joy to Him Who gave
salvation to us, and Who set us free.
We are restored to peace and holiness.
There is no room in us for fear today,
for we have welcomed love into our hearts.

## WHAT IS THE LAST JUDGMENT?

Christ's Second Coming gives the Son of God this gift: To hear the Voice for God proclaim that what is false is false, and what is true has never changed. And this the judgment is in which perception ends. At first you see a world that has accepted this as true, projected from a now corrected mind. And with this holy sight, perception gives a silent blessing and then disappears, its goal accomplished and its mission done.

The Final Judgment on the world contains no condemnation. For it sees the world as totally forgiven, without sin and wholly purposeless. Without a cause, and now without a function in Christ's sight, it merely slips away to nothingness. There it was born, and there it ends as well. And all the figures in the dream in which the world began go with it. Bodies now are useless, and will therefore fade away, because the Son of God is limitless.

You who believed that God's Last Judgment would condemn the world to hell along with you, accept this holy truth: God's Judgment is the gift of the Correction He bestowed on all your errors, freeing you from them, and all effects they ever seemed to have. To fear God's saving grace is but to fear complete release from suffering, return to peace, security and happiness, and union with your own Identity.

God's Final Judgment is as merciful as every step in His appointed plan to bless His Son, and call him to return to the eternal peace He shares with him. Be not afraid of love. For it alone can heal all sorrow, wipe away all tears, and gently waken from his dream of pain the Son whom God acknowledges as His. Be not afraid of this. Salvation asks you give it welcome. And the world awaits your glad acceptance, which will set it free.

This is God's Final Judgment: "You are still My holy Son, forever innocent, forever loving and forever loved, as limitless as your Creator, and completely changeless and forever pure. Therefore awaken and return to Me. I am your Father and you are My Son."

## LESSON 311

**I judge all things as I would have them be.**

Judgment was made to be a weapon used against the truth. It separates what it is being used against, and sets it off as if it were a thing apart. And then it makes of it what you would have it be. It judges what it cannot understand, because it cannot see totality and therefore judges falsely. Let us not use it today, but make a gift of it to Him Who has a different use for it. He will relieve us of the agony of all the judgments we have made against ourselves, and re-establish peace of mind by giving us God's Judgment of His Son.

*Father, we wait with open mind today,
to hear Your Judgment of the Son You love.
We do not know him, and we cannot judge.
And so we let Your Love decide what he
whom You created as Your Son must be.*

## LESSON 312

**I see all things as I would have them be.**

Perception follows judgment. Having judged, we therefore see what we would look upon. For sight can merely serve to offer us what we would have. It is impossible to overlook what we would see, and fail to see what we have chosen to behold. How surely, therefore, must the real world come to greet the holy sight of anyone who takes the Holy Spirit's purpose as his goal for seeing. And he cannot fail to look upon what Christ would have him see, and share Christ's Love for what he looks upon.

*I have no purpose for today except
to look upon a liberated world,
set free from all the judgments I have made.
Father, this is Your Will for me today,
and therefore it must be my goal as well.*

## LESSON 313

**Now let a new perception come to me.**

*Father, there is a vision which beholds
all things as sinless, so that fear has gone,
and where it was is love invited in.
And love will come wherever it is asked.
This vision is Your gift. The eyes of Christ
look on a world forgiven. In His sight
are all its sins forgiven, for He sees
no sin in anything He looks upon.
Now let His true perception come to me,
that I may waken from the dream of sin
and look within upon my sinlessness,
which You have kept completely undefiled
upon the altar to Your holy Son,
the Self with Which I would identify.*

Let us today behold each other in the sight of Christ. How beautiful we are! How holy and how loving! Brother, come and join with me today. We save the world when we have joined. For in our vision it becomes as holy as the light in us.

## LESSON 314

**I seek a future different from the past.**

From new perception of the world there comes a future very different from the past. The future now is recognized as but extension of the present. Past mistakes can cast no shadows on it, so that fear has lost its idols and its images, and being formless, it has no effects. Death will not claim the future now, for life is now its goal, and all the needed means are happily provided. Who can grieve or suffer when the present has been freed, extending its security and peace into a quiet future filled with joy?

*Father, we were mistaken in the past,
and choose to use the present to be free.
Now do we leave the future in Your Hands,
leaving behind our past mistakes, and sure
that You will keep Your present promises,
and guide the future in their holy light.*

## LESSON 315

**All gifts my brothers give belong to me.**

Each day a thousand treasures come to me with every passing moment. I am blessed with gifts throughout the day, in value far beyond all things of which I can conceive. A brother smiles upon another, and my heart is gladdened. Someone speaks a word of gratitude or mercy, and my mind receives this gift and takes it as its own. And everyone who finds the way to God becomes my savior, pointing out the way to me, and giving me his certainty that what he learned is surely mine as well.

*I thank You, Father, for the many gifts that come to me today and every day from every Son of God. My brothers are unlimited in all their gifts to me. Now may I offer them my thankfulness, that gratitude to them may lead me on to my Creator and His memory.*

## LESSON 316

**All gifts I give my brothers are my own.**

As every gift my brothers give is mine, so every gift I give belongs to me. Each one allows a past mistake to go, and leave no shadow on the holy mind my Father loves. His grace is given me in every gift a brother has received throughout all time, and past all time as well. My treasure house is full, and angels watch its open doors that not one gift is lost, and only more are added. Let me come to where my treasures are, and enter in where I am truly welcome and at home, among the gifts that God has given me.

*Father, I would accept Your gifts today. I do not recognize them. Yet I trust that You Who gave them will provide the means by which I can behold them, see their worth, and cherish only them as what I want.*

## LESSON 317

**I follow in the way appointed me.**

I have a special place to fill; a role for me alone. Salvation waits until I take this part as what I choose to do. Until I make this choice, I am the slave of time and human destiny. But when I willingly and gladly go the way my Father's plan appointed me to go, then will I recognize salvation is already here, already given all my brothers and already mine as well.

*Father, Your way is what I choose today. Where it would lead me do I choose to go; what it would have me do I choose to do. Your way is certain, and the end secure. The memory of You awaits me there. And all my sorrows end in Your embrace, which You have promised to Your Son, who thought mistakenly that he had wandered from the sure protection of Your loving Arms.*

## LESSON 318

**In me salvation's means and end are one.**

In me, God's holy Son, are reconciled all parts of Heaven's plan to save the world. What could conflict, when all the parts have but one purpose and one aim? How could there be a single part that stands alone, or one of more or less importance than the rest? I am the means by which God's Son is saved, because salvation's purpose is to find the sinlessness that God has placed in me. I was created as the thing I seek. I am the goal the world is searching for. I am God's Son, His one eternal Love. I am salvation's means and end as well.

*Let me today, my Father, take the role You offer me in Your request that I accept Atonement for myself. For thus does what is thereby reconciled in me become as surely reconciled to You.*

## LESSON 319

**I came for the salvation of the world.**

Here is a thought from which all arrogance has been removed, and only truth remains. For arrogance opposes truth. But when there is no arrogance the truth will come immediately, and fill up the space the ego left unoccupied by lies. Only the ego can be limited, and therefore it must seek for aims which are curtailed and limiting. The ego thinks that what one gains, totality must lose. And yet it is the Will of God I learn that what one gains is given unto all.

*Father, Your Will is total. And the goal which stems from it shares its totality. What aim but the salvation of the world could You have given me? And what but this could be the Will my Self has shared with You?*

## LESSON 320

**My Father gives all power unto me.**

The Son of God is limitless. There are no limits on his strength, his peace, his joy, nor any attributes his Father gave in his creation. What he wills with his Creator and Redeemer must be done. His holy will can never be denied, because his Father shines upon his mind, and lays before it all the strength and love in earth and Heaven. I am he to whom all this is given. I am he in whom the power of my Father's Will abides.

*Your Will can do all things in me, and then extend to all the world as well through me. There is no limit on Your Will. And so all power has been given to Your Son.*

## WHAT IS CREATION?

Creation is the sum of all God's Thoughts,
in number infinite, and everywhere
without all limit. Only Love creates,
and only like Itself. There was no time
when all that It created was not there.
Nor will there be a time when anything
that It created suffers any loss.
Forever and forever are God's Thoughts
exactly as they were and as they are,
unchanged through time and after time is done.

God's Thoughts are given all the power that
their own Creator has. For He would add
to Love by its extension. Thus His Son
shares in creation, and must therefore share
in power to create. What God has willed
to be forever one will still be one
when time is over; and will not be changed
throughout the course of time, remaining as
it was before the thought of time began.

Creation is the opposite of all
illusions, for creation is the truth.
Creation is the holy Son of God,
for in creation is His Will complete
in every aspect, making every part
container of the Whole. Its oneness is
forever guaranteed inviolate;
forever held within His holy Will,
beyond all possibility of harm,
of separation, imperfection and
of any spot upon its sinlessness.

We are creation; we the Sons of God.
We seem to be discrete, and unaware
of our eternal unity with Him.
Yet back of all our doubts, past all our fears,
there still is certainty. For Love remains
with all Its Thoughts, Its sureness being theirs.
God's memory is in our holy minds,
which know their oneness and their unity
with their Creator. Let our function be
only to let this memory return,
only to let God's Will be done on earth,
only to be restored to sanity,
and to be but as God created us.

Our Father calls to us. We hear His Voice,
and we forgive creation in the Name
of its Creator, Holiness Itself,
Whose holiness His Own creation shares;
Whose holiness is still a part of us.

## LESSON 321

**Father, my freedom is in You alone.**

*I did not understand what made me free,
nor what my freedom is, nor where to look
to find it. Father, I have searched in vain
until I heard Your Voice directing me.
Now I would guide myself no more. For I
have neither made nor understood the way
to find my freedom. But I trust in You.
You Who endowed me with my freedom as
Your holy Son will not be lost to me.
Your Voice directs me, and the way to You
is opening and clear to me at last.
Father, my freedom is in You alone.
Father, it is my will that I return.*

Today we answer for the world, which will be freed along with us. How glad are we to find our freedom through the certain way our Father has established. And how sure is all the world's salvation, when we learn our freedom can be found in God alone.

## LESSON 322

**I can give up but what was never real.**

I sacrifice illusions; nothing more. And as illusions go I find the gifts illusions tried to hide, awaiting me in shining welcome, and in readiness to give God's ancient messages to me. His memory abides in every gift that I receive of Him. And every dream serves only to conceal the Self Which is God's only Son, the likeness of Himself, the Holy One Who still abides in Him forever, as He still abides in me.

*Father, to You all sacrifice remains
forever inconceivable. And so
I cannot sacrifice except in dreams.
As You created me, I can give up
nothing You gave me. What You did not give
has no reality. What loss can I
anticipate except the loss of fear,
and the return of love into my mind.*

## LESSON 323

**I gladly make the "sacrifice" of fear.**

*Here is the only "sacrifice" You ask
of Your beloved Son; You ask him to
give up all suffering, all sense of loss
and sadness, all anxiety and doubt,
and freely let Your Love come streaming in
to his awareness, healing him of pain,
and giving him Your Own eternal joy.
Such is the "sacrifice" You ask of me,
and one I gladly make; the only "cost"
of restoration of Your memory
to me, for the salvation of the world.*

And as we pay the debt we owe to truth,— a debt that merely is the letting go of self-deceptions and of images we worshipped falsely —truth returns to us in wholeness and in joy. We are deceived no longer. Love has now returned to our awareness. And we are at peace again, for fear has gone and only love remains.

## LESSON 324

**I merely follow, for I would not lead.**

*Father, You are the One Who gave the plan
for my salvation to me. You have set
the way I am to go, the role to take,
and every step in my appointed path.
I cannot lose the way. I can but choose
to wander off a while, and then return.
Your loving Voice will always call me back,
and guide my feet aright. My brothers all
can follow in the way I lead them. Yet
I merely follow in the way to You,
as You direct me and would have me go.*

So let us follow One Who knows the way. We need not tarry, and we cannot stray except an instant from His loving hand. We walk together, for we follow Him. And it is He Who makes the ending sure, and guarantees a safe returning home.

## LESSON 325

**All things I think I see reflect ideas.**

This is salvation's keynote: What I see reflects a process in my mind, which starts with my idea of what I want. From there, the mind makes up an image of the thing the mind desires, judges valuable, and therefore seeks to find. These images are then projected outward, looked upon, esteemed as real and guarded as one's own. From insane wishes comes an insane world. From judgment comes a world condemned. And from forgiving thoughts a gentle world comes forth, with mercy for the holy Son of God, to offer him a kindly home where he can rest a while before he journeys on, and help his brothers walk ahead with him, and find the way to Heaven and to God.

*Our Father, Your ideas reflect the truth,*
*and mine apart from Yours but make up dreams.*
*Let me behold what only Yours reflect,*
*for Yours and Yours alone establish truth.*

## LESSON 326

**I am forever an Effect of God.**

*Father, I was created in Your Mind,*
*a holy Thought that never left its home.*
*I am forever Your Effect, and You*
*forever and forever are my Cause.*
*As You created me I have remained.*
*Where You established me I still abide.*
*And all Your attributes abide in me,*
*because it is Your Will to have a Son*
*so like his Cause that Cause and Its Effect*
*are indistinguishable. Let me know*
*that I am an Effect of God, and so*
*I have the power to create like You.*
*And as it is in Heaven, so on earth.*
*Your plan I follow here, and at the end*
*I know that You will gather Your effects*
*into the tranquil Heaven of Your Love,*
*where earth will vanish, and all separate thoughts*
*unite in glory as the Son of God.*

Let us today behold earth disappear, at first transformed, and then, forgiven, fade entirely into God's holy Will.

## LESSON 327

**I need but call and You will answer me.**

I am not asked to take salvation on the basis of an unsupported faith. For God has promised He will hear my call, and answer me Himself. Let me but learn from my experience that this is true, and faith in Him must surely come to me. This is the faith that will endure, and take me farther and still farther on the road that leads to Him. For thus I will be sure that He has not abandoned me and loves me still, awaiting but my call to give me all the help I need to come to Him.

*Father, I thank You that Your promises*
*will never fail in my experience,*
*if I but test them out. Let me attempt*
*therefore to try them, and to judge them not.*
*Your Word is one with You. You give the means*
*whereby conviction comes, and surety*
*of Your abiding Love is gained at last.*

## LESSON 328

**I choose the second place to gain the first.**

What seems to be the second place is first, for all things we perceive are upside down until we listen to the Voice for God. It seems that we will gain autonomy but by our striving to be separate, and that our independence from the rest of God's creation is the way in which salvation is obtained. Yet all we find is sickness, suffering and loss and death. This is not what our Father wills for us, nor is there any second to His Will. To join with His is but to find our own. And since our will is His, it is to Him that we must go to recognize our will.

*There is no will but Yours. And I am glad*
*that nothing I imagine contradicts*
*what You would have me be. It is Your Will*
*that I be wholly safe, eternally*
*at peace. And happily I share that Will*
*which You, my Father, gave as part of me.*

## LESSON 329

**I have already chosen what You will.**

*Father, I thought I wandered from Your Will, defied it, broke its laws, and interposed a second will more powerful than Yours. Yet what I am in truth is but Your Will, extended and extending. This am I, and this will never change. As You are One, so am I one with You. And this I chose in my creation, where my will became forever one with Yours. That choice was made for all eternity. It cannot change, and be in opposition to itself. Father, my will is Yours. And I am safe, untroubled and serene, in endless joy, because it is Your Will that it be so.*

Today we will accept our union with each other and our Source. We have no will apart from His, and all of us are one because His Will is shared by all of us. Through it we recognize that we are one. Through it we find our way at last to God.

## LESSON 330

**I will not hurt myself again today.**

Let us this day accept forgiveness as our only function. Why should we attack our minds, and give them images of pain? Why should we teach them they are powerless, when God holds out His power and His Love, and bids them take what is already theirs? The mind that is made willing to accept God's gifts has been restored to spirit, and extends its freedom and its joy, as is the Will of God united with its own. The Self Which God created cannot sin, and therefore cannot suffer. Let us choose today that He be our Identity, and thus escape forever from all things the dream of fear appears to offer us.

*Father, Your Son can not be hurt. And if we think we suffer, we but fail to know our one Identity we share with You. We would return to It today, to be made free forever from all our mistakes, and to be saved from what we thought we were.*

## WHAT IS THE EGO?

The ego is idolatry; the sign
of limited and separated self,
born in a body, doomed to suffer and
to end its life in death. It is the "will"
that sees the Will of God as enemy,
and takes a form in which it is denied.
The ego is the "proof" that strength is weak
and love is fearful, life is really death,
and what opposes God alone is true.

The ego is insane. In fear it stands
beyond the Everywhere, apart from All,
in separation from the Infinite.
In its insanity it thinks it has
become a victor over God Himself.
And in its terrible autonomy
it "sees" the Will of God has been destroyed.
It dreams of punishment, and trembles at
the figures in its dreams; its enemies,
who seek to murder it before it can
ensure its safety by attacking them.

The Son of God is egoless. What can
he know of madness and the death of God,
when he abides in Him? What can he know
of sorrow and of suffering, when he
lives in eternal joy? What can he know
of fear and punishment, of sin and guilt,
of hatred and attack, when all there is
surrounding him is everlasting peace,
forever conflict-free and undisturbed,
in deepest silence and tranquility?

To know reality is not to see
the ego and its thoughts, its works, its acts,
its laws and its beliefs, its dreams, its hopes,
its plans for its salvation, and the cost
belief in it entails. In suffering,
the price for faith in it is so immense
that crucifixion of the Son of God
is offered daily at its darkened shrine,
and blood must flow before the altar where
its sickly followers prepare to die.

Yet will one lily of forgiveness change
the darkness into light; the altar to
illusions to the shrine of Life Itself.
And peace will be restored forever to
the holy minds which God created as
His Son, His dwelling place, His joy, His love,
completely His, completely one with Him.

## LESSON 331

### There is no conflict, for my will is Yours.

*How foolish, Father, to believe Your Son
could cause himself to suffer! Could he make
a plan for his damnation, and be left
without a certain way to his release?
You love me, Father. You could never leave
me desolate, to die within a world
of pain and cruelty. How could I think
that Love has left Itself? There is no will
except the Will of Love. Fear is a dream,
and has no will that can conflict with Yours.
Conflict is sleep, and peace awakening.
Death is illusion; life, eternal truth.
There is no opposition to Your Will.
There is no conflict, for my will is Yours.*

Forgiveness shows us that God's Will is one,
and that we share it. Let us look upon
the holy sights forgiveness shows today,
that we may find the peace of God. Amen.

## LESSON 332

### Fear binds the world. Forgiveness sets it free.

The ego makes illusions. Truth undoes
its evil dreams by shining them away.
Truth never makes attack. It merely is.
And by its presence is the mind recalled
from fantasies, awaking to the real.
Forgiveness bids this presence enter in,
and take its rightful place within the mind.
Without forgiveness is the mind in chains,
believing in its own futility.
Yet with forgiveness does the light shine through
the dream of darkness, offering it hope,
and giving it the means to realize
the freedom that is its inheritance.

*We would not bind the world again today.
Fear holds it prisoner. And yet Your Love
has given us the means to set it free.
Father, we would release it now. For as
we offer freedom, it is given us.
And we would not remain as prisoners,
while You are holding freedom out to us.*

## LESSON 333

### Forgiveness ends the dream of conflict here.

Conflict must be resolved. It cannot be
evaded, set aside, denied, disguised,
seen somewhere else, called by another name,
or hidden by deceit of any kind,
if it would be escaped. It must be seen
exactly as it is, where it is thought
to be, in the reality which has
been given it, and with the purpose that
the mind accorded it. For only then
are its defenses lifted, and the truth
can shine upon it as it disappears.

*Father, forgiveness is the light You chose
to shine away all conflict and all doubt,
and light the way for our return to You.
No light but this can end our evil dream.
No light but this can save the world. For this
alone will never fail in anything,
being Your gift to Your beloved Son.*

## LESSON 334

### Today I claim the gifts forgiveness gives.

I will not wait another day to find
the treasures that my Father offers me.
Illusions are all vain, and dreams are gone
even while they are woven out of thoughts
that rest on false perceptions. Let me not
accept such meager gifts again today.
God's Voice is offering the peace of God
to all who hear and choose to follow Him.
This is my choice today. And so I go
to find the treasures God has given me.

*I seek but the eternal. For Your Son
can be content with nothing less than this.
What, then, can be his solace but what You
are offering to his bewildered mind
and frightened heart, to give him certainty
and bring him peace? Today I would behold
my brother sinless. This Your Will for me,
for so will I behold my sinlessness.*

## LESSON 335

### I choose to see my brother's sinlessness.

Forgiveness is a choice. I never see my brother as he is, for that is far beyond perception. What I see in him is merely what I wish to see, because it stands for what I want to be the truth. It is to this alone that I respond, however much I seem to be impelled by outside happenings. I choose to see what I would look upon, and this I see, and only this. My brother's sinlessness shows me that I would look upon my own. And I will see it, having chosen to behold my brother in its holy light.

*What could restore Your memory to me, except to see my brother's sinlessness? His holiness reminds me that he was created one with me, and like myself. In him I find my Self, and in Your Son I find the memory of You as well.*

## LESSON 336

### Forgiveness lets me know that minds are joined.

Forgiveness is the means appointed for perception's ending. Knowledge is restored after perception first is changed, and then gives way entirely to what remains forever past its highest reach. For sights and sounds, at best, can serve but to recall the memory that lies beyond them all. Forgiveness sweeps away distortions, and opens the hidden altar to the truth. Its lilies shine into the mind, and call it to return and look within, to find what it has vainly sought without. For here, and only here, is peace of mind restored, for this the dwelling place of God Himself.

*In quiet may forgiveness wipe away my dreams of separation and of sin. Then let me, Father, look within, and find Your promise of my sinlessness is kept; Your Word remains unchanged within my mind, Your Love is still abiding in my heart.*

## LESSON 337

### My sinlessness protects me from all harm.

My sinlessness ensures me perfect peace, eternal safety, everlasting love, freedom forever from all thought of loss; complete deliverance from suffering. And only happiness can be my state, for only happiness is given me. What must I do to know all this is mine? I must accept Atonement for myself, and nothing more. God has already done all things that need be done. And I must learn I need do nothing of myself, for I need but accept my Self, my sinlessness, created for me, now already mine, to feel God's Love protecting me from harm, to understand my Father loves His Son; to know I am the Son my Father loves.

*You Who created me in sinlessness are not mistaken about what I am. I was mistaken when I thought I sinned, but I accept Atonement for myself. Father, my dream is ended now. Amen.*

## LESSON 338

### I am affected only by my thoughts.

It needs but this to let salvation come to all the world. For in this single thought is everyone released at last from fear. Now has he learned that no one frightens him, and nothing can endanger him. He has no enemies, and he is safe from all external things. His thoughts can frighten him, but since these thoughts belong to him alone, he has the power to change them and exchange each fear thought for a happy thought of love. He crucified himself. Yet God has planned that His beloved Son will be redeemed.

*Your plan is sure, my Father, –only Yours. All other plans will fail. And I will have thoughts that will frighten me, until I learn that You have given me the only Thought that leads me to salvation. Mine alone will fail, and lead me nowhere. But the Thought You gave me promises to lead me home, because it holds Your promise to Your Son.*

## LESSON 339

**I will receive whatever I request.**

No one desires pain. But he can think
that pain is pleasure. No one would avoid
his happiness. But he can think that joy
is painful, threatening and dangerous.
Everyone will receive what he requests.
But he can be confused indeed about
the things he wants; the state he would attain.
What can he then request that he would want
when he receives it? He has asked for what
will frighten him, and bring him suffering.
Let us resolve today to ask for what
we really want, and only this, that we
may spend this day in fearlessness, without
confusing pain with joy, or fear with love.

*Father, this is Your day. It is a day*
*in which I would do nothing by myself,*
*but hear Your Voice in everything I do;*
*requesting only what You offer me,*
*accepting only Thoughts You share with me.*

## LESSON 340

**I can be free of suffering today.**

*Father, I thank You for today, and for*
*the freedom I am certain it will bring.*
*This day is holy, for today Your Son*
*will be redeemed. His suffering is done.*
*For he will hear Your Voice directing him*
*to find Christ's vision through forgiveness, and*
*be free forever from all suffering.*
*Thanks for today, my Father. I was born*
*into this world but to achieve this day,*
*and what it holds in joy and freedom for*
*Your holy Son and for the world he made,*
*which is released along with him today.*

Be glad today! Be glad! There is no room
for anything but joy and thanks today.
Our Father has redeemed His Son this day.
Not one of us but will be saved today.
Not one who will remain in fear, and none
the Father will not gather to Himself,
awake in Heaven in the Heart of Love.

## WHAT IS A MIRACLE?

A miracle is a correction. It
does not create, nor really change at all.
It merely looks on devastation, and
reminds the mind that what it sees is false.
It undoes error, but does not attempt
to go beyond perception, nor exceed
the function of forgiveness. Thus it stays
within time's limits. Yet it paves the way
for the return of timelessness and love's
awakening, for fear must slip away
under the gentle remedy it brings.

A miracle contains the gift of grace,
for it is given and received as one.
And thus it illustrates the law of truth
the world does not obey, because it fails
entirely to understand its ways.
A miracle inverts perception which
was upside down before, and thus it ends
the strange distortions that were manifest.
Now is perception open to the truth.
Now is forgiveness seen as justified.

Forgiveness is the home of miracles.
The eyes of Christ deliver them to all
they look upon in mercy and in love.
Perception stands corrected in His sight,
and what was meant to curse has come to bless.
Each lily of forgiveness offers all
the world the silent miracle of love.
And each is laid before the Word of God,
upon the universal altar to
Creator and creation in the light
of perfect purity and endless joy.

The miracle is taken first on faith,
because to ask for it implies the mind
has been made ready to conceive of what
it cannot see and does not understand.
Yet faith will bring its witnesses to show
that what it rested on is really there.
And thus the miracle will justify
your faith in it, and show it rested on
a world more real than what you saw before;
a world redeemed from what you thought was there.

Miracles fall like drops of healing rain
from Heaven on a dry and dusty world,
where starved and thirsty creatures come to die.
Now they have water. Now the world is green.
And everywhere the signs of life spring up,
to show that what is born can never die,
for what has life has immortality.

## LESSON 341

**I can attack but my own sinlessness,**
**And it is only that which keeps me safe.**

*Father, Your Son is holy. I am he*
*on whom You smile in love and tenderness*
*so dear and deep and still the universe*
*smiles back on You, and shares Your Holiness.*
*How pure, how safe, how holy, then, are we,*
*abiding in Your Smile, with all Your Love*
*bestowed upon us, living one with You,*
*in brotherhood and Fatherhood complete;*
*in sinlessness so perfect that the Lord*
*of Sinlessness conceives us as His Son,*
*a universe of Thought completing Him.*

Let us not, then, attack our sinlessness,
for it contains the Word of God to us.
And in its kind reflection we are saved.


## LESSON 342

**I let forgiveness rest upon all things,**
**For thus forgiveness will be given me.**

*I thank You, Father, for Your plan to save*
*me from the hell I made. It is not real.*
*And You have given me the means to prove*
*its unreality to me. The key*
*is in my hand, and I have reached the door*
*beyond which lies the end of dreams. I stand*
*before the gate of Heaven, wondering*
*if I should enter in and be at home.*
*Let me not wait again today. Let me*
*forgive all things, and let creation be*
*as You would have it be and as it is.*
*Let me remember that I am Your Son,*
*and opening the door at last, forget*
*illusions in the blazing light of truth,*
*as memory of You returns to me.*

Brother, forgive me now. I come to you
to take you home with me. And as we go,
the world goes with us on our way to God.


## LESSON 343

**I am not asked to make a sacrifice**
**To find the mercy and the peace of God.**

*The end of suffering can not be loss.*
*The gift of everything can be but gain.*
*You only give. You never take away.*
*And You created me to be like You,*
*so sacrifice becomes impossible*
*for me as well as You. I, too, must give.*
*And so all things are given unto me*
*forever and forever. As I was*
*created I remain. Your Son can make*
*no sacrifice, for he must be complete,*
*having the function of completing You.*
*I am complete because I am Your Son.*
*I cannot lose, for I can only give,*
*and everything is mine eternally.*

The mercy and the peace of God are free.
Salvation has no cost. It is a gift
that must be freely given and received.
And it is this that we would learn today.


## LESSON 344

**Today I learn the law of love; that what**
**I give my brother is my gift to me.**

*This is Your law, my Father, not my own.*
*I have not understood what giving means,*
*and thought to save what I desired for*
*myself alone. And as I looked upon*
*the treasure that I thought I had, I found*
*an empty place where nothing ever was*
*or is or will be. Who can share a dream?*
*And what can an illusion offer me?*
*Yet he whom I forgive will give me gifts*
*beyond the worth of anything on earth.*
*Let my forgiven brothers fill my store*
*with Heaven's treasures, which alone are real.*
*Thus is the law of love fulfilled. And thus*
*Your Son arises and returns to You.*

How near we are to one another, as
we go to God. How near is He to us.
How close the ending of the dream of sin,
and the redemption of the Son of God.

## LESSON 345

**I offer only miracles today,  
For I would have them be returned to me.**

*Father, a miracle reflects Your gifts  
to me, Your Son. And every one I give  
returns to me, reminding me the law  
of love is universal. Even here,  
it takes a form which can be recognized  
and seen to work. The miracles I give  
are given back in just the form I need  
to help me with the problems I perceive.  
Father, in Heaven it is different,  
for there, there are no needs. But here on earth,  
the miracle is closer to Your gifts  
than any other gift that I can give.  
Then let me give this gift alone today,  
which, born of true forgiveness, lights the way  
that I must travel to remember You.*

Peace to all seeking hearts today. The light has come to offer miracles to bless the tired world. It will find rest today, for we will offer what we have received.

## LESSON 346

**Today the Peace of God envelops me,  
And I forget all things except His Love.**

*Father, I wake today with miracles  
correcting my perception of all things.  
And so begins the day I share with You  
as I will share eternity, for time  
has stepped aside today. I do not seek  
the things of time, and so I will not look  
upon them. What I seek today transcends  
all laws of time and things perceived in time.  
I would forget all things except Your Love.  
I would abide in You, and know no laws  
except Your law of love. And I would find  
the peace which You created for Your Son,  
forgetting all the foolish toys I made  
as I behold Your glory and my own.*

And when the evening comes today, we will remember nothing but the peace of God. For we will learn today what peace is ours, when we forget all things except God's Love.

## LESSON 347

**Anger must come from judgment. Judgment is  
The weapon I would use against myself,  
To keep the miracle away from me.**

*Father, I want what goes against my will,  
and do not want what is my will to have.  
Straighten my mind, my Father. It is sick.  
But You have offered freedom, and I choose  
to claim Your gift today. And so I give  
all judgment to the One You gave to me  
to judge for me. He sees what I behold,  
and yet He knows the truth. He looks on pain,  
and yet He understands it is not real,  
and in His understanding it is healed.  
He gives the miracles my dreams would hide  
from my awareness. Let Him judge today.  
I do not know my will, but He is sure  
it is Your Own. And He will speak for me,  
and call Your miracles to come to me.*

Listen today. Be very still, and hear the gentle Voice for God assuring you that He has judged you as the Son He loves.

## LESSON 348

**I have no cause for anger or for fear,  
For You surround me. And in every need  
That I perceive, Your grace suffices me.**

*Father, let me remember You are here,  
and I am not alone. Surrounding me  
is everlasting Love. I have no cause  
for anything except the perfect peace  
and joy I share with You. What need have I  
for anger or for fear? Surrounding me  
is perfect safety. Can I be afraid,  
when Your eternal promise goes with me?  
Surrounding me is perfect sinlessness.  
What can I fear, when You created me  
in holiness as perfect as Your Own?*

God's grace suffices us in everything that He would have us do. And only that we choose to be our will as well as His.

## LESSON 349

**Today I let Christ's vision look upon
All things for me and judge them not, but give
Each one a miracle of love instead.**

*So would I liberate all things I see,
and give to them the freedom that I seek.
For thus do I obey the law of love,
and give what I would find and make my own.
It will be given me, because I have
chosen it as the gift I want to give.
Father, Your gifts are mine. Each one that I
accept gives me a miracle to give.
And giving as I would receive, I learn
Your healing miracles belong to me.*

Our Father knows our needs. He gives us grace to meet them all. And so we trust in Him to send us miracles to bless the world, and heal our minds as we return to Him.

## LESSON 350

**Miracles mirror God's eternal Love.
To offer them is to remember Him,
And through His memory to save the world.**

*What we forgive becomes a part of us,
as we perceive ourselves. The Son of God
incorporates all things within himself
as You created him. Your memory
depends on his forgiveness. What he is,
is unaffected by his thoughts. But what
he looks upon is their direct result.
Therefore, my Father, I would turn to You.
Only Your memory will set me free.
And only my forgiveness teaches me
to let Your memory return to me,
and give it to the world in thankfulness.*

And as we gather miracles from Him, we will indeed be grateful. For as we remember Him, His Son will be restored to us in the reality of Love.

## WHAT AM I?

*I am God's Son, complete and healed and whole,*
*shining in the reflection of His Love.*
*In me is His creation sanctified*
*and guaranteed eternal life. In me*
*is love perfected, fear impossible,*
*and joy established without opposite.*
*I am the holy home of God Himself.*
*I am the Heaven where His Love resides.*
*I am His holy Sinlessness Itself,*
*for in my purity abides His Own.*

Our use for words is almost over now.
Yet in the final days of this one year
we gave to God together, you and I,
we found a single purpose that we shared.
And thus you joined with me, so what I am
are you as well. The truth of what we are
is not for words to speak of nor describe.
Yet we can realize our function here,
and words can speak of this and teach it, too,
if we exemplify the words in us.

We are the bringers of salvation. We
accept our part as saviors of the world,
which through our joint forgiveness is redeemed.
And this, our gift, is therefore given us.
We look on everyone as brother, and
perceive all things as kindly and as good.

We do not seek a function that is past
the gate of Heaven. Knowledge will return
when we have done our part. We are concerned
only with giving welcome to the truth.

Ours are the eyes through which Christ's vision sees
a world redeemed from every thought of sin.
Ours are the ears that hear the Voice for God
proclaim the world as sinless. Ours the minds
that join together as we bless the world.
And from the oneness that we have attained
we call to all our brothers, asking them
to share our peace and consummate our joy.

We are the holy messengers of God
who speak for Him, and carrying His Word
to everyone whom He has sent to us,
we learn that it is written on our hearts.
And thus our minds are changed about the aim
for which we came, and which we seek to serve.
We bring glad tidings to the Son of God,
who thought he suffered. Now is he redeemed.
And as he sees the gate of Heaven stand
open before him, he will enter in
and disappear into the Heart of God.

## LESSON 351

**My sinless brother is my guide to peace.
My sinful brother is my guide to pain.
And which I choose to see I will behold.**

*Who is my brother but Your holy Son?
And if I see him sinful I proclaim
myself a sinner, not a Son of God;
alone and friendless in a fearful world.
Yet this perception is a choice I make,
and can relinquish. I can also see
my brother sinless, as Your holy Son.
And with this choice I see my sinlessness,
my everlasting Comforter and Friend
beside me, and my way secure and clear.
Choose, then, for me, my Father, through Your Voice.
For He alone gives judgment in Your Name.*

## LESSON 352

**Judgment and love are opposites. From one
Come all the sorrows of the world. But from
The other comes the peace of God Himself.**

*Forgiveness looks on sinlessness alone,
and judges not. Through this I come to You.
Judgment will bind my eyes and make me blind.
Yet love, reflected in forgiveness here,
reminds me You have given me a way
to find Your peace again. I am redeemed
when I elect to follow in this way.
You have not left me comfortless. I have
within me both the memory of You,
and One Who leads me to it. Father, I
would hear Your Voice and find Your peace today.
For I would love my own Identity,
and find in It the memory of You.*

## LESSON 353

**My eyes, my tongue, my hands, my feet today
Have but one purpose; to be given Christ
To use to bless the world with miracles.**

*Father, I give all that is mine today
to Christ, to use in any way that best
will serve the purpose that I share with Him.
Nothing is mine alone, for He and I
have joined in purpose. Thus has learning come
almost to its appointed end. A while
I work with Him to serve His purpose. Then
I lose myself in my Identity,
and recognize that Christ is but my Self.*

## LESSON 354

**We stand together, Christ and I, in peace
And certainty of purpose. And in Him
Is His Creator, as He is in me.**

*My oneness with the Christ establishes
me as Your Son, beyond the reach of time,
and wholly free of every law but Yours.
I have no self except the Christ in me.
I have no purpose but His Own. And He
is like His Father. Thus must I be one
with You as well as Him. For who is Christ
except Your Son as You created Him?
And what am I except the Christ in me?*

## LESSON 355

**There is no end to all the peace and joy,  
And all the miracles that I will give,  
When I accept God's Word. Why not today?**

*Why should I wait, my Father, for the joy  
You promised me? For You will keep Your Word  
You gave Your Son in exile. I am sure  
my treasure waits for me, and I need but  
reach out my hand to find it. Even now  
my fingers touch it. It is very close.  
I need not wait an instant more to be  
at peace forever. It is You I choose,  
and my Identity along with You.  
Your Son would be Himself, and know You as  
his Father and Creator, and his Love.*

## LESSON 356

**Sickness is but another name for sin.  
Healing is but another name for God.  
The miracle is thus a call to Him.**

*Father, You promised You would never fail  
to answer any call Your Son might make  
to You. It does not matter where he is,  
what seems to be his problem, nor what he  
believes he has become. He is Your Son,  
and You will answer him. The miracle  
reflects Your Love, and thus it answers him.  
Your Name replaces every thought of sin,  
and who is sinless cannot suffer pain.  
Your Name gives answer to Your Son, because  
to call Your Name is but to call his own.*

## LESSON 357

**Truth answers every call we make to God,  
Responding first with miracles, and then  
Returning unto us to be itself.**

*Forgiveness, truth's reflection, tells me how  
to offer miracles, and thus escape  
the prison house in which I think I live.  
Your holy Son is pointed out to me,  
first in my brother; then in me. Your Voice  
instructs me patiently to hear Your Word,  
and give as I receive. And as I look  
upon Your Son today, I hear Your Voice  
instructing me to find the way to You,  
as You appointed that the way shall be:*

*"Behold his sinlessness, and be you healed."*

## LESSON 358

**No call to God can be unheard nor left  
Unanswered. And of this I can be sure;  
His answer is the one I really want.**

*You Who remember what I really am  
alone remember what I really want.  
You speak for God, and so You speak for me.  
And what You give me comes from God Himself.  
Your Voice, my Father, then is mine as well,  
and all I want is what You offer me,  
in just the form You choose that it be mine.  
Let me remember all I do not know,  
and let my voice be still, remembering.  
But let me not forget Your Love and care,  
keeping Your promise to Your Son in my  
awareness always. Let me not forget  
myself is nothing, but my Self is all.*

## LESSON 359

**God's answer is some form of peace. All pain
Is healed; all misery replaced with joy.
All prison doors are opened. And all sin
Is understood as merely a mistake.**

*Father, today we will forgive Your world,
and let creation be Your Own. We have
misunderstood all things. But we have not
made sinners of the holy Sons of God.
What You created sinless so abides
forever and forever. Such are we.
And we rejoice to learn that we have made
mistakes which have no real effects on us.
Sin is impossible, and on this fact
forgiveness rests upon a certain base
more solid than the shadow world we see.
Help us forgive, for we would be redeemed.
Help us forgive, for we would be at peace.*

## LESSON 360

**Peace be to me, the holy Son of God.
Peace to my brother, who is one with me.
Let all the world be blessed with peace through us.**

*Father, it is Your peace that I would give,
receiving it of You. I am Your Son,
forever just as You created me,
for the Great Rays remain forever still
and undisturbed within me. I would reach
to them in silence and in certainty,
for nowhere else can certainty be found.
Peace be to me, and peace to all the world.
In holiness were we created, and
in holiness do we remain. Your Son
is like to You in perfect sinlessness.
And with this thought we gladly say "Amen."*

# FINAL LESSONS

## Introduction

Our final lessons will be left as free of words as possible. We use them but at the beginning of our practicing, and only to remind us that we seek to go beyond them. Let us turn to Him Who leads the way and makes our footsteps sure. To Him we leave these lessons, as to Him we give our lives henceforth. For we would not return again to the belief in sin that made the world seem ugly and unsafe, attacking and destroying, dangerous in all its ways, and treacherous beyond the hope of trust and the escape from pain.

His is the only way to find the peace that God has given us. It is His way that everyone must travel in the end, because it is this ending God Himself appointed. In the dream of time it seems to be far off. And yet, in truth, it is already here; already serving us as gracious guidance in the way to go. Let us together follow in the way that truth points out to us. And let us be the leaders of our many brothers who are seeking for the way, but find it not.

And to this purpose let us dedicate our minds, directing all our thoughts to serve the function of salvation. Unto us the aim is given to forgive the world. It is the goal that God has given us. It is His ending to the dream we seek, and not our own. For all that we forgive we will not fail to recognize as part of God Himself. And thus His memory is given back, completely and complete.

It is our function to remember Him on earth, as it is given us to be His Own completion in reality. So let us not forget our goal is shared, for it is that remembrance which contains the memory of God, and points the way to Him and to the Heaven of His peace. And shall we not forgive our brother, who can offer this to us? He is the way, the truth and life that shows the way to us. In him resides salvation, offered us through our forgiveness, given unto him.

We will not end this year without the gift our Father promised to His holy Son. We are forgiven now. And we are saved from all the wrath we thought belonged to God, and found it was a dream. We are restored to sanity, in which we understand that anger is insane, attack is mad, and vengeance merely foolish fantasy. We have been saved from wrath because we learned we were mistaken. Nothing more than that. And is a father angry at his son because he failed to understand the truth?

We come in honesty to God and say we did not understand, and ask Him to help us to learn His lessons, through the Voice of His Own Teacher. Would He hurt His Son? Or would He rush to answer him, and say, "This is My Son, and all I have is his"? Be certain He will answer thus, for these are His Own Words to you. And more than that can no one ever have, for in these Words is all there is, and all that there will be throughout all time and in eternity.

## LESSONS 361 TO 365

**This holy instant would I give to You.
Be You in charge. For I would follow You,
Certain that Your direction gives me peace.**

And if I need a word to help me, He will give it to me. If I need a thought, that will He also give. And if I need but stillness and a tranquil, open mind, these are the gifts I will receive of Him. He is in charge by my request. And He will hear and answer me, because He speaks for God my Father and His holy Son.

# EPILOGUE

This course is a beginning, not an end.
Your Friend goes with you. You are not alone.
No one who calls on Him can call in vain.
Whatever troubles you, be certain that
He has the answer, and will gladly give
it to you, if you simply turn to Him
and ask it of Him. He will not withhold
all answers that you need for anything
that seems to trouble you. He knows the way
to solve all problems, and resolve all doubts.
His certainty is yours. You need but ask
it of Him, and it will be given you.

You are as certain of arriving home
as is the pathway of the sun laid down
before it rises, after it has set,
and in the half-lit hours in between.
Indeed, your pathway is more certain still.
For it can not be possible to change
the course of those whom God has called to Him.
Therefore obey your will, and follow Him
Whom you accepted as your voice, to speak
of what you really want and really need.
His is the Voice for God and also yours.
And thus He speaks of freedom and of truth.

No more specific lessons are assigned,
for there is no more need of them. Henceforth,
hear but the Voice for God and for your Self
when you retire from the world, to seek
reality instead. He will direct
your efforts, telling you exactly what
to do, how to direct your mind, and when
to come to Him in silence, asking for
His sure direction and His certain Word.
His is the Word that God has given you.
His is the Word you chose to be your own.

And now I place you in His hands, to be
His faithful follower, with Him as Guide
through every difficulty and all pain
that you may think is real. Nor will He give
you pleasures that will pass away, for He
gives only the eternal and the good.
Let Him prepare you further. He has earned
your trust by speaking daily to you of
your Father and your brother and your Self.
He will continue. Now you walk with Him,
as certain as is He of where you go;
as sure as He of how you should proceed;
as confident as He is of the goal,
and of your safe arrival in the end.

The end is certain, and the means as well.
To this we say "Amen." You will be told
exactly what God wills for you each time
there is a choice to make. And He will speak
for God and for your Self, thus making sure
that hell will claim you not, and that each choice
you make brings Heaven nearer to your reach.
And so we walk with Him from this time on,
and turn to Him for guidance and for peace
and sure direction. Joy attends our way.
For we go homeward to an open door
which God has held unclosed to welcome us.

We trust our ways to Him and say "Amen."
In peace we will continue in His way,
and trust all things to Him. In confidence
we wait His answers, as we ask His Will
in everything we do. He loves God's Son
as we would love him. And He teaches us
how to behold him through His eyes, and love
him as He does. You do not walk alone.
God's angels hover near and all about.
His Love surrounds you, and of this be sure;
that I will never leave you comfortless.

# MANUAL FOR TEACHERS

## HOW IS CORRECTION MADE?

*You but mistake interpretation for*
*the truth. And you are wrong. But a mistake*
*is not a sin, nor has reality*
*been taken from its throne by your mistakes.*
*God reigns forever, and His laws alone*
*prevail upon you and upon the world.*
*His Love remains the only thing there is.*
*Fear is illusion, for you are like Him.*

## WHAT IS THE RESURRECTION?

All living hearts are tranquil with a stir of deep anticipation, for the time of everlasting things is now at hand. There is no death. The Son of God is free. And in his freedom is the end of fear. No hidden places now remain on earth to shelter sick illusions, dreams of fear and misperceptions of the universe. All things are seen in light, and in the light their purpose is transformed and understood. And we, God's children, rise up from the dust and look upon our perfect sinlessness. The song of Heaven sounds around the world, as it is lifted up and brought to truth.

Now there are no distinctions. Differences have disappeared and Love looks on Itself. What further sight is needed? What remains that vision could accomplish? We have seen the face of Christ, His sinlessness, His Love behind all forms, beyond all purposes. Holy are we because His holiness has set us free indeed! And we accept His holiness as ours; as it is.

As God created us so will we be forever and forever, and we wish for nothing but His Will to be our own. Illusions of another will are lost, for unity of purpose has been found.

These things await us all, but we are not prepared as yet to welcome them with joy. As long as any mind remains possessed of evil dreams, the thought of hell is real. God's teachers have the goal of wakening the minds of those asleep, and seeing there the vision of Christ's face to take the place of what they dream. The thought of murder is replaced with blessing. Judgment is laid by, and given Him Whose function judgment is. And in His final judgment is restored the truth about the holy Son of God. He is redeemed, for he has heard God's Word and understood its meaning. He is free because he let God's Voice proclaim the truth. And all he sought before to crucify are resurrected with him, by his side, as he prepares with them to meet his God.

## AS FOR THE REST...

And now in all your doings be you blessed.
God turns to you for help to save the world.
Teacher of God, His thanks He offers you,
And all the world stands silent in the grace
You bring from Him. You are the Son He loves,
And it is given you to be the means
Through which His Voice is heard around the world,
To close all things of time; to end the sight
Of all things visible; and to undo
All things that change. Through you is ushered in
A world unseen, unheard, yet truly there.
Holy are you, and in your light the world
Reflects your holiness, for you are not
Alone and friendless. I give thanks for you,
And join your efforts on behalf of God,
Knowing they are on my behalf as well,
And for all those who walk to God with me.

AMEN

# CLARIFICATION OF TERMS

## THE EGO – THE MIRACLE

Illusions will not last. Their death is sure
and this alone is certain in their world.
It is the ego's world because of this.
What is the *ego*? But a dream of what
you really are. A thought you are apart
from your Creator and a wish to be
what He created not. It is a thing
of madness, not reality at all.
A name for namelessness is all it is.
A symbol of impossibility;
a choice for options that do not exist.
We name it but to help us understand
that it is nothing but an ancient thought
that what is made has immortality.
But what could come of this except a dream
which, like all dreams, can only end in death?

What is the ego? Nothingness, but in
a form that seems like something. In a world
of form the ego cannot be denied
for it alone seems real. Yet could God's Son
as He created him abide in form
or in a world of form? Who asks you to
define the ego and explain how it
arose can be but he who thinks it real,
and seeks by definition to ensure
that its illusive nature is concealed
behind the words that seem to make it so.

There is no definition for a lie
that serves to make it true. Nor can there be
a truth that lies conceal effectively.
The ego's unreality is not
denied by words nor is its meaning clear
because its nature seems to have a form.
Who can define the undefinable?
And yet there is an answer even here.

We cannot really make a definition
for what the ego is, but we *can* say
what it is not. And this is shown to us
with perfect clarity. It is from this
that we deduce all that the ego is.
Look at its opposite and you can see
the only answer that is meaningful.

The ego's opposite in every way,–
in origin, effect and consequence –
we call a miracle. And here we find
all that is not the ego in this world.
Here is the ego's opposite and here
alone we look on what the ego was,
for here we see all that it seemed to do,
and cause and its effects must still be one.

Where there was darkness now we see the light.
What is the ego? What the darkness was.
Where is the ego? Where the darkness was.
What is it now and where can it be found?
Nothing and nowhere. Now the light has come:
Its opposite has gone without a trace.
Where evil was there now is holiness.
What is the ego? What the evil was.
Where is the ego? In an evil dream
that but seemed real while you were dreaming it.
Where there was crucifixion stands God's Son.
What is the ego? Who has need to ask?
Where is the ego? Who has need to seek
for an illusion now that dreams are gone?

What is a *miracle*? A dream as well.
But look at all the aspects of *this* dream
and you will never question any more.
Look at the kindly world you see extend
before you as you walk in gentleness.
Look at the helpers all along the way
you travel, happy in the certainty
of Heaven and the surety of peace.
And look an instant, too, on what you left
behind at last and finally passed by.

This was the ego - all the cruel hate,
the need for vengeance and the cries of pain,
the fear of dying and the urge to kill,
the brotherless illusion and the self
that seemed alone in all the universe.
This terrible mistake about yourself
the miracle corrects as gently as
a loving mother sings her child to rest.
Is not a song like this what you would hear?
Would it not answer all you thought to ask,
and even make the question meaningless?

Your questions have no answer, being made
to still God's Voice, Which asks of everyone
one question only: "Are you ready yet
to help Me save the world?" Ask this instead
of what the ego is, and you will see
a sudden brightness cover up the world
the ego made. No miracle is now
withheld from anyone. The world is saved
from what you thought it was. And what it is,
is wholly uncondemned and wholly pure.

The miracle forgives; the ego damns.
Neither need be defined except by this.
Yet could a definition be more sure,
or more in line with what salvation is?
Problem and answer lie together here,
and having met at last the choice is clear.
Who chooses hell when it is recognized?
And who would not go on a little while
when it is given him to understand
the way is short and Heaven is his goal?

## FORGIVENESS – THE FACE OF CHRIST

How lovely does the world become in just
that single instant when you see the truth
about yourself reflected there. Now you
are sinless and behold your sinlessness.
Now you are holy and perceive it so.
And now the mind returns to its Creator;
the joining of the Father and the Son,
the Unity of unities that stands
behind all joining but beyond them all.
God is not seen but only understood.
His Son is not attacked but recognized.

## TRUE PERCEPTION – KNOWLEDGE

The world stands like a block before Christ's face.
But true perception looks on it
as nothing more than just a fragile veil,
so easily dispelled that it can last
no longer than an instant. It
is seen at last for only what it is.
And now it cannot fail to disappear,
for now there is an empty place made clean
and ready. Where destruction was perceived
the face of Christ appears,
and in that instant is the world forgot,
with time forever ended as the world
spins into nothingness from where it came.

A world forgiven cannot last. It was
the home of bodies. But forgiveness looks
past bodies. This is its holiness;
this is how it heals.
The world of bodies is the world of sin,
for only if there were a body is
sin possible. From sin comes guilt as surely
as forgiveness takes all guilt away.
And once all guilt is gone what more remains
to keep a separated world in place?
For place has gone as well, along with time.
Only the body makes the world seem real,
for being separate it could not remain
where separation is impossible.
Forgiveness proves it is impossible
because it sees it not.
And what you then will overlook will not
be understandable to you, just as
its presence once had been your certainty.

This is the shift that true perception brings:
What was projected out is seen within,
and there forgiveness lets it disappear.
For there the altar to the Son is set,
and there his Father is remembered. Here
are all illusions brought to truth and laid
upon the altar. What is seen outside
must lie beyond forgiveness, for it seems
to be forever sinful. Where is hope
while sin is seen as outside? What remedy
can guilt expect? But seen within your mind,
guilt and forgiveness for an instant lie
together, side by side,
upon one altar. There at last
are sickness and its single remedy
joined in one healing brightness. God has come
to claim His Own. Forgiveness is complete.

And now God's *knowledge*, changeless, certain, pure
and wholly understandable,
enters its kingdom.

Gone is perception, false and true alike.
Gone is forgiveness, for its task is done.
And gone are bodies in the blazing light
upon the altar to the Son of God.
God knows it is His Own, as it is his.
And here they join, for here the face of Christ
has shone away time's final instant, and
now is the last perception of the world
without a purpose and without a cause.
For where God's memory has come at last
there is no journey, no belief in sin,
no walls, no bodies, and the grim appeal
of guilt and death is there snuffed out forever.

O my brothers, if you only knew
the peace that will envelop you and hold
you safe and pure and lovely in the Mind
of God, you could but rush to meet Him where
His altar is. Hallowed your name and His,
for they are joined here in this holy place.
Here He leans down to lift you up to Him,
out of illusions into holiness;
out of the world and to eternity;
out of all fear and given back to love.

## JESUS – CHRIST

There is no need for help to enter Heaven
for you have never left.
But there is need for help beyond yourself
as you are circumscribed by false beliefs
of your Identity, Which God alone
established in reality.
Helpers are given you in many forms,
although upon the altar they are one.
Beyond each one there is a Thought of God,
and this will never change.
But they have names which differ for a time,
for time needs symbols, being itself unreal.
Their names are legion, but we will not go
beyond the names the course itself employs.
God does not help because He knows no need.
But He creates all Helpers of His Son
while he believes his fantasies are true.
Thank God for them for they will lead you home.

The name of *Jesus* is the name of one
who was a man but saw the face of Christ
in all his brothers and remembered God.
So he became identified with *Christ*,
a man no longer, but at one with God.
The man was an illusion, for he seemed
to be a separate being,
walking by himself,
within a body that appeared to hold
his self from Self, as all illusions do.
Yet who can save unless he sees illusions
and then identifies them as what they are?
Jesus remains a Savior because he saw

the false without accepting it as true.
And Christ needed his form
that He might appear to men
and save them from their own illusions.

In his complete identification with
the Christ - the perfect Son of God,
His one creation and His happiness,
forever like Himself and one with Him
– Jesus became what all of you must be.
He led the way for you to follow him.
He leads you back to God because he saw
the road before him, and he followed it.
He made a clear distinction,
still obscure to you,
between the false and true. He offered you
a final demonstration that it is
impossible to kill God's Son;
nor can his life in any way be changed
by sin and evil, malice, fear or death.

And therefore all your sins have been forgiven
because they carried no effects at all.
And so they were but dreams. Arise with him
who showed you this because you owe him this
who shared your dreamsthat they might be
dispelled.
And shares them still, to be at one with you.

Is he the Christ? O yes, along with you.
His little life on earth was not enough
to teach the mighty lesson that he learned
for all of you. He will remain with you
to lead you from the hell you made to God.

And when you join your will with his,
your sight will be his vision, for
the eyes of Christ are shared.
Walking with him is just as natural
as walking with a brother whom you knew
since you were born, for such indeed he is.
Some bitter idols have been made of him
who would be only brother to the world.
Forgive him your illusions, and behold
how dear a brother he would be to you.
For he will set your mind at rest at last
and carry it with you unto your God.

Is he God's only Helper? No, indeed.
For Christ takes many forms with different names
until their oneness can be recognized.
But Jesus is for you the bearer of
Christ's single message of the Love of God.
You need no other. It is possible
to read his words and benefit from them
without accepting him into your life.
Yet he would help you yet a little more
if you will share your pains and joys with him,
and leave them both to find the peace of God.
Yet still it is his lesson most of all
that he would have you learn, and it is this:

*There is no death because the Son of God
is like his Father. Nothing you can do
can change Eternal Love. Forget your dreams
of sin and guilt, and come with me instead
to share the resurrection of God's Son.
And bring with you all those whom He has sent
to you to care for as I care for you.*

# EPILOGUE

Forget not once this journey is begun
the end is certain. Doubt along the way
will come and go and go to come again.
Yet is the ending sure. No one can fail
to do what God appointed him to do.
When you forget, remember that you walk
with Him and with His Word upon your heart.
Who could despair when Hope like this is his?
Illusions of despair may seem to come,
but learn how not to be deceived by them.
Behind each one there is reality
and there is God. Why would you wait for this
and trade it for illusions, when His Love
is but an instant farther on the road
where all illusions end? The end *is* sure
and guaranteed by God. Who stands before
a lifeless image when a step away
the Holy of the Holies opens up
an ancient door that leads beyond the world?

You *are* a stranger here. But you belong
to Him Who loves you as He loves Himself.
Ask but my help to roll the stone away,
and it is done according to His Will.
We *have* begun the journey. Long ago
the end was written in the stars and set
into the Heavens with a shining Ray
that held it safe within eternity
and through all time as well. And holds it still;
unchanged, unchanging and unchangeable.

Be not afraid. We only start again
an ancient journey long ago begun
that but seems new. We have begun again
upon a road we travelled on before
and lost our way a little while. And now
we try again. Our new beginning has
the certainty the journey lacked till now.
Look up and see His Word among the stars,
where He has set your name along with His.
Look up and find your certain destiny
the world would hide but God would have you see.

Let us wait here in silence, and kneel down
an instant in our gratitude to Him
Who called to us and helped us hear His Call.
And then let us arise and go in faith
along the way to Him. Now we are sure
we do not walk alone. For God is here,
and with Him all our brothers. Now we know
that we will never lose the way again.
The song begins again which had been stopped
only an instant, though it seems to be
unsung forever. What is here begun
will grow in life and strength and hope, until
the world is still an instant and forgets
all that the dream of sin had made of it.

Let us go out and meet the newborn world,
knowing that Christ has been reborn in it,
and that the holiness of this rebirth
will last forever. We had lost our way
but He has found it for us. Let us go
and bid Him welcome Who returns to us
to celebrate salvation and the end
of all we thought we made. The morning star
of this new day looks on a different world
where God is welcomed and His Son with Him.
We who complete Him offer thanks to Him,
as He gives thanks to us. The Son is still,
and in the quiet God has given him
enters his home and is at peace at last.

www.ingramcontent.com/pod-product-compliance
Lightning Source LLC
Chambersburg PA
CBHW081125170426
43197CB00017B/2751